Getting Started with Oracle BPM Suite 11gR1

A Hands-On Tutorial

Learn from the experts – teach yourself Oracle BPM Suite 11g with an accelerated and hands-on learning path brought to you by Oracle BPM Suite Product Management team members

Heidi Buelow

Manoj Das

Manas Deb

Prasen Palvankar

Meera Srinivasan

[PACKT] PUBLISHING

enterprise
professional expertise distilled

BIRMINGHAM - MUMBAI

Getting Started with Oracle BPM Suite 11gR1
A Hands-On Tutorial

First published: September 2010

Production Reference: 1060910

Published by Packt Publishing Ltd.
32 Lincoln Road
Olton
Birmingham, B27 6PA, UK.

ISBN 978-1-849681-68-1

www.packtpub.com

Cover Image by Sandeep Babu (sandyjb@gmail.com)

Credits

Authors
Heidi Buelow

Manoj Das

Manas Deb

Prasen Palvankar

Meera Srinivasan

Acquisition Editor
James Lumdsen

Technical Editors
Alfred John

Aanchal Kumar

Manasi Poonthottam

Indexer
Hemangini Bari

Rekha Nair

Editorial Team Leader
Aanchal Kumar

Proofreader
Aaron Nash

Graphics
Geetanjali Sawant

Production Coordinator
Shantanu Zagade

Cover Work
Shantanu Zagade

Foreword

Oracle released the BPM Suite 11gR1 product in April, 2010. This is part of the 11gR1 release cycle for the Oracle Fusion Middleware (FMW) family of products that started in the summer of 2009. This release marks the unification of features of the Aqua Logic BPM (ALBPM) product that Oracle obtained as part of its BEA acquisition in 2008, and that BEA had in turn acquired from Fuego, with Oracle BPEL PM, SOA Suite, and the FMW framework. As with all FMW products, BPM Suite 11gR1 follows the guiding principles behind the FMW products: complete, integrated, open, and best-of-breed in its Business Process Management Suite (BPMS) offering. At the time of the BEA acquisition, ALBPM was an industry-leading BPM product – the BPM Suite 11g release preserves and enhances the best of ALBPM features such as ease of modeling, simulation, and basic process analytics. It also adds a significant set of capabilities that leverage other synergistic products from the FMW family, such as strong support for backend integration, event handling, Business Activity Monitoring (BAM), Web 2.0 and Enterprise 2.0 style collaboration, extended process analytics and actionable insights, and superior performance, scalability and system reliability.

With BPM adoption, organizations aim to generate high-value business benefits via increased efficiency, visibility, and agility. However, often such initiatives fail to produce satisfactory results due to a variety of reasons—certain limitations in their chosen BPMS tool set account for some of these reasons. For example, many BPM products specialize in addressing either human, document, system, or decision-centric projects, or cater to either small departmental projects with simpler GUI but limited capabilities, or large enterprise deployments that have complex and fragmented IDEs and execution engines. Also, traditionally BPM tools with enhanced features for developers have been difficult for business users to use. A key goal of Oracle's BPM Suite 11g offering is to eliminate such barriers to successful BPM adoption by providing a comprehensive and unified BPM product that addresses all flavours of BPM projects, provides the best tools for every persona engaged in the BPM lifecycle, and evolves seamlessly from simple projects to more complete scenarios.

Typical BPM solutions involve the modeling of complex human interactions, business rules, and connections to a variety of IT systems. Such solutions also need to incorporate security policies, exception handling, and the handling of business events. These applications are commonly deployed as distributed applications. To get maximum productivity and value from these projects, in addition to a good product you need a good understanding of the applicable software tools. To help you in understanding the tools better, the BPM Suite product management team has put together this getting-started tutorial.

The authors of this book have been instrumental in defining and designing the product, and creating, delivering, and rolling-out BPM Suite 11gR1 training programs internally and externally to partners and customers. In this book they take a step-by-step approach to incrementally building a non-trivial BPM application. They utilize a broad range of product features providing click-by-click guidance at every step. If your goal is to get started quickly with BPM Suite 11gR1, you will find the content and style of this book highly appropriate. BPM Suite 11g is a best-in-class product with an eye to the future, and I hope you will enjoy working with it.

Michael Weingartner
Vice President, Product Development
Oracle

About the Authors

Heidi Buelow is a BPM Product Manager with Oracle and is responsible for Oracle BPM Suite and programs such as beta and technical previews. Heidi joined Oracle in 2006, and previously was Chief Application Architect developing a Business Process Management engine, developer toolset, and application framework. Heidi started her career as a software developer at Xerox working on the Xerox Network Services and Star Workstation products, where she first learned to appreciate object-oriented and services-oriented technologies. She holds a Bachelor of Science degree in Computer Science from the University of Southern California.

Manoj Das is Director of Product Management at Oracle, responsible for Oracle's BPM Suite of products. Manoj's BPM journey started at Siebel Systems, where he was responsible for the next generation, process-centric and insight-driven application platform. He plays a leading role setting BPM and SOA industry standards, especially in BPMN 2.0, BPEL, and Business Rules. He is widely recognized at industry conferences and from Information Technology publications. Manoj has a BS in Computer Science from IIT Kanpur and an MBA from UC Berkeley. He has held senior Product Management, Development Management, and Product Development positions at Oracle, Siebel, Mentor Graphics, and others.

Manas Deb is a senior director in the Fusion Middleware/SOA, BPM, Governance Suites Product Group at Oracle HQ. He currently leads outbound product management and many strategic engagement initiatives for Oracle's SOA, BPM and Governance solutions, worldwide. He is also responsible for Oracle/HQ-based SOA Methodology initiatives. He has worked in the software industry for over 20 years, most of which have been spent in software product management/marketing and on architecting and leading a wide variety of enterprise-level application development and business integration projects in a range of industries. A graduate of The Indian Institute of Technology (KGP), Manas attended post-graduate studies at the University of Texas at Austin. He received his PhD in an inter-disciplinary program comprising Computer Science, Applied Mathematics, and Engineering. Manas also holds an MBA with specialization in international business.

Prasen Palvankar is a Director of Product Management at Oracle and is responsible for outbound SOA Suite and BPM Suite product-related activities such as providing strategic and architectural support to Oracle's SOA Suite and BPM Suite (current and prospective) customers, and also field and partner enablement, and training. Prasen joined Oracle in 1998 and worked as a Technical Director in the Advanced Technology Solutions group in Oracle Consulting delivering large-scale integration projects before taking on his current role five years ago. Prior to joining Oracle, he worked as a Principal Software Engineer at Digital Equipment Corporation.

Meera Srinivasan is a BPM Product Manager with Oracle and is responsible for Oracle BPM Suite and Oracle BPA Suite. She has 15 years of extensive experience in integration, SOA, BPM, and EA technologies, and represents Oracle at OMG, OASIS, and other industry consortia. Meera joined Oracle in 2003, and was part of the SOA Product Management team managing Adapters. Prior to joining Oracle, she spent seven years with TIBCO Software, a pioneer in electronic trading, message-oriented middleware, and enterprise integration. At TIBCO, she was an Engineering Manager involved in managing the development of various Adapters and EAI technologies. She holds a Master of Science degree in Computer Science from the University of Florida at Gainesville.

Acknowledgement

The authors would like to thank the Oracle BPM Suite 11*g* development and product management teams, and the leadership team of Bhagat Nainani, David Shaffer, Michael Weingartner, Hasan Rizvi, and Thomas Kurian for their vision, strategy and creation of the industry-leading BPM and process-enabling software suite that was used in this book. The work presented here has substantially benefited from the input and feedback of many, including members of business integration software product management and the enterprise architecture groups, over five hundred training attendees within and outside of Oracle, and the instructors who delivered the training to them. We specifically would like to mention the direct contributions of Avinash Dabholkar, Eduardo Chiocconi, Yogeshwar Kuntawar, Payal Srivastava, and Mark Wilkins. Thanks also to our former colleague Dan Atwood who is currently with Avio Consulting. Dan provided great feedback on many of the chapters. In addition, we would like to acknowledge and give thanks for help received from Sheila Cepero and Todd Adler in handling all the necessary legal steps within Oracle associated with the publishing of this book.

The publishing team at Packt Publishing was wonderful to work with — the enthusiasm, promptness, and guidance of James Lumsden, Aanchal Kumar, Alfred John, and Manasi Poonthottam throughout the evolution of this book are particularly worthy of mention.

Finally, we would like to expressly thank our families for their love and support as we took on the challenge of putting this book together on top of our already very busy schedules and borrowed heavily from the invaluable family time.

Table of Contents

Preface

The adoption of Business Process Management (BPM) is increasingly becoming one of the most popular approaches for boosting overall organizational excellence. As per industry analyst reports such as those from Gartner, Forrester, and IDC, BPM has been at the top of the senior management focus list for the last three to four years and BPM spending has been at a multi-billion dollar level with healthy double-digit percentage growth in BPM investment; analysts project this trend to stay strong for the upcoming years. BPM is a big deal for most organizations and for most business integration vendors.

By BPM of course we mean the comprehensive treatment of all lifecycle phases of business processes in an organization, including continuous process improvement activities. A BPM initiative needs to cater for a variety of projects where some or all of human workflows, manoeuvring of documents, system automation, and complex decision making might be involved. There are also many different stakeholders with their individual skills and goals. Business analysts, enterprise and solution architects, process designers, developers, and testers focus on concept-to-implementation phases and continuous improvement activities of processes; operation teams manage deployed solutions; process operators and business users are more interested in the outcome that the process generates. A key goal of Oracle BPM Suite 11g has been to deliver on all these requirements in the same platform without over burdening any specific participant.

Built on Oracle's SOA (Service Oriented Architecture) Suite infrastructure, BPM Suite 11g provides enhanced support for application integration services and business events, Web 2.0 and E2.0 style collaborations, and high scalability. It is a full-featured, enterprise-grade BPMS that has sufficient easy-to-use features to make it also suitable for small departmental quick-win projects. The main purpose of this book is to provide an accelerated learning path to master the essentials of the product framework and the key features of this feature-rich tool set.

The authors of this book are part of the Oracle BPM Suite product management team, and the book benefits from their in-depth experience of the product. The content is based on dozens of successful BPM Suite trainings conducted by the author team; these trainings have been rolled out world-wide and have been well received by a large audience of Oracle consultants, partners, and customers. Since the goal of this book is to get the reader quickly ramped up on the use of the product, it focuses more on breadth of features rather than on depth—in that sense it is not a reference manual or a handbook. However, from the outcomes of the many trainings that we have already done, we do expect that this tutorial will provide you with a very good understanding of what is possible with the BPM Suite 11*g* tool set and thus will help you choose the right feature for the problem in hand.

What this book covers

The principal aim of this book is to get you operational with the Oracle BPM Suite 11*g* R1 product quickly and easily. In this spirit, the largest part of this book is dedicated towards a set of hands-on step-by-step exercises that build a realistic BPM application that you can deploy, test, run, monitor, and manage.

Chapter 1, Business Process Management starts the book off with a quick refresher on the essential BPM concepts, historical perspective, and evolution BPM discipline and standards. The chapter ends with a discussion on BPM benefits.

Chapter 2, Getting Started with BPM follows with an overview of strategies and planning steps helpful in starting individual BPM projects and broader BPM initiatives.

Chapter 3, Product Architecture and *Chapter 4, Functional Overview* describe the product architecture and key functionalities of BPM Suite 11*g*. The tutorial uses a Sales Quote process as the base example for creating all the hands-on labs.

Chapter 5, The Tutorial Project: Sales Quote Processing describes this process and the steps that are completed in different follow-on chapters that ultimately lead to the target BPM application.

Chapter 6, Product Installation guides you through the product installation and configuration.

Chapter 7, Process Modeling using BPMN 2.0 covers the essentials of BPMN 2.0 modeling.

Chapter 8, Process Organization Model discusses the representation of roles and organizations units being critical in modeling human activities and interactions.

Chapter 9, Simulation and Analysis of the Business Process describes the process simulation techniques in BPM Suite 11*g* and their use in process analysis and improvement.

Chapter 10, Implementation of the Business Process discusses how BPMN 2.0 provides execution semantics so that a process model can be executed in a process engine and how this is accomplished in BPM Suite 11*g*.

Chapter 11, Using Process Composer covers the application BPM Suite 11*g* tool set, which includes a web browser-based, zero-install application called Process Composer which lets you access, modify, and share a process model.

Chapter 12, Using Process Spaces and Workspace Application discusses how in BPM Suite 11*g*, collaboration among various process participants and during different lifecycle phases of a process are facilitated by Web 2.0 and Enterprise 2.0 style portals called "Spaces". Such collaboration also includes task reassignment. Also, concepts and use of Spaces are explored in this chapter.

Chapter 13, Process Analytics and Business Activity Monitoring shows how BPM suite 11*g* allows you to easily generate a variety of analytics, management dashboards, and to connect selected process output events to Oracle Business Activity Monitoring (BAM) and how these functionalities are accomplished.

Chapter 14, Using Business Rules illustrates the different ways business rules could be used with BPM Suite 11*g* to control the behaviour of a process and to boost the agility the process.

Chapter 15, Using Human Task Patterns and Other Concepts and *Chapter 16, User Interface Development for Human Tasks* are focused on handling human tasks including the creation of user interfaces using the Java Server Faces (JSF)-based Oracle Application Development Framework (ADF).

Chapter 17, Events and Exception Handling and *Chapter 18, Customizing and Extending Process Spaces* look at more advanced topics such as handling of exception and events, and Process Space customization.

Chapter 19, Administering the BPM Environment discusses how Oracle Enterprise Manager (EM) unifies operational monitoring and management of Fusion Middleware applications such as one created by BPM Suite 11*g*.

Chapter 20, Concluding Remarks briefly discusses some of the ways you could use such BPM Suite applications to provide business benefits.

Who this book is for

This book is primarily intended for BPM developers and process architects with some basic understanding of web services and XML technologies. No prior knowledge of Oracle middleware products including BPM or SOA is assumed. While this is a getting started tutorial, people familiar with Oracle BPM and SOA technologies will find this as a useful refresher tying together various components of the BPM and SOA products.

While the hands-on exercises in this book may be too detailed for business or process analysts, they may find this book useful, skipping or glossing over the details, to get familiar with BPM concepts at a level of detail that is not usually found in analyst targeted books and training. Increasingly, as business and process analysts want to take a more proactive approach in BPM initiatives, such understanding may be critical for them to separate themselves from the rest.

Conventions

In this book, you will find a number of styles of text that distinguish between different kinds of information. Here are some examples of these styles, and an explanation of their meaning.

Code words in text are shown as follows: "Specify `webcenter.jks` as the keystore in `jps_config` as follows."

A block of code is set as follows:

```
setDiscussionForumConnectionProperty(appName='webcenter',
name='local-jive', key='keystore.location', value=jks_loc)
setDiscussionForumConnectionProperty(appName='webcenter',
name='local-jive', key='keystore.type', value= 'jks')
setDiscussionForumConnectionProperty (appName='webcenter',
name='local-jive', key='keystore.password', value= 'welcome1')
```

When we wish to draw your attention to a particular part of a code block, the relevant lines or items are set in bold:

```
setDiscussionForumConnectionProperty(appName='webcenter',
name='local-jive', key='keystore.location', value=jks_loc)
setDiscussionForumConnectionProperty(appName='webcenter',
name='local-jive', key='keystore.type', value= 'jks')
setDiscussionForumConnectionProperty (appName='webcenter',
name='local-jive', key='keystore.password', value= 'welcome1')
```

New terms and **important words** are shown in bold. Words that you see on the screen, in menus or dialog boxes for example, appear in the text like this: "Select the two, set **Change State** to **Online**, and then click on **Save**".

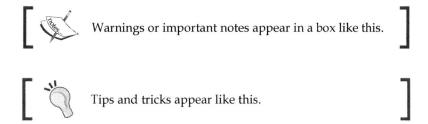

Reader feedback

Feedback from our readers is always welcome. Let us know what you think about this book—what you liked or may have disliked. Reader feedback is important for us to develop titles that you really get the most out of.

To send us general feedback, simply send an email to feedback@packtpub.com, and mention the book title via the subject of your message.

If there is a book that you need and would like to see us publish, please send us a note in the **SUGGEST A TITLE** form on www.packtpub.com or email suggest@packtpub.com.

If there is a topic that you have expertise in and you are interested in either writing or contributing to a book on, see our author guide on www.packtpub.com/authors.

Customer support

Now that you are the proud owner of a Packt book, we have a number of things to help you to get the most from your purchase.

Downloading the example code for this book

You can download the example code files for this book from http://www.oracle.com/technetwork/middleware/bpm/learnmore/index.html.

Errata

Although we have taken every care to ensure the accuracy of our content, mistakes do happen. If you find a mistake in one of our books—maybe a mistake in the text or the code—we would be grateful if you would report this to us. By doing so, you can save other readers from frustration, and help us to improve subsequent versions of this book.

If you find any errata, please report them by visiting http://www.packtpub.com/support, selecting your book, clicking on the **errata submission form** link, and entering the details of your errata. Once your errata are verified, your submission will be accepted and the errata will be uploaded on our website, or added to any list of existing errata, under the Errata section of that title.

Any existing errata can be viewed by selecting your title from http://www.packtpub.com/support.

Piracy

Piracy of copyright material on the Internet is an ongoing problem across all media. At Packt, we take the protection of our copyright and licenses very seriously. If you come across any illegal copies of our works, in any form, on the Internet, please provide us with the location address or web site name immediately so that we can pursue a remedy.

Please contact us at copyright@packtpub.com with a link to the suspected pirated material.

We appreciate your help in protecting our authors, and our ability to bring you valuable content.

Questions

You can contact us at questions@packtpub.com if you are having a problem with any aspect of the book, and we will do our best to address it.

1
Business Process Management

A business, whether it is a commercial or a government organization, and whether it pursues for profit or not-for-profit goals, conducts itself within some defined norms, policies, practices, and a set of **activities**. A business process is essentially a collection of related business activities with specified logic for coordination between such activities and the governing norms, policies, and practices. Business processes are often graphically represented using flowchart diagrams. A business process may be defined at a pretty high-level using coarse-grain business activities that are sometimes identified with what are called **enterprise value chains**. These coarse grain activities may be further decomposed into finer activities or tasks that may also be related through lower-level processes or sub-processes. Typically, it is the lower level activities or tasks that are actually executed, either by humans or by machines, and the results rolled up to the coarser-grain activities so as to provide higher-level business sense. For example, an order-to-cash process can be described by a handful of high-level business activities such as order entry, order fulfillment, payment receipt, and so on. Each of these activities will most likely be comprised of finer activities; for example, order fulfillment could include activities related to handling the distribution channels and some of these activities may even be outsourced or done by partners.

Business Process Management (BPM) is a disciplined approach for treating business processes as assets, managing their lifecycle, and seeking to improve and optimize them. Using some of the key benefits of BPM, Gartner defined it to be something that *provides governance of a business's process environment to improve agility and operational performance*. BPM scope includes process analysis, modeling, execution, monitoring, and improvement. As such a BPM adoption involves certain changes to organizational behavior, pursuance of suitable BPM methodology, and the use of appropriate software tools often categorized as **Business Process Management System (BPMS)**, each contributing their part within the broad BPM scope.

Our goal in this book is to introduce the reader to one such BPMS, the Oracle BPM Suite 11*g*, using a series of hands-on exercises. There are of course many easy-to-find books and publications that go into the general strategies and procedural details of BPM adoption.

> BPM is a management practice that provides for governance of a business's process environment toward the goal of improving agility and operational performance. BPM is a structured approach employing methods, policies, metrics, management practices, and software tools to manage and continuously optimize an organization's activities and processes. — *Gartner report "Business Process Management: Preparing for the Process-Managed Organization", 2005.*

A business process may be explicit (that is, clearly documented) or implicit (that is, based only on the understanding of those that are involved in executing the process), and may be manual (that is, tasks are done by humans) or automated (that is, tasks are handled by machine applications). Enterprise software applications such as **Customer Relationship Management (CRM)**, **Enterprise Resource Planning (ERP)**, **Human Resource Planning (HRM)** and **Supply Chain Management (SCM)** typically embed (portions of) many business processes while many other business processes are implemented in a layer above and independent of applications, the **middleware** layer. In reality, many business processes exhibit characteristics that are mixtures of some of the above traits. This book will focus on explicit business processes implemented in middleware that may include a combination of automated and manual tasks.

BPM—context and historical perspective

Roughly two decades ago, the US economy was going through a bit of crisis, a brief recession of sorts; consumer confidence was low leading to reduced expenditure and less goods sold. Manufacturers were looking to become efficient, which often meant reducing the total cost to produce, and deliver goods and services. So, the **Harvard Business Review (HBR)** article by Michael Hammer titled *Re-engineering Work: Don't Automate, Obliterate*, published in late 1990 was not only catchy but also timely. This and similar articles, and then popular books such as *Re-engineering the Corporation* by Hammer and Champy (which made to it into the national best-sellers list), *The Process Engineering Workbook* by Harbour, and *Process Innovation* by Davenport were focused on eliminating work that was thought to be dragging down efficiency and were starting to advocate the use of (information) technology to boost efficiency of work. Of course, **processes**, the targets of these re-engineering drives, are the so-called **business processes**, and such re-engineering efforts came to be known as **BPR** or **Business Process Re-engineering**. As launched, BPR initiatives were narrowly focused on few specific aspects of process dynamics as opposed to being a wholesome treatment of related business activities. In addition, in the zeal of achieving large benefits through BPR, most companies had set unachievable goals and proceeded to execute them without holistic plans, and in the name of waste elimination many of them laid off a lot of the workforce. There were few successes and, although BPR quickly fell out of favor, the movement had raised the visibility of business processes quite high.

About a decade later, another HBR article, this time by Nicholas Carr, titled *IT Doesn't Matter* and his book *Does IT Matter? Information Technology and the Corrosion of Competitive Advantage* that soon followed the HBR article, generated a storm of opinions, some for and many against Carr's observations and conclusions. According to Carr, IT had gotten mostly commoditized, such as the railroads and electricity, and thus, did not offer much competitive advantage anymore. Those who argued against Carr's conclusions pointed to his narrow scope of data-centric IT. It was interesting to note, however, that as debates progressed, the importance of business processes and BPM as enablers of organizational excellence and competitiveness were again in the lime-light (see, for example, *Business Process Management: The Third Wave* by Smith and Fingar).

Of course, the discipline of dealing with processes started much earlier than the excitement caused by the likes of Hammer or Carr. In the late 18th century, the famous economist Adam Smith used the notion of a process to describe the activities in a pin factory using some 18 different operations comprised of relatively easy tasks that ranged from drawing the wire, straightening it, cutting it, sharpening its end, fitting the head, and so on, up to coloring it for a particular type of application. By using the ideas of division of labor and work specialization the process of pin making could achieve over 200 times the original productivity! In the early 1900s, Frederic Winslow Taylor of Philadelphia published his monograph titled *Shop Management* based on his work on process management at Midvale Steele Company. Taylor's goal was also to improve worker productivity by streamlining activities and by division of labor. Similar ideas were also used by Henry Ford around the same time to create efficient assembly line processes for producing automobiles.

Over time, statistical quality controls brought significant enhancements to the early workflow systems inspired by Taylor, Ford, Gantt, and so on. During the mid-to-late 1900s, workflow and process improvement methods such as **Six Sigma**, **Total Quality Management (TQM)**, **Lean**, and **BPR** were being practiced. While the methods become more sophisticated, process management continued to mainly focus on improvements in labor productivity till around early 21st century, and then these ideas were expanded to cover most of the business activities, and the phrase **BPM** became more appropriate and popular.

It may be interesting to point out here that the acronym BPM sometimes has also been used to refer to business process modeling, business process monitoring, and business performance monitoring or management.

Evolution of BPM tools and standards

Software tools supporting process management have also been evolving steadily over the last two decades. There were multiple paths of evolution. Modern workflow management systems started emerging in the 80s. These systems were mainly focused on keeping track of a sequence of activities by individual (human) workers or **agents** and the flow of associated documents. Over time, these systems became capable of handling automated agents such as computer applications and databases. By the late 1990s, enterprise application (**EAI**) tools started adding some workflow capabilities with user interfaces and basic process modeling capabilities on top of their otherwise stronger system-to-system integration capabilities. In the early 2000s, a handful of **pure-play** vendors, mostly start-ups, created a market focus for process modeling and analysis tools. These specialized tools had relatively advanced features with better graphics and were aimed also at business analysts as opposed to only technical programmers. However, often these pure-play offerings essentially focused on human-centric processes and lacked strong system-level integration support.

Business Process Management Suite (BPMS)

It was becoming apparent that a suitable combination of the functionalities provided by the various forms of process tools was required to create general purpose process management platforms and would best serve the end user requirements. The analyst firm Gartner introduced the idea of **Business Process Management Suites** (**BPMS**) to capture a comprehensive set of functionalities for an enterprise class BPM platform. These capabilities included support of structured and unstructured processes, human tasks, forms and documents, rules and policies, participant roles and responsibilities, organizational structures, work-item routing, collaboration, business events, handling of design-time changes, integration with software services, and process monitoring and management. Due to the breadth and the depth of a typical BPMS, bigger middleware platform vendors were more suitable to take up the challenge of BPMS offering—**Oracle Business Process Management Suite 11g**, the tool set used in this book is an example of a full-featured BPMS.

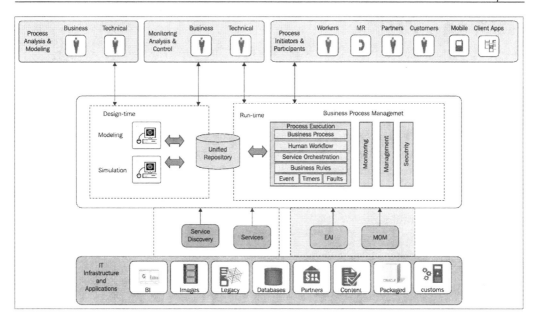

Most business processes cut across functional and departmental silos, and connect disparate applications, information, and people. Thus, a full-featured BPMS must cater to the requirements of many stakeholders, ranging from business users and analysts to IT developers and operations people. They must also handle the challenges of integration of systems, events, information, documents, and human workers, and keeping with the emerging trend of increasing digital communication must facilitate employee and partner collaboration. Given rapid changes in the business environment, a modern BPMS should also make the job of adapting existing processes easy. As will be shown later in the book, Oracle BPM Suite 11*g* has been designed from the groundup to handle such challenges.

SOA and BPM

A contemporary IT trend called **Service Oriented Architecture (SOA)**, where the development and use of computer applications utilize the concept of **services** can be seen as complementary to BPM. Services are a type of encapsulation of technology-based functionalities that, philosophically speaking, resemble the idea of services in our day-to-day life. SOA-based applications access services through well-defined **service interfaces and operations**, and are expected to receive service responses that are in line with published **service contracts**. Services facilitate reuse of functionality and easier composition of SOA-based applications. Such applications are characterized as **loosely coupled** as the service consumers are isolated from the inner working of the services—this helps in making such application significantly more resilient to change.

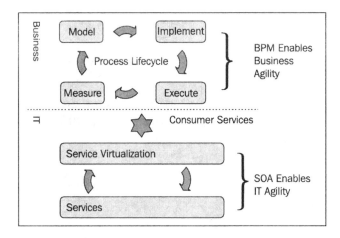

Business processes can be built by orchestration of such software services, particularly when functionalities from other applications need to be accessed; in this scenario business processes can be viewed as types of SOA-based applications. While SOA and BPM both provide business benefits on their own, when practiced in tandem, these benefits increase significantly. In a SOA-enabled BPM setting, business analysts and IT developers are closely aligned yet also enjoy the benefits of separation of concerns—business analysts focusing on the process descriptions and technical developers dealing with the intricacies of service implementation and collaborating through service interfaces and contracts. As will be shown later in this book, Oracle BPM Suite 11*g* provides an integrated platform for SOA-enabled BPM, thus easing the challenges of adopting SOA-enabled BPM.

Notational standards in BPM—BPEL and BPMN

As the process management tools evolved and were being adopted more broadly, the emergence of standards to describe modeling, exchange and execution of such processes was natural. Two noteworthy standards are the **Business Process Execution Language (BPEL)** and **Business Process Modeling Notation (BPMN)**. BPEL, an XML-based language, was inspired by IBM's **Web Services Flow Language (WSFL)** and its directed graph approach, as well as Microsoft's XLANG and its block-structured approach. BPEL is now backed by most of the software vendors in the process management space and has received a broad industry uptake; pervasive adoption of a wide variety of **Web Services** standards (**WS-***) like those for software functionality encapsulation, interfacing and policy enforcement, and message-based connectivity, which BPEL heavily leverages, has contributed significantly to this popularity. BPEL 1.0 was proposed in 2002 followed by BPEL 1.1 in 2003 when it was also submitted to OASIS (`www.oasis-open.org`) for making it an industry standard. BPEL 2.0 was proposed in 2005 and was accepted as a standard in 2007. BPEL provides strong execution semantics, and thus supports construction of standards-based process execution engines (for example, as found in products such as Oracle's SOA Suite).

Definitions from Wikipedia:

Business Process Execution Language (BPEL), short for Web Services Business Process Execution Language (WS-BPEL) is an OASIS standard executable language for specifying interactions with Web Services. Processes in Business Process Execution Language export and import information by using Web Service interfaces exclusively.

Business Process Modeling Notation (BPMN) is a graphical representation for specifying business processes in a business process modeling.

However, BPEL is viewed as something that requires technical savvy and is seen as difficult for business analysts to handle. Besides, BPEL's block-structured syntax limits its ability to handle certain process modeling requirements, such as complex human interactions and tasks, and extensive roles and responsibility management. Almost contemporary to the BPEL efforts is another initiative called **Business Process Management Initiative (BPMI)** with the aim of meeting the business analyst challenges resulted in BPMN specification. BPMN followed concepts familiar to business analysts such as flow-charts and **swim-lanes**, and supported highly flexible interaction graphs. BPMI's BPM activities were merged with OMG (`www.omg.org`) in 2005 and BPMN 1.0 and 1.1 versions emerged in 2006 and 2007, respectively. BPMN 1.x provided a powerful approach to process modeling but it did not include the discipline for execution of those models. With the emergence of BPMN 2.0, a version that is nearing final acceptance by OMG at this time, standards specs added the necessary enhancements to BPMN so that execution engines would be able to interpret the model and execute the process. As Oracle's BPM Suite and SOA Suite use the same modeling and run-time infrastructure (more explanations on this later in the book), the end user has the ability to both model and execute both BPMN and BPEL processes, and even combine them in process composites.

It is perhaps worth mentioning that many of the process modeling languages either exhibit similarities with or were influenced by more rigorous mathematical models for communicating processes, for example, **Pi Calculus** and **Petri Nets**. The connections between Pi Calculus with process modeling are along the lines of themes such as flow control, communication through messaging, and dynamic assignments of process **end-points**. The focus of Petri Net concepts is on the process graphs, states, and state transition. BPMN is closer to Petri Nets while BPEL, due its heritage, exhibits certain conceptual commonalities with both Pi Calculus and Petri Nets. Interested readers may catch a short and introductory review of Pi Calculus and Petri Nets, and their relationships with BPEL and BPMN in the 2005 article *BPM Theory for Laymen* by Michael Harvey (`http://soa.sys-con.com/node/89786`)

The promise of BPM – key benefits

The overall promise of BPM is to get organizational excellence that manifests in an organization's ability to outperform its competition. This means doing better at producing higher revenue and profit margins, introducing products and services better and faster than the competition, and achieving better customer satisfaction. A successful adoption of BPM adoption helps improve organizational excellence by enabling business-IT alignment, by improving operational efficiency, visibility, and predictability, and by increasing organizational agility.

Business-IT alignment is critical for the healthy functioning of any modern business. In the presence of such alignment, IT delivers functionality required by business promptly and efficiently, and innovations in IT lead to business innovation. BPMS provides a great platform for business-IT alignment. Model-driven BPMS, such as Oracle BPM Suite 11*g* with business-friendly interfaces for process analysis and modeling, empower business analysts to quickly and accurately specify the process steps and execution logic through graphical process models. In a unified BPMS such as Oracle 11*g*, these process models are embellished (for example, refined) by IT developers where necessary so that a process model can be executed. Conversely, IT developers can create reusable assets, typically lower level processes and services, which can be easily combined by business users very quickly to support business innovation or faster time-to-market requirements.

Efficiency	Visibility	Agility
Better, faster and more cost effective than your current alternative	Know the current status and outcome of your processes & business	Adapt quickly to changing business conditions

Metrics

Efficiency	Visibility	Agility
• Utilization, capacity • Throughput, speed • Quality, yield, exceptions	• Financial • Organizational • SLA failure rate • Rate of non-compliance	• Speed to create & change processes • Time to market

Results

Efficiency	Visibility	Agility
• Reduced Cost • Improved productivity/ROI • Effective resource utilization • Better quality / service	• Managed, lower risk • Compliance • Financial accountability • Lower capital reserves • Better visibility	• New revenue growth • Market share growth • Increased competitiveness • Thought leadership

BPM increases operational efficiency in several ways. By integrating functionalities of other systems and computer calculation of applicable rules associated with processes, it increases the level of automation in process execution, which in turn decreases process cycle time and increases process volume. Reduction in human activities reduces human errors thus increasing reliability and reducing exceptions. In case of processes where automated tasks and human activities are combined, BPM makes the human participation explicit and precise which leads to productivity improvements. BPMS such as Oracle BPM Suite 11*g* adds another critical productivity booster—advanced participant collaboration facilitating what may be called **Social BPM**. Using Web 2.0 and Enterprise 2.0 (E 2.0) style collaboration portals, participants can share and influence process design and certain decision making activities during process execution as opposed to (or in some cases in addition to) traditional styles involving email, document attachments, and web-based or face-to-face meetings.

Explicit description of processes as captured by the BPMS helps tracking of process execution at many levels; for example, the overall health of the end-to-end process execution at the business level or system problems at infrastructure levels, and specific events or milestones such as alerts and exceptions. Comprehensive tracking, increased visibility, and timely alerting during process execution are crucial for achieving high customer satisfaction, leveraging of potential up-sell and cross-sell opportunities, for managing a wide variety of regulatory compliance mandates, and for early detection system failures.

Clear process description, better visibility into process execution states, and appropriate processing of events generated during process execution can be used to predict possible outcomes of a process, often well in time to take appropriate remedial actions so as to reverse potential bad outcomes (for example, SLA violations, event storms generated by excessive alerts due to a few known exceptions, unacceptable system performance, and so on). Such predictive capabilities afforded by BPMS can significantly lower business execution risks.

In order to remain competitive, modern businesses have to often act very quickly to changing business requirements. Ability to sense-and-respond fast in a cost effective manner is the essence of business agility which BPM can boost significantly. Good business-IT alignment reduces communication gap between business need and speeds up delivery of quality IT functionality. **User-centric** features of BPMS as in Oracle BPM Suite 11*g*, where interactions with BPM toolset are designed to specifically cater to the needs of different participants through the lifecycle of processes, reduce the time and cost of process design, implementation and execution, and improve the overall quality. Reuse of established processes (and corresponding services in SOA-enabled BPM) also reduces both cost and implementation time. A BPMS such as Oracle BPM Suite 11*g* provides easy editing of existing processes and hot-deployable changes in process execution behavior through business rules, thus leading to high business agility.

BPM excellence is fast becoming popular as a corporate goal—contemporary reports by many industry analyst firms such as Gartner and Forrester, surveys done by BPM vendors such as Oracle, and personal experiences of the authors strongly support this trend. As with most things of value, the adoption of BPM does require some corporate will and appropriate adoption strategy.

Summary

In this chapter, we reviewed the evolution of BPM both as a discipline as well as the tools and standards used. We discussed how BPM delivers an overall benefit of organizational excellence and how it gets you there by aligning the business with IT using a unified BPMS. In the next chapter, we will briefly discuss these topics and offer some guidance regarding starting BPM initiatives in an organization.

2
Getting Started with BPM

As we discussed in Chapter 1, BPM yields high business benefits in many dimensions when adopted successfully. Thus it is prudent to be familiar, right from the start, with the essential considerations that lead to a successful BPM adoption, and conversely, the absence of which is likely to lead to failure and frustration. However, before we dive into a discussion on how we should prepare for BPM projects, a couple of clarifications are in order.

First, we should point out that not all *processes* are *business processes*. A process, particularly a digital description of a process, is essentially a depiction of a sequence of activities along with applicable flow control and business logic. In digital applications such processes appear in a variety of places. Take for example a "customer information update" activity with cross-departmental scope. This may involve updating multiple back-end IT applications, and the exact update operation may differ from application to application in how much to update and in what format to communicate with the application; there may be conditions under which certain updates may or may not take place, and so on. Often, processes are used to explicitly state all the individual tasks and associated logic behind a complex activity such as this system-wide customer information update. While such a customer information update activity will be recognized as an important and essential process at a business level, its lower level details may be expressed by an *information mediation process* that may be of little interest to a line of business owner. Thus, the associated process is not a business process. In general, business processes will involve activities with direct relevance to the business and the process itself will typically embody all, or a significant part, of some *business value-chain*.

Compared to the processes that guide data exchange between applications, business processes also typically engage more roles, often played by human participants, and involve complicated decision making, some of which requires sophisticated articulation of business rules; some others require live actions by the human participants. Depending on the situation, certain tasks in a business process may have to be transferred from one participant to the other. In some cases, a business task may require joint activity of several participants, as in collaboration.

These behind-the-scenes, technical workflow processes that exchange data between applications and perform other integration flows in support of the business tasks are generally referred to as *service orchestrations* to distinguish them from core business processes.

The second clarification concerns the abbreviation **BPM,** which is commonly used to imply Business Process Modeling, or Business Process Monitoring, or even Business Performance Management. Here we are referring to the full lifecycle of business processes of which modeling and monitoring are specific parts. Business performance management has a finance focus, and of course, business processes can feed useful information to such financial calculations.

Areas of focus for successful BPM adoption

Successful BPM adoption often involves changes in organizational behavior and focus, acquisition of skills in the necessary technology and tools, and implementation of suitable working practices. These practices range from planning to implementation of business processes, working with process instances, and monitoring and management of such processes, including post-implementation process improvement activities.

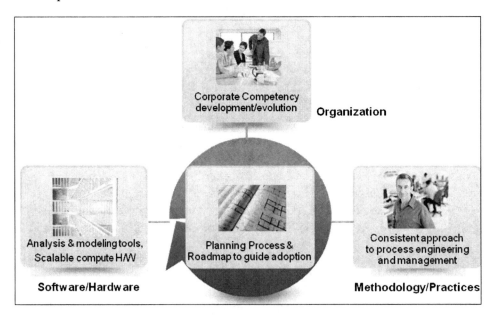

These are areas of focus that are critical for BPM adoption success. Process-centric or process-driven organizations behave differently than others, in that their leaders are strongly committed to business process excellence, and their employees at all levels are better aware how the business conducts itself. Their processing of business transactions has clearer definition, better visibility, and end-to-end traceability. Such organizations make necessary investments in improving their existing processes and creating newer ones faster than their competition. Suitable change in organizational behavior, when warranted, is critical for successful BPM adoption. The implementation of such organizational changes concerns various aspects of organizational development, such as organizational culture, managerial actions and incentive compatibility, and is not strongly tied to a specific BPMS.

Mastering adequate skills in a BPMS suitable for the scope of BPM adoption is critical for efficient and successful delivery of individual projects. BPM practice, that is, the discipline and organized activities that lead to successful BPM projects, combines BPM methodology with proper use of tools and can be seen as one of the ways an organization committed to process excellence conducts itself. This chapter will focus on some of the practice aspects of a BPM project while the rest of this book is dedicated to helping you get started with a full-featured BPMS, that is, Oracle BPM Suite 11*g*.

The scope of a BPM project can also vary from company to company. A BPM project may be limited to simply working on a specific process, either creating a new one or improving an existing one. We would call this a *tactical* project. On the other hand, a BPM project may be the starting point of a broader scoped BPM adoption that is intended to span multiple sub-organizations and is meant to include families of BPM applications. We would call this a *strategic* initiative. Of course, you may also be dealing with a BPM project that is one of many being executed under a bigger BPM program. Clearly, your preparation will be somewhat different depending on what type of project you are involved in.

Regardless of the scope of your BPM project, an essential step in assuring project success is to identify the **Critical Success Factors (CSFs)** of your project. You need to also ensure that these CSFs are relevant to the key stakeholders of the project, including those who fund the project or own or use the outcome of the project.

Once you know the scope of your BPM adoption, an immediate question is, do you have the right capabilities, both in type and level, to execute the chosen initiative successfully? Oracle's BPM methodology provides a BPM Capability Maturity Model framework to articulate your BPM capabilities. It groups nearly a hundred individual capabilities into eight *capability domains*: business and strategy, organization, governance, project process and service portfolios, architecture, information, infrastructure, and operations, administration, and management—the first half of this list focuses more on organizational aspects while latter half is more technology focused.

Oracle's BPM maturity model also classifies an organization on its level of expertise within each of the capabilities (and thus within each of the capability domains) in one of five maturity levels: *Ad-hoc*, *Opportunistic*, *Systematic*, *Managed*, and *Optimized*. The higher the level of maturity, the higher is the ability to execute; conversely, lower levels of maturity identify areas that may require improvement. Target maturity levels for each of the capability domains depend on the scope and goals of a BPM initiative, and any gap between the required and available maturity levels for any of the capabilities, if not remedied, can be a potential source of risk adversely affecting successful execution of the BPM initiative. (Given the nature of this book, a detailed discussion on topics such as BPM maturity model that is part of Oracle's BPM methodology is out of its scope.) The following diagram shows capability types and maturity levels per Oracle's BPM methodology:

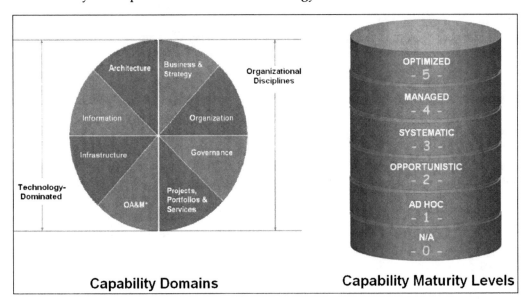

Starting with the right business process

Something that begins in the right way has a better chance of ending well. This is no different in the case of BPM projects. So, what process would you pick as the focus of your BPM project? In other words, what are the important process selection criteria?

Processes can be characterized by the amount of complexity they exhibit in terms of their suitability for explicit representation (as this is needed for digital modeling), number of activities, amount of logic, diversity of process stakeholders, number and spread of the back end application they connect to, and the type and number of human user interfaces the process needs to support. Process complexity can also be interpreted as a cost and/or risk measure. Processes can also be classified on the basis of the business impact they are likely to make—this is a benefit measure. Thus, processes that have low cost or complexity and a high business impact or benefit are easy picks for starting BPM projects and should be assigned the highest priority. Conversely, processes with high complexity and low business impact should be given the lowest priority.

Other possible combinations of process cost and benefit would have intermediate priorities. Of course, this cost-benefit analysis is useful when you have the possibility of choosing one or few processes from a larger set of possible candidate processes. In some cases certain organizational mandates may require you to consider a process which has been prioritized according to more diverse cost-benefit rankings, for example, a process that may be needed for ensuring certain legal compliance.

Once a process is chosen for a BPM project, it is advisable for the program or project managers to assess BPM capability maturity of the teams involved in the project in the context of the requirements of that project. Should significant gaps be found between the as-is and the required capabilities, strategies for timely bridging of such gaps should be included as part of the project plan.

Creating a process-based application

Some of the key goals of BPM initiative are to capture streams of business activities and associated logic and to create digital a rendition of these activities and logic, that is, the process model and to execute this model as a computer application. As with most computer applications, the lifecycle stages of a business process involves discovery, analysis, design, solution development and deployment, and operational management of deployed solution. Of course there can be iteration between and across these stages. Occasionally, the entire process, or some select process steps, may be subject to evaluation for the purpose of future improvement.

The goal of the first two stages—process discovery and analysis—is to get a deep understanding of the process itself and its interactions with its ecosystem. This includes individual activities and their flow; cost of executing these activities, business logic, and rules that govern the flow of these activities; data that the process uses or generates; process exceptions, in particular the manual ones that have to be handled; and the various roles, whether they are computer applications or human process operators, that are engaged in advancing the process flow. In addition, process discovery captures how the process impacts the business, relevant process analytics and the **Key Performance Indicators** (**KPIs**), and anticipated future change requirements to the process. Typically, *as-is* and *to-be* analyses are done to depict existing and desired versions of the process. The execution of process discovery could be done as a top-down or a bottom-up activity or as a combination of the two (as long as sufficient strategic analysis and selection have been done already). In the top-down approach, you will start with the higher level business problem and make your way down to finer details; in bottom-up approach, you will start with finding out finer grain tasks that actually happen in the context of a business process and roll them up to match the high-level business problem. Regardless of how you gather the information, all the stakeholders need to participate in validating the collected information from their points-of-view.

The end result of the discovery and analysis stages is a process definition. As business processes are connected to enterprise value chains, often the high-level definitions are not suitable for computer implementation. Process decomposition is a technique to break-down high level process definitions into finer grain (sub) processes. The decomposition is repeated several times, for example, starting from business function, to process groups, to core business processes, to business activities, to a task, and finally to a step. Typically, business tasks or steps are the ones that are actually implemented, and their actions are rolled up to realize the high-level business processes that reflect business value chains. Functional decomposition is a popular technique to conduct such an exercise. In many industry verticals, standardized process definitions are often leveraged; for example, SCOR for supply chain or eTOM for telecom systems.

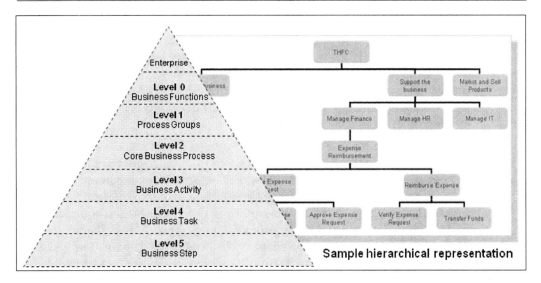

Sample hierarchical representation

Once a process has been defined from its business functionality point of view, technical analysis can follow. The focus of a technical analysis is to identify IT-related aspects of the process. Examples include the systems it needs to connect to, data it needs to access, business events the process needs to respond to or the business events it needs to generate, software and hardware servers needed to execute the process, and a variety of considerations related to manageability, scalability, reliability, and security aspects of the solution.

Analysis leads to the design phase where the process is described in a manner that it can be encoded in a BPMS, ultimately leading to the creation of a process-based application.

Roles in BPM projects

A typical BPM initiative touches many systems and a variety of people in an organization. Roles are used to articulate and manage participation of systems and people at different stages of the lifecycle of a BPM project. BPMN modeling notation also uses the roles concept for the purpose of categorizing participants involved in a business process application. Here we will mainly discuss the roles of people participating in the delivery of a BPM project. While there are no industry-wide standards for BPM roles yet, the following list is representative of popular practice:

- **Process sponsor**: Process sponsor, typically a business person, is the initiator of the project and provides the senior management connection to the project. Often the sponsor also provides the funding for the project.

- **Process owner**: This is the role that leads and maintains the overall context of the BPM project. A process owner is familiar with, and influences the high-level characteristics of, the project and the process, goals and KPIs, process variabilities, and future change requirements. He also has an oversight of the key milestones and deliverables. A "process context map" that summarizes all the important aspects of the process is often a useful tool used by this role.

- **Program/project manager**: Often, several related projects are grouped under a program, and hence the role of a program manager may be useful in addition to that of the project manager. The project management role is primarily responsible for creating the **Work Breakdown Structure (WBS)** for the project, managing schedule, resource and deliverables, and coordination among other roles engaged in the project. The program/project manager is also attentive to capability maturity of the project participants and risks involved in the project. The program/project manager uses executive reporting to keep process sponsor and process owner up-to-date on the project status.

- **Enterprise architect/business analyst**: Depending on the organization and the project scope, these may be separate roles. The focus here is to capture relevant business architecture, value chains, and strategy maps, and align the target process with them. The business analyst specifies all the business level requirements for the process for the *as-is* and *to-be* states. These roles own the use-case level documentation of the processes and also define the process KPIs.

- **Business user**: This role, sometimes included with in the business analyst role, is a key contributor to the business process discovery activities, and is tasked with continual review of the process model and making changes to business processes that are (relatively) small and not highly technical. In some cases, expert *end users* (that is, those who work with BPM applications to execute process based transactions) can play this role. One key benefit is to have the business users directly implement such process modifications without initiating new or additional IT involvement.

- **Process analyst/architect**: This role pertains more to the actual implementation of the process. He may conduct process simulation and suggest incremental refinements. He also contributes to the definitions of the exceptions, and of business indicators and KPIs, and formulates mechanisms to collect necessary input and to compute such metrics. He also provides the necessary technical details required to create the actual process model. In the event that the analyst and architect roles are handled by different individuals, the analyst focuses mainly on the business aspects.

- **Process designer/developer**: This role is responsible for producing the digital rendition of the process model, encoding business rules, designing the user interfaces, and creating the executable version of the process. Depending on the BPMS and the division of labor in an organization, an additional and more technical role called the IT Developer may supplement this role and perform the tasks of creating and connecting process end-points, some of which can be software *services* (as in SOA).

Besides the above roles, some of the traditional functions that exist in most IT endeavors, for example, system administration, governance, and release management, are also equally relevant to BPM projects. It should be pointed out here that while roles in the above list are sufficiently distinct, depending on the size and scope of the project, a particular person may handle multiple roles, that is, wear multiple hats, so to say.

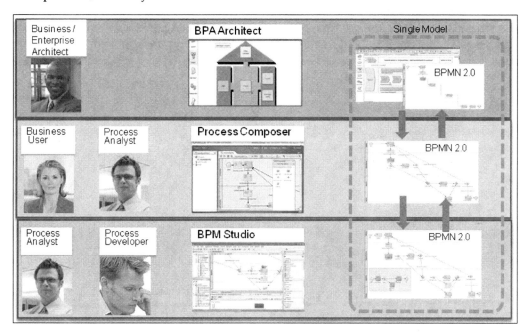

Different tools or tool components are better suited for the different BPM roles. As an example, business analyst/enterprise architects can make use of the **Oracle BPA (Business Process Analysis)** product for their activities — these activities correspond closely with BPMN's *descriptive* level of modeling. The fully web-based and light-weight Process Composer is better suited for the business user role. The full-featured development environment provided by BPM Studio would be the main work-horse of the process (and IT) developers handling activities that are closely aligned with BPMN's *execution* level modeling. The analysts may use either Process Composer or the BPM Studio depending on their needs — the analysis activities are aligned with the *analytical* level of BPMN modeling.

Summary

In this chapter, we briefly discussed how to prepare before you actually get deep into working with a BPMS tool set such as Oracle BPM Suite 11*g*. We also touched on the various roles that are involved in a BPM project and the types of tool support that are appropriate for some of the key roles.

3
Product Architecture

While there are many BPM tools available today, fitting one pattern of usage or another nicely, a long-term strategic investment in BPM requires a product built on a robust architecture that can evolve with changing requirements and scale as deployment matures. Selecting the best product for current needs and making a strategic choice should not be a trade-off, and that is Oracle BPM's promise.

Guiding principles

- BPM's success is greater and realized sooner when business users are empowered to drive BPM initiatives. Empowering business users not only requires easy-to-use, user-centric tools, but also standards-based skills.

- Collaboration is essential in all phases of the BPM lifecycle, spanning from process discovery, to implementation, to change management.

- Over time business processes do not fit within a silo of system-centric, human-centric, document-centric, or decision-centric. To achieve continued success with end-to-end process management, a comprehensive and unified BPM product is needed.

- A well-unified stack delivers lower **total-cost-of-ownership** (TCO), as well as enables taking on more complex projects.

Design environment

Oracle BPM includes two design tools—JDeveloper-based BPM Studio and web-based Process Composer.

User-centric design tools

Process Composer is targeted at **line-of-business** (**LOB**) process owners, business users, and business analysts. BPM Studio is targeted at process analysts/architects and developers. Both of these tools are in turn role based and provide different users a different experience, based on and optimized for their role selection.

These two design tools work on the same metadata artifacts (that is, no generation or translation) that are shared between the two using **Oracle Meta Data Store** (**MDS**). BPM Studio also integrates with **Source Code Control Systems** (**SCCS**) leveraging JDeveloper framework's rich capabilities in this regard. The following figure shows the BPM Tooling Architecture:

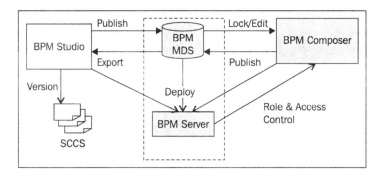

Composite BPM project

One of the core tenets of BPM is business visibility and rapid development through model driven development. While the process model has historically been the focus of attention for BPM vendors, fitting all problems to one model does not work well. Instead, domain-specific modeling support is needed for different categories of use cases, such as business rules, service orchestration, service mediation, data transformations, and so on. Oracle BPM addresses this by treating BPM projects as a composite of these model types. The following figure shows a sample BPM composite:

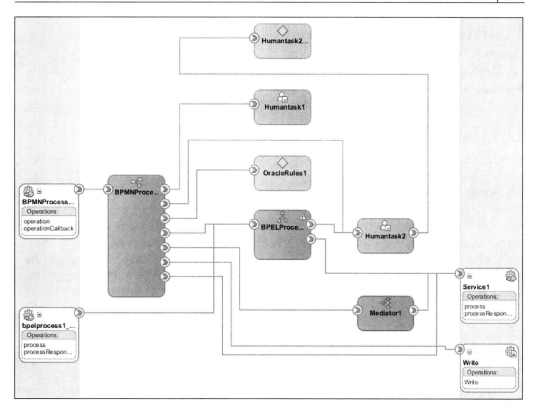

As we can see, a BPMN process may invoke a human task, business rules, BPEL process, mediator, adapter services, and various other service references. These other components can in turn invoke each other; for example, a human task can invoke business rules for rules-driven routing. A BPMN process may also be invoked by other BPMN processes, BPEL processes, and mediator services; the latter is particularly interesting as it allows BPMN process to subscribe to events through mediator.

A composite project is a unit of reuse. Any component of the composite that is desired to be reused should be exposed as a service from composite. Most components, including BPMN processes, BPEL processes, human tasks, business rules, and mediator can be exposed as a service so that other projects and other clients can use them.

A composite project is also deployed and versioned as one, simplifying the lifecycle management of a complex BPM project. However, as business rules are expected to change more often than other process models, business rules can be changed for a deployed composite without requiring the full composite to be versioned; these are referred to as **Design Time at Run Time (DT@RT)** changes.

Runtime architecture

Oracle SOA and BPM products leverage a **Service Component Architecture (SCA)** server that provides a unified services and events infrastructure. Various service engines plug into this infrastructure.

Unified SCA server

For each model type, there is a service engine that provides direct execution of the model. For example, BPMN service engine to execute BPMN 2.0 natively, BPEL service engine executes BPEL natively, business rules service engine executes business rules, and so on. The underlying SCA server provides highly optimized binding between these service engines, without incurring any overheads typically associated with such cross-model interactions. This allows process analysts and developers to select the right model for the right usage, without worrying about the performance implications. The SCA server also provides for policy enforcement on the wire. The following figure shows the architecture of a BPM unified server:

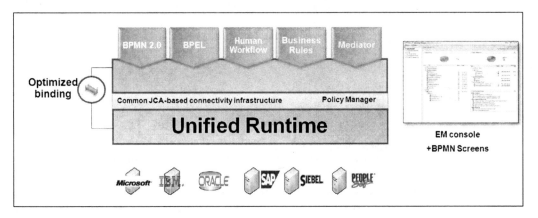

In addition to the unification accomplished through SCA Server, the BPMN 2.0 and BPEL service engines share a common process core that handles common process infrastructure activities such as service invocations, instance dehydration, alarm scheduling, and so on. This also means that the two service engines share APIs, and customers using BPEL APIs, in most cases, should be able to use them with BPMN as well.

Workflow architecture

In accordance with WS-Human Task architecture, Oracle BPM separates handling details of human task activities such as managing deadlines, access, and presentation to a separate service engine. In addition to achieving the right separation of concerns, this architecture also means that same human task components may be used by BPMN 2.0, BPEL, or stand-alone (for example, when the use case is an approval workflow). The following figure shows the workflow architecture:

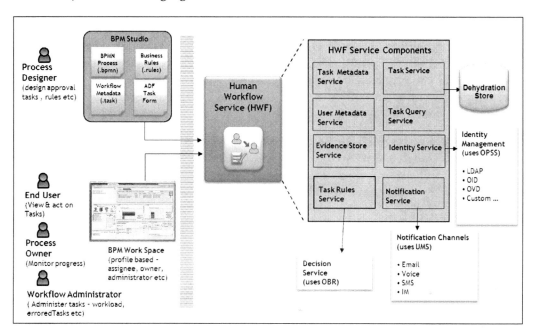

As shown in the preceding figure, **Human Workflow Service** (HWF) may be invoked by a BPMN (or BPEL) process; once the task is completed, HWF notifies the invoking process through call-back. The call-back mechanism may also be configured to notify the invoking process or the Java handler about finer grained state changes of the task.

Human tasks may be exposed as a service from the composite and invoked directly. As human tasks in Oracle BPM can be complex multi-step tasks, this allows for applications that need to manage approvals to use human tasks without a surrounding process.

HWF is tightly integrated with business rules and can invoke business rules to determine both assignment and routing. This is more powerful than invoking business rules in the process and then using the outcome within the task because when rules are used directly from human tasks, they are invoked each time an assignment or routing decision needs to be made or when different participants act on their tasks.

The workflow service engine exposes a rich set of APIs for accessing and interacting with the tasks. These APIs are abstracted and wrapped in an **Oracle Application Development Framework (ADF) Data Control (ADF DC)**. The ADF DC allows drag-and-drop binding of user interface elements to human task data within the ADF designer (in BPM Studio). The ADF DC is also exposed through ADF Desktop Integration for creating Excel interfaces in a zero-code fashion. Customers who need user interface technologies other than ADF or Excel use the underlying APIs, which are available both in Java and as web services.

HWF integrates with **Oracle Unified Messaging Service (UMS)** to deliver notifications through a variety of channels and based on a user's personal preferences. HWF also supports actionable e-mail messages that are able to handle task actions through in-bound e-mail.

Integration with identity directories and the authorization architecture is discussed later in the *Security* section.

Process analytics

Achieving the promise of continuous process improvement requires robust process analytics. Oracle BPM includes standard dashboards, native custom dashboards, process STAR schema, and seamless integration with Oracle BAM.

The process STAR schema, called **Process Cubes**, provides storage of standard and process-specific metrics — measures and dimensions. The standard and native custom dashboards are built on top of the process cubes. Process cubes may also be used with **Oracle Business Intelligence (BI)** or other business intelligence tools.

The BPMN audit engine, which is responsible for maintaining audit, pushes the needed process analytic data to the process cubes. It can also push these events to Oracle BAM by using BAM Adapter. Oracle BAM Process Monitor provides dashboards for standard process metrics out-of-the-box. For process-specific metrics, BAM Data Objects are set up to receive these events. Business users using Oracle BAM Studio can create their own dashboards. The following figure shows the architecture of process analytics:

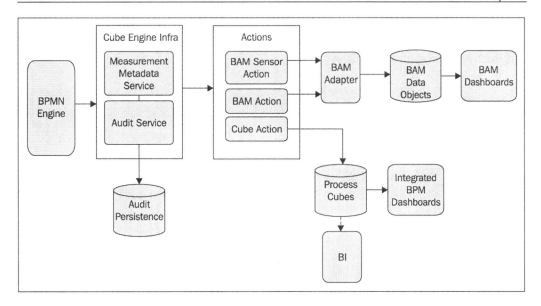

Deployment topology

Oracle BPM follows Oracle Fusion Middleware's scalability and high availability architecture. It can scale both horizontally and vertically. Horizontal scaling is achieved by grouping different managed servers together to share a workload. Oracle Fusion Middleware provides great vertical scaling by allowing multiple managed servers to the same node based on its hardware specs.

To briefly summarize Oracle Fusion Middleware scalability and high availability concepts—a **Domain** is a unit of WebLogic Server Administration. A domain consists of one or more WebLogic server instances that are managed by an **Administration Server**. A domain can be configured to have additional WebLogic Server instances called **Managed Servers**. For example, SOA/BPM is a managed server, and so is BAM; WebCenter may have multiple managed servers for spaces, portlets, and services. Managed servers in a domain may be grouped together in a **Cluster**, running simultaneously and working together for increased scalability and reliability. In a cluster, most resources and services are deployed identically to each managed server, enabling fail-over and load-balancing. Both **active-active** and **active-passive** failover patterns are supported; active-active failover requires an external load balancer to detect failure and automatically redirect requests. **Disaster Recovery** is accomplished by configuring a passive site and by using disk-replication technologies to periodically update the passive site; for the database, Oracle Data Guard is recommended.

The following figure shows a sample deployment topology. It shows a possible deployment topology. In this topology, an external load balancer is used as well as Oracle RAC database configuration.

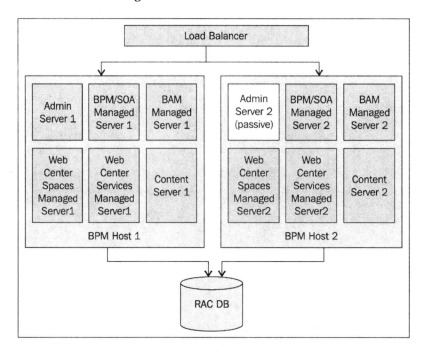

In the figure above, two nodes — BPM1 and BPM2 — run the WebLogic server configured with managed servers for running SOA/BPM, BAM, and WebCenter. The managed servers are configured in an active-active manner.

Depending on the hardware specs of the underlying physical servers, it may be preferable to run BAM and/or WebCenter on different nodes as shown in the next diagram:

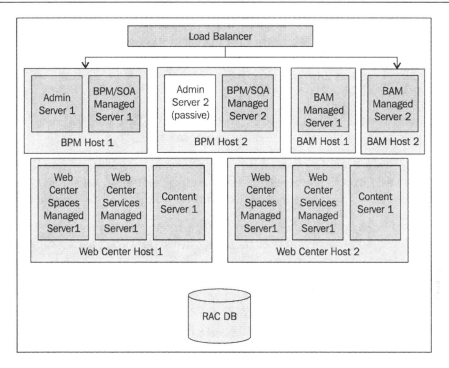

The figure above shows alternative deployment topology.

Security

Oracle BPM uses a two-tier architecture for managing user identities and authorization.

User authentication and authorization

Actual users and groups are leveraged from the identity directory in use at the customer site. BPM supports the concept of process roles that can be mapped to the actual users and groups, enabling a BPM specific abstraction.

Oracle BPM relies on **Oracle Platform Security Services (OPSS)** for integrating with identity directories, including Oracle Identity Manager, Oracle Access Manager, Netscape LDAP, and Active Directory among others. Configuration of identity providers for authentication and authorization is therefore done at the OPSS layer.

Oracle BPM supports process roles, which are BPM-specific application roles. (Application roles are an OPSS concept for applications such as BPM to better manage granting of privileges.) These process roles are then mapped to actual users and groups by a process administrator from Workspace (or BPM Studio). A swim lane in a BPMN model is a process role.

Organization roles are a special type of process roles that are mapped using query specifications (also sometimes known as **parametric roles**).

Approval groups are another special type of process roles that allow specification of sequencing in addition to membership. For example, a process admin may specify that `Tier3ApprovalGroup` requires `wfaulk` and `cdoyle`, and in that sequence.

Assignment of tasks and granting of other BPM privileges is typically done to a process role, instead of an actual user or group; however, direct assignment of tasks to actual users and groups is supported as well.

Policy-driven security

An enterprise-grade BPM deployment requires that security policies on processes and other services can be specified, enforced, and audited. Moreover, this needs to work in a heterogeneous environment.

Oracle BPM and SOA products support WS-* standards for security and security policies. Some examples of concerns addressed are: who can access which service, how credentials are passed between services, and what data needs to be encrypted.

To allow separation of security concerns from process development, Oracle BPM and SOA supports policy-driven security specification—this alleviates hard-coded security in process and application logic. In addition, this enables the specification of security policies to be deferred and delegated to security architects, and policies to be changed without requiring re-deployments. Policies may be specified from Oracle Enterprise Manager, as well as from BPM Studio. Oracle Enterprise Manager provides a unified console where all security-related aspects such as credential-stores, roles, and policies can be configured.

The enforcement and auditing of security policies is managed by **Oracle Web Services Manager (OWSM)**, which is built into the SCA Server.

Management

Oracle Enterprise Manager (**EM**) is the single unified technical monitoring and management tool for Oracle products. While this provides significant TCO savings for customers using multiple Oracle products, its cutting edge management features provide even pure BPM customers significant value beyond most other products in this space.

Among other capabilities, Oracle EM provides the following:

- **Administration** of the BPM infrastructure (including SOA, WebCenter, and related components). This is where different settings can be configured.
- **Management** of BPM projects (composite), including deployment, un-deployment, redeployment, start, and stop.
- **Monitoring** BPM composites and its components for exceptions and faults. It also provides end-to-end monitoring of process instances (discussed in the next section.)
- **Performance** analysis and tuning for both BPM composites as well as BPM infrastructure.
- **Security Policy** specification as discussed earlier.

End-to-end monitoring

The Oracle BPM and SOA console within Oracle EM provides end-to-end instance (or transaction) tracing. A process instance may traverse multiple components in a composite; the audit trail traces the instance's path through all the components. The following figure shows an end-to-end audit trail:

Drilling down into a particular component, such as business process or business rules, provides an audit trail specific to that component. These audit trails also include sufficient information for diagnostics based on the configured audit level.

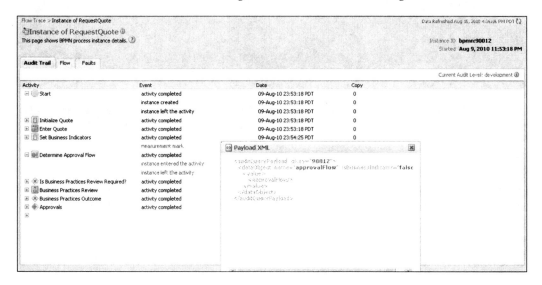

The figure above shows a BPMN audit trail.

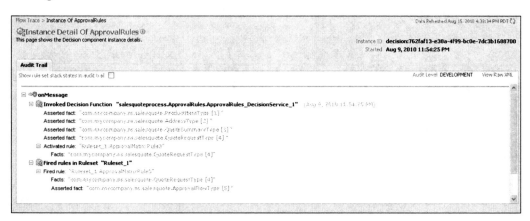

The figure above shows a business rules audit trail.

In addition, an instance is assigned an ECID tag that is unique across the deployment and can be used to trace an instance spanning multiple composites.

Policy-driven exception handling

While Oracle BPM supports explicit exception handling as per the BPMN 2.0 and BPEL standards, it is usually desired that not every process designer be burdened with exception handling and that there is a centralized and consistent framework for handling exceptions. Oracle BPM and SOA supports policy-driven exception handling that enables specifying how to handle various exceptions that have not been explicitly handled in the process. Oracle EM provides a centralized dashboard from where exceptions requiring manual intervention can be handled. From Oracle EM, one can drill down into a faulted process composite, and retry, replay, abort, and re-throw the exception or continue processing.

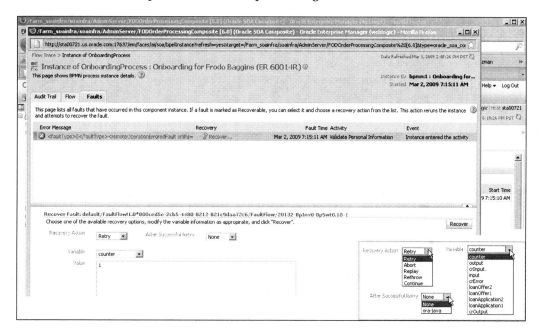

The figure above shows fault recovery from EM.

Deployment

BPM projects are SOA composites and follow the same rules for deployment. Three options are provided for deployment:

1. **JDeveloper**: Individual BPM projects as well as a combination of BPM projects can be deployed to runtime servers. This involves setting up a deployment profile, which is usually automatically set up during project creation, and then deploying by using the deployment profile. To deploy multiple projects as a unit, a deployment profile with **SOA Bundle**, target type needs to be configured. Moreover, shared artifacts that are used across projects can be deployed by creating a deployment profile with **JAR** target type.

2. **Ant**: Deployment can be scripted using **ant** scripts. Ant scripts, including `ant-sca-compile.xml`, `ant-sca-package.xml`, `ant-sca-deploy.xml`, are provided in the `Middleware_Home\SOA_Suite_Home\bin` directory. WLST scripts may also be used.

3. **EM**: EM provides capabilities to deploy, un-deploy, redeploy, as well as start and stop BPM composites. This option requires the SAR or corresponding file to be created using one of the above two options.

Test–to–production

To facilitate moving projects from one environment to another, typically from development to test to production, Oracle BPM and SOA features support **Configuration Plans** to modify environment-specific values easily, such as JDBC connection strings and host names of servers. Configuration plans enable the changing of any composite, service component, reference, service, and binding properties in the composite from environment to environment. These include attribute values (such as locations) for binding, `schemaLocation` of an import in a WSDL or XSD, location attribute of a WSDL, and properties in the JCA adapter files.

A configuration plan may be created in either Oracle JDeveloper or with **WebLogic Scripting Tool (WLST)** commands. A configuration plan file may be attached to an SOA composite application JAR file or ZIP file (if deploying a SOA bundle) during deployment with one of JDeveloper, EM, or WLST. During process deployment, the configuration plan is used to search the SOA project for values that must be replaced to adapt the project to the next target environment. The following code is a snippet of a sample configuration plan file:

```
<?xml version="1.0" encoding="UTF-8"?>
<SOAConfigPlan
 xmlns:jca="http://platform.integration.oracle/blocks/adapter/fw/
```

```
metadata"
 xmlns:wsp="http://schemas.xmlsoap.org/ws/2004/09/policy"
 xmlns:orawsp="http://schemas.oracle.com/ws/2006/01/policy"
 xmlns:edl="http://schemas.oracle.com/events/edl"
 xmlns="http://schemas.oracle.com/soa/configplan">
  <composite name="FileAdaptorComposite">
    <service name="readPO">
      <binding type="*">
        <property name="inFileFolder">
          <replace>/mytestserver/newinFileFolder</replace>
        </property>
      </binding>
    </service>
  </composite>
  <!-- For all composite replace host and port in all imports wsdls
-->
  <composite name="*">
    <imports>
      <searchReplace>
        <search>myserver17</search>
        <replace>test-server</replace>
      </searchReplace>
      <searchReplace>
        <search>8888</search>
        <replace>8198</replace>
      </searchReplace>
    </imports>
    <reference name="*">
      <binding type="ws">
        <attribute name="location">
          <searchReplace>
            <search>myserver17</search>
            <replace>test-server</replace>
          </searchReplace>
          <searchReplace>
            <search>8888</search>
            <replace>8198</replace>
          </searchReplace>
        </attribute>
      </binding>
    </reference>
  </composite>
</soaConfigPlan>
```

In addition to moving the project from one environment to another, it may also be desired to move configuration such as role mappings, view definitions, flex field mappings, and so on, from environment to environment. As all such runtime configuration is stored in MDS, they can be easily migrated. Oracle BPM includes a tool, **Data Migrator**, to do this migration. Data migrator is available as an ant target (ORACLE_HOME/bin/ant-t2p-worklist.xml) and uses a properties file, migration. properties, for specifying the parameters for migration.

In addition, WebLogic supports cloning, enabling easy replication of the environment with all patches applied consistently from one environment to another.

Summary

Oracle BPM Suite provides a comprehensive and seamlessly unified BPM platform that is built on an enterprise-grade platform providing superior manageability, scalability, and reliability. While providing business friendly features such as BPMN 2.0 and business rules modeling complemented with a high-degree of collaboration, it also provides robust features for application management such as test-to-production migration that are useful not only for enterprise-grade deployments, but also for departmental projects.

Functional Overview

The previous chapter discussed the architecture of Oracle BPM Suite 11*g* on top of an enterprise-grade architecture. Oracle BPM Suite 11*g* packs many best-of-breed features to enable customers to realize the potential of BPM. In this chapter, you'll see a brief summary of some of the key features of Oracle BPM Suite 11*g*.

Business-friendly modeling

Oracle BPM Suite 11*g* empowers business users through business-friendly modeling in the following ways:

- A comprehensive set of business modeling tools seamlessly unified within one integrated modeling environment. Different model types fit naturally to different types of business logic, and having access to a broad set of model types provides for easier and more transparent expression of the business problem.

- A combination of zero-code and what-you-model-is-what-you-execute paradigms where a business model becomes executable through progressive refinement instead of coding or some other transformation.

- Web-based process and rules, modeling, and change.

- A collaborative workspace.

BPM Studio

BPM Studio is a comprehensive integrated modeling environment. It supports persona-based profiles, allowing a process analyst persona to have access only to BPM modeling. However, a developer persona may also have access to XML, web services, and Java development.

BPM Studio includes the following model types.

BPMN 2.0

Business Process Modeling Notation (BPMN) 2.0 is a standard from Object Management Group (OMG). BPM Studio includes rich support for BPMN 2.0 modeling and simulation.

Oracle BPM Suite 11*g* supports BPMN 2.0 natively (that is, no transformation to another language or technology) and BPM Studio enables execution semantics to be associated with BPMN models via declarative property specifications. Through the usage of BPMN 2.0 constructs, such as gateways (exclusive, parallel, and complex) and events/event handlers, very complex process logics can be easily expressed.

The swim lanes in the BPMN process may be used as an assignment mechanism. They are logical process roles that are mapped to physical users and groups in an identity store, such as LDAP.

BPM Studio also enables simulation of one or more BPMN 2.0 processes using modeled process scenarios. Simulation enables what-if analysis of various metrics including time and cost metrics under different scenarios. Queue build-ups are visualized on the process model itself and resources may be dynamically changed to resolve such build-ups.

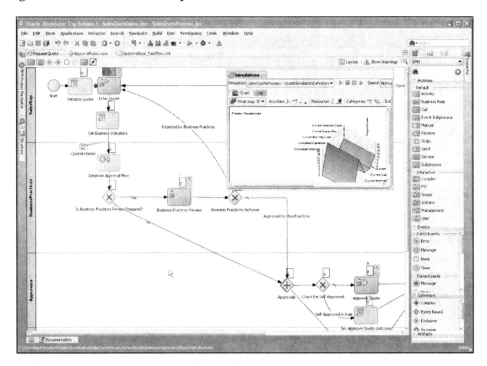

In addition to BPMN 2.0, Oracle BPM Studio also includes support for **Business Process Execution Language (BPEL)**. BPEL is particularly useful for integration flows and for service orchestrations.

Business Rules

Oracle BPM includes **Oracle Business Rules**, a RETE algorithm-based (see, for example, `http://en.wikipedia.org/wiki/Rete_algorithm`) true inference rules engine. BPM Studio includes business-friendly modeling of rules, including both if-then and decision-table metaphors. A **decision-table** uses a spreadsheet-type arrangement for expressing business rules and supports conflict (or overlap) detection as well as gap analysis. The gap analysis feature can also automatically create the table structure for the missing conditions.

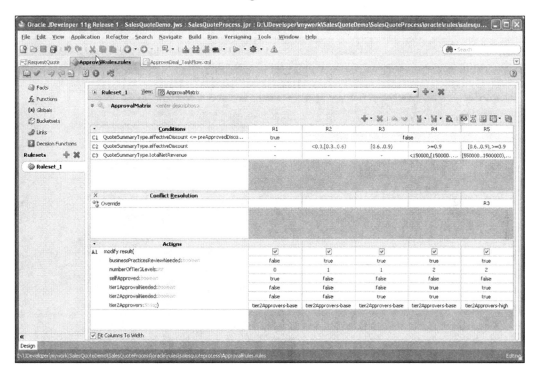

User interface (task forms)

Oracle BPM leverages **Oracle Application Development Framework** (ADF) for task forms (or user interfaces). ADF is a framework based on the industry-standard Java Server Faces (JSF) and includes:

- Visual drag-and-drop ADF designer
- Rich palette of highly interactive controls as well as data visualization elements (charts, graphs, trees, and so on)
- Declarative specification of complex UI behavior
- Consistent abstraction of backend data sources including BPM processes, databases, and web services, enabling easy composition of mashed-up pages
- A rich page-flow technology known as **ADF Task Flows** that not only provides for screen navigation but also allows invocation of automated services, evaluation of conditionals, and save/restore of state

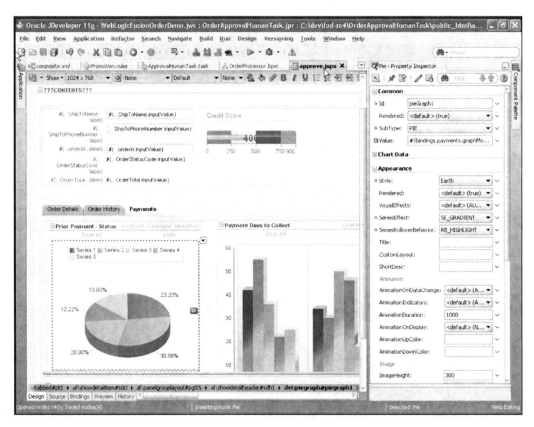

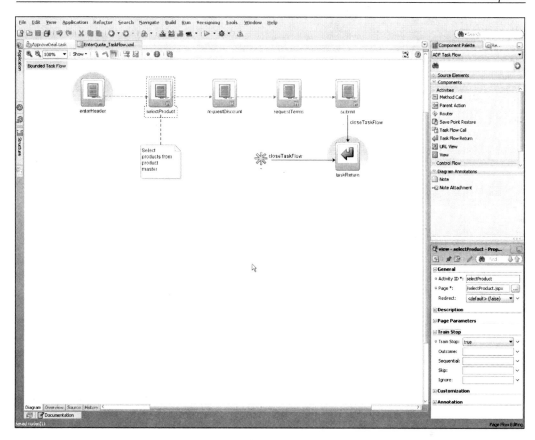

Also, Oracle BPM Studio includes wizards for generating the ADF views and Task Flows either completely automatically or based on user guidance. These generated UI elements may be used as-is or can be further enhanced in the ADF designer.

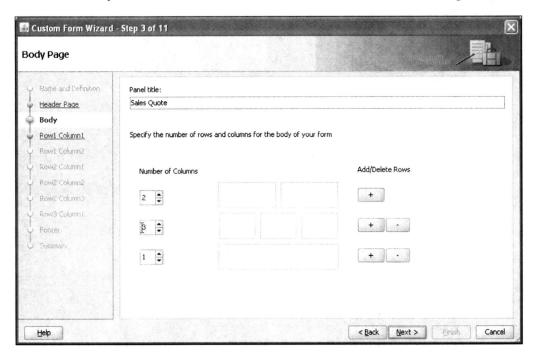

SCA Composite

The **SCA** (**Service Component Architecture**, refer to this link: `www.osoa.org`) The Composite model provides a component-level wiring diagram. It is automatically created and maintained as part of BPM modeling and its existence may be totally transparent to process analysts. Process developers would use the SCA editor as it provides access to web services and application or technology adapters, as well as to other Oracle SOA Suite components, such as Mediator. The services that developers create in this view gets added to the business catalog and is available to be used by process analysts in their BPMN processes.

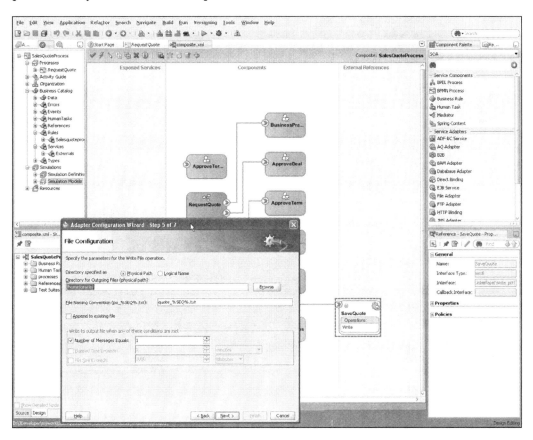

Process Composer

In addition to the BPM Studio, Oracle BPM Suite 11*g* includes a web-based process (BPMN 2.0) and business rules modeling and editing environment.

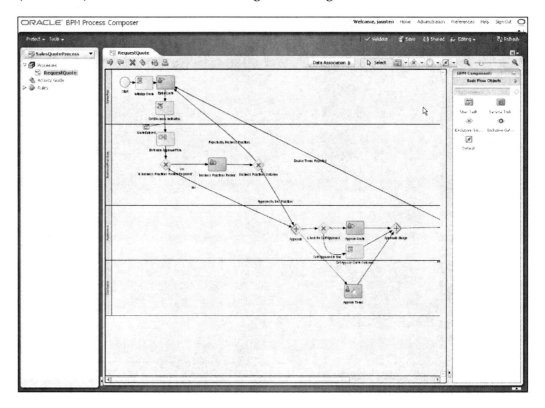

In addition to providing an easier to use interface, especially for users not wanting to install a tool on their desktop, **Process Composer** is also a role-based collaborative application. The role based access feature of Process Composer enables the Business Analyst to share the process definition with various stakeholders, many of whom may just have view-only access.

Modeling Space

Modeling Space is an out-of-the-box collaborative Oracle Web Center Space that facilitates team work and collaboration around the process model definition and evolution. The modeling team can use features such as discussions, documents, issues, Wikis, and blogs to collaborate more effectively as a team.

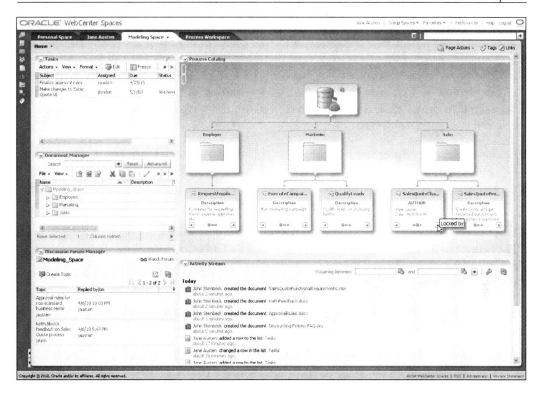

Process analysis

As discussed earlier, one of the big benefits of adopting BPM is the ability to continually analyze and optimize the processes. Oracle BPM Suite 11*g* features rich process analytics and change-edit features to enable this benefit.

The first aspect of process analysis is process simulation. Oracle BPM Studio enables specification of various scenarios for a given process, where a scenario includes probability distributions for various process events as well as a \resourcing and costing model. Multiple processes can be simulated simultaneously based on these scenarios. Various metrics including cost, unit, and time can be charted and analyzed. Also, queue build-ups are displayed overlaid on the process model and resources can be dynamically changed during a simulation run, to do what-if analysis. (See the screenshot in the *BPM Studio* section).

The second aspect of process analysis is to monitor and analyze interesting business indicators during process execution. Oracle BPM Suite 11*g* includes many out-of-the-box dashboards to analyze common business indicators such as cycle time, work distribution, work performance, and so on. In addition, process-specific business indicators may be specified by business analysts along with the process models. End users can create their own dashboards using these process-specific business indicators as well as standard indicators.

The dashboarding capability is also well integrated with Oracle Business Activity Monitoring (BAM). **Oracle BAM** is an events-based, real-time monitoring product that can aggregate events from a variety of sources, including Oracle BPM Suite 11*g* and supporting backend applications, correlate them, and present true end-to-end dashboards.

BPM Suite 11*g* has a STAR schema, called Process Cubes, underlying the dashboarding capabilities. Oracle BI EE and other business intelligence tools can easily work against this schema.

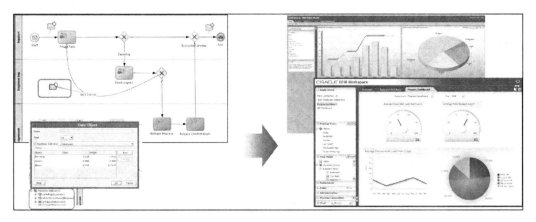

Also, Oracle BPA Suite, a complementary product for detailed business process analysis, enables modeling of various aspects of processes and their supporting environments, including objectives, risks, strategies, business capabilities, business services, applications, standards, and their inter-relationships. Rich reports and analyses can be produced based on such modeled information.

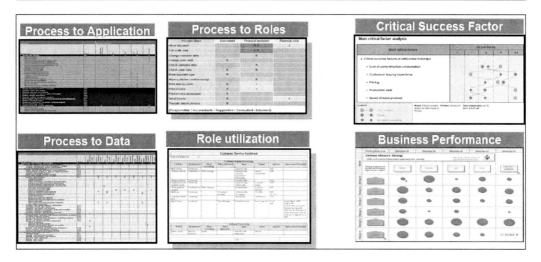

Productive work management

BPM should not only deliver efficiency through streamlined business processes and intelligent resource allocation, it should also help process participants in doing their job better. Oracle BPM Suite 11*g* includes many features to facilitate the performance of work from an end user's perspective, and thus not only increases their productivity but also makes them more enthusiastic in adopting BPM.

Process Spaces (Social BPM)

Process Spaces is an out-of-the-box collaborative and social application with composite and tailored interfaces that makes end users more productive through better collaboration.

Process Workspace

Process Workspace is a collaborative space composed of BPM task lists and other components such as dashboards, and Enterprise 2.0 functionalities such as discussions, documents, and so on. Using the built-in Page Composer, business users can customize the space and its pages, rearranging components as well as including other components available in the catalog. Other Oracle products such as Oracle BI may populate the catalog with their components; customers can add custom/external portlets as well as ADF applications to the catalog. Everything in the catalog is available to the business user editing a page in Page Composer, enabling them to compose mashed-up interfaces.

Process Workspace makes end users more productive in the following ways:

- Integrated document manager ensures that relevant policies and best practices are always available to process participants

- Best practices, tips, techniques, and issues can be discussed leveraging the integrated discussions forum

- Ability to compose mashed-up interfaces mean that process participants have, at the point of action, all the insights and information needed to make the best decisions

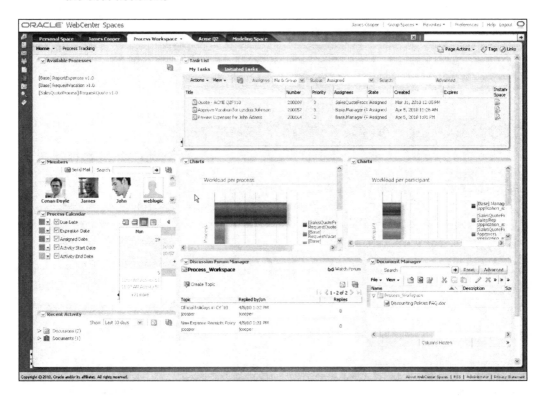

Process instance space

Some processes are very collaborative and ad hoc in nature. In typical BPM products, the collaboration and ad hoc interactions happen outside of the BPM product, creating a rich shadow process that unfortunately is not traceable or auditable.

Chapter 4

Oracle BPM Suite 11*g* supports the creation of a collaboration space specific to a process instance. In this space, process participants can not only see and manage the process instance as modeled and executed in the BPM Suite process execution engine, but also use its team collaboration capability to collaborate on the process completion. For example, a sales team working on a specific opportunity can create a collaboration space tied to the process instance (RequestQuote process) and use that space to manage all the documents, discussions, and events associated with closing the opportunity.

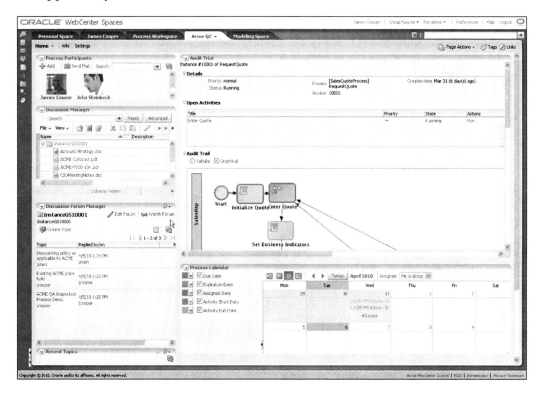

Work organization and management

In addition to the collaboration features described earlier, Oracle BPM Suite 11*g* includes features enabling process participants to organize and streamline their work.

[55]

Views

Views enable organization of work. A view is essentially a search criteria; it can also have display attributes including columns to include and sort order. Views can be used not only to organize one's work but also as a delegation mechanism—entire views may be delegated.

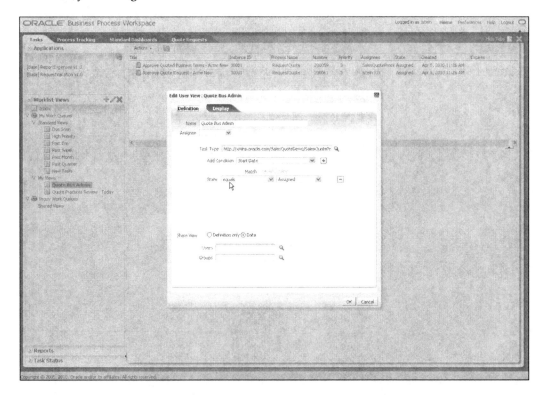

Personal and group rules

Oracle BPM Suite 11*g* features rules-driven work management. Using a very simple-to-use interface, end users can write rules to handle work assigned to them. These rules may reassign, delegate, or automatically complete the work. Users managing groups can also write rules handling work assigned to the group. In this scenario, out-of-the-box as well as custom load balancing algorithms may be used.

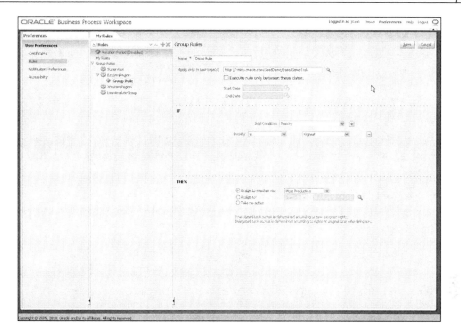

Dashboard-driven filtering

Earlier in the chapter, we discussed Oracle BPM Suite 11*g*'s support for out-of-the-box as well as custom business indicators and dashboards. These dashboards may also be used to filter the process instances. For users dealing with a large work load, who need some intelligent analysis on what to focus on, the ability to drill down from process dashboards to a filtered list of instances is very helpful.

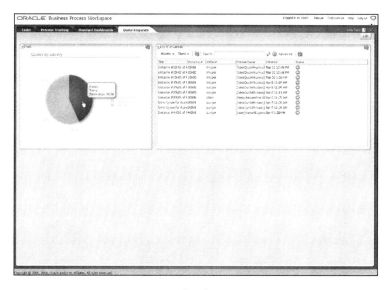

Built for change

Agility, or the ability to respond with speed, is an important benefit of BPM. Agility comes from at least the following three aspects of BPM:

- BPM projects can be rapidly developed and deployed using tooling discussed earlier.

- BPM processes have optimized cycle times, both through streamlining of the process as well as through enhanced productivity of end users as discussed in the previous section.

- Once the operating environment changes, a BPM process can rapidly react to that change. This section describes how Oracle BPM Suite 11*g* supports rapid change.

The first aspect of being able to react to change is to build the processes to be resilient to change. The most common way this can be accomplished is by leveraging business rules—rules that can be changed independent of the process as needed.

Oracle BPM Suite 11*g* not only integrates business rules seamlessly into process definitions but also leverages rules more pervasively to provide more resilience to change. Some such usages beyond a process using business rules as a decision activity include:

- A process activity can be dynamically bound to its implementation based on business rules. This is an elegant pattern to handle variance in processes arising from differences in geographies, products, and so on.

- Business rules can drive task assignment and routing.

- End users can define their own work management rules as discussed in previous section.

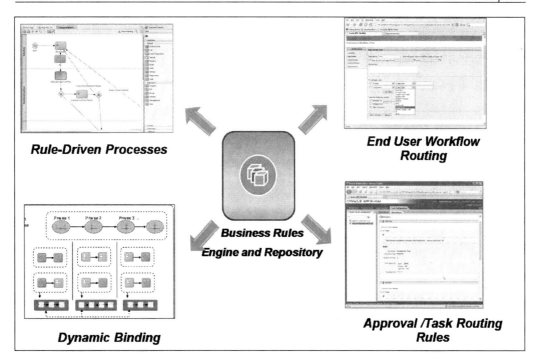

Rule-Driven Processes

End User Workflow Routing

Business Rules Engine and Repository

Dynamic Binding

Approval /Task Routing Rules

In spite of building the process to be resilient to change, it may not be possible to foresee all possible variances or exceptions. In such scenarios, Oracle BPM Suite 11*g* enables an appropriately privileged user to change the process in an ad hoc fashion. Such changes include:

- Reassignment of current task
- Re-routing of current task, including adding additional participants

- Re-routing of future task, including adding additional participants

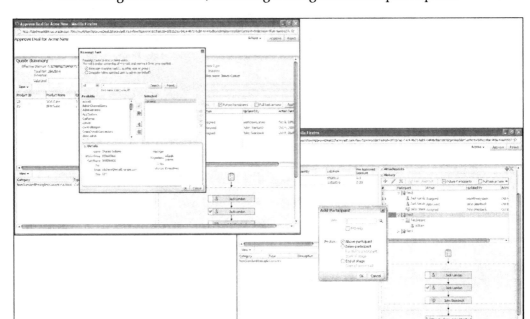

Finally, there are situations where the process definition needs to be changed. Process Composer (discussed earlier) enables rapid change to process definition. By enabling business users or analysts to change the processes themselves and deploy without requiring any IT engagement is a key enabler of agility. While addressing the need to change rapidly, Process Composer also features governance mechanisms to protect from bad changes. These mechanisms include:

- The ability to specify in the process model what can and cannot be changed
- Support for change approval workflows

Summary

Oracle BPM Suite 11*g* includes a rich set of features in a very complete and unified product. These features deliver on BPM's promise of efficiency, visibility, and agility in the following ways:

- Business-friendly modeling tools that allow the business users to model and manage their business processes
- Rich process analysis capabilities that enable the discipline of continuous process improvement as well as allows the process initiatives to be aligned with business drivers and IT landscape
- Easy to use, collaborative, and social interfaces that enable end users to be more productive as well as make better decisions leveraging more enterprise knowledge and insight
- The ability to handle anticipated and unanticipated changes

5
The Tutorial Project: Sales Quote Processing

Throughout this book, you will be incrementally building a business process-based composite application, exploring functionalities of all of the key components in the Oracle BPM Suite, and how they can be used together.

Structure of the tutorial

The tutorial is laid out to mimic a typical BPM life cycle. You begin purely from a Business Analyst perspective and end with a fully-functional running process providing real-time reports on the progress and the health of the process.

The following diagram illustrates this development process. In reality, the whole development process may be (and is recommended to be) iterative in the form of a closed-loop cycle. For the tutorial, you will be progressing through the steps illustrated in the diagram.

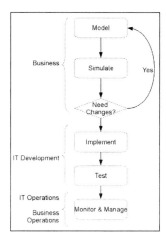

You start off as a Business Analyst, modeling a process for processing a Sales Quote—from the point it is created by a sales representative to the point it is sent to an ERP application for further processing. A Business Analyst should not be concerned with technical details, such as database interactions, service end points, and so on. The model he or she creates should describe the series of activities that when executed, either managed manually or by a process execution engine, results in the expected business outcome.

You will see how Oracle BPM 11*g* keeps the modeling unpolluted from technical details in *Chapter 7, Process Modelling using BPMN 2.0*. The chapter introduces the BPMN 2.0 standard and its modeling elements such as activities, gateways, and events. You will use these to create the process model for the Sales Quote process use case.

A typical process has multiple user tasks that a person or group of persons need to perform. BPMN defines a concept of a **Lane**, which maps to roles and is used to associate roles to user tasks. This association, in most cases defines the initial performer of a given user task. The relationship between roles, user, user groups, and the organization of these roles, as it pertains to the process, is defined using the Organizational Model. *Chapter 8, Process Organization Model*, discusses these aspects in detail.

Once modeled, a process may go through a simulation exercise where what-if scenarios are used to observe how the process performs, given a set of constraints. The BPM Studio in Oracle BPM 11*g* includes a simulation engine which allows you to do just that. You will learn, in *Chapter 9, Simulation and Analysis of the Business Process*, what simulation definitions and simulation models are, and how to run different simulations to identify bottlenecks in the process.

Once a business process model is complete from a business functionality perspective, it is then handed over to SOA/BPM developers to add technical details to it so that it can run on a process server such as the Oracle BPM 11*g* process engine. *Chapter 10, Implementation of the Business Process*, gives details on how to add implementation details for the different types of tasks, such as User Tasks and Service Tasks. It also covers handling of data in a process using business object types and process variables.

Oracle BPM 11*g* also provides a 100 percent web-browser based-process modeling tool called **BPM Composer**, which is ideal for business users. It allows for template-based modeling where business users can create new processes from pre-built process templates and related assets. The composer is also an ideal tool for doing customizations to existing processes without using a heavy-duty IDE like JDeveloper. All these feature and usages are described in *Chapter 11, Using Process Composer*, along with step-by-step instructions on converting the Sales Quote process to a template using JDeveloper and then using that template in the composer.

Oracle BPM Workspace is the primary user interface for interacting with the user tasks. This is a rich, web-based work-list management application that BPM end users will use to perform their assigned tasks. This tool also provides all the administrative functions for managing different aspects of user task flows such as user-role mapping, management of approval groups, calendar management, and so on. *Chapter 12, Using Process Spaces and Workspace Application,* describes these and many more features offered by the BPM Workspace. It also introduces Process Spaces, which is an Oracle WebCenter-based workspace that integrates Web 2.0 features with BPM Suite for collaboration during process modeling as well as on resolving issues on one or more instances of a running process.

Chapter 13, Process Analytics and Business Activity Monitoring, introduces process analytics and reporting using the BPM Workspace. It describes the steps for adding measurement points in the process for enabling reporting, and for creating reports and dashboards end user consumption. This chapter walks you through for creating a custom report tab in the BPM Workspace that shows measurements for the Sales Quote process. The same measurement data can also be sent to **Oracle Business Activity Monitor (BAM)** for creating real-time dashboards. This chapter also provides step-by-step instructions for integration with BAM as well as for creating custom reports in the BPM Workspace.

In *Chapter 14, Using Business Rules,* you will enhance the process by putting in a decision step that evaluates the Sales Quote to determine whether a business practices compliance review is required. It will also establish, based on certain rules, the types of approvals needed. All this will be done using a **Decision Table** in the **Oracle Business Rules Engine** and without writing a single line of code.

You will further enrich the process by converting one of the user tasks to use the output of the Business Rules Engine to perform a complex task flow for approving the sales quote. *Chapter 15, Using Human Task patterns and other concepts,* discusses different task flow patterns available out of the box, such as Simple Task, Management Task, Group Task, FYI Task, and so on. Also, it provides steps to create a complex task flow using these core patterns.

You will learn how to build non-trivial Rich Internet Applications (RIA) for the human tasks modelled in the process in *Chapter 16, User Interface Development for Human Tasks.* This chapter provides a brief introduction to Oracle Application Development Framework (ADF) and provides step-by-step instructions for creating complex, rich web-based user interfaces using ADF components such as ADF Task Flows, ADF Faces components, ADFBC task-flow data controls, and so on.

Chapter 17, Events and Exception Handling, goes into some of the advanced modelling concepts and discusses event handling and modeling for exception handling. This chapter covers different types of start, intermediate, and end events the BPM 2.0 defines. It also explains the use of event subprocesses and multi-instance subprocesses.

One of the powerful features of Oracle BPM 11*g* is collaborative BPM. Collaboration is achieved by using Web 2.0 features, such as discussion groups, forums, mash-ups, and so on, in the context of a BPM project, a process, or an instance. Oracle WebCenter spaces is the underlying technology that allows you to create a complex composite UI using different services and provides a highly customizable user interface. *Chapter 18, Customizing and Extending Process Spaces,* introduces Work Space customization using step-by-step, hands-on exercises. It covers end user personalization, process spaces customization and explains different customization capabilities based on roles such as administrator, moderator, developer, and so on.

Monitoring and managing your BPM environment is the focus of *Chapter 19, Administering the BPM Environment.* It covers both, BPM administration from a functional point of view as well as administration of the BPM system. In explaining BPM administration, the chapter uses a couple of short exercises to illustrate the various functions available to the BPM Administrator. For system administrators responsible for managing and maintaining the Oracle BPM 11*g* system, the chapter provides details on managing the BPM process life cycle and end-to-end tracking of instances. Since Oracle BPM 11*g* is part of the unified Fusion Middleware platform and provides a single management console for managing all components in the platform, this chapter focuses primarily on the ones relevant to BPM.

The tutorial progressively builds up to the final solution and hence the labs have to be completed in sequence. In case you want to skip one or more of the chapters, we provide complete working solutions for each chapter. For example, if you are already familiar with BPMN 2.0 modeling and are interested in learning about the implementation details, you can use the completed solution for that chapter as the starting point for your implementation chapter. The following diagram illustrates the flow of the hands-on exercises:

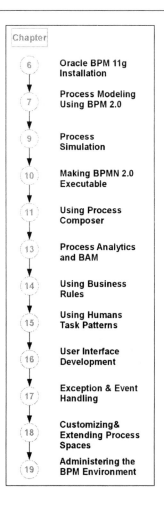

Sales Quote tutorial scenario

You will be modeling and creating a BPM application for creating new Sales Quotes. The process starts with the sales representative creating a new sales quote and submitting it for approval.

The quote is then checked to see if any special approvals are required. If the quote requires special review, it is sent to the Business Practices reviewers for checking business practices compliance.

If the quote does not warrant a business practices review or if the business practices review approves the quote, then it is sent for approval to the appropriate management levels. The levels of management that the quote needs to go up to are determined based on the value of the quote and rate of discount offered.

At the same time that the quote is sent for management approval, it is also sent to the contract review team for review and for approving terms and conditions attached to the quote.

Once both the quote price approval by management and terms and conditions approval by the contracts teams completes with an overall approval outcome, the quote is sent to the contracts team for finalizing the contract and recording the quote into a backend ERP system. If any of the approvals results in a rejection, the quote is sent back to the sales representative who created the quote. The following process illustrates the flow:

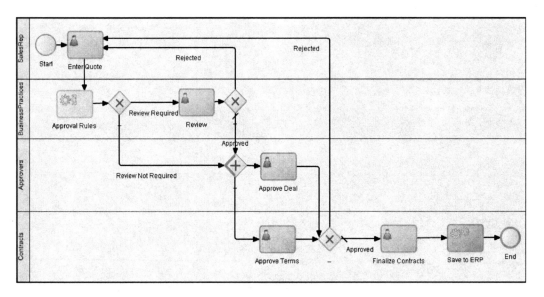

The business requirements are as follows. The sales quote needs to capture:

- Customer information, including the industry the customer belongs to, any customer contacts, and so on.
- List of items that the quote is being prepared for with any discounts being offered. Only those items can be quoted which are listed in the published price list.
- Any terms and conditions that need to be added.
- Each item will have some preapproved discount limits.
- If effective total discount for all the items in the quote is less than preapproved discount, no special approvals are required and the quote is treated as having been automatically approved.

- If effective discount exceeds preapproved discounts the quote needs to be reviewed for business practices compliance.

- If discount exceeds 89 percent, additional approval from a higher-level manager is required.

- If the net quote value exceeds 0.5 million, two managers need to approve the deal.

- All quotes, irrespective of the discount offered or the net value of the quote, have to always go through contractual review for terms and conditions and the final quote.

- Once complete, the quote needs to be sent to the company's ERP system.

Tutorial files

To build this tutorial you will need a few files such as the XML schema for the quote data object, scripts for creating the database objects, and so on. These files can be downloaded as a single compressed archive from the Oracle Technology Network at: `http://www.oracle.com/technetwork/middleware/bpm/learnmore/index.html`.

The ZIP archive is structured as follows:

- `input` — contains sample input data

- `sql` — database scripts for creating the quote schema required for the lab exercises

- `schemas` — XML schema definitions

- `solutions / chh#` — a completed, working solution as a JDeveloper project for each chapter

- `adflib` — page templates library needed for Chapter 16

- `lib` — pre-compiled java classes needed for Chapter 16

After unzipping the `SOA11gFoundationTutorial.zip` file, move or copy it to `c:\bpm`.

The instructions in this book assume that you are on the Microsoft Windows operating system and that you will be using this default path of `c:\bpm`. Note that you can of course use another location for the tutorial. In that case you will need to remember to adjust instructions accordingly when `c:\bpm` is referenced.

Summary

Now that you know what you are going to build in this tutorial and you have the artifacts you need to build it, it's time to get started. The next chapter describes the installation process.

6

Product Installation

This chapter provides the instructions for installing and configuring the Oracle BPM Suite server and the Oracle JDeveloper development tool needed to run the tutorial. These instructions are for the GA version of 11*g* Release 1 (11.1.1.3.0), dated April 2010.

These instructions are Windows-based but Linux users should have no difficulty adjusting them for their environment.

Checking your installation

If you already have BPM Suite and BPM Studio (JDeveloper) installed, confirm that you have the correct version and configuration by following the steps in the following section called *Testing your installation*. In addition, you may choose to complete the items in the section called *Additional Actions*.

What you will need and where to get it

Before you can begin the installation, you need to check your machine, download installation files, and check your database, browser, and JDK versions. Follow the instructions in this section carefully for a successful install.

What to install

BPM Suite 11*g*R1 and SOA Suite 11*g*R1 PS2 installation binaries are the same. That is, the binaries you download are the same whether you want to install BPM Suite or SOA Suite, and both get installed when you install. With BPM Suite, you also can choose to install the Process Spaces component, which requires WebCenter.

This document describes how to install BPM Suite from scratch. It does not describe how to upgrade from SOA Suite PS1.

If you want more details about other installation options or how to install other components, see the *Oracle Fusion Middleware 11g Release 1 Documentation* at http://www.oracle.com/technology/documentation/middleware.html

For BPM Suite you install the following components. For Process Spaces you also install WebCenter. The rest of this document describes the process.

Database	WebLogic Server	RCU
SOA	JDeveloper	WebCenter

Memory and disk space requirements

Without WebCenter, the software requires a minimum of 3 GB available memory to run, but more is recommended. With WebCenter on the same machine, the minimum is 4 GB but more is recommended.

If you have less, separate the installation of the database, the servers, and JDeveloper onto different machines.

Without WebCenter, you need about 10 GB of disk space to download the install files plus about 10 GB to install everything. WebCenter requires an additional 10GB. Your database takes an additional 5 GB (or so, depending on your configuration).

Disk and Memory Requirements	Download Disk Space	Memory	Installed Disk Space without database
Without WebCenter	10 GB	3 GB minimum	Approx 5 GB
With WebCenter	40 GB	4 GB minimum	Approx 20 GB

Downloading files

1. Create c:\stageFMW to hold the download files used for installation. If you already have this directory from a previous install, empty it first.

This document assumes this directory. If you save the files somewhere else then make sure there are no spaces in your path and adjust accordingly when c:\stageFMW is referenced in this document.

2. Locate your download location from where you will download the installation files. You can download from eDelivery or from Oracle Technology Network at `http://www.oracle.com/technology/products/soa/soasuite/index.html`

3. Download the following to `c:\stageFMW`. Some file names may be slightly different. The database component is handled later in this document.

    Some components are generic and some are platform specific. Some components require multiple files. You will be installing both PS1 and PS2. Read the list carefully.

    ° **WebLogic Server** (select WLS + Coherence option) — `wls1033_win32.exe`

    ° **RCU** (includes both BPM and SOA) — `ofm_rcu_win_11.1.1.3.0_disk1_1of1.zip`

    ° **SOA** (includes both BPM and SOA, PS1 and PS2) — `ofm_soa_generic_11.1.1.2.0_disk1_1of1.zip`, and `ofm_soa_generic_11.1.1.3.0_disk1_1of1.zip`

    ° **WebCenter** (only if installing Process Spaces) — `ofm_wc_generic_11.1.1.2.0_disk1_1of1.zip`, and `ofm_wc_generic_11.1.1.3.0_disk1_1of1.zip` `ofm_ucm_generic_10.1.3.5.1_disk1_1of1.zip` `ofm_webtier_win_11.1.1.2.0_32_disk1_1of1.zip`, and `ofm_webtier_win_11.1.1.3.0_32_disk1_1of1.zip`

    ° **JDeveloper** — `jdevstudio11113install.exe` or `jdevstudio11113install.jar`

    ° **JDeveloper extensions for SOA and BPM**

       (optional download, can update automatically with JDeveloper) — `bpm-jdev-extension.zip` `soa-jdev-extension.zip`

    ° **Demo Community** — `workflow-001-DemoCommunitySeedApp.zip` you can find this on the Human Workflow samples page: `http://www.oracle.com/technology/sample_code/products/hwf/index.html`

4. Extract the installation files as follows:

    ° `ofm_soa_generic_11.1.1.2.0_disk1_1of1.zip` to `c:\stageFMW\SOAPS1`

    ° `ofm_soa_generic_11.1.1.3.0_disk1_1of1.zip` to `c:\stageFMW\SOAPS2`

        °   `ofm_rcu_win_11.1.1.3.0_disk1_1of1.zip` to
             `c:\stageFMW\RCU`

5. If installing Process Spaces, extract the following:

        °   `ofm_wc_generic_11.1.1.2.0_disk1_1of1.zip` to
             `c:\stageFMW\WCPS1`

        °   `ofm_wc_generic_11.1.1.3.0_disk1_1of1.zip` to
             `c:\stageFMW\WCPS2`

        °   `ofm_ucm_generic_10.1.3.5.1_disk1_1of1.zip` to
             `c:\stageFMW\UCM`

        °   `ofm_webtier_win_11.1.1.2.0_32_disk1_1of1.zip` to
             `c:\stageFMW\WTPS1`

        °   `ofm_webtier_win_11.1.1.3.0_32_disk1_1of1.zip` to
             `c:\stageFMW\WTPS2`

6. Finally, extract the following:

        °   `workflow-001-DemoCommunitySeedApp.zip` to
             `c:\stageFMW\democommunity`

Checking your browser

- Enterprise Manager requires Firefox 3 or IE 7+:

    ° Firefox 3 — use `http://portableapps.com` and keep Firefox 2 if you use Rules Author in 10gR3

    ° Firefox 2 and IE 6 do not work in 11*g*

- BAM requires IE 7:

    ° IE 7 without special plugins (there's a Pro-search plugin that causes problems)

    ° IE 8 does not work. IE 6 has a few UI issues. Firefox does not work

Checking your JDK

The WebLogic server installation `exe` is packaged with a JDK. If you install JDeveloper from an `exe` then that also comes with a JDK. The JDeveloper installation `jar` does not.

You can use the install `jar` to install on Windows or non-Windows. If you are going to install the WebLogic server and JDeveloper on the same machine you use the JDK from WebLogic for JDeveloper too. However, if you are going to install on separate machines, you need to have Oracle Sun Java 1.6 update 18 JDK for JDeveloper. You can get it from the Oracle Sun downloads page. Be sure to get the JDK not the JRE: `http://java.sun.com/products/archive/`.

Installation

Now you have all of the files required for the installation of BPM Suite 11*g*R1 except possibly the database. The first step is to confirm your database installation and install a database if necessary.

Installing the database

Database	WebLogic Server	RCU
SOA	JDeveloper	WebCenter

Determine which database version you have already, if any, and then decide which database version you will use for your BPM installation. Oracle XE Universal is the recommended choice for development due to its small footprint.

You need one of the following:

- XE Universal or Standard database version 10.2.0.1
- 10g database version 10.2.0.4+
- 11*g* database version 11.1.0.7+

You may see problems with installing XE when you already have 10g installed on Windows. The Windows registry sometimes gets the database file locations confused. If you need to uninstall a database, you should follow these instructions.

- If you need to uninstall XE, be sure to follow these instructions:
    - ° *Oracle Database Express Edition Installation Guide*
    - ° *10g Release 2 (10.2) for Microsoft Windows*
    - ° *Part Number B25143-03, Section 7,Deinstalling Oracle Database XE*:
      `http://download.oracle.com/docs/cd/B25329_01/doc/install.102/b25143/toc.htm#CIHDDHJD`

- If you need to uninstall 10.2, be sure to follow these instructions:

  ° *Oracle Database Installation Guide*

  ° *10g Release 2 (10.2) for Microsoft Windows (32-Bit)*

  ° *Part Number B14316-04, Section 6, Removing Oracle Database Software*:
    `http://download.oracle.com/docs/cd/B19306_01/` `install.102/b14316/deinstall.htm#CIHDGGJJ`.

- If needed, install `OracleXEUniv.exe` or `OracleXE.exe`

  This is recommended for small footprint database. You may see problems with installing XE when you already have 10g installed. You can get XE from here: `http://www.oracle.com/technology/software/products/` `database/xe/index.html`.

- If needed, configure Oracle XE.

When you are using Oracle XE, you must update database parameters if you have never done this for your database installation. You only have to do this once after installing. Set the processes parameter to `>=300` as follows.

The shutdown command can take a few minutes. Sometimes the shutdown/startup command fails. In that case, simply restart the XE service in the **Control Panel | Administrative Tools | Services** dialog after setting your parameters.

```
sqlplus sys/welcome1@XE as sysdba
SQL> show parameter session
SQL> show parameter processes
SQL> alter system reset sessions scope=spfile sid='*';
SQL> alter system set processes=300 scope=spfile;
SQL> shutdown immediate
SQL> startup
SQL> show parameter session
SQL> show parameter processes
```

Installing WebLogic server

Database	WebLogic Server	RCU
SOA	JDeveloper	WebCenter

Once your database is ready, you can install the next step, the WebLogic server.

If you want to upgrade from SOA PS1 instead of installing from scratch, see the first section on where to find information about upgrading. This document only includes instructions for installing from scratch.

If you have installed BPM 11*g* or SOA 11*g* before and want to install again in the same location, you must uninstall the previous one first. See the section at the end of this document on uninstalling.

When you are ready to install, complete the following:

1. Open a command window and enter:

    ```
    cd c:\stageFMW
    wls1033_win32.exe
    ```

2. When the install wizard comes up, click on the **Next** window. Select **Create a new Middleware Home** and enter **c:\Oracle\Middleware\home_ps2**. This document assumes that path. If you use a different middleware home then adjust accordingly when C:\Oracle\Middleware\home_ps2 is referenced throughout this document.

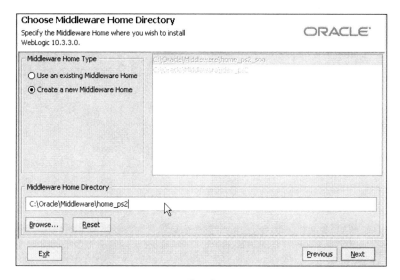

3. Click on the **Next** button.

4. Enter e-mail to register for security alerts or disable the checkbox and decline whichever you prefer, click on **Next**.

5. Select **Typical**, click on **Next**.

6. Review installation directories.

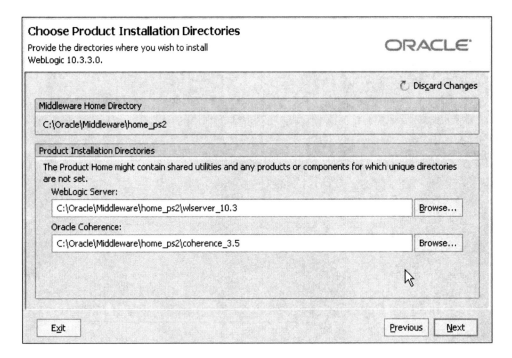

7. Click on **Next**.

8. Select **All Users Start Menu folder**, click on **Next**.

9. Review the summary.

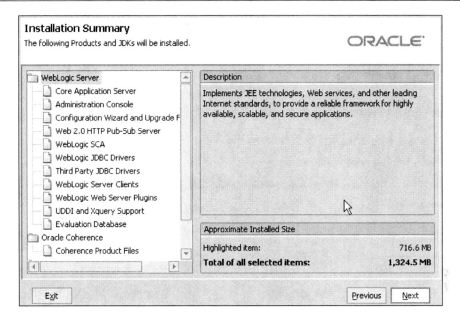

10. Click on **Next** to start the installation process. Install takes about five minutes.

11. When the install is complete, disable the **Run Quickstart** checkbox and click on **Done**.

Installing database schema using RCU

Database	WebLogic Server	RCU
SOA	JDeveloper	WebCenter

Now it is time to set up the database schema.

If you have installed BPM or SOA 11*g* before and you are not upgrading, you must drop your existing database schema before reinstalling or create a second schema for this installation. You cannot reuse an existing schema. See the section in this document on uninstalling to drop an existing schema. After you drop the existing schema, come back here to configure the new schema.

If you want to upgrade from SOA PS1, see the first section in this document about where to find information about upgrading. This document includes instructions only for installing from scratch.

Configuring schema

Now create the new schema. Open a command window and enter the following:

```
cd c:\stageFMW\RCU\bin
rcu.bat
```

The Repository Creation Utility opens.

1. On the welcome screen, click on the **Next** button.

2. Select the **Create** option.

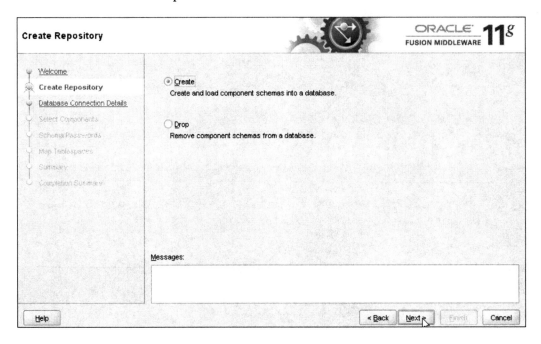

3. Click on **Next**.

4. Enter the database information.

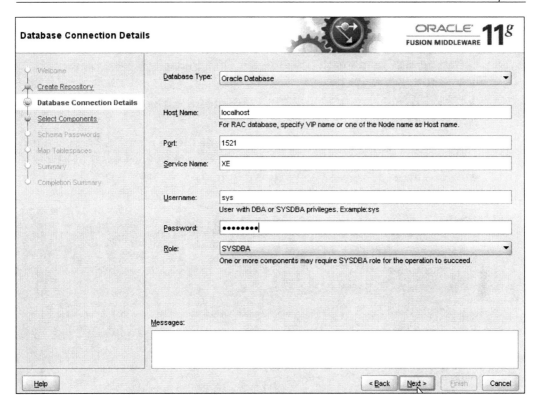

5. Click on **Next**.

6. If you are using XE, you will see a warning when you install the schema that this version is too old. You can safely ignore this warning as it applies only to production environments.

If you are using XE Standard, not Universal, you will also see a warning about character sets. You can safely ignore this warning. If you wish to use extended character sets you must use XE Universal.

7. The pre-requisites are reviewed. When complete, click on the **OK button**. The utility moves to the next page with a slight delay, just wait for it.

8. On the **Select Components** screen, enter **DEV** in the field for creating a new prefix.

9. Select the component **SOA and BPM Infrastruture**. Dependent schemas are selected automatically.

10. If you choose to select other components, these install instructions may not match your experience. Also, you may have to increase processes in XE (you will get a message telling you what is required).

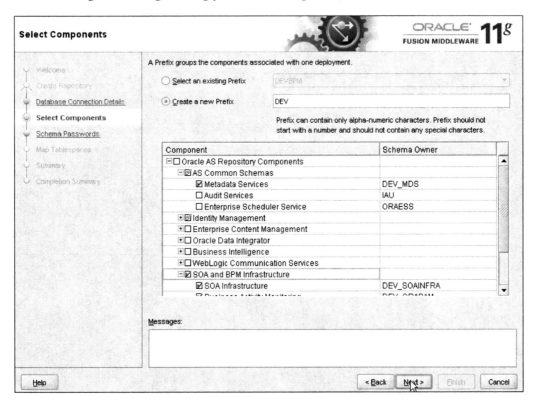

11. Click on the **Next** button.

12. The pre-requisites for this step are checked. When completed, click on **OK**.

13. Select the radio button to **Use the same password for all schemas**. Enter a schema password. The password **welcome1** is assumed in this document but you should choose your own secure password or a different one for each schema and be sure to record your passwords as you will need them later.

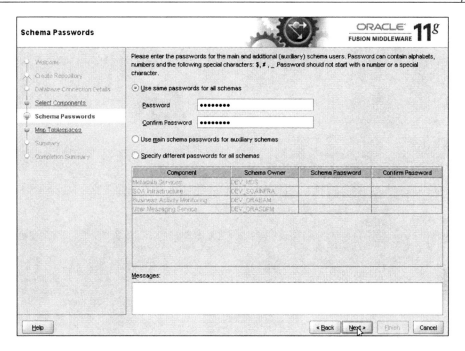

14. Click on the **Next** button.

15. Review the tablespaces and schema owners for the components.

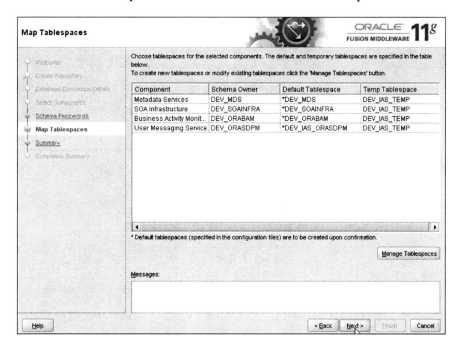

16. Accepting the defaults, click on **Next** and then click on **OK** to create the tablespaces.

17. When the pre-requisites for this step are completed, click on **OK**.

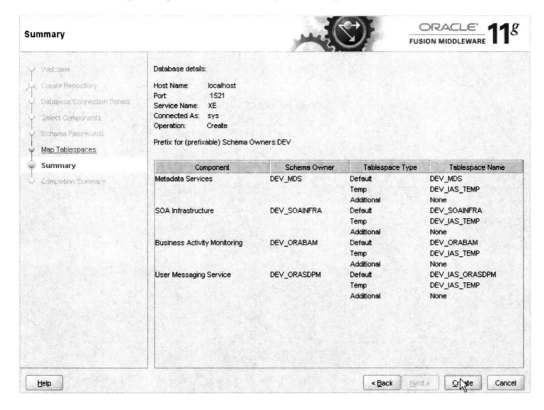

18. Click on **Create** to create the tablespaces. This takes about two minutes.

19. When completed, click on **Close**.

Installing BPM

Database	WebLogic Server	RCU
SOA	JDeveloper	WebCenter

Once the schema has been created, you are ready to install the BPM server.

To install BPM 11*g*R1 (also known as SOA 11*g*R1 PS2), you first install SOA 11*g*R1 PS1 and then SOA 11*g*R1 PS2.

Installing SOA PS1

Locate the JDK directory path within the installed middleware home. You use this path in the next command. The JDK location is jdk160_18.

1. In a command window enter:

    ```
    cd c:\stageFMW\SOCPS1\Disk1
    setup -jreLoc C:\Oracle\Middleware\home_ps2\jdk160_18
    ```

2. When the install wizard welcome screen comes up, click **Next**.

    Wait for the pre-requisite check to complete (it's quick!)

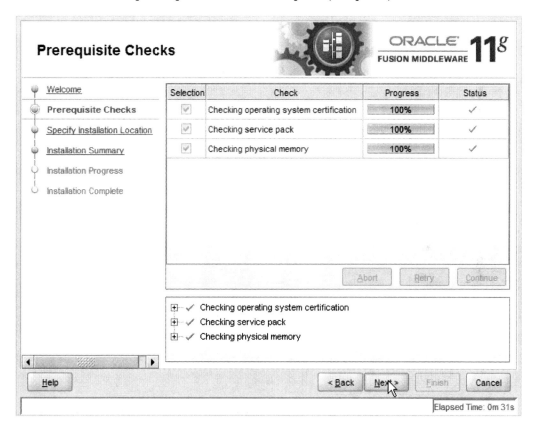

3. Click on the **Next** button.

4. On the **Specify Installation Location** screen, select the **Middleware** home:
    `C:\Oracle\Middleware\home_ps2`.

5. Enter **Oracle Home Directory: Oracle_SOA1**. If you use a different Oracle home then adjust accordingly when Oracle_SOA1 is referenced throughout this document.

6. Click on the **Next** button.
7. Review the summary.

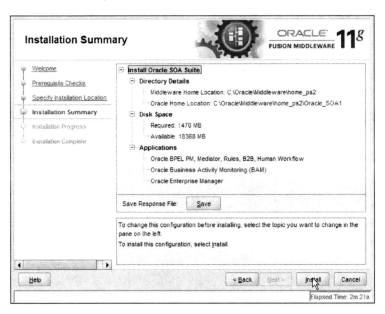

8. Click on **Install**.

9. Wait for the install to complete—it takes a few minutes.

10. When install reaches 100 percent, click on **Next** and then click on the **Finish** button.

Installing SOA PS2 with BPM 11gR1

This step is exactly the same as the previous step for SOA but you run setup from the SOAPS2 directory. BPM is installed with SOA Suite 11gR1 PS2.

1. In a command window enter:

```
cd c:\stageFMW\SOAPS2\Disk1
setup -jreLoc C:\Oracle\Middleware\home_ps2\jdk160_18
```

Complete the remaining screens in the wizard as described for installing SOA above and be sure to use the same Oracle home location, for example Oracle_SOA1, when you get to step 3 of the wizard. You will need to edit this value since it defaults to a unique Oracle home.

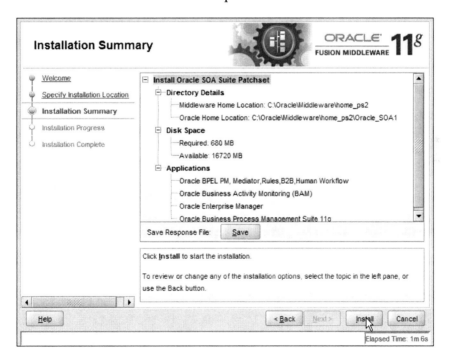

2. Confirm that the installation summary is correct and select **Install**. Wait for the install to complete—it takes a few minutes.

3. When install reaches 100 percent, click on **Next** and then click on **Finish**.

Creating domain

Now that you have the software installed, you can create the WebLogic domain for the server.

1. In a command window enter:

    ```
    cd C:\Oracle\Middleware\home_ps2\Oracle_SOA1\common\bin
    config.cmd
    ```

2. When the configuration wizard welcome screen comes up, select **Create a new WebLogic domain**, and then click **Next**.

3. Select **Generate a domain** and select **BPM Suite, SOA Suite, Enterprise Manager**, and **Business Activity Monitoring**. Dependent products are selected automatically. If you are installing Process Spaces, you add this at a later step.

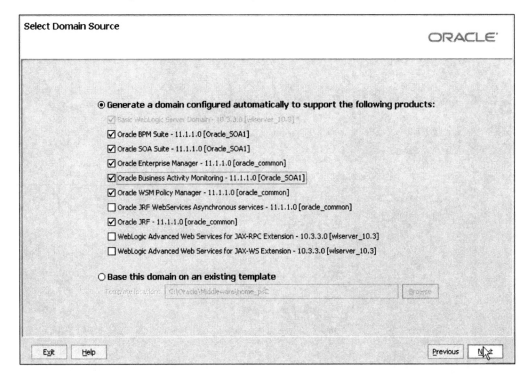

4. Click on **Next**.

5. Enter the **Domain name**: **domain1**.

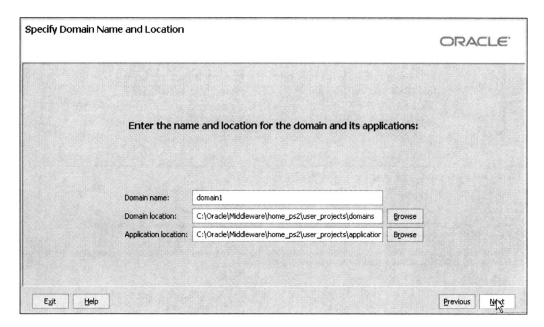

6. Click on **Next**.

7. Enter username **weblogic** and a password. The password, **welcome1**, is assumed in this document but you should choose your own secure password and remember it for later in the document when the password is referenced.

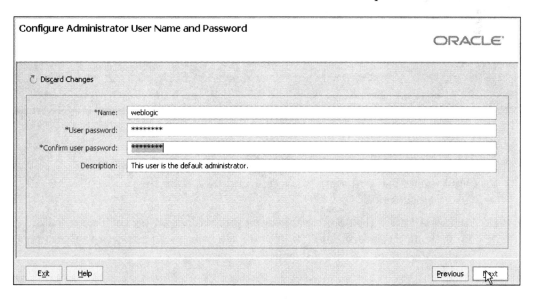

8. Click on **Next**.

9. Select either the Sun or JRockit SDK 1.6_18 and leave Development
   Mode checked.

 There is an issue with editing BAM reports with Oracle Sun JDK
1.6_18. If you will be using BAM, choose Oracle JRockit or, if you
need to use the Sun JDK you will need an updated version — see *My
Support* for the correct JDK. You can change your JDK post-install.

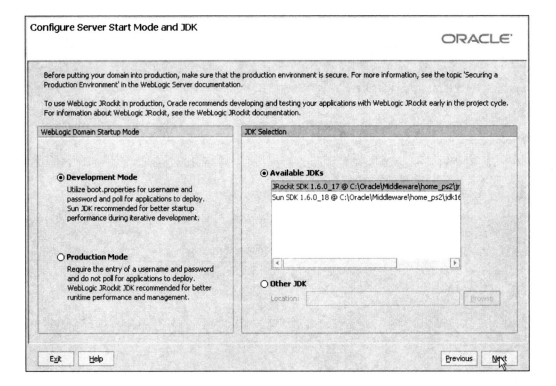

10. Click on **Next**.

11. On the **Configure JDBC Component Schema** screen, you select the
    components that you want to change, and then enter the property value for
    those components.

12. First, select all of the components and enter **welcome1** for the password in
    the **Schema Password** field. Or, if you used a different password when you
    created the schema with RCU, enter that password.

13. With all of the checkboxes still enabled, enter the **Service**, **Host**, and **Port** values.

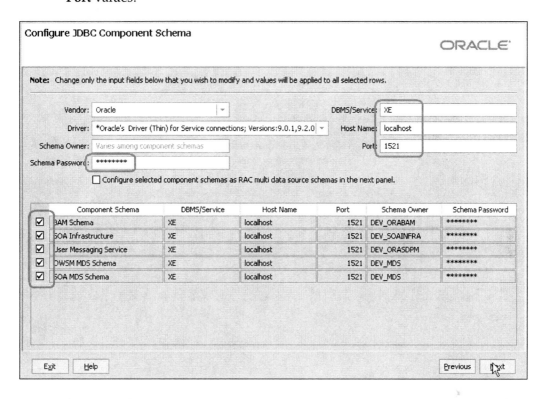

14. Now, look at the table. Review the **Schema Owner** column and confirm that the values are the same as what you configured in the *Configure Schema* section of this document when you ran the RCU. Go back and review the screenshots in that section of this document for the schema owners if you do not remember them.

15. Complete the following steps if the schema owners need to be updated, for example, BAM:

    ° Deselect all the component checkboxes

    ° Select **BAM Schema** only

    ° Enter the **Schema Owner**, **MY_ORABAM** (or as appropriate)

    ° Next, deselect **BAM Schema** and select the next one

    ° Enter the schema owners one-by-one by pre-pending the correct prefix to the defaulted value

    ° Continue until all schema owners are entered

16. Click on **Next**.

17. The data source connections are all tested.

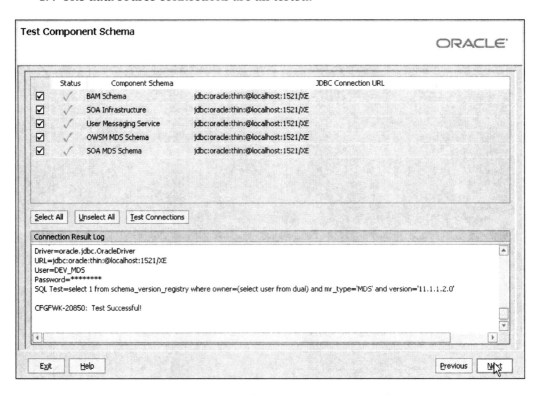

18. If all are successful, click on **Next**, otherwise click on **Previous** and correct any errors.

   Now you must choose whether to have your server run as a managed server or in a single server configuration. Except for Windows, use the single server configuration for a 32-bit system. For Windows and for all 64-bit configurations, use the managed server configuration. This is due to the way in which Windows 32-bit utilizes memory resources.

19. If you want the managed server configuration, just click on **Next**. This takes you to the **Summary** page and you can jump ahead in the document to that point.

If you want the single server configuration, complete the following steps:

1. For the single server configuration, on the **Optional Configuration** screen, select **Managed Servers, Clusters and Machines**.

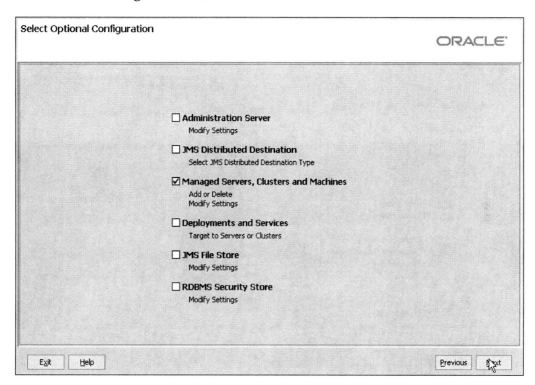

2. Click on **Next**.
3. On the **Configure Managed Servers** screen, select the BAM server.
4. Click on **Delete**. When the server is removed from the Managed Server configuration it runs on the Admin Server. This is a single-server configuration.
5. Select and delete the SOA server as well.

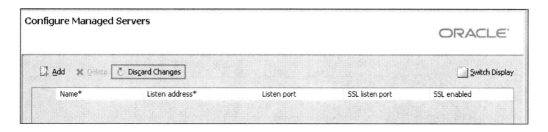

6. Click on **Next** four times to move through the remaining optional configuration screens without making any changes, and you reach the **Configuration Summary** screen.

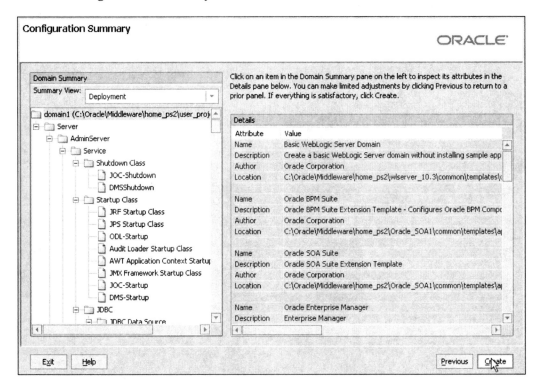

7. This is the summary page for both the Managed Server and single server configuration options. Click on **Create** to create the domain.

8. Wait for the create to finish—it takes just a minute.

9. Click on **Done**.

Your server is now installed. You can install JDeveloper next or jump ahead to the section called *Additional Actions* for configuration settings and details about starting your server.

Installing JDeveloper

Database	WebLogic Server	RCU
SOA	JDeveloper	WebCenter

JDeveloper installation has three parts—JDeveloper IDE, SOA Composite Editor, and BPM Studio. The BPM Studio 11*g* is the BPM design editor that runs in JDeveloper.

Installing and starting JDeveloper

If you are installing JDeveloper on a machine that is not the same as your WebLogic server installation, you need to have installed the JDK 6 update 18 first. JDeveloper uses the 32-bit version of the Oracle Sun JDK. See the section called *Check your JDK* for the download location. The Oracle JRockit JDK is not available as an independent install. JDeveloper does not use a 64-bit JDK.

If you want to uninstall an existing JDeveloper first, see the last section on uninstalling. Do not install into an existing install directory.

1. Open a command window and enter the following. Make sure there is no space after the = sign and eliminate trailing spaces.

   ```
   cd c:\stageFMW
   ```

   ```
   jdevstudio11113install.exe
   ```

   or

   ```
   set JAVA_HOME=C:\Oracle\Middleware\home_ps2\jdk160_18
   %JAVA_HOME%\bin\java.exe -jar jdevstudio11113install.jar
   ```

   You will see a message that the jar is extracting:

   ```
   >%JAVA_HOME%\bin\java.exe -jar jdevstudio11113install.jar
   Extracting 0%........................
   ```

2. When it reaches 100 percent the installation wizard opens. This takes a few minutes.

If you see the splash screen briefly but then you do not see the extracting message and the installation wizard does not open, it's probably because the Java JDK is the wrong version. Enter %JAVA_HOME%\bin\java.exe version to see the version. It must be version 1.6_18.

Complete the installation wizard as follows. Note that this does install an embedded WebLogic server that you can use for testing Java applications. You won't use it if you are creating only BPM and SOA applications. Although you can deselect the WebLogic server using the custom install option, most of the subcomponents are still required by JDeveloper anyway. It's your choice.

3. You will see the Welcome Screen Now; click on the **Next** button.

4. Choose **Middleware Home Directory**: select **Create a new Middleware Home** and enter **C:\Oracle\Middleware\jdev_ps2**. This document assumes that path. If you enter something else then adjust accordingly when **C:\Oracle\Middleware\jdev_ps2** is referenced.

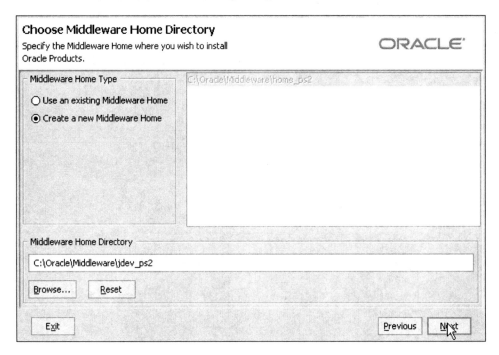

5. Click on **Next**.

6. Choose Install Type: **Complete**, and click on **Next**.

7. **JDK Selection**: You will see your JAVA_HOME.

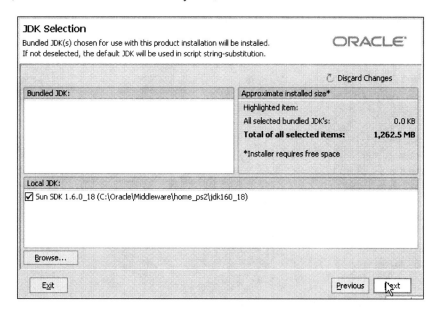

8. Click on **Next**.

9. Confirm **Product Installation Directories**. You should see:
Middleware Home Directory: C:\Oracle\Middleware\jdev_ps2
JDeveloper and ADF: C:\Oracle\Middleware\jdev_ps2\jdeveloper
WebLogic Server: C:\Oracle\Middleware\jdev_ps2\wlserver_10.3.

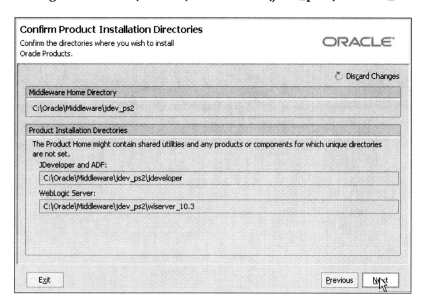

10. Click on **Next**.

11. Choose Shortcut location: **All Users** and click on Next.

12. Review **Installation Summary**.

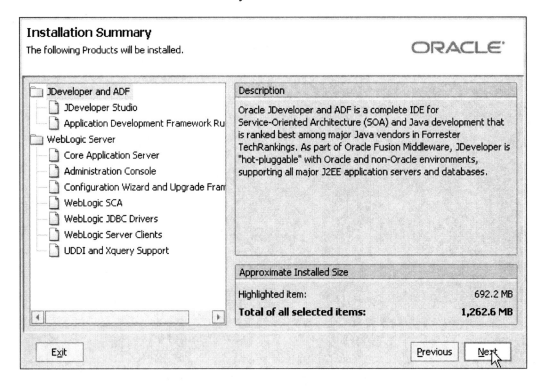

13. Click on **Next** and the installation starts.

14. Wait for the installation to complete—it'll take a few minutes.

15. When installation completes, deselect **Run Quickstart** and click on **Done**.

16. Start JDeveloper Studio 11.1.1.3.0 from the Windows Programs menu:
    Oracle Fusion Middleware 11.1.1.3.0 or run `C:\Oracle\Middleware\jdev_ps2\jdeveloper\jdeveloper.exe`.

During startup, select the following when prompted:

17. Select **Default Role**, deselect **Show this dialog every time**, and click on **OK**.

18. If you see the **Confirm Import Preferences** dialog click on **Yes** or on **No** as desired; usually **No** is appropriate.

19. If you are prompted to select file extensions to associate with JDeveloper, deselect everything or select whichever ones you would like for your machine and continue.

 When the file extension is associated with JDeveloper, double-clicking on that file type opens the file in JDeveloper, starting up JDeveloper, if necessary. Usually only the `jws` extension (JDeveloper workspace file) is appropriate but select whichever ones for which you would like this behavior.

Now, you must update JDeveloper with the SOA and BPM design editors. These are JDeveloper extensions. They are added to JDeveloper one at a time.

Updating JDeveloper with latest SOA

SOA design time in JDeveloper requires a JDeveloper extension called SOA Composite Editor. While this is normally updated over the network, you can update from a local file if you have the extension file. The extension is about 200 MB and can take some time to download.

1. Start JDeveloper if it is not already started.

2. Select **Help/Check For Updates**, Click on **Next**.

3. Select **Fusion Middleware Products and Official Extensions**.

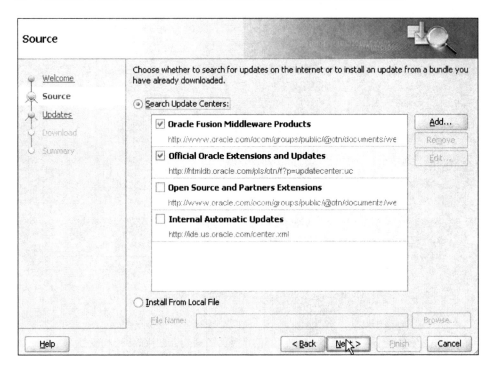

If there is a problem connecting to the Update Center, it may be caused by a proxy setting. You are prompted to set the proxy server and proxy exclusions to appropriate values for your environment. Then, restart JDeveloper.

4. Click on **Next**.

5. In the **Updates** list scroll down to **SOA Composite Editor** or type **SOA** in the **Available Updates** search box and enable the check box for the **SOA Composite Editor**.

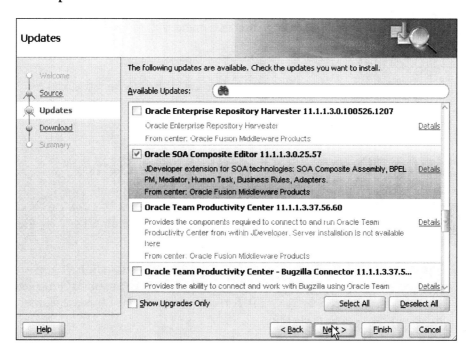

6. Click on **Next**.

7. Check that the update has finished downloading successfully.

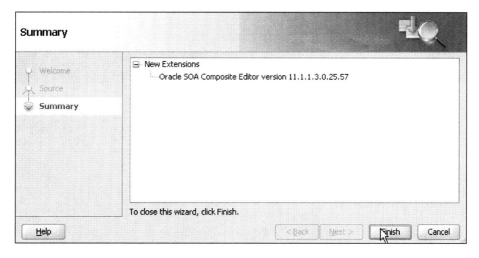

The Update Center provides the most recent version of the SOA Composite Editor that is compatible with your version of JDeveloper and you may have a newer version than the one listed here. The last two numbers, **25.57**, refer to the version that was released in April 2010.

8. Click on **Finish**.

9. Restart JDeveloper when prompted. During startup, you are asked to select **Yes** or **No** again to the import preferences question. **No** is the appropriate response.

Updating JDeveloper with latest BPM

Like SOA, BPM design time in JDeveloper requires a JDeveloper extension called BPM Studio. Again, this is normally updated over the network but you can update from a local file if you have the extension file. The extension is about 60 MB and can take some time to download.

1. First make sure you have already installed the SOA extension. If you are not sure, in JDeveloper, use the **Help** menu and select **About** and then check on the **Version** tab that you have the correct version of the SOA extension, as shown in the previous section.

2. When you are ready to install the BPM extension, select **Help/Check For Updates**. Click on **Next**.

3. Follow the same steps as in the previous section. This time, you are looking for the BPM Studio. When it has finished downloading, confirm the version number: **11.1.1.3.0.6.84**.

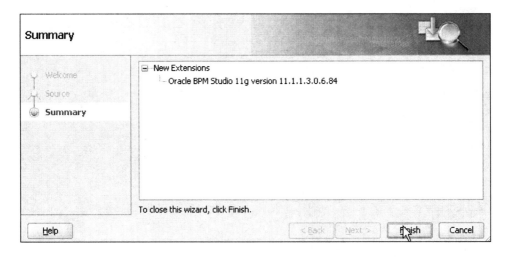

> The Update Center provides the most recent version of the BPM Studio that is compatible with your version of JDeveloper and you may have a newer version than the one listed here. The last two numbers, **6.84**, refer to the version that was released in April2010.

4.   Click on the **Finish** button.

5.   Restart JDeveloper when prompted. During restart, you will say **Yes** or **No** again to the import preferences question. **No** is the appropriate response.

Additional actions

In the following section, you perform additional configuration that is optional but will greatly improve performance and usability in the context of the development work you are about to start with the tutorial.

Setting memory limits

1.   Open for editing, the SOA domain environment file found here (make sure you have the SOA Domain environment file):

    ```
    C:\Oracle\Middleware\home_11gbeta\user_projects\domains\
    domain1\bin\setSOADomainEnv.cmd
    ```

2.   Set memory values.

> On Windows 32 bit, if you increase the Xmx too much, then you cannot use the PermSize parameter. The heap size is calculated as -Xmx + PermMaxSize. If these two add up to more than 1408 MB then WLS will not start.

Here is the recommendation for Windows 32 bit:
```
set DEFAULT_MEM_ARGS=-Xms512m -Xmx1024m
```
```
set DEFAULT_MEM_ARGS=%DEFAULT_MEM_ARGS% -XX:PermSize=128m -XX:
MaxPermSize=512m
```

Here is the recommendation for linux:
```
set DEFAULT_MEM_ARGS=-Xms512m -Xmx1536m
```

These values are dependent on your machine's resources and may need to be adjusted for your machine. These values are appropriate for a 3 GB memory, 32-bit machine.

Starting and stopping

Follow these instructions to start and stop your managed servers or your single-server configuration.

Before starting the servers for the first time, exit all unnecessary programs on your machine, including JDeveloper. After the first time, the server startup memory requirements are slightly lower.

Starting servers

1. If you have a single-server configuration, open one command window. If you have a managed server configuration, open three command windows, one for the WebLogic admin server, one for the SOA managed server, and one for the BAM managed server (you only start BAM when you need it for a BAM lab).

2. Start the Admin Server.

   ```
   cd c:\Oracle\Middleware\home_ps2\user_projects\domains\domain1
   startWebLogic.cmd
   ```

3. Wait for the Admin Server to finish starting up. It takes a few minutes — watch for the status **RUNNING** in the log console window.

```
.>
<Aug 29, 2010 2:47:21 PM PDT> <Notice> <Server> <BEA-002613> <Channel "Default[4
]" is now listening on 127.0.0.1:7001 for protocols iiop, t3, ldap, snmp, http.>

<Aug 29, 2010 2:47:21 PM PDT> <Warning> <Server> <BEA-002611> <Hostname "hbuelow
-lap.us.oracle.com", maps to multiple IP addresses: 10.159.223.154, 192.168.1.5,
192.168.146.1, 192.168.153.1>
<Aug 29, 2010 2:47:21 PM PDT> <Notice> <WebLogicServer> <BEA-000331> <Started We
bLogic Admin Server "AdminServer" for domain "domain1" running in Development Mo
de>
<Aug 29, 2010 2:47:21 PM PDT> <Notice> <WebLogicServer> <BEA-000365> <Server sta
te changed to RUNNING>
<Aug 29, 2010 2:47:21 PM PDT> <Notice> <WebLogicServer> <BEA-000360> <Server sta
rted in RUNNING mode>
```

4. If you have a single-server configuration, continue to wait for the SOA server to start. Watch for the startup messages in the console window as described in the following steps.

5. For the managed server, start the SOA Managed Server in the second command window as shown. This start script is in the `bin` directory. You can choose to cd to the `bin` directory instead.

   ```
   cd C:\Oracle\Middleware\home_ps2\user_projects\domains\domain1
   bin\startManagedWebLogic.cmd soa_server1
   ```

6. When prompted, enter the user name **weblogic** and password **welcome1**.

After the first time you start the managed server, create a file called `boot.properties` with the following content:

password=welcome1

username=weblogic

Store it to the following directory:
`C:\Oracle\Middleware\home_ps2\user_projects\domains\domain1\`
`servers\soa_server1\security`

This folder does not exist until you have started the server the first time (you have to create the security folder). This file allows your managed server to startup without prompting for a password. The file is encrypted the first time it is accessed.

If you set the `boot.properties` as described above, you are no longer prompted during startup.

The server is started when you see the message, **INFO: FabricProviderServlet. stateChanged SOA Platform is running and accepting requests**.

```
INFO: SSLSocketFactoryManagerImpl.getSSLSocketFactory Could not obtain keystore
location or password
INFO: SSLSocketFactoryManagerImpl.getKeystoreLocation SOA Keystore location: C:/
ORACLE/MIDDLE~1/home_ps2/USER_P~1/domains/domain1/config/fmwconfig/default-keyst
ore.jks
INFO: SSLSocketFactoryManagerImpl.getKeystorePassword Obtained null or empty key
store password
INFO: SSLSocketFactoryManagerImpl.getKeyPassword Obtained null or empty key pass
word
INFO: SSLSocketFactoryManagerImpl.getSSLSocketFactory Could not obtain keystore
location or password
INFO: DeploymentEventPublisher.invoke Publishing deploy event for default/Simple
Approval!1.0*soa_7776277e-cb52-40d4-8dc9-72abb0e63a74
looking up version 11.1.1.3.0
SchemaVersion actual dbVersion=11.1.1.3.0, expected dbVersion=11.1.1.3.0
INFO: FabricProviderServlet.stateChanged SOA Platform is running and accepting r
equests
```

7. When needed, start the BAM Managed Server in the third command window:
```
cd C:\Oracle\Middleware\home_ps2\user_projects\domains\domain1
bin\startManagedWebLogic.cmd bam_server1
```

8. When prompted, enter the user name **weblogic** and password **welcome1**. After the first time you start the server, set the `boot.properties` as described above. Watch for the **RUNNING** status.

Console URLS

Log in with **weblogic/welcome1** for all consoles.

Use port `7001` in all URLs if you have a single-server configuration, otherwise use `8001` or `9001` as noted. For the workspace and composer, you can also log in as an end user.

- Weblogic console: `http://localhost:7001/console`
- Enterprise Manager console: `http://localhost:7001/em`
- BAM (must use IE browser): `http://localhost:9001/OracleBAM`
- BPM workspace: `http://localhost:8001/bpm/workspace`
- BPM composer: `http://localhost:8001/bpm/composer`

Stopping servers

Whenever you need to stop the server complete the following steps:

1. Stop the managed servers first by entering **CTRL-C** in the command window. Wait until stopped.
2. After the managed server stops, stop the admin server by entering **CTRL-C** in the command window.

WebLogic server console settings

There are three suggested changes to make in the WebLogic server console.

First, you occasionally view the application deployments using the WebLogic server console. This is a lot more convenient if you change the settings not to show libraries as this makes the list a lot shorter and you can find what you need more quickly.

1. Start the WebLogic Admin Server (WLS), if it is not already running.
2. Open a browser and log in to the WLS console `http://localhost:7001/console`
3. Click **Deployments** in the left navigation bar.
4. Click **Customize this table** at the top of the **Deployments** table.
5. Change the number of rows per page to **100** (there are only about 30).
6. Enable the checkbox to exclude libraries and click on **Apply**.

Second, there are many applications installed and running by default but you won't need all of these during the tutorial. Turn off as many as you can to save resources on your machine.

1. Enable the checkbox next to as many applications as you think you won't need and then from the **Stop** menu, select **Force Stop Now**.

> Some examples of applications you can stop are worklist and composer, since you will more likely use the BPM Workspace and BPM Composer instead. You may also want to turn off b2bui and Oracle Apps Adapter.
>
> If you are unsure, leave it running as it may be used by the BPM infrastructure.

And third, when the server is started, by default internal applications like the WLS console are not deployed completely and you see a slight delay when you first access the console. You saw this delay just now when you first accessed the console URL. You can change this behavior to deploy internal applications at startup instead and then you don't get the delay when you access the console. This is convenient for demos (if you want to show the console) and also if you tend to use the console.

1. Click on **domain1** in the left navigation bar in the WLS console.

2. Click on the **Configuration | General** tab.

3. Disable the **Enable on-demand deployment of internal applications** check box.

4. Click on the **Save** button.

EM settings for development

The **Enterprise Manager Fusion Middleware Control** (**EM**) can provide different levels of information about composite runtime instances based on a property setting. During development it is helpful to have a higher setting to get more information. These settings are not used on production machines except when specifically needed for debugging purposes.

1. Start your servers if they are not already running.

2. Log in to the EM console at `http://localhost:7001/em`.

3. Right-click on the **soa-infra (soa_server1)** in the left navigation bar to open the SOA menu and select **SOA Administration | Common Properties**.

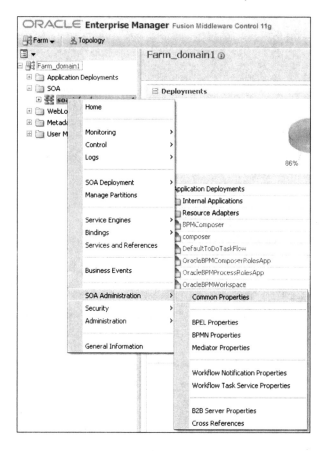

4. Select **Audit Level: Development** and enable the checkbox for **Capture Composite Instance State**.

5. Click on **Apply** and click on **Yes**.

Configuration

This tutorial uses a demo user community. To configure your server for this tutorial, you need to seed the demo users in to the LDAP directory.

Seed demo users

You usually need a set of users and groups to use during development testing and all of the samples in SOA Suite and BPM Suite use a provided set of users called demo users.

To install the demo users, open `c:\stageFMW\demo-community` and follow the instructions in the `readme.txt`. When completed, you have a community as shown in the following image:

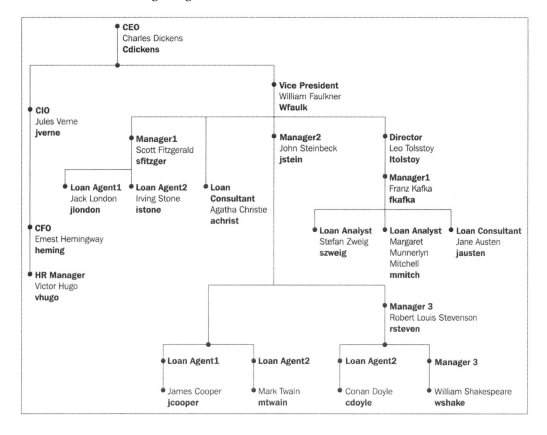

Installing WebCenter

Database	WebLogic Server	RCU
SOA	JDeveloper	WebCenter

The following instructions provide a simplified path through installation of WebCenter and configuration of its services. For more complete instructions and details on the various options, refer to the product documentation library:

`http://download.oracle.com/docs/cd/E15523_01/install.1111/e12001/toc.htm`

`http://download.oracle.com/docs/cd/E15523_01/webcenter.1111/e12405/toc.htm`

If you have not already downloaded and unzipped the files that you need for this installation, see the *Downloading files* section at the top of this chapter.

 WebCenter installation includes three more managed servers: WebCenter Services, WebCenter Spaces, and WebCenter Portlet. In addition, install Web Tier and Unified Content Manager. This installation will not fit on a 3GB system.

Preparing for installing UCM

Web Tier installation is a pre-requisite for installing **Unified Content Management** (**UCM**) along with WebCenter. Note that you can use an existing install of UCM or install it later. Skip this step if you are not installing UCM with WebCenter.

In addition, the following instructions assume that you need to install an HTTP server. If you can use an existing HTTP server, skip relevant steps below.

Installing Web Tier

Web Tier is installed similar to SOA. Both PS1 and PS2 Web Tier are installed. WLS and SOA managed servers must be running.

1. In a command window enter:

```
cd c:\stageFMW\WTPS1\Disk1
setup -jreLoc C:\Oracle\Middleware\home_ps2\jdk160_18
```

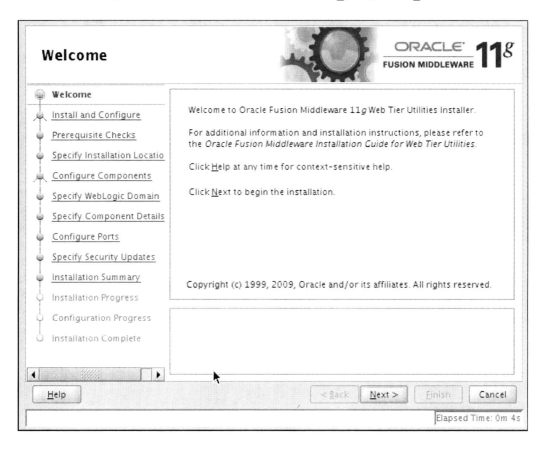

2. Click on **Next.**

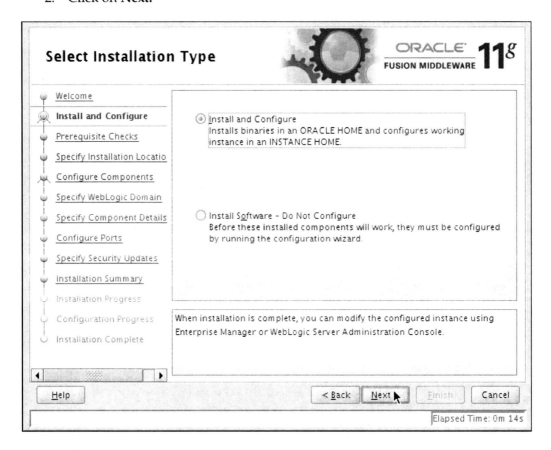

3. Select **Install and Configure** and click on **Next.**

4. When the pre-requisites check completes, click on **Next**.

5. Select your Middleware home from the list and enter the Web Tier home directory. If you are using a different Oracle home, then adjust accordingly when `Oracle_WT1` is referenced throughout this document.

6. Click on **Next**.

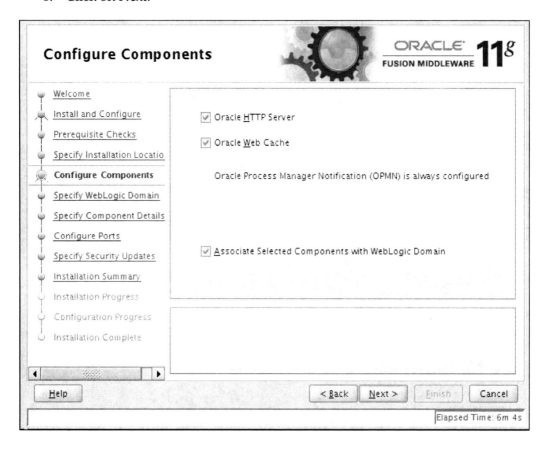

7. Select the components, **Oracle HTTP Server**, **Oracle Web Cache**, and the checkbox for **Associate Selected Components with WebLogic Domain**. Click on **Next**.

8. Enter the field values for the WebLogic domain and click on **Next**.

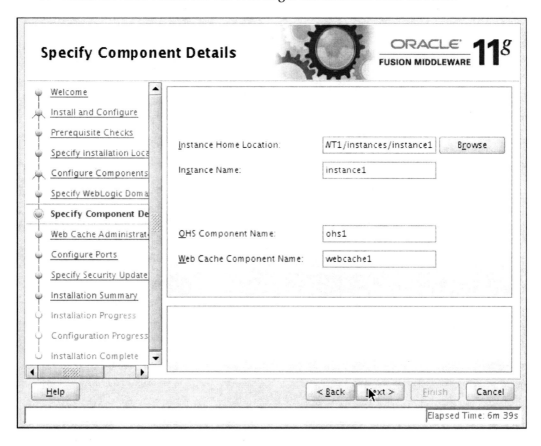

9. Specify the component details. The default values are fine here. If you use something instead of the default values, remember these for use later in this chapter. Click on **Next**.

10. Enter a password for the Web Cache Administrator. The password, **welcome1**, is assumed in this chapter but you should choose and remember your own secure password. Click on **Next**.

11. Select **Auto Port Configuration** and click on **Next**.

12. The Web Tier configuration continues until completion. When it is finished, click on **Next**.

13. On the Web Tier Installation Summary page, select **Install** to start the installation.

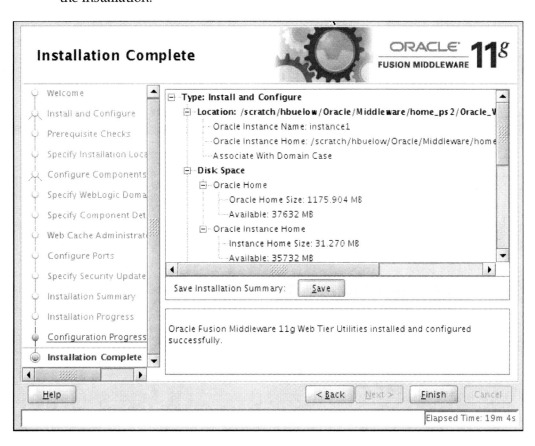

14. When the installation is complete, click on **Save Installation Summary** to save the summary to a file. This includes configuration and port information you may need later.

15. Click on **Finish**.

16. Now install PS2 for Web Tier. In a command window enter:

```
cd c:\stageFMW\WTPS2\Disk1
setup -jreLoc C:\Oracle\Middleware\home_ps2\jdk160_18
```

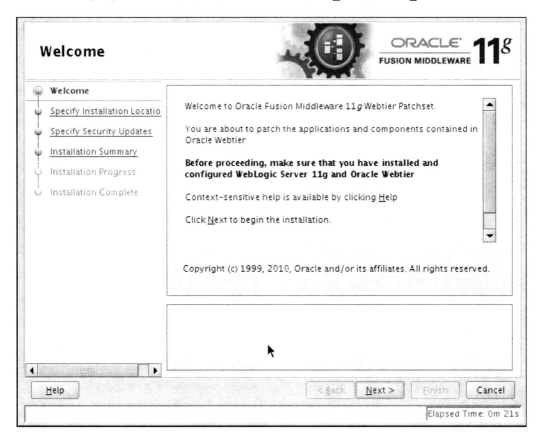

17. Click on **Next**.

18. Enter the same **Oracle Home Directory** as before. Click on **Next**.

19. On the **Installation Summary** page, click on **Install.** If you get an error during installation about the process being unable write file, wait for 10 seconds and click on **Retry**. Installation will continue (repeat the wait and retry if it happens again).

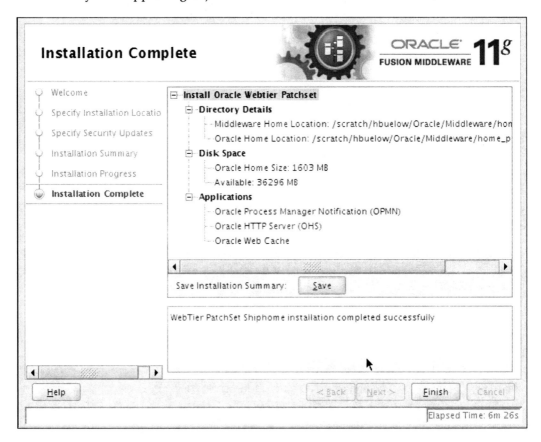

20. When the installation is complete, click on **Save Installation Summary** to save the summary to a file. This includes configuration and port information you may need later. Click on **Finish**.

At the moment, the Web Tier is installed but not running. It gets started later in the installation process.

Installing WebCenter RCU, Server, and UCM

The first step in installing the WebCenter is to set up the schemas; then you install the WebCenter binaries, and finally the UCM.

RCU

In case you did not create the schemas for WebCenter during RCU step for SOA/ BPM, do so now.

1. Open a command window and enter the following:

    ```
    cd c:\stageFMW\RCU\bin
    rcu.bat
    ```

    The Repository Creation Utility opens.

2. On the welcome screen, click on **Next.**

3. Select **Create**.

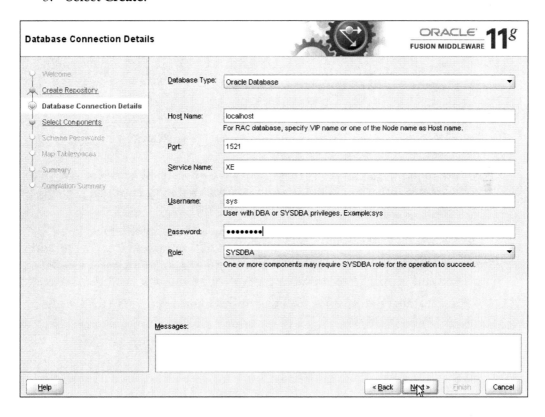

4. Complete the database information and click on **Next**.

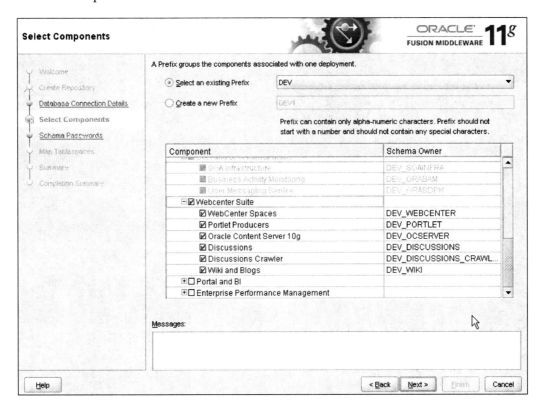

5. Be sure to use the same prefix that you used earlier for BPM and select **WebCenter Suite**. Dependent schemas are selected automatically. Click on **Next**.

6. Select the radio button to **Use the same password for all schemas**. Enter a schema password. The password, **welcome1**, is assumed in this chapter but you should choose your own secure password or a different one for each schema and be sure to record your passwords as you will need them later.

7. Review the next two screens and click through until you get to the **Create** screen. Click on **Create**.

Installing WebCenter server

Once the schema is ready, you can install WebCenter. This is similar to the SOA installation. Install both PS1 and PS2 for WebCenter. This also installs the UCM.

1. In a command window enter:

```
cd c:\stageFMW\WCPS1\Disk1
setup -jreLoc C:\Oracle\Middleware\home_ps2\jdk160_18
```

2. Click on **Next**.

---

3. When the pre-requisites check completes, click on **Next**.

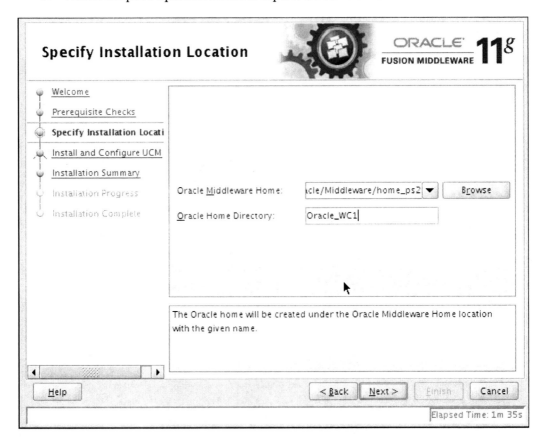

4. Select the Middleware home and enter the **Oracle Home Directory**. Click on **Next**.

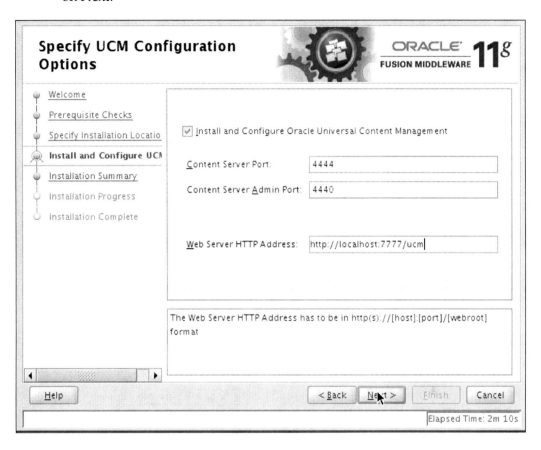

5. Enter the **Web Server HTTP Address** as `http://localhost:7777/ucm`. The webroot is `ucm`. The port, `7777` is your HTTP port. Click on **Next**.

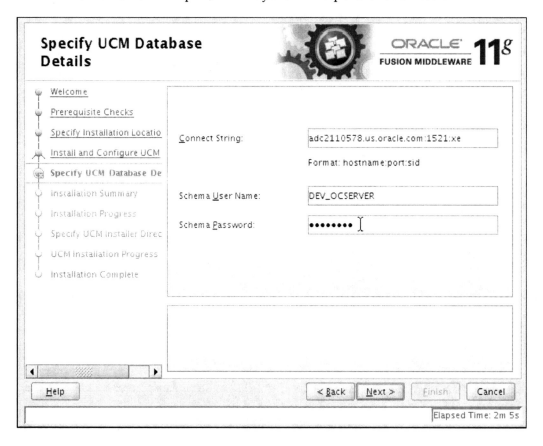

6. Enter the **Connect String** for the database and enter `DEV_OCSERVER` for the **Schema User Name** for UCM. Click on **Next**.

7. On the Installation Summary screen, click on **Install** to install WebCenter.

8. On the UCM Installer Directory screen, enter the location in the stage directory for the UCM installation, `C:\stageFMW\UCM\ContentServer`. Click on **Next**.

9. When the installation is complete, click on **Save Installation Summary** to save the summary to a file. This includes configuration and port information you may need later. Click on **Finish**.

10. Now install PS2 for WebCenter. In a command window enter:

```
cd c:\stageFMW\WCPS2\Disk1
setup -jreLoc C:\Oracle\Middleware\home_ps2\jdk160_18
```

11. Click on **Next**.

12. Select the Middleware home and enter the same **Oracle Home Directory** as you entered for PS1 WebCenter. Click on **Next**.

13. On the Installation Summary screen, click on **Install**.

14. When the installation is complete, click on **Save Installation Summary** to save the summary to a file. This includes configuration and port information you may need later. Click on **Finish**.

Configuring WebCenter

Now that WebCenter and UCM are installed, you need to configure WebCenter to join your WLS domain.

1. In a command window enter:

```
cd C:\Oracle\Middleware\home_ps2\Oracle_WC1\common\bin
config.cmd
```

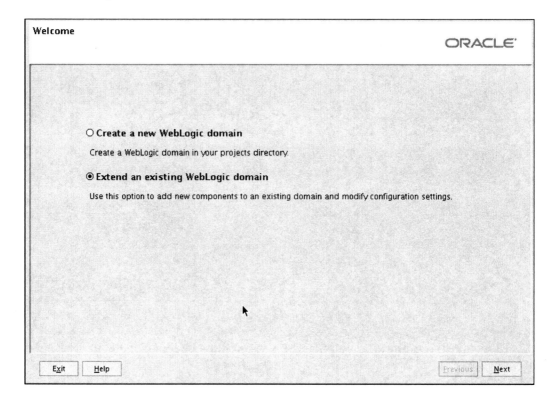

2. Choose **Extend an existing WebLogic** domain and click on **Next**.

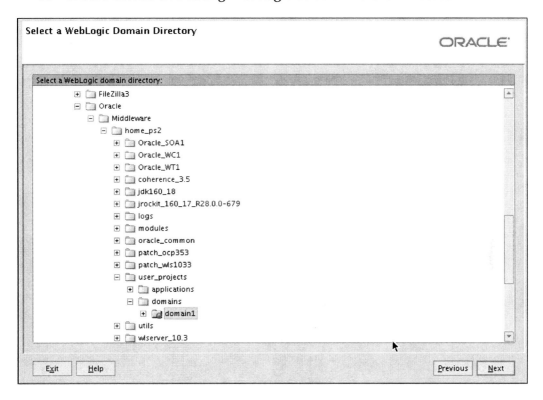

3. Locate the SOA domain, select it, and click on **Next**.

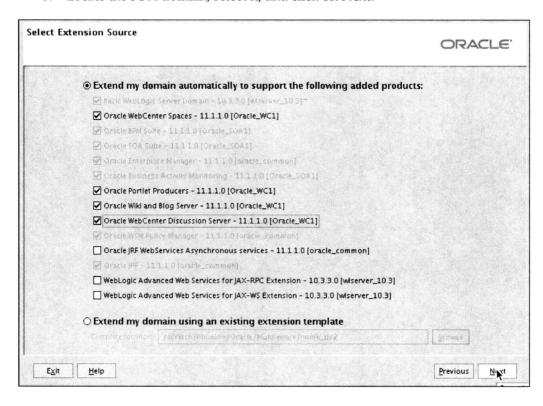

4. Select all the WebCenter components and click on **Next**.

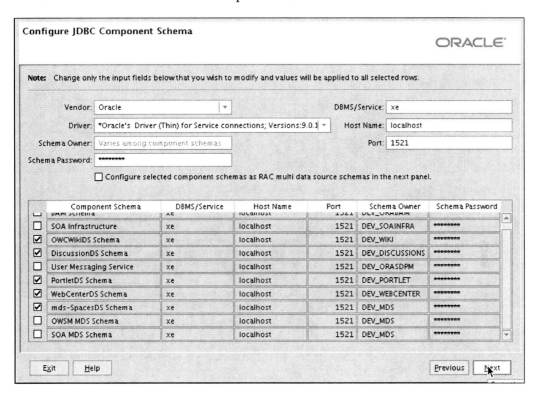

5. On the **Configure JDBC Component Schema** screen, select the new schemas, and enter the password, service, and hostname. Click on **Next**.

6. When the schemas all test successfully, click on **Next**. If there is a failure, click on **Previous** and fix any errors; click on **Next** to test, and click on **Next** when successful.

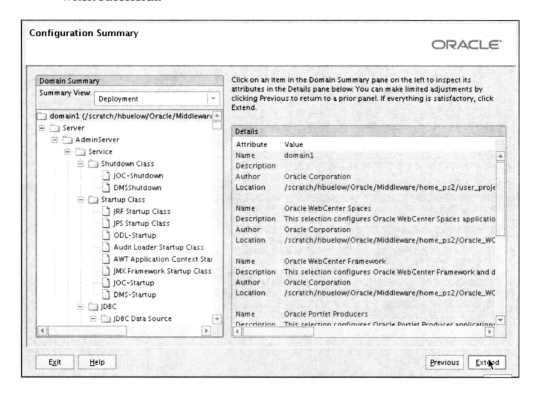

7. On the summary screen, click on **Extend**. When it is finished, click on **Done**. This takes less than a minute.

Now that the domain is configured, it's time to start the WebCenter servers.

1. Start the WLS Managed Servers in a command window. This start script is in the `bin` directory. You can choose to `cd` to the `bin` directory instead:

   ```
   cd C:\Oracle\Middleware\home_ps2\user_projects\domains\domain1
   bin\startManagedWebLogic.cmd WLS_Portlets
   ```

2. When you see the `RUNNING` status, repeat for WLS_Services and WLS_Spaces, each in its own command window.

3. Refer to the earlier section in this chapter, *Starting servers*, for details on setting up a `boot.properties` file after the managed server has started for the first time.

4. Access the WebCenter login page at: `http://localhost:8888/webcenter/spaces`

Configuring UCM

Now, everything is installed and running. It's time to configure.

For clarity, the follow paths are defined and then used in this section. Replace with the full path when executing commands:

- `MW_HOME=C:\Oracle\Middleware\home_ps2`
- `UCM_HOME=$MW_HOME/Oracle_WC1/ucm`
- `WT_HOME=$MW_HOME/Oracle_WT1`

1. Allow IPs for Socket:

   ° Open `$UCM_HOME/config/config.cfg` and ensure that it has the following line:
   `SocketHostAddressSecurityFilter=127.0.0.1`

   ° Copy the above line to `$UCM_HOME/admin/bin/intradoc.cfg`.

2. Restart UCM:

   `$UCM_HOME/etc/idcserver_restart`
   `$UCM_HOME/admin/etc/idcadmin_restart`

3. Configure HTTP server for UCM:

   ```
   cp $WT_HOME/instances/instance1/config/OHS/ohs1/httpd.conf $WT_
   HOME/instances/instance1/config/OHS/ohs1/httpd.conf.orig
   cat >> $WT_HOME/instances/instance1/config/OHS/ohs1/httpd.conf
   <<EOF
   include "$UCM_HOME/data/users/apache22/apache.conf"
   EOF
   ```

4. Restart HTTP server:

   `$MW_HOME/Oracle_WT1/instances/instance1/bin/opmnctl stopall`
   `$MW_HOME/Oracle_WT1/instances/instance1/bin/opmnctl startall`

Configuring security for UCM

You need to set up UCM to use the embedded LDAP.

Setting up password for embedded LDAP

1. Log into Console, typically `http://localhost:7001/console`.

2. Select the domain on the far left navigation bar, and set its password to `welcome1` as follows:

     ° Select the **Security** tab

     ° Select the **Embedded LDAP** sub-tab

     ° Specify **Credential** and **Confirm Credential** as `welcome1`

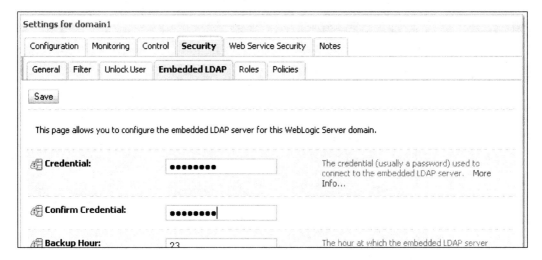

3   Restart admin server, and managed servers.

Configuring LDAP provider in UCM

1. Log into UCM console, at `http://localhost:7777/ucm`:

   ° User: `sysadmin`

   ° Pw: `idc`

2. Expand **Administration** in the left-hand side panel and select **Providers**.

3. In the **Create a New Provider** section, find the row for **ldapuser** and click on **Add**

4. Specify the following settings:

Field Name	Field Type
Source Path	$MWHOME (expanded value)
LDAP Server	`localhost`
LDAP Suffix	`ou=people,ou=myrealm,dc=domain1`
LDAP Port	`7001`
LDAP Attribute Map	`cn:dFullName`
	`mail:dEmail`
	`title:dUserType`
LDAP Admin DN	`cn=Admin`
LDAP Admin Password	`welcome1`

Add LDAP Provider

Provider Name	EmbeddedLDAP
Provider Description	EmbeddedLDAP
Provider Class	intradoc.provider.LdapUserProvider
Connection Class	intradoc.provider.LdapConnection
Configuration Class	
Source Path	c:\Oracle\Middleware\home_ps2
LDAP Server	localhost
LDAP Suffix	ou=people,ou=myrealm,dc=domain1
LDAP Port	7001
Number of connections	5
Connection timeout	10
Priority	1
Credential Map	

5. For the **Attribute Map**, add the values one by one, matching the following table:

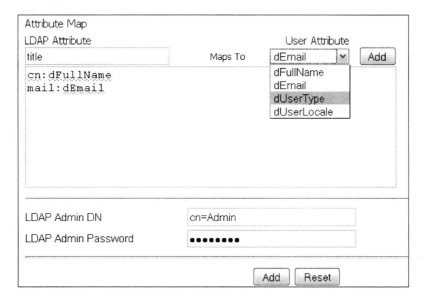

6. Restart UCM:

  ○ `$UCM_HOME/etc/idcserver_restart`

  ○ `$UCM_HOME/admin/etc/idcadmin_restart`

7. Log back into UCM console, navigate to **Providers**, and verify that the LDAP provider created above is working.

Configuring discussions security

For discussions security, you need a keypair. To learn more about keypairs and security, please see this document in the product documentation library: `http://download.oracle.com/docs/cd/E15523_01/webcenter.1111/e12405/wcadm_security.htm#BGBFBJJF`

The Sun JDK has a keystore tool. That is what you use in the following commands to set up the keypair.

1. Create a keypair in your home directory:

```
mkdir ~/keystore
cd ~/keystore
set JAVA_HOME=yourjavahome

$JAVA_HOME/bin/keytool -genkeypair -keyalg RSA -dname "cn=space
s,dc=bpmdemo,dc=com" -alias orakey -keypass welcome1 -keystore
webcenter.jks -storepass welcome1 -validity 1064
keytool -exportcert -v -alias orakey -keystore webcenter.jks -
storepass welcome1 -rfc -file orakey.cer
keytool -importcert -alias webcenter_spaces_ws -file orakey.cer -
keystore webcenter.jks -storepass welcome1
keytool -importcert -alias df_orakey_public -file orakey.cer -
keystore owc_discussions.jks -storepass welcome1
```

2. For the last two commands, say `yes` when prompted.

3. Create `keystore.properties` file:

```
cat > keystore.properties <<EOF
org.apache.ws.security.crypto.provider=org.apache.ws.security.
components.crypto.Merlin
org.apache.ws.security.crypto.merlin.keystore.type=jks
org.apache.ws.security.crypto.merlin.keystore.password=welcome1
org.apache.ws.security.crypto.merlin.keystore.alias=df_orakey_
public
org.apache.ws.security.crypto.merlin.file=`pwd`/owc_discussions.
jks
EOF
```

4. Copy `webcenter.jks` file to `fmwconfig` dir:

```
cp webcenter.jks $DOMAIN_HOME/config/fmwconfig
```

5. Create a JAR `df_props.jar` with above `keystore.properties` file and copy it to domain's classpath:

```
jar cvf df_props.jar keystore.properties
cp df_props.jar $DOMAIN_HOME/lib
```

6. Configure Jive to use the above keys as follows:

   ° Go to Jive admin, typically located at `http://localhost:8890/owc_discussions/admin`.

   ° Log in as `weblogic`/`welcome1` (Jive is pre-configured to use same LDAP as WebCenter)

° Click on **System Properties** under **Forum System** to display
the **Jive Properties** page.

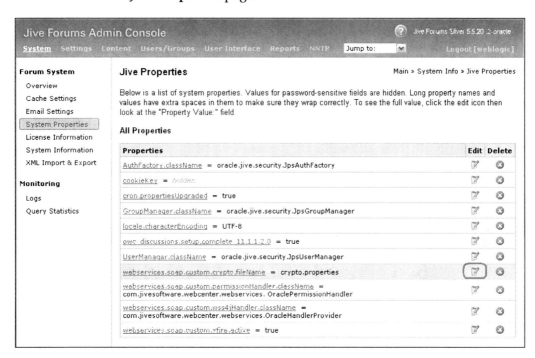

7. Modify the system property webservices.soap.custom.crypto.fileName
as keystore.properties.

8. Click on **Save Property** and restart the WLS_Services Managed Server.

 You need to modify WebCenter to use the same key as well; you will do this in the next section using WLST along with creating connections.

Configuring connections

In this section, you use WLST to configure connections, as well as to set up the security for Jive on WebCenter end.

1. Specify `webcenter.jks` as the keystore in `jps_config` as follows:

   ° Open `$DOMAIN_HOME/config/fmwconfig/jps-config.xml` in an editor.

   ° Locate the `<serviceInstance>` node for the `keystore. provider` Provider.

   ° Specify the location as `./webcenter.jks` (earlier we copied the `webcenter.jks` keystore file to `$DOMAIN_HOME/config/ fmwconfig`).

2. Create `wlst_props.txt` with the following text and change as appropriate for your configuration:

   ° Create `wlst_props.txt` in `$WC_HOME/common/bin` with the following content:

   ```
   user=weblogic
   pw=welcome1
   admin_url=t3://localhost:7001
   disc_url=http://localhost:8890/owc_discussions
   wiki_url=http://bpm2:8890/
   jks_loc=/home/oracle/bpm/user_projects/domains/domain1/
   config/fmwconfig/webcenter.jks
   ucm_host=localhost
   ucm_port=4444
   bpm_url=http://localhost:8001
   ```

 Using `localhost` for `wiki_url` location will not work. Edit for your host.

3. Copy the following as `wcsetup.py`:

```
print "Connecting"
connect (user, pw, admin_url)


print "Creating credentials"
createCred(map="oracle.wsm.security", key="keystore-csf-key",
user="owsm", password="welcome1", desc="Keystore key")
createCred(map="oracle.wsm.security", key="enc-csf-key",
user="orakey", password="welcome1", desc="Encryption key")
createCred(map="oracle.wsm.security", key="sign-csf-key",
user="orakey", password="welcome1", desc="Signing key")


print "Creating discussion forum connection"
createDiscussionForumConnection(appName='webcenter', name='local-
jive', url=disc_url, adminUser='weblogic', secured=true,
default=true)
setDiscussionForumConnectionProperty(appName='webcenter',
name='local-jive', key='keystore.location', value=jks_loc)
setDiscussionForumConnectionProperty(appName='webcenter',
name='local-jive', key='keystore.type', value= 'jks')
setDiscussionForumConnectionProperty (appName='webcenter',
name='local-jive', key='keystore.password', value= 'welcome1')
setDiscussionForumConnectionProperty (appName='webcenter',
name='local-jive', key='encryption.key.alias', value='orakey')
setDiscussionForumConnectionProperty (appName='webcenter',
name='local-jive', key='encryption.key.password', value=
'welcome1')
setDiscussionForumConnectionProperty(appName='webcenter',
name='local-jive', key='group.mapping', value= 'category')


print "Configuring Wiki"
createCred(map="owc_wiki",key="wsPasscode",user="owc_wiki",passwor
d="welcome1",desc="OWC Wiki Web Services passcode")
createWikiserverConnection(appName='webcenter', name='local-wiki',
url=wiki_url, passcode='welcome1', default=true)


print "Configuring content server connection"
createJCRContentServerConnection(appName='webcenter', name='local-
ucm', socketType='socket', serverHost=ucm_host, serverPort=ucm_
port, isPrimary=true)
setDocumentsSpacesProperties(appName='webcenter', spacesRoot='/
Spaces', adminUserName='sysadmin', applicationName='Spaces')


print "Creating BPEL connection"
```

```
createBPELConnection(appName='webcenter', name='local-bpm',
url=bpm_url, policy='oracle/wss10_saml_token_client_policy')
addWorklistConnection(appName='webcenter', name='local-bpm')
```

4. Run WLST with this property file as shown:

```
$WC_HOME/common/bin/wlst.sh -loadProperties wlst_props.txt
wcsetup.py
```

For more information on configuring discussions, you may refer to `http://download.oracle.com/docs/cd/E15523_01/web.1111/e13813/custom_webcenter_admin.htm#WLSTC668`

> The above instructions do not set up SSO with wiki—SSO setup instructions can be found along with supporting scripts at:
> `http://www.oracle.com/wocportal/page/wocprod/ver-22/ocom/technology/products/webcenter/pdf/owcs_r11_saml_sso_config_wp.pdf`

Testing WebCenter installation

Log into WebCenter at `http://localhost:8888/webcenter/spaces`, and make sure that all services are working as desired.

Installing Process Spaces

For BPM, installing WebCenter includes adding the BPM Process Spaces panels. These are provided as templates. Complete the following to add these panels to your WebCenter installation:

1. Extract the templates:

```
cd $MW_HOME/Oracle_SOA1/bpm/
unzip processportal.zip -d processportal
```

2. Edit `process-portal-install.properties` appropriately for your environment, and also:

   ° Set `wcConfigServices` to `false`
   ° Set `extendSoa` to `true`

3. Use ant to install process portal:

```
export ANT_ARGS=
"-lib $MW_HOME/modules/net.sf.antcontrib_1.0.0.0_1-0b2/lib"
ant -f install.xml (you will find ant under $MW_HOME/modules/org.
apache.ant_1.7.0)
```

4. Restart admin and managed servers of WebCenter.

Verifying and configuring Process Spaces

1. Log into WebCenter as weblogic at http://localhost:8888/webcenter/
spaces.

2. Go to **Administration**, and make the imported templates online as follows:

   ° Click on the **Administration** link on the main menu bar.

   ° Click on the **Group Spaces** sub-tab.

   ° If the **Modeling Space** and **Process Space** are not listed,
     click on the refresh icon next to the **Search** control within the
     Manage Group Spaces section.

   ° When the refresh is done, **Modeling Space** and **Process
     Workspace** should show up in the list of spaces; their state
     will be **Offline**.

○ Select the two, set **Change State** to **Online**, and then click on **Save**.

3. Go to Process Workspace space settings to add users:

 ○ Add users to the space:

  ○ jcooper,**jlondon,wfaulk,cdoyle,mtwain** as participant.

  ○ jstein as moderator.

○ Select the **Services** tab, select **Discussions**, click on the search icon, create a forum, and select it.

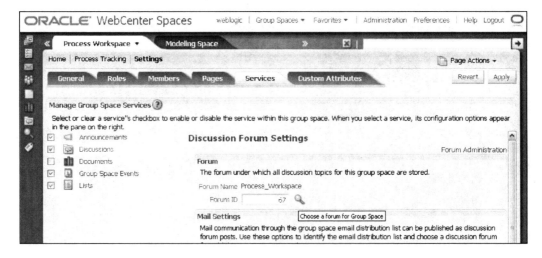

    ° Go to roles and set up privileges for services (if not set correctly already).

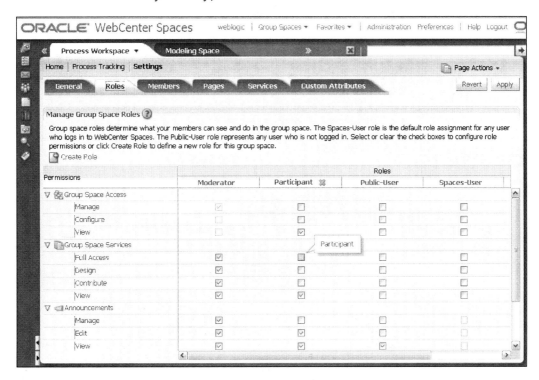

    ° Repeat the above steps for Modeling Space

You have completed the installation of Process Spaces.

Testing your installation

This section shows you how to verify your installation and configuration.

After installing BPM Suite and BPM Studio (JDeveloper), confirm that you have the correct 11.1.1.3.0 version.

You have five things to check.

1. JDeveloper: Start JDeveloper and select from the toolbar, **Help | About**. You should see this build: **JDEVADF_11.1.1.3.PS2_GENERIC_100408.2356.5660**.

2. SOA Composite Editor: Select the **Version** tab on the JDeveloper **Help/About** dialog. You should see this value: **11.1.1.3.0.25.57**.

3. BPM Studio: Select the **Version** tab on the JDeveloper **Help/About** dialog. You should see this value: **11.1.1.3.0.6.84**.

4. SOA Server: Run `soaversion.cmd` from `C:\Oracle\Middleware\home_11gR1\Oracle_SOA1\bin` and you should see this build: **PCBPEL_11.1.1.3.0_GENERIC_ 100415.2045.2557**.

5. Confirm the demo community setup: with the server running, open in a browser and log in as **jcooper/welcome1**, `http://localhost:7001/bpm/workspace` (use **8001** if you have a managed server configuration).

Uninstalling

If you need to uninstall everything, complete the following steps:

1. First save anything you want to keep from here: `C:\Oracle\Middleware\jdev_ps2\jdeveloper\mywork`.

2. Run **Uninstall** from the program menu to completion for both JDeveloper and WLS.

3. Delete `C:\Oracle\Middleware\jdev_ps2` and `C:\Oracle\Middleware\home_ps2`.

4. Delete program groups from `C:\Documents and Settings\All Users\Start Menu\Programs\`.
   ° Oracle Fusion Middleware 11.1.1.1.0
   ° Oracle SOA 11*g* — Home1
   ° Oracle WebLogic

5. To drop your existing schema, run the RCU Drop command. Copy the following into a command window:
   ```
   cd c:\stageFMW\rcuHome\bin
   rcu.bat
   ```

The Repository Creation Utility opens.

1. Click on the **Next** button.
2. Select **Drop**.

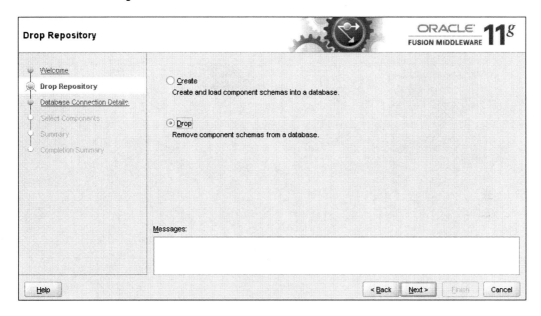

3. Click on the **Next** button.
4. Complete the database information.

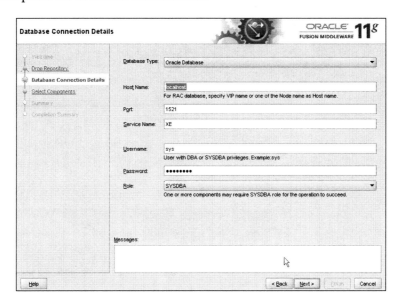

5. Click on the **Next** button.

6. The pre-requisites are reviewed. When completed, click on **OK**. The utility moves to the next page — there's a slight delay, just wait for it.

7. The utility finds the existing schemas and offers the dropdown list of all **Schema Owner Prefixes**. Check that the prefix is correct and review the schema.

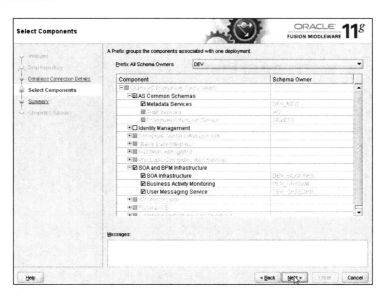

8. Click on **Next**.

9. On the drop schema warning, click on **OK**.

10. The pre-requisites for this step are reviewed. When completed, click on **OK** to move to the next page—again there's a slight delay, just wait for it.

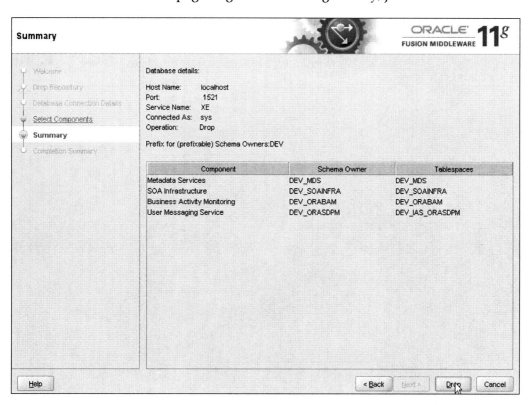

11. Click **Drop** to drop the schema. This only takes a minute or so.
12. When it is finished, click on the **Close** button.

Summary

You have now installed and configured all the software required to go through the tutorial. All installation steps were condensed into one single chapter and there was a lot to do! By the end of this tutorial, you will have a good understanding of the very extensive and capable set of tools that you now have at your disposal. Open the next chapter and begin.

7
Process Modeling using BPMN 2.0

This chapter provides a brief overview of **Business Process Modeling Notation** (BPMN) concepts with particular emphasis on the **BPMN 2.0** additions. In addition, it describes the steps involved in modeling the Sales Quote Process described in the case study chapter using Oracle BPM Studio.

BPMN 2.0 concepts

BPMN stands for **Business Process Modeling Notation** and is a public standard maintained by **OMG**. It describes a business-friendly, flow chart-like graphical notation that business process analysts and business users can use to model business processes and has support for process interactions, exception handling, compensation semantics, and so on. It is widely accepted by both commercial and open source BPMS tooling vendors. It is highly adaptable and can be used to capture everything from abstract process outlines to detailed process flows to implementation ready processes. One of the main value propositions of BPMN besides being a diagram standard is the precise semantics behind the diagram. The shape, the symbols (also referred to as markers), the borders, the placement of the BPMN diagram elements, as well as their properties have well defined meanings and have to be interpreted in the same manner by all tools.

While **BPMN 1.1** comprehensively addresses process modeling notations, it's failure to address an interchange format (for diagram exchange) has resulted in implementation vendors adopting different standards (**BPEL**, **XPDL**, other proprietary formats) to store BPMN process models leading to not only a loss of portability across tools but also making it difficult to communicate across the various stakeholders. The vision of BPMN is to have a single specification for notation, metamodel, and interchange. In addition, BPMN 2.0 has been expanded to include orchestrations and choreography of process models.

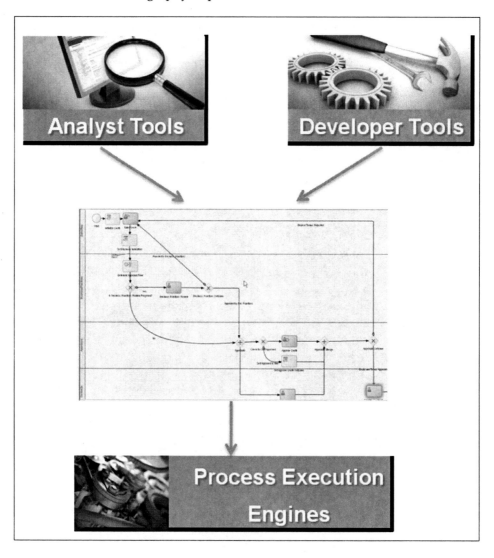

Salient enhancements to **BPMN 2.0** are as follows:

- BPMN 2.0 includes both diagram interchange as well as model interchange (the interchange formats can be either XML or UML) enabling portability of BPMN models across tool vendors.

- Formal execution semantics for all BPMN elements—BPMN 2.0 can not only be used to capture process models but can be used as an implementation model as well. IT simply layers the process execution details on top of the business process model leading to effective business-IT collaboration. Historically, business process models developed by business people have been technically separated from the process representations required by systems designed to implement and execute those processes. Thus, there was a need to manually translate the original business process models to the execution models. Vendors used standards such as BPEL and XPDL to save as well as execute BPMN Process models. Such translations are subject to errors and the impedance mismatch made it difficult for the process model and the executable process to be in sync with each other, as changes were made to both during the process development life cycle. With BPMN 2.0, there is no translation involved and the model is the implementation as well.

- Defines an extensibility mechanism for both Process model extensions and graphical extension.

- Refines event composition and correlation.

- Extends the definition of human interactions and aligns BPEL4People with the BPMN specification.

- Defines a Choreography model.

A quick introduction to BPMN

At its heart, BPMN has only three main elements, also referred to as Flow Objects—Activity (rectangle), Events (circle), and Gateways (diamond). An Activity represents some work done; Gateway represents a decision point or parallel forking or merge or join; Event represents either a trigger generated by the process or received by the process (from external source or from some other part of the process).

These **Flow Objects** are linked by connections referred to as Sequential Flows. These Sequential Flows represent the chronological sequence of process steps. The preceding steps pass control to the following step(s) along the connection. The data is also passed along the connection flow.

The **Activity** can be either a **Task** (an atomic process step) or **Embedded Sub-process** (compound process step). The Embedded Sub-Process can be either expanded or collapsed and has access to the process data. BPMN 2.0 supports different flavors of Tasks, namely: **User Task** for a human step managed by the workflow component of the BPM run-time engine; Manual Task for a human step that is not managed by the BPM run-time engine); **Service Task** for synchronous system interactions; **Send Task** and **Receive Task** for asynchronous system interactions; **Script Task** for scripting needs; **Call Task** for invoking another BPMN process (process chaining). The different task types have different symbols or markers to visually distinguish them.

In BPMN, the lane objects are used to group activities based on the categories (can be human resources or system resources) that they are associated for better visualization purpose. In Oracle BPM Studio, the lanes are associated with the BPM Role object and the Performer of the User Task is automatically set to the BPM Role object associated with the lane.

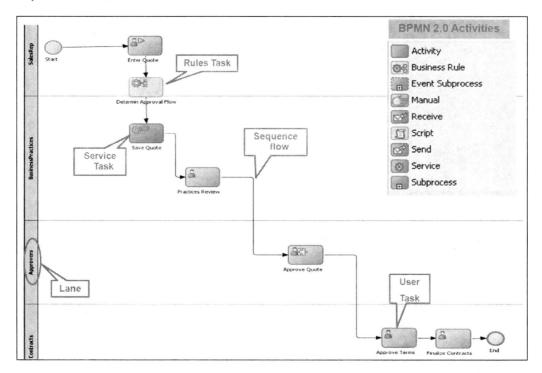

The User Task is associated with Process Participants or Performers who represent the business users who need to carry out the User Task. The associated Task (work to be performed) is shown in the inbox of the assigned Performers when the User Task is triggered. The actual work is performed only when the Performer executes on his Task. The Task is presented to the Performers through a browser-based worklist application. In BPM Studio the Process Participant or Performer is a BPM Role object in the Organization model.

Oracle BPM Suite supports out-of-the-box workflow patterns. **Workflow patterns** allow users to declaratively specify approval chains, notifications, and escalation and expiration policies. This simplifies the process logic by encapsulating approval chains within reusable task components. It is always possible to model the approval pattern using simple Tasks, Gateways, and Events within the BPMN process — but for many processes it is more convenient to define workflow patterns as well as notification, expiration, and escalation policies as part of the user task definition. BPM Studio exposes these workflow patterns through six flavors of Interactive Tasks.

The User Task refers to the Single Approver pattern and the participant or assignee is the member of the Role associated with the BPMN Process swim lane. The Management Task refers to the sequential management pattern and there are multiple participants assigned to the Task in a sequential pattern. Further, these participants are based on the Management hierarchy defined as part of LDAP and have the notion of a starting participant as well as the number of levels to be traversed up the management chain from the starting participant. The Group Task refers to the Parallel Voting pattern and the participants are members of the Role associated with the BPMN Process swim lane. The tasks are assigned in parallel to the participants in this case and the task is completed when a percentage of defined voting outcomes are reached. The FYI Task refers to the notification pattern and the participants are based on the Role associated with the BPMN Process swim lane. The task is completed as soon as the work items are assigned to the Task Inbox of the participants. Finally, the Complex Task for complex patterns involving task chaining and in this case the participants are not tied to the BPMN Process swim lanes.

The **Gateways** are used for conditional data splits, conditional merge, parallel forking and parallel joins. The conditional data splits can be exclusive (XOR Gateway — one and only one path can be taken) or inclusive (OR Gateway — one or more paths can be taken. The XOR Gateway is used for exclusive conditional merges and the OR Gateway for inclusive conditional merges). The parallel forking (AND) is used to indicate parallel paths. The AND Gateway is also used for joining parallel paths.

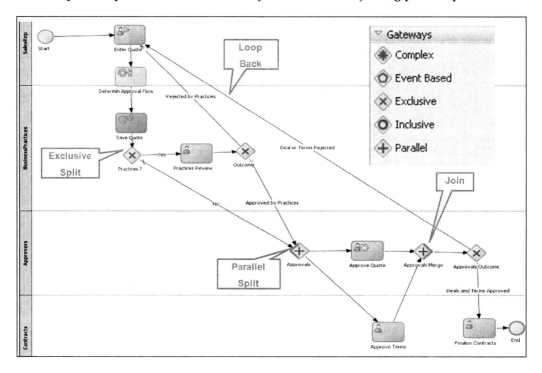

The Events can occur at the beginning (Start Events) or at the end (End Events) or in the middle (Intermediate) of the process. The Events can be of catch (receive trigger) or throw (send trigger) type. The Start Events are always of catch type and the End Events are always of throw type. The Intermediate Events can be either of throw or catch type. Similar to Activities, there are various flavors of Events to denote the type of trigger.

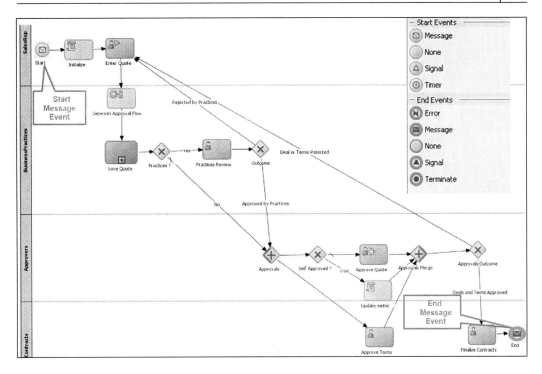

The Event Types are listed as follows:

- Message Events—send or receive messages
- Timer Events—are always of catch type and used to signify waiting for a specific time condition to evaluate to true
- Signal Events—are used for publish and subscribe of signals
- Error Events—are used for exception handling and they can occur only at the end of the process
- Termination Event—to abruptly terminate the process and can occur only at the end of the process
- Conditional Event—for rule-based trigger
- Escalation Event—has been newly introduced in BPMN 2.0 to handle escalation conditions
- Compensation Events—to handle compensation

There can be multiple End Events and the process completes only when all parallel paths complete. The exception to this is the Error End Event (as shown in the following figure). When the process encounters the Error End Event, it abruptly terminates irrespective of whether there are other parallel paths which are still being executed.

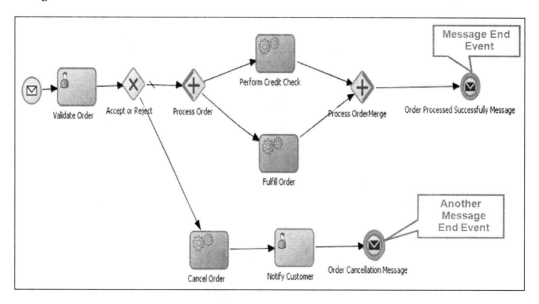

Sales Quote Process Flow

In order to analyze and optimize the business process, you need to create an accurate representation of the process with a model and then simulate how the process performs under different conditions. Oracle JDeveloper with the BPMN Editor extension is called Oracle BPM Studio. BPM Studio provides business user friendly process modeling and simulation. Using BPM Studio, a process analyst can model a business process including activities in the process, transitions between each activity, and roles associated with each activity. BPM Studio also allows the process analyst to define business rules and business indicators in the context of business processes. You can simulate processes based on certain assumptions to perform throughput analysis, to identify bottlenecks, and to determine the optimal resource requirements to achieve a specified SLA. The following details have to be captured before you design the process model:

- Process Flow: What are the sequence of steps in the Process Flow and how are they connected to each other?

- Process Participants: Who are the business users and groups responsible for the various human steps in the process?

- Business Data: What are the inputs/outputs of the various process steps and the process as a whole?

- Task Outcomes: What are the possible outcomes for the human steps (managed by a workflow engine)? Do these outcomes affect the flow of the process?

- Exception Paths: How to handle errors and external events.

The Sales Quote process flow for creation of Sales Quote process model is described below. The business process implements a solution for Sales Representatives to submit Sales Quotes and manage all the approvals within a particular Sales organization. A quick recap on the business process definition and its flow is detailed below:

1. The Sales Representative receives a Quote in his/her Task Inbox. He/She needs to complete the Quote. This is a human step, the Sales Representative role is the participant (task performer) and the input as well as output data is the Quote.

2. The next step is to review and approve the Quote by Business Practices role. This is a human step; the Business Practices role is the participant and Quote is the input as well as output data. The **Business Practices Review** step can have two possible outcomes:

   - APPROVE: Quote is approved by Business Practices role.
   - REJECT: Quote is rejected by Business Practices role.

3. The APPROVE outcome continues the process on the forward going path.

4. On the other hand, the REJECT outcome redirects the process to the Enter Quote Details step so that the Sales Representative can refine the quote and resubmit.

5. If the Quote gets approved by the Business Practices step, it then has to get approved in parallel for the deal structure and the terms. The Approve Deal step is used for approving the deal structure of the Quote and the Approve Terms step is used for approving the terms of the Quote, respectively.

6. The Approve Quote step is a human step executed by individuals belonging to the Approvers role. The input and output data is the Quote.

7. The Approve Terms step is a human step as well, executed by individuals belonging to the Contracts role.

8. Similar to the Business Practices Review step, the Approve Deal and the Approve Term steps can have two possible outcomes—APPROVE and REJECT.

9. The APPROVE outcome for both Approve Deal and Approve Terms steps continues the process on the forward going path.

10. On the other hand, the REJECT outcome for one or both of these steps redirects the process to the Enter Quote Details step so that the Sales Representative can refine the Quote and resubmit.

11. If both Approve Deal and Approve Terms steps have been approved, then the process proceeds to the Finalize Contracts step. This is a human step executed by an individual in the Contracts role.

12. Finally the Quote data is saved.

13. Quote is the only business data. Use the Quote.xsd provided with the sample.

Creating a BPM Application

The BPM Application consists of a set of related business processes and associated shared artifacts such as Process Participants and Organization models, User Interfaces, Services, and Data. The process-related artifacts such as Services and Data are stored in the Business Catalog. The Business Catalog facilitates collaboration between the various stakeholders involved in the development of the business process. It provides a mechanism for Process Developer (IT) to provide building blocks that can in turn be used by the process analyst in implementing the business process.

Start BPM Studio using **Start | Programs | Oracle Fusion Middleware 11.1.1.3 | Oracle JDeveloper 11.1.1.3**. BPM Studio supports two roles or modes of process development. The BPM Role is recommended for Process Analysts and provides a business perspective with focus on business process modeling. The Default Role is recommended for Process Developers for refinement of business process models and generation of implementation artifacts to complete the BPM Application for deployment and execution.

Tutorial: Creating SalesQuote project and modeling RequestQuote process

This is the beginning of the BPM 11*g*R1 hands-on tutorial. Start by creating the BPM Application and then design the Sales Quote business process.

1. Open BPM Studio by selecting the BPM Process Analyst role when you start JDeveloper or if JDeveloper is already open, select **Preferences** from the **Tools** menu and in the **Roles** section, select **BPM Process Analyst**. Go to **File | New** to launch the Application wizard.

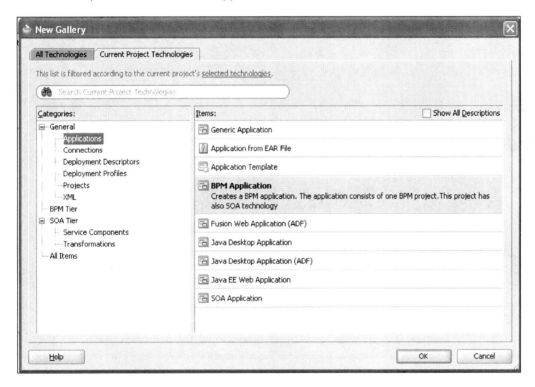

2. In the **New Gallery** window, select **Applications** in the **Categories** panel. Select **BPM Application** in the **Items** panel. Specify the **Application Name** — **SalesQuoteLab**; the folder name should also be set to SalesQuoteLab.

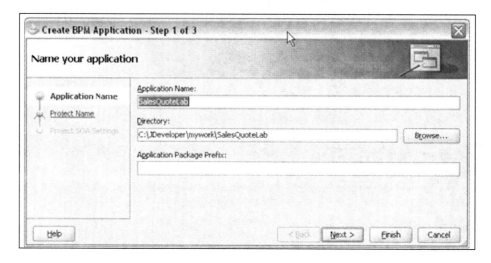

3. Click on the **Next** button. Enter QuoteProcessLab for the **Project Name**. Click on the **Finish** button.

4. Go to the **View | BPM Project Navigator**. The **BPM Project Navigator** opens up the **QuoteProcessLab – BPM Project** that you just created.

 A single BPM Project can contain multiple related business processes. Notice that the BPM Project contains several folders. Each folder is used to store a specific type of BPM artifact. The Processes folder stores BPMN business process models; the Activity Guide folder is used to store the process milestones; the Organization folder stores Organization model artifacts such as Roles and Organization Units; the Business Catalog folder stores Services and Data; the Simulation folder stores simulation models to capture what-if scenarios for the business process and the Resources folder holds XSLT data transformation artifacts.

5. To create a new business process model, you need to right-click on **Processes** and select **New | Process**. This launches the **Create BPMN Process** wizard. Select **From Pattern** option and select the **Manual Process** pattern. Recall that the Sales Quote Process is instantiated when Enter Quote task gets assigned to the Sales Representative role. The Asynchronous Service and the Synchronous Service patterns are used to expose the BPMN process as a Service Provider.

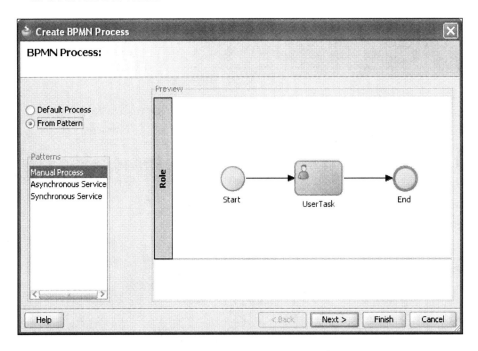

6. Click on the **Next** button. Specify the name for the Process — RequestQuoteLab. Click on the **Finish** button. This creates a RequestQuoteLab process with a Start Event (thin circle) and End Event (thicker circle) of type None with a User Task in between. The User Task represents a human step that is managed by the BPM run-time engine — workflow component. The Start Event of type None signifies that there is no external event triggering the process. The first activity after the Start Event creates the process instance. In addition, a default swim lane — Role, gets created.

In BPM Studio, the swim lanes in the BPMN process point to logical roles. A logical role represents a process participant (user or group) and needs to be mapped to physical roles (LDAP users/groups) before the process is deployed. This is addressed in *Chapter 8, Organization and Roles*.

7. Right-click on the **User Task** step, select **Properties**, and specify the name **Enter Quote Details** for the step. Click on the **OK** button.

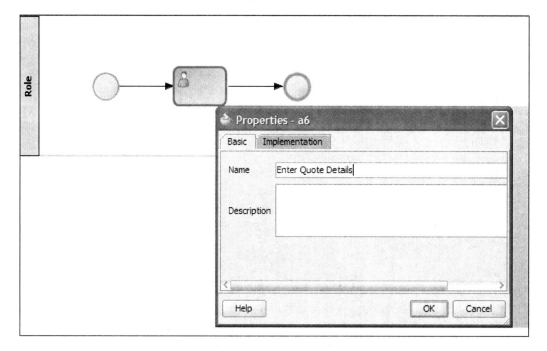

8. The next step is to rename the default created role to SalesRep. Navigate to **QuoteProcessLab – BPM Project** node and select the **Organization** node underneath it. Right-click on the **Organization** node and select **Open**. This opens up the Organization pane.

9. Highlight the default role named Role and use the pencil icon to edit it to be `SalesRep`. Click on the **+** sign to add the following roles—**Approvers**, **BusinessPractices**, and **Contracts**. The following screenshot shows the list of roles that you just created:

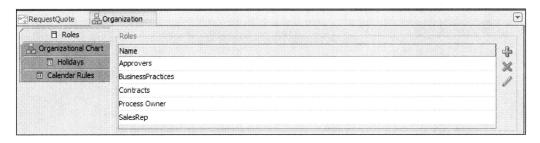

10. Close the **Organization** window. Go back to the **RequestQuoteLab**—process model. The participant for the Enter Quote Details—User Task is now set to the SalesRep role. Ignore the yellow triangular symbol with the exclamation for now. It indicates that certain configuration information is missing for the activity. Implementing the business process is covered in Chapter 10.

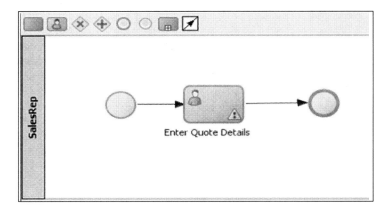

11. Right-click on the process diagram just below the SalesRep-Lane. Choose the **Add Role** option.

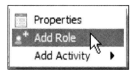

12. Choose **Business Practices** from the list of options available. Click on the **OK** button.

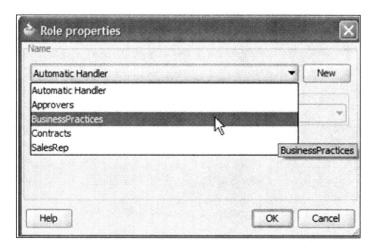

13. Open the **View | Component Palette**. Drag and drop a **User Task** from the **Interactive Tasks** section of the **BPMN Component Palette**.

Note: The Interactive Tasks refers to a step that is managed by the workflow engine. The Assignees (Participants) represent the business users who need to carry out the Interactive Task. The associated Task (work to be performed) is shown in the inbox of the assignees (similar to Email Inbox) when the Interactive Task is triggered. The User Task is the simplest type of Interactive Task where the assignee of the task is set to a single role. The actual work is performed only when the Assignee executes on his Task. The Task is presented to the Assignee through a browser based worklist application. In BPM Studio, the Assignee is automatically set to the role associated with the swim lane into which the Interactive Task is dropped.

14. Place this new User Task after the existing Enter Quote Details—User Task by hovering on the center of the connector until it turns blue and name it **Business Practices Review**. The connection lines are automatically created.

15. Drag the new Business Practices Review—User Task to the Business Practices lane. The performer or assignee for the Business Practices Review—User Task is automatically set to Business Practices—role.

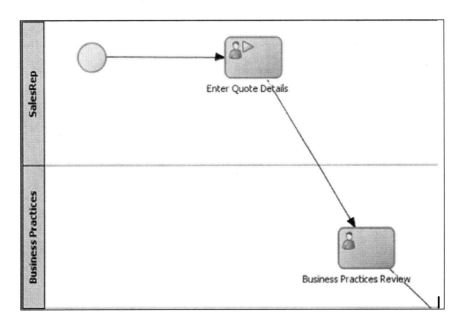

16. Create two more lanes for Approvers and Contracts. Drag and drop three User Tasks on to the process diagram, one following the other, and name them `Approve Deal`, `Approve Terms`, and `Finalize Contracts` respectively. Pin the Approve Deal step to the Approvers Lane. Pin the other two User Tasks—Approve Terms and Finalize Contracts steps to the Contracts Lane. Finally add a Service Task right after the Finalize Contracts step from the BPM Component Palette and name it `Save Quote`. The modified diagram should look like the following:

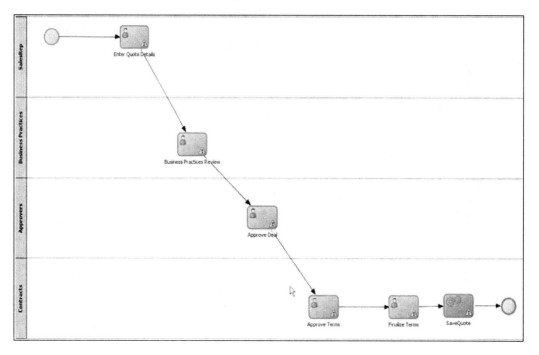

The high-level outline of the process is complete. The next step is to modify the process further to promote Approve Deal and Approve Terms steps as parallel and concurrent activities. This can be achieved through a Parallel (AND) Gateway.

1. Drag-and-drop a **Parallel Gateway** from the Gateway Pane and place it right before the Approve Deal step. Click on **OK**. This creates a pair of Parallel Gateways to indicate the parallel split and parallel join (merge).

2. Right-click on the **Parallel Split Gateway** to bring up the **Properties Editor** and set the Name to **Approvals**.

3. Right-click on the **Parallel Merge Gateway** to bring up the **Properties Editor** and set the Name to **Approvals Merge**.

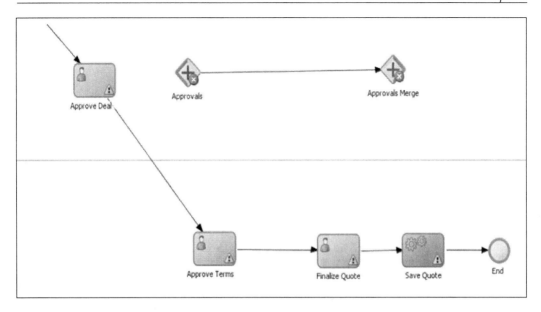

4. Rewire the outgoing connection from the Business Practices Review step to point to Approvals Gateway.

5. Select Approve Deal incoming and outgoing sequence flows, right-click, and choose the **Delete** option to delete the incoming and outgoing sequence flows.

6. Move the Approve Deal User Task and insert it between the **Approvals** and **Approvals Merge Gateways**.

7. Right-click on the **Approvals Gateway** and select the **Add Sequence Flow to Converging Gateway** option to create a parallel path.

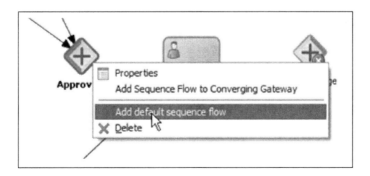

8. Delete the outgoing sequence flow from Approve Terms step. Now drop the Approve Terms step to the newly created parallel path between Approvals and Approvals Merge gateways.

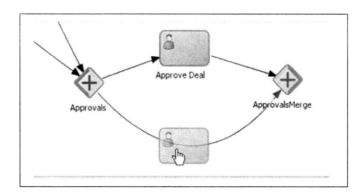

9. Rewire the connections such that the outgoing connection from the Approvals Merge- Gateway is now pointing to the Finalize Contracts step. Do this by right-clicking on the Approvals Merge Gateway task and clicking on Add default sequence flow:

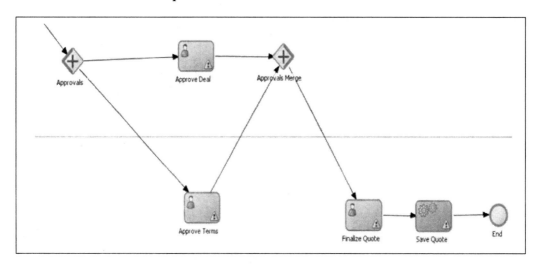

10. There is one last modification to be done before completing the outline. The Business Practices Review, Approve Deal, and Approve Terms — User Tasks can have two possible outcomes — APPROVE or REJECT. The APPROVE outcome continues the process on the happy path. On the other hand, the REJECT outcome redirects the process to the Enter Quote Details step so that the Sales Representative can refine the quote and resubmit. The Exclusive (XOR) Gateway can be used to create a loop. Drag and drop an Exclusive Gateway — **Business Practices Outcome** just after the Business Practices Review step. Change outgoing sequence flow from Business Practices Review to Business Practices Outcome gateway by first selecting the connection leaving Business Practices review and then dragging the connection's arrow over to the new Business Practices Outcome Gateway task.

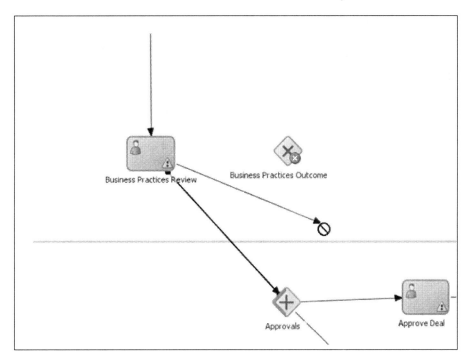

11. The outgoing business exception path from the newly added Exclusive Gateway should redirect the process flow to the Enter Quote Details step. Right click on the Business Practices Outcome Gateway and select **Add conditional sequence** flow. Join the connection to Enter Quote Details step. Right-click on this new connection and select **Properties**. Enter `Business Practices Reject` as the connection name. Right-click on the Business Practices Outcome Gateway and select **Add default sequence flow**. The connection line appears and you need to join it to the Approvals step. Name the default path to **Business Practices Approve**.

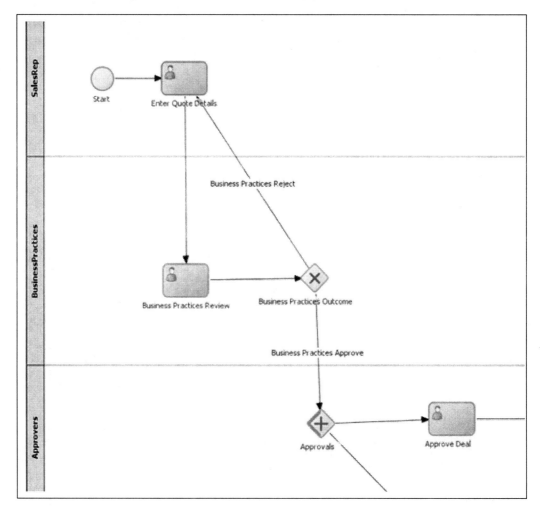

12. Similarly, the process flow goes to Enter Quote Details step if the Approve Terms step or Approve Deal step outcome is REJECT. Drag and drop an **Exclusive Gateway** and name it **Approvals Outcome** just after the Approvals Merge step. The outgoing business exception path from the newly added Exclusive Gateway should redirect the process flow to the Enter Quote Details step as shown in the figure below. Change outgoing sequence flow from Approvals Merge Parallel Join Gateway to flow to the newly added Approvals Outcome XOR Gateway.

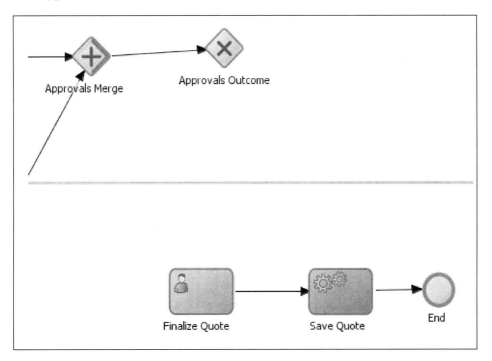

13. Right-click on **Approvals Outcome** — Exclusive (XOR) Gateway and select the **Add default sequence flow** option. A connection appears and you need to join it to Finalize Contracts step. Right-click on the default connection to bring up the Properties wizard. Go to the **Description** tab. Type in **Approved** for the connection name.

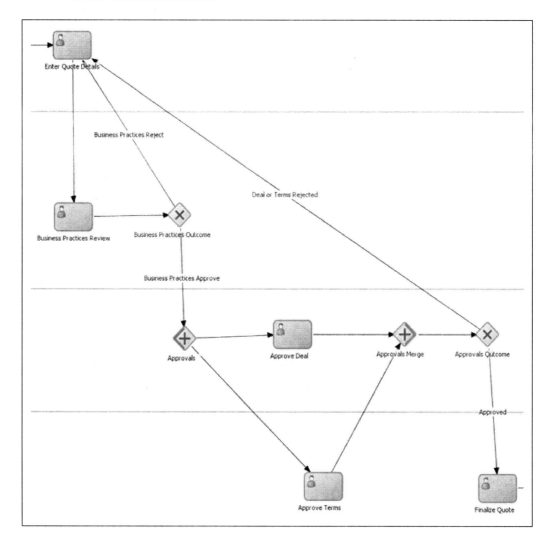

14. Right-click on Approvals Outcome — Exclusive (XOR) Gateway again and select the **Add conditional sequence flow** option. A connection appears and you need to join it to the Enter Quote Details step. Right-click on the conditional connection to bring up the **Properties** wizard. Go to the **Description** tab. Type in **Deal or Terms Rejected** for the connection name. The completed process outline looks like the following diagram. Save the process.

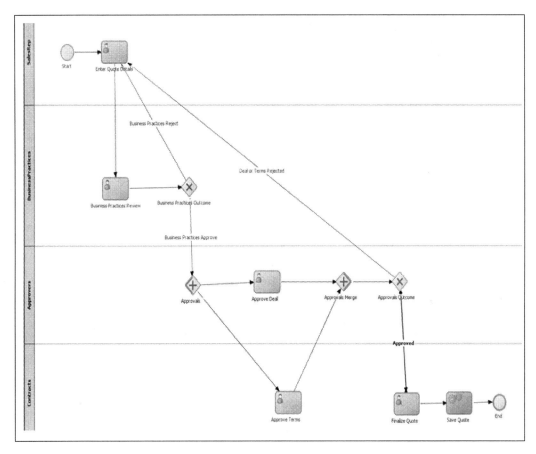

Summary

In this chapter you learned about creating a BPM Project, modeling BPMN processes, and roles. The simplicity and expressiveness of BPMN extends modeling to a wider business audience. It enables business users to get involved in understanding and improving their own processes. In addition, the BPMN models allow high fidelity mapping between business requirements and the actual executable process, as the model is the implementation. This business-empowered, model-driven execution allows business and IT stakeholders to collaborate throughout the process development life cycle.

8
Process Organization Model

In the previous chapter, we saw the steps to build the process design prototype for the sales quote process. In this chapter, process prototype will be linked to actual roles, its employees, and its various departments. In addition, you will understand and define the organizational structure for **Sales Quote process**. You will learn to use **Oracle BPM Studio** to define:

- Organizational units (for example, departments or regions)
- Roles (for example, manager, clerk, instructor, teller, and claims adjuster)
- Participants (end users or employees)
- Holiday and calendar rules

Typically, a select small group of people on a project define an organizational structure. This task is not the responsibility of every process designer or developer. However, in reality, developers often establish their own unit test environments. Moreover, the responsibilities of developers, designers, and administrators often differ from project to project, and you may be called upon occasionally to define an organization's structure. For this reason, you will want to understand how to use the **Oracle BPM Studio's Organization Manager** to define organization units, roles, and participants.

Concepts

This section provides an overview of the various Organization assets in
BPM Suite 11*g*.

Role

A **Role** is a title or job function performed by participants in the project. For example,
a role could be supervisor or finance administrator. It is also referred to as an abstract
or logical role as it defines the responsibility in the context of the business process
and needs to be mapped to a real-world user or group. The logical roles are often
mapped to LDAP Group(s) or User(s) at deployment time. The human steps of the
process need to be tied to roles or process participants in order to execute them.
Each swim lane in the BPMN process in Oracle BPM Studio represents a unique role.
In BPM Studio, the Interactive Tasks represent the human steps managed by the
workflow component of the BPM runtime engine and the process participants/role
of the Interactive Tasks are automatically derived from the swim lane role that they
are associated with. There is no limit as to the amount of roles that can be created,
but the general practice is to think about responsibilities in the organization where
the process is deployed.

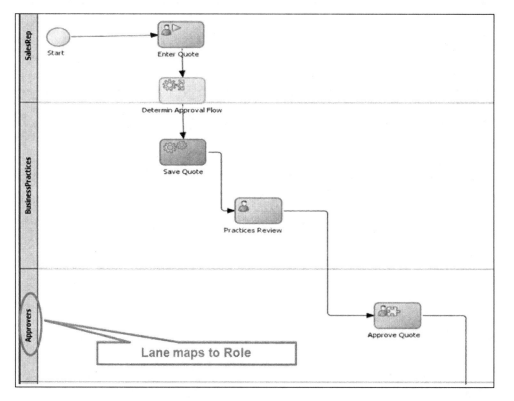

Organization unit

Organization units represent departments or divisions within an organization. Typically, they are organized in a hierarchy. Once the **Organizational units** have been defined, the employees of the company defined as process participants might be assigned to one of the organizational units in the hierarchy. Processes can be deployed for one of the organizational units defined here. Only participants in that **Organizational unit** and in lower levels within the hierarchy are able to perform tasks in such processes.

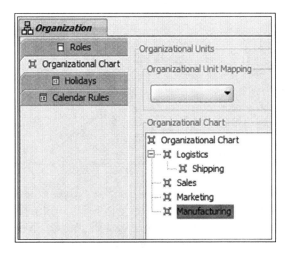

Calendar and holiday rules

Calendar rules and **holiday rules** define the work hours, time zone, and holiday rule assignment for organizational units. Holiday Rules are used to define non working days. **Calendar rules** are used to define **working hours** for individuals in an **organization**. Together they determine the scheduling of activity deadlines. Multiple **calendar rules** can be created as needed for different organizational units—for example, day shift, night shift, east coast, west coast, and so on.

The following screenshot shows **holiday rules** defined for the Sales Quote process for the three different regions:

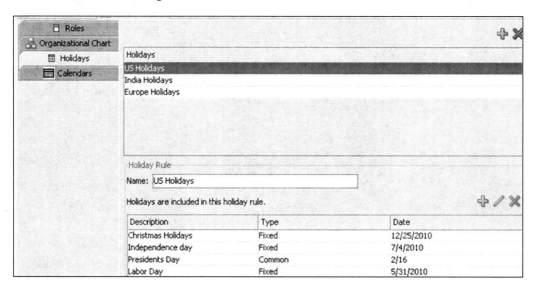

Calendar rules can be assigned one or more holiday rules. You can create as many holiday rules as needed for different calendar rules. The following screenshot shows the working hours and the holidays for regular shift for the Sales Quote process. Note that the **US Holidays**, a holiday rule is assigned to the **Regular Shift**, a calendar rule.

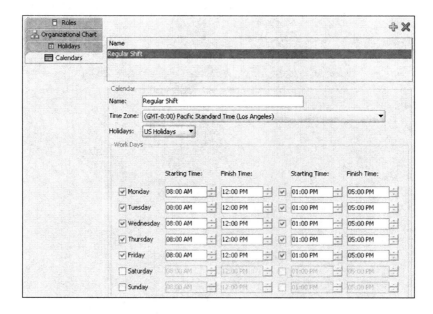

Calendar rules can be associated with organizational units, and each organizational unit can have a different calendar rule associated with it. This enables the BPM runtime engine to calculate deadlines according to the time zones and work schedules of the organizational unit where the processes are deployed. To determine which calendar rule should be applied, the BPM runtime engine looks for the organizational unit where the process of the instance being executed is deployed. If the engine finds no calendar rule for the organizational unit, then it looks in the upper levels of the organizational hierarchy until it finds one. If the engine finds no calendar rule, then it assumes that all days are working days.

The following screenshot shows the mapping between **Sales**, an organization unit and **Regular Shift**, a calendar rule:

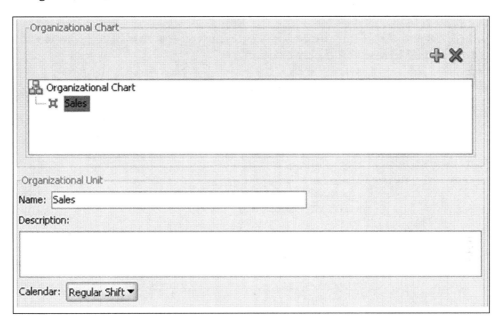

Calendar rules can be associated with roles as well. The BPM runtime engine takes into account both the calendar rule associated with the organizational unit where the process is deployed and the activity role where the instance is running. The BPM runtime engine evaluates the calendar rule set at the role level first. This rule overrides any rules defined for the organization unit.

Organizational Artifacts Mapping, Application Roles, and Approval Groups

Organization units and roles defined in BPM Studio are abstract. They help define and mimic responsibilities of an individual in the Enterprise. They need to be mapped to your real-world organization. During deployment of your project, the components of the modeled organization and roles are mapped to your real-world organization. They are usually mapped to LDAP users and groups.

Application roles

Application roles are part of the Oracle Fusion Middleware policy store and used across various Oracle Fusion Middleware components. They are policy-related roles outside of corporate directory store. They promote reuse across BPM projects and in turn are mapped to real-world organization.

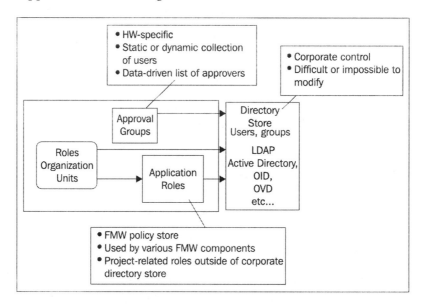

Approval groups

Approval groups are specific to the **Human Workflow Component** of the Oracle **BPM Suite 11g** platform. They can be a static or dynamic collection of users and are used for data-driven scenarios.

Tutorial: Defining organizational model for SalesQuote

Each BPM Project, in addition to having a processes folder, also has an organization folder. This node is used to define the:

- Organizational units to create department hierarchies and help segregate process deployment
- Roles (Abstract) to be used in the business process
- Participants (LDAP users/groups) that can be mapped to roles and organization units
- Holiday and calendar rules to embed declarative time sensitive constraints

The following screenshot shows the different type of assets that can be created under the BPM Project Organization node:

Adding a role

Roles can be added in two ways.

Adding a swim lane to the BPMN process model automatically creates a role in the Organization Chart. Note that in Chapter 7 during process modeling, four swim lanes—SalesRep, Approvers, BusinessPractices, and Contracts—were created to represent the roles of the Sales Quote process. To view the roles of the Sales Quote process, go to the Organization node in the BPM Project Navigator. Right-click and select **Open**. Highlight **Roles**. This shows the four roles that were already created—**SalesRep**, **Approvers**, **Contracts**, and **Business Practices**. In addition, there is a **Process Owner** role in the Organizational Chart of the Sales Quote BPM Project. This is the default role and represents the process owner of the business process. The **Process Owner** role has special administrative privileges and can do re-assignment of tasks for all tasks belonging to the business process.

Roles can also be explicitly created in the **Organizational Chart**. To add a role, follow these steps:

1. Go to the **BPM Project Navigator** tab.

2. Expand **Organization** node, and right-click on it.

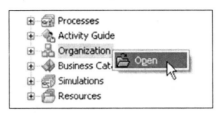

3. Select **Open**.

4. Select **Roles** and use the + button to add roles.

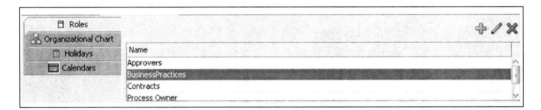

Adding members to the role

Members or participants are the end users (people) enabled to track and perform activities for the instances as they flow through a process. You can add LDAP users, groups, or BPM application roles as members for the role.

 BPM application roles promote reuse of roles across BPM projects and they are defined at the BPM runtime engine level.

You will add the members to the roles in a later chapter because you can not add members while using the BPM Process Analyst role in BPM Studio.

Adding an organization unit

This section describes the steps for adding an organization unit and assigning members to it.

1. To add an organizational unit, go to the **BPM Project Navigator** tab, expand **Organization** node, right-click on it, and select **Open**.

2. Select the **Organizational Chart** on the left-hand section. Click on + and enter the new organization unit called **Sales** and click on the **OK** button. You can create a hierarchy of organization units. In the following screenshot, the Sales organization unit is further classified into **North American Sales**, **Latin American Sales**, **Asian Sales**, and **European Sales**:

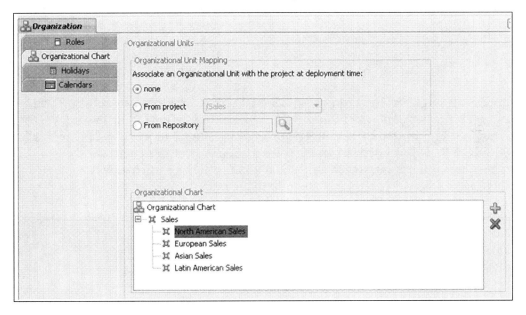

An organization unit can be associated to the project at deployment. The participant is assigned a task only if he belongs to both the role associated with the task and the organization unit of the BPM project to which this task belongs. The organization unit mapping section enables you to specify the organizational unit to associate with a project at deployment. Mapping an organization unit to a BPM project is optional and you can choose the **none** option if you wish to skip the organizational unit mapping. There are two possible options for organization unit mapping:

3. **From Project**: Pick an organization unit from the ones already defined in the current project.

4. **From Repository**: Pick an organization unit defined in the BPM runtime server.

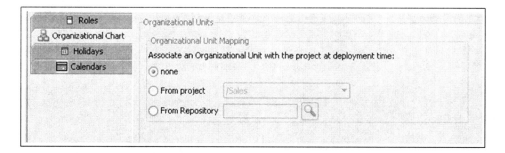

Participants might belong to an organizational unit so that they can only perform tasks on processes deployed in that organizational unit or any of the lower levels within the organization hierarchy. The process activities that participants are authorized to perform depend on the roles they have been assigned and the organization units under which they come under. All the participants of the Sales Quote process belong to the default organization unit.

Adding members to the organization unit follows the exact same steps as adding members to the role.

Creating holiday rules

This section describes the steps to create holiday rules.

1. To create a holiday rule, go to the **Organization** node and select the **Holidays** option on the left-hand side. This opens up the **Holiday Rule** editor.

2. Click on the **+** sign to add a holiday rule and provide a meaningful name:

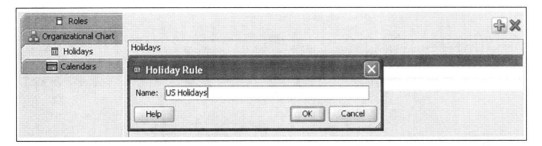

3. For each holiday rule, you can add more holidays by selecting the **+** symbol in the bottom section:

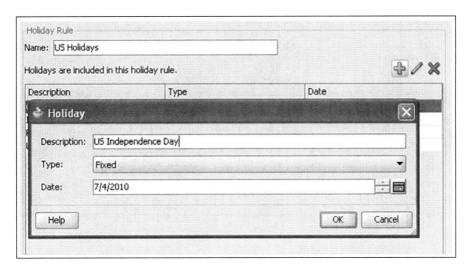

Creating calendar rules

This section describes the steps to create calendar rules.

1. To create a calendar rule, go to the **Organization** node and select the **Calendars** option on the left-hand side. This opens up the **Calendar Rule** editor.

2. Click on the **+** sign to add a calendar rule and provide a meaningful name.

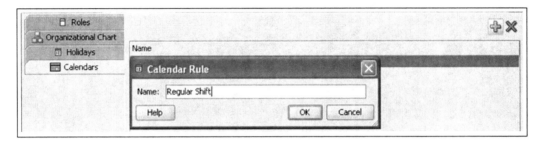

3. Pick the **Time Zone,** the **Holidays,** the **Work Days,** and the **Hours** in the bottom section for completing the configuration of the calendar rule, as shown in the following screenshot:

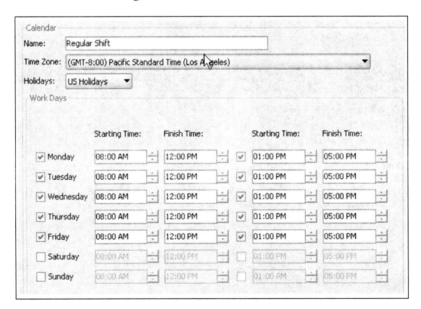

Creating and mapping organization artifacts inside BPM Workspace

Roles and **organization units** can be created at deployment time inside Oracle BPM Workspace by a Process Administrator role. The **Oracle BPM Workspace** component is a standalone web application for end user work management, process monitoring, and administration. The approval groups can only be created from BPM Workspace. You have to log in as an administrator to Oracle BPM Workspace to create and administer role mappings.

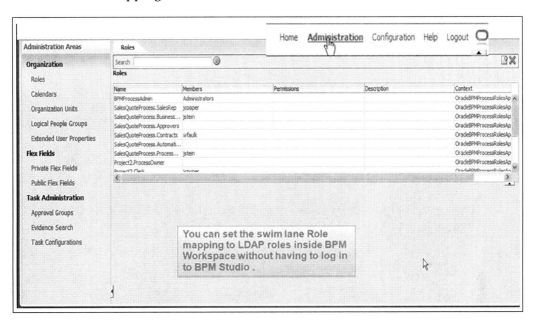

This section describes the steps involved in creating roles and mapping of members to role inside BPM Workspace.

1. Log in to BPM Workspace as an administrator (that is, `weblogic`) at `http://localhost:8001/bpm/workspace`.

2. Go to the **Administration** tab on the main menu.

3. Go to **Approval Groups**.

4. This opens up the approval groups editor on the right-hand side. Use the **+** symbol to add **Approval Groups**.

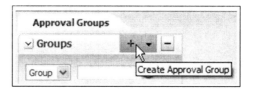

5. Choose **static** from the list of options.

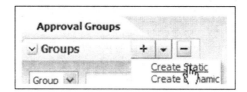

6. Then click on the **+** symbol on the right-hand pane to add users. In this case, we are adding the user **cdoyle**.

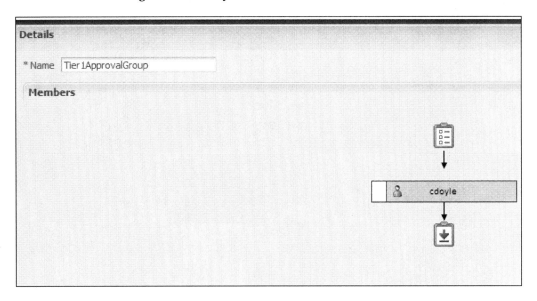

Summary

Organizational Charts enable the BPM platform to manage which people should participate within a process, when they should participate, and how much authority they should have. To manage process participants, Studio's Organization Manager is used to define the organization, any organizational units, roles, users, and any calendar rules that may apply. End users interact with a process using the Oracle BPM Workspace. This is a web-based application that requires a login and enforces the roles and permissions as defined in the organization settings, and as such, only displays activities relevant to the logged on individual. When a process activity requires human participation, the Oracle BPM Engine simply *pushes* work to them for access through the Workspace.

9
Simulation and Analysis of the Business Process

Simulating enables determination of the process throughput, generate process performance statistics, locate bottlenecks, measure user allocations, and pinpoint optimizations that will improve performance and reduce cost of the process. Simulator helps analyze and fine-tune the business process based on meaningful assumptions without having to actually implement and execute the process. Simulation is a powerful tool and enables understanding of process design issues that could affect performance before process implementation. It helps run "what-if" experiments to see what will be the impact of:

- Reducing or increasing the number of people assigned to an activity
- A sudden increase in the number of instances flowing through the process
- Changing the approval ratio from 70% approved 30% disapproved to a worse case 50% approved 50% disapproved

This can help avoid the embarrassment and cost of launching a new process with a flaw that only becomes obvious on day three of production. It can verify that the desired output meets the metric objectives and easily finds bottlenecks in redesigned processes and leads to breakthroughs. In this chapter, the Sales Quote process developed in the previous chapter is simulated, analyzed, and improved to produce a future optional version of the process.

Simulation concepts

The simulation algorithm is based on discrete events that can process events in a serial fashion as they occur in time. The Process Simulation Models and Project Simulation Definitions have to be created to run simulation. The **Process Simulation Model** captures a "what-if scenario" for a particular business process model. There can be multiple Process Simulation Models for a particular business process model. This allows creation of different simulations based on different combinations of resource allocations and activity behavior. The **Project Simulation Definition** is used to take the dependency and shared resources across processes in to account. It consists of a Process Simulation Model of multiple processes. The simulation does not execute the actual code of each activity within the process. However, by configuring parameters within the Process Simulation Models and Project Simulation Models, the behavior of the business processes in real-life can be mimicked. In order to perform simulation, the processes need to be complete and semantically valid.

Simulation steps

In order to analyze and optimize the business process, the Process Simulation model that represents simulation scenario needs to be created. BPM Studio does not mandate the creation of Process Simulation Model. A default scenario is automatically created by the tool. The key steps for running a simulation are as follows:

1. Define meaningful assumptions:

   Before simulating the process, the process analyst must collect the following information about the business processes. The information can be based on historical data or based on a best guess or be a combination of both.

   ° Time settings: Expected average processing time for the process activities. The average processing time need not be a constant value and statistical distributions can be used to closely mimic the anticipated processing time of the business process if it were to be executed.

   ° Routing settings: Probability of taking one path versus the other in the case of conditional splits.

   ° Cost settings: Cost for processing the activity and cost of the activity plus the cost of the resource if it is an interactive human centric step.

   ° Instance settings: Amount and rate of process instances created. This can either be a constant or statistical distribution such as normal, uniform, exponential, and so on.

   ° Role allocation: Number of people allocated to a particular role.

2. Define one or more simulation models (what-if scenarios) for the business processes.

3. Define one or more simulation projects and select the business processes to be analyzed. Then pick a simulation model for each of the selected business processes.

4. Run the simulation.

5. Analyze simulation results.

Tutorial: Simulating SalesQuote

To do simulation, first create the simulation model and then the simulation definition.

Creating the Process Simulation Model

The Oracle BPM Studio is a modeling cum simulation tool. This section explains the simulation steps for analyzing the Sales Quote business process model created in *Chapter 7*.

1. Start the BPM Studio 11*g* and open up the **SalesQuoteLab** application workspace.

2. Switch to the BPM Navigator Pane. If the pane is not seen, it can be opened with the menu item **View | BPM Project Navigator**.

3. Open up the **Processes** node.

4. Double-click on the **RequestQuoteLab** element. This opens the **Request Quote Lab** main process and the process diagram is displayed in the main panel in the standard Business Process Modeling Notation (BPMN).

5. In the **BPM Project Navigator** go to the **Simulations** node and expand the node by clicking the **+** icon.

6. Underneath this node, there are two folders—**Simulation Definitions** for storing Project Simulation Definitions and **Simulation Models** for storing Process Simulation Models.

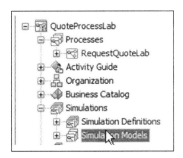

7. Select the **Simulation Models** folder, right-click on it, and choose the **New Process Simulation**.

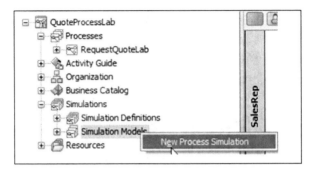

8. Select **RequestQuoteLab** process in the **Process** drop-down box. Type in **NormalLoad** for the **Simulation Model Name** and click on the **OK** button. The newly created NormalLoad Process Simulation Model opens.

A Process Simulation Model can configure the following settings for a process:

- ○ Process settings.
- ○ Amount and rate of instances created in the process. This can either be a constant or statistical distribution such as normal, uniform, exponential, and so on.
- ○ Activity Settings: Average Execution Time — this is the time that the activity is actually executing as opposed to the waiting time of instances that might queue at the activity. This can either be a constant or a statistical distribution. In addition, if it is a User Task (human step), the number of people associated with the participant role needs to be specified.

- ○ Routing Settings: Probability percentage of instances routed through the different outgoing transitions of conditional gateways.
- ○ Cost Settings: Cost for processing the activity and cost of the activity + the cost of the resource if it is an interactive human centric step.

9. On the **Process Information** tab, set the number of processes to run for your simulation. Alternatively, the simulation can be set up to run for a period of (simulated) time by setting the activity based setting on the start event.

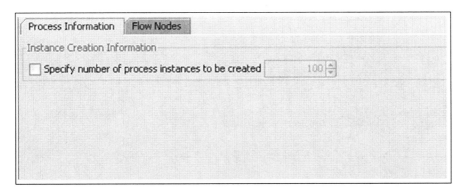

10. To set the activity based parameters, select the **Flow Nodes** tab.

11. To configure the frequency of process instances created select the start node. Set the instances creation **Distribution Type** to **Constant** with a **Period** of five minutes. This creates one instance every five minutes.

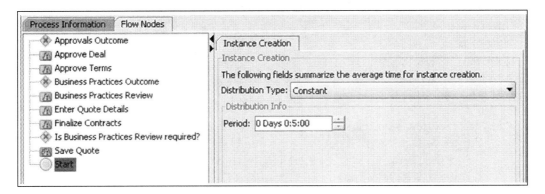

12. Now set the parameters for the activities as shown in the table (except for Is Business Practices Review Required? gateway, which is added in a later step). The estimated time that it takes a user to complete each activity is set. In addition, the probability that a gateway branch will go one way or another is also set. The number of resources assigned to each user task are not defined in the Process Simulation Model but are specified later in the Project Simulation Definition.

Activity Name	Duration (Distribution type, Mean, Std Deviation)	Cost	Transitions
Approve Deal	Normal, 20 minutes, 3 seconds	$100	N/A
Approve Terms	Normal, 10 minutes, 3 seconds	$50	N/A
Business Practices Review	Normal, 20 minutes, 3 seconds	$100	N/A
Enter Quote Details	Normal, 20 minutes, 3 seconds	$30	N/A
Finalize Contracts	Normal, 20 minutes,3 seconds	$60	N/A
Is Business Practices Review Required?—Gateway	N/A	-	Business Practices Review—1 (10%) Approvals—.9 (90%)
Business Practices Outcome—Gateway	N/A	-	Approvals—1 (100%) Enter Quote Details—0
Approvals Outcome—Gateway	N/A	-	Finalize Contracts—1 (100%) Enter Quote Details—0

13. The next few steps show the specification of simulation properties for the Approve Deal step. Select the **Approve Deal** step on the left-hand section. Select the **Duration** tab. Set the **Distribution type** to **Normal, Mean** to **0 Days 0:20:0** (20 minutes), and **Standard Deviation** to **0 Days 0:0:3** (3 seconds).

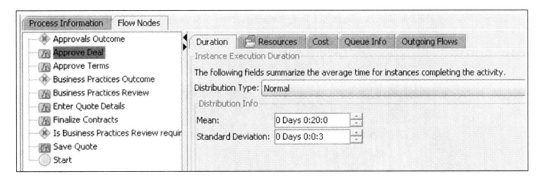

14. The Approver role is the assignee or participant for the Approve Deal activity. Select the **Use Organization Resource** option. The number of people for the Approvers role is specified as part of the Project Simulation Definition.

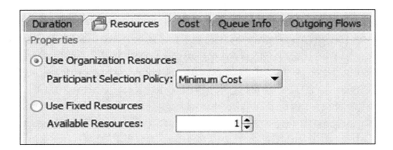

15. There are two ways in which the cost can be calculated for an activity base cost and base cost plus resource cost. In the former case, the cost of the resource is not taken in to consideration while in the latter the cost of the resource is added to the base cost of the activity while calculating the total cost of an activity during the simulation run. Choose the Fixed Base Cost option for this sample. The resource cost will be specified during the definition of the Project Simulation Definition in the next section.

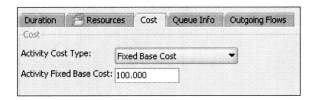

16. Choose the default options for **QueueInfo** as shown in the following screenshot:

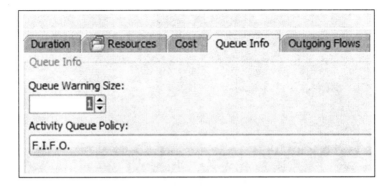

17. If there is more than one outgoing path, the probabilities to indicate how often a specific path is traversed versus the others needs to be specified. For an Exclusive Conditional Gateway (XOR) where one and only one of the outgoing paths can be chosen, the sum of the probabilities has to be equal to 1. For example, if there are two outgoing paths and if the probability of the conditional path is 90% then the probability of the default path (the other path) has to be 10%. For an Inclusive Conditional Gateway (OR), more than one outgoing paths can be taken and hence the sum of the probabilities of the outgoing path doesn't need to add up to 1. It can be greater than 1. If the probability for the paths are not specified, then all the paths are considered equally likely. An example screenshot for setting probability of outgoing flow for Business Practices Review? — XOR Gateway is shown below. The slide bar has to be moved to change the probability.

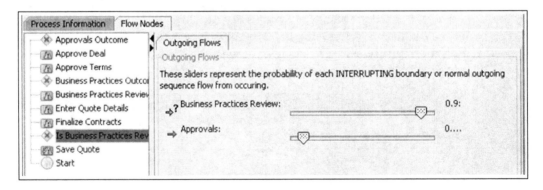

18. Save the NormalLoad Process Simulation Model.

Creating the project simulation definition

BPM projects can consist of many processes. Similarly, each project simulation can consist of one or more processes and their corresponding simulation models. In this step, a Project Simulation Definition is created. A Project Simulation Model determines which processes and Process Simulation Models should be used and how resources (some of which can be shared) should be configured for the simulation.

1. In the **BPM Project Navigator/Simulations** tab, note that there are two *simulations* folders—**Simulation Definitions** and **Simulation Models**. As shown below, right-click on the **Simulation Definitions** folder and click **New Simulation**:

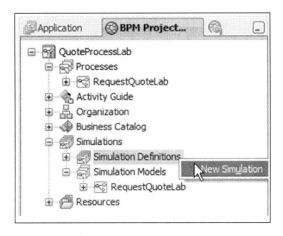

2. Enter **AsIsSalesQuoteSimulation** as **the Simulation Name**. Click on the **OK** button and the simulation definition opens.

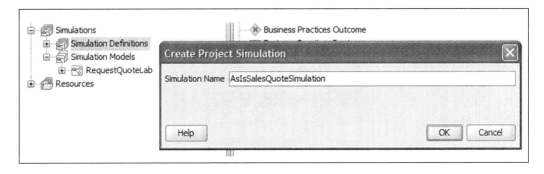

3. The Process Simulation Models available are displayed. The NormalLoad Process Simulation Model is the only item in the list and is chosen.

4. Set the **Duration** to **0 Months 0 Days 10:0:0** (10 hours). Enable the checkbox beside **Let in-flight instances finish before the simulation ends**. Enable the checkbox for **Include in simulation**.

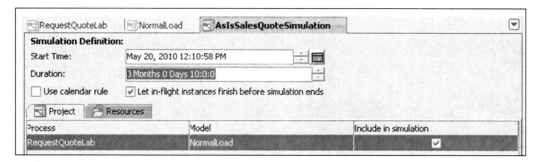

5. Click on the **Resources** tab. In this panel, the current number of people available to perform the activities in their roles is specified. Click on the **+** button to set the participants for the roles defined as part of the BPM project. The capacity for each resource is set as shown in the following screenshot:

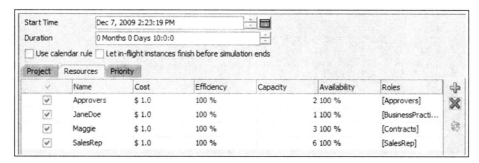

6. To select the predefined roles, double-click the **Roles** cell and click on the magnifying glass to open the roles list.

7. Save the project.

Running the simulation

Now that the simulation model has been defined, you can run the simulation.

1. Click on the **Simulation** tab in the bottom window as shown in the following screenshot. Open the simulation view from the menu by clicking **View | Simulations**.

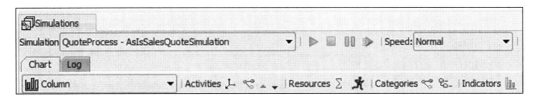

2. With the process diagram open in the top window, click on the ▷ button in the **Simulations** tab. This starts simulation in an interactive mode and the animation allows the progress to be viewed on the process diagram.

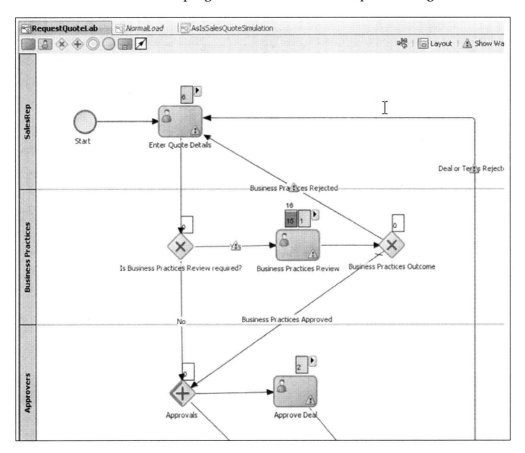

3. During simulation, the tool supports adjusting the queue sizes for interactive activities to prevent bottlenecks from forming when you have Fixed Resources set in the model. To adjust the queue size of an interactive activity, click the arrow button next to the activity. This expands a small control panel. Inside the panel the number of resources assigned to this activity can be adjusted. The speed of the simulation can be increased by selecting the **Speed** drop-down box and choosing the **Faster** or **Fastest** options.

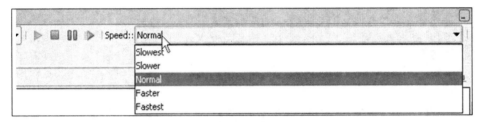

4. To complete the simulation without waiting, click on the Run to end button in the Simulation View.

Analyzing the simulation results

Now that the simulation is run, the next step is to analyze the results. The first step is to find out how many instances have completed and how many are pending.

1. Click on the **Indicators** on the right-hand side of the simulation chart tool bar. Select the **Units** checkbox. Choose **Current Queue Size** and **Completed Instances** from the **Units** category of **Indicators**.

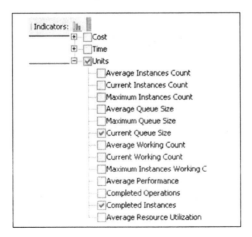

2. The default chart is **Column** type. The number of process instances is shown on the vertical axis and the completed versus queued buckets are shown on the horizontal axis. Observe that the only 26 instances were completed and 80+ instances are still pending. This is of course not desirable.

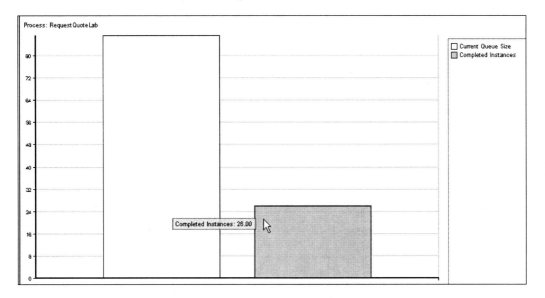

3. The process performance can be displayed by choosing the **Time** option under **Indicators**.

4. Choose **Average processing time** from the list of metrics.

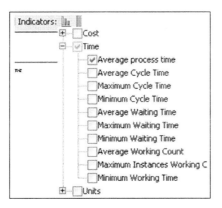

5.   Change the report type to **Bar** in the drop-down just below the **Chart** tab in the left-hand side of the simulation view. This will make the chart more readable by showing the activities on the vertical axis and values out on the horizontal axis.

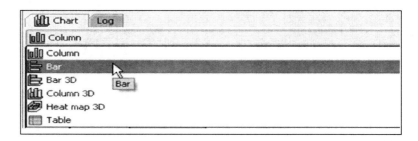

6.   The chart shows one big bar for the overall average process time for the quote process. It took 4+ hours to process the quote.

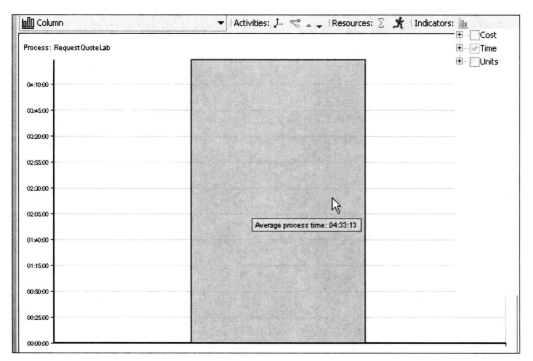

7. To investigate why the process is taking this long to process orders, drill down in to simulation results for **Activities**, as shown in the following screenshot:

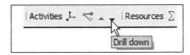

8. Select the  icon to filter out the activities that have a negligent processing time.

9. Drill into the process to see the average times for processing for each activity. The Business Practices Review step has an average cycle time of nearly 3+ hours, which is unacceptable.

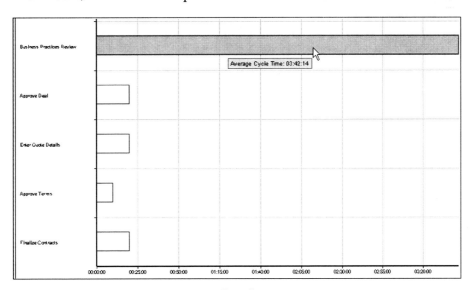

10. The Business Practices step takes much more time than any of the other activities combined. This is a surprise because it takes only 20 minutes, approximately, to complete the step. Maybe there is a bottleneck here? To find out, go to **Indicators | Time | Average waiting time**. The maximum average waiting time is nearly 3+ hours. The delay is due to the quotes that need Business Practices being backed up for most of the processing time with no one working on them.

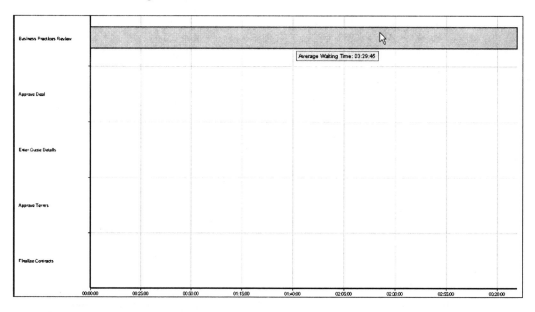

11. Calculate the total cost of activities by going to **Indicators | Cost | Total cost**. Observe that the total cost for the Business Practices Review step is pretty high at $ 15000+. The immediate solution of throwing more resources at it might come with a high price.

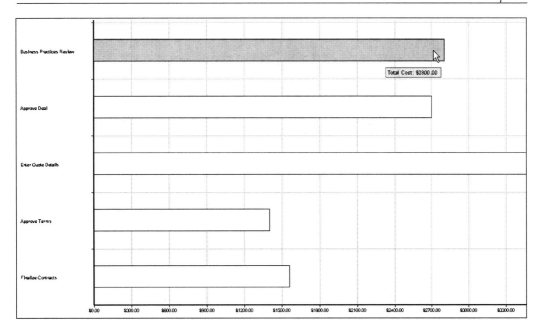

Improving the process

Based on the analysis of the simulation results in the previous section, the as-is Sales Quote process model is used as the starting point and modified to produce the to-be Sales Quote process model. Simulation of the to-be Sales Quote process model helps to determine the benefits of the changes introduced in a rapid fashion. There might be many versions of to-be process models that need to be produced and analyzed before arriving at an optimal process model for execution. The shorter wait time at the Business Practices Review and Approve Deal steps will result in shorter quote processing time. This in turn will help improve customer satisfaction and increase the chances of converting more quotes into orders. The main changes proposed for the to-be Sales Quote process model will now be discussed.

Summary of revisions:

- The Business Practices Review step is a bottleneck and increasing the number of people assigned to the Business Practices role will result in a substantial increase in cost. Hence, the improvement is to bypass the Business Practices Review step for quotes with discounts that are less than or equal to pre- approved discounts and revenue below $ 1 million. Usage of more complex business rules to determine whether the Business Practices Review is required or not will be dealt in later chapters.

- The Approve Deal is another step that is a potential bottleneck. Bypassing the Approve Deal step is not a possible option currently, and hence the optimization is to increase the number of people assigned to the Approvers role from two to five.

Creating the to-be Sales Quote process

Now create the improved process.

1. Drag and drop an Exclusive Conditional gateway near Business Practices Review — user task.
2. Right-click on the gateway and select **Properties**. Type in **Is Business Practices Review required?**
3. Select the **Is Business Practices Review required?** gateway. Right-click and choose the **Add conditional sequence flow** option to create the conditional path to the Business Practices Review step.
4. Select the conditional path, right-click, select **Properties**, and set the name of this path to **Yes**.
5. Select the **Is Business Practices Review required?** gateway. Right-click and choose the **Add default sequence flow** option to create the default path to the Approvals gateway.
6. Select the default path, right-click, select **Properties,** and set the name of this path to **No**.

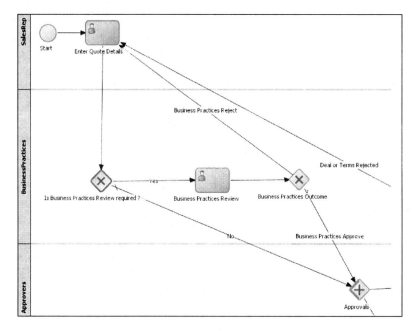

Modifying the Simulation Model for Sales Quote process

Change the Probabilities for the Business Practices Review.

1. Edit the NormalLoad Process Simulation Model and set the probabilities for the **Yes** and **No** paths as shown in the following screenshot:

Outgoing Paths	Probability
Yes path connecting Is Business Practices Review required? – Gateway and Business Practices Review step.	0.1
No path connecting Is Business Practices Review required? – Gateway and Approvals Gateway.	0.9

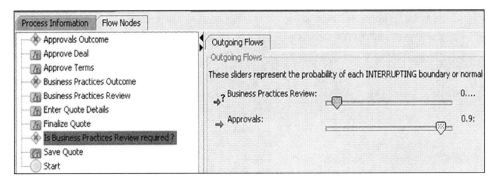

Modifying the Project Simulation Definition

Now edit the parameters for the simulation model. This should address the bottleneck seen earlier.

1. The next step is to increase the number of people assigned to the Approvers role. Go to As Is Simulation Definition. Select the **Resources** tab.

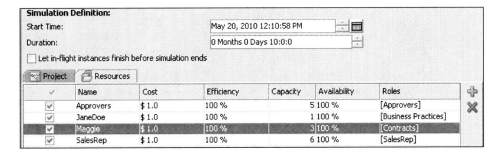

2. For the Approvers role (a participant who is an Approver is capable of approving the quote deal), click inside the **Capacity** column and increase the number to **5**. The **Efficiency** which points to the skill level is set to **100%** in the preceding example. The **Cost** is set to **$1.0** for all participants.

3. Save the Project Simulation Definition.

Re-running the simulation

Re-run the simulation to see how the changes affect the results.

1. In the simulation view, click on the "Run to end fast-forward" button to run the simulation with the new parameters. Switch to the Average Processing Time chart if you're not already on it.

2. This results in some dramatic improvements. The number of completed instances has now increased from 32+ to 65+.

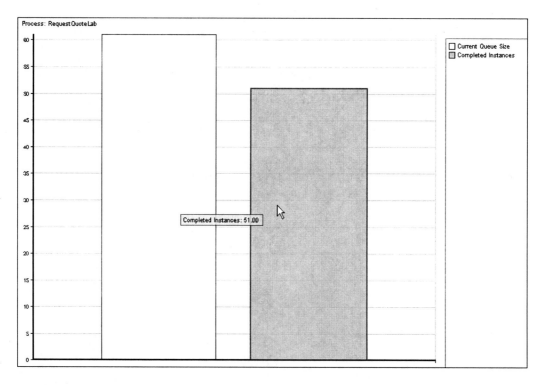

3. Drill down in to activities by clicking on the icon. Choose **Indicators | Unit | Current Queue Size**. The queue size for Business Practices Review has reduced to 0.

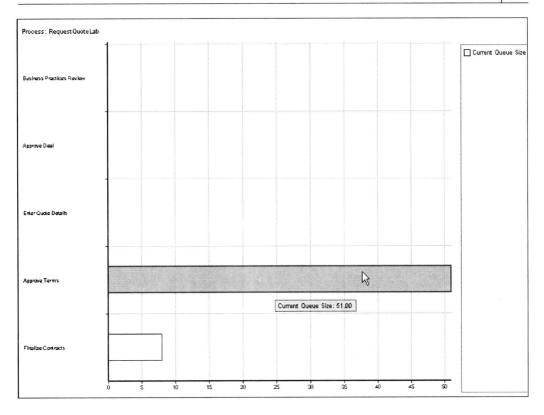

4. Choose **Indicators | Time | Average Processing Time**. The average processing time for the Business Practices Review step has reduced from approx 3 hours 20 minutes to approx 20 minutes.

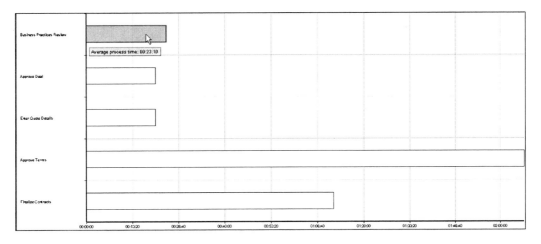

5. Note that this was a direct result of a corresponding reduction in the Average Waiting Time for Business Practices Review step. This is significantly lower than the second simulation model. This ensures a better guarantee on agreed upon service level to the customers.

Summary

In this exercise, you have seen how a Business Analyst can dive right into processes currently running in an organization and how simulation can be leveraged to analyze processes and propose improvements. This is all done without involving any technical resources. It is easy to share your findings with the business owners because the diagrams, charts, and reports are easy for business people to understand.

10
Implementation of the Business Process

BPMN 2.0 can not only be used to capture process models but can be used to drive implementation as well. It simply layers the process execution details on top of the business process model leading to effective business-IT collaboration. Historically, business process models developed by business people have been technically separated from the process representations required by systems designed to implement and execute those processes. Thus, there was a need to manually translate the original business process models to the execution models. Vendors used standards such as BPEL and XPDL to save as well as execute BPMN process models. Such translations are subject to errors and the impedance mismatch made it difficult for the process model and the executable process to be in sync with each other as changes were made to both during the process development life cycle. With BPMN 2.0, there is no translation involved and the model is the implementation as well. The implementation properties are overlaid on top of the process model and the model that is the implementation leads to agile and collaborative process development.

The process model created in *Chapter 7, Process Modelling using BPMN 2.0* has to be implemented before it can be executed on the BPM run-time engine. The process developer/IT developer role is responsible for the implementation. Implementation of the process model involves creation of implementation artifacts, creation of data types and data mapping, handling of exception conditions, transactional conditions, and compensation logic. For system steps, adapters can be used to integrate and reuse existing assets and wrap existing application logic as services. The BPM Suite platform allows browsing of external services and also supports wrapping of Java code and invoking them as services.

For human steps managed by the BPM engine, the human task implementation artifacts and their associated user interfaces have to be implemented. In addition, the roles have to be mapped to an LDAP user or group before deployment. Similarly, the business rules have to be implemented for rule steps. Further, these business rules can be dynamically changed by the business user at runtime to meet the changing needs of the business. Finally, implementation of the process model involves creation of complex data types, variables, and transformation logic to convert data from one format to another. BPM Studio provides a unified, wizard-driven, design-time environment that is IT-friendly for the implementation of the process model.

Concepts

A **BPM Project** contains one or more related process models, shared artifacts such as organization models, services, data types, events, and so on. In addition, it also contains simulation models and documentation for these processes. It is deployed as a unit on the BPM runtime engine.

BPM Projects and BPM Project Templates

BPM Project Templates are derived from BPM Projects and promote creation of processes that are slightly different from each other in specific areas but fundamentally the same in many ways. BPM Project Templates promote reusability and include customization constraints that promote governance across the customization of variants. The BPM Project Template allows for defining permissions that control what portions of the processes inside a BPM Project can be changed or cannot be changed or must be changed. The BPM Project Template cannot be deployed to the runtime engine. A BPM Project must be created from the BPM Project Template and all the the steps that must be implemented have to be completed before it can be deployed.

Business Catalog

Business Catalog contains process related artifacts such as services, data types, events, rules, human task implementations, and exceptions that can be shared and reused across the various business processes in a BPM Project. It promotes both top-down and bottom-up process development.

1. In the top-down approach, the web-based, role-based BPM Process Composer can be used to create BPMN process models annotated for completion by process developers (sans implementation details) and then publish it to **Metadata Services Repository** (**MDS**) for further refinements inside BPM Studio by a process developer role.

2. In the bottom-up approach, the process developer/process analyst can create a BPM Project or a BPM Project Template, populate the Business Catalog with re-usable artifacts, and publish it to MDS. The business user can modify/compose new processes from these published BPM Projects/BPM Project Templates to tailor-fit their business use case.

The BPM Suite 11g platform supports a combination of top-down and bottom-up approaches to complete the development of process models.

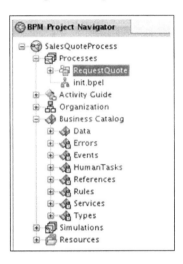

There are different folders for holding different types of BPM artifacts. The **Human Tasks** folder contains human task implementation artifacts. The **Rules** folder contains the business rules artifacts, the **Services** folder contains the system services (these can be BPEL processes, adapter services, or other services), the **References** folder contains external services, and the **Types** folder contains data types related to the implementation artifacts.

In Oracle BPM Suite 11g, the process steps in the BPMN process model are abstract until they are bound to implementation artifacts. Interactive tasks are bound to Human Task implementation artifacts, and Rule Tasks are bound to Oracle Business Rule implementation artifacts. Likewise, the Service, Send, and Receive Tasks are bound to system services and these system services can be adapter services (the BPM Suite 11g product comes with a rich set of technology and application adapters) or BPEL processes or external services, or even other BPMN processes exposed as a service. Some folders in the Business Catalog, namely **Rules**, **Events**, **Human Tasks**, **References**, **Services**, and **Types** have a lock symbol to indicate that the artifacts inside them cannot be deleted as they are bound to process steps. Custom folders to hold Events, Business Exceptions, and Business Objects can be created as well.

Business Objects refer to complex data types, and Business Exceptions refer to exceptions that can be thrown and caught by the business processes inside the BPM Project. Events refer to the events generated by the underlying event-driven platform of the Oracle BPM Suite 11g product. BPMN has a special type of event called **Signal Event** to signify publishing/subscription of events based on broadcast mechanisms.

Business Object

Complex types are referred to as **Business Objects** in BPM Studio and represented by XML Schema. Business Objects are stored under the `Business Catalog` folder. There are two ways to create a Business Object:

1. Create from scratch
2. Browse an external schema definition and create Business Objects from it

Data Objects

Data Objects represent variables. Data Objects can be process-level variables or project-level variables. The former are referred to as Process Data Objects and the latter are referred to as Project Data Objects. **Process Data Objects** are global variables visible throughout the process and persisted through the life cycle of the process instance. On the other hand, **Project Data Objects** are visible across process instances of all the processes inside a BPM Project. The Project Data Object allows for greater reuse and sharing across processes in a BPM Project. The Data Object has a type. The type can be a scalar or native type: `String`, `Integer`, `Decimal`, `Boolean`, `Array`, or it can be a complex type defined by a Business Object.

Tutorial: Making SalesQuote executable and testing it

The first step is to define the data types and variables used in the Sales Quote process. Next, define the user interface, service details, and data associations.

Creation of Business Objects for Sales Quote process

In the Sales Quote example, a Business Object named `Quote` defined by the `QuoteRequest` element in the `Quote.xsd` file is the input to the business process. The following steps illustrate how to create a Business Object:

1. Launch BPM Studio and if prompted for the role, select **Default** or if not prompted, be sure Default is selected under **Tools | Preferences | Roles.** The BPM Studio is the tool for various personas such as business analyst, process analyst, process developer, and IT developer. The process analyst/business analyst, depending on the information available and their skill level, can model at a very high level as well as drill down in to more detailed process flows and make certain implementation choices. The Process Developer/IT Developer design the implementation artifacts, the user interfaces (Forms) associated with Human Task steps, the dashboards, exposing backend applications as services using adapters and other technologies. When logged in using the BPM role, the BPM Studio displays a limited set of navigators, palettes, components, and wizards tailored to a business audience. The focus is on creation of the process model, organization charts, simulation models, and business indicators, and work is primarily done inside the BPM Project Navigator. When logged in as the Default Role, all palettes, components, navigators, and wizards are enabled. To check this, go to **Applications Navigator**, highlight your **BPM Project**, **QuoteProcessLab**, and right-click on **Properties**. Go to **Technology Scope** and see that both **BPM** and **SOA** are in the **Selected** pane on the right. If necessary, add the technology to the pane as shown in the following screenshot:

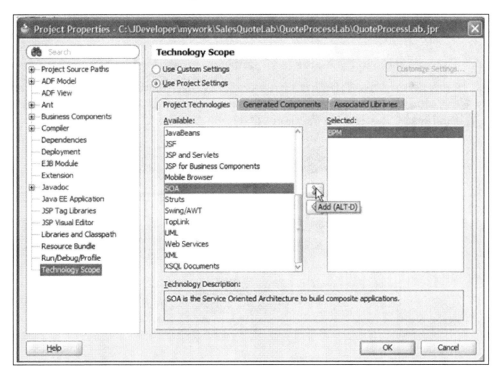

2. In the **BPM Project Navigator**, right-click on **Business Catalog**, select **New**, and then select **Business Object**.

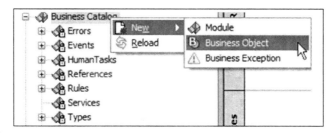

3. This brings up the **Create Business Object** dialog.

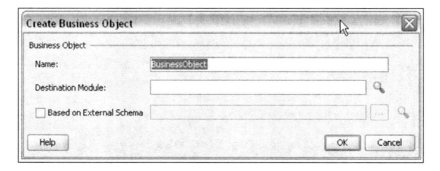

4. Type in **Quote** in the **Name** field, replacing the default text **BusinessObject**.

5. Click on the browse button next to the **Destination Module**. This brings up the **Module List** dialog. Click on the **New** symbol to add a module under **Business Catalog** with the name **Data**.

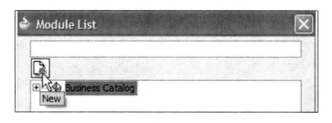

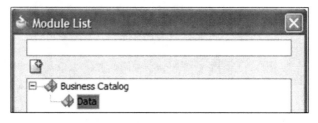

6. Click on the **OK button.**

7. Select the **Based on External Schema** option and click on the **Schema Browser** icon. This brings up the **Type Chooser** dialog. Click on the **Import Schema Files** icon on the top right corner to import an XSD file into your BPM Project.

8. Select the **Copy to Project** option in the **Import Schema File** dialog and select the browse icon at the end of the **URL** field.

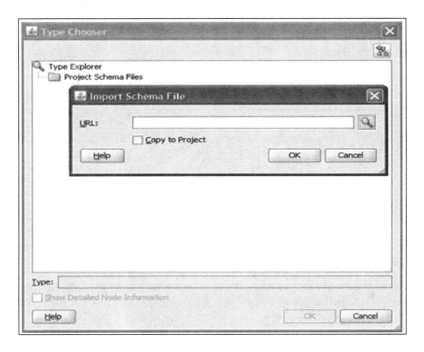

9. This brings up the **SOA Resource Browser** window. Locate and select the Quote.xsd file in the lab materials schemas folder.

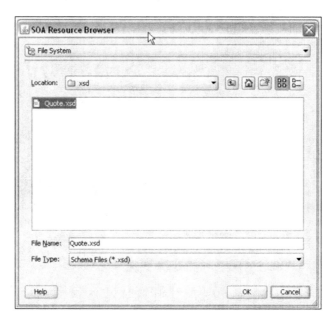

10. Click on the **OK** button to close the **SOA Resource Browser** and click on the **OK** button again on the **Localize Files** dialog.

11. Expand the `Project Schema Files` folder in the **Type Chooser** and expand `Quote.xsd` and select the `QuoteRequest` element. Click on the **OK** button and then click on the **OK** button again in the next window.

12. The Quote Business Object opens. The description and documentation details can be added here as desired. When finished, close the Quote window. This completes the creation of the Quote Business Object.

Creating Data Objects for Sales Quote process

In the Sales Quote process, there are three String variables for the outcomes of Business Practices Review, Approve Deal, and Approve Terms activities, a Boolean variable used to determine if the Business Practices Review step is required or not, and a complex variable of the `QuoteRequest` type in `Quote.xsd` using the Business Object created for `QuoteRequest`. The Data Objects for the Sales Quote process are captured in the following table:

Process Data Object	Type
approveDealOutcome	String
approveTermsOutcome	String
businessPracticesOutcome	String
businessPracticesReviewRequired	Boolean
quote	QuoteRequest in Quote.xsd (using the Quote Business Object already created)

The following steps show the creation of the approveDealOutcome Process Data Object:

1. In the **BPM Project Navigator**, highlight your **RequestQuoteLab** process to view the **Structure** pane in the lower left of the screen. If the **Structure** pane is not visible, select **View | Structure** and select the process in the **BPM Project Navigator**. Right-click on the **Process Data Objects** folder and select **New** to launch the **Create Data Object** window.

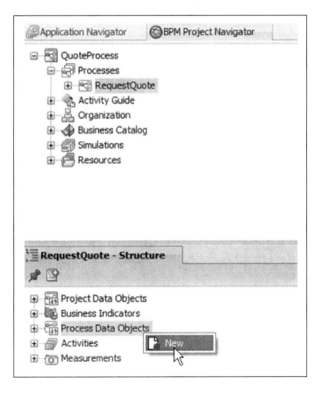

2. Enter **approveDealOutcome** for the **Name** field, replacing the default text **dataObject1**, and select **String** for **Type**.

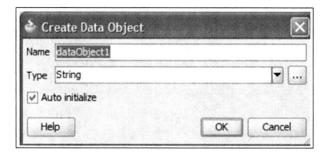

3. Create the other scalar Process Data Objects in the same manner.

4. To create the quote Process Data Object of complex data type, right-click on **Process Data Objects** in the **Structure Pane** and select **New**. This brings up the **Create Data Object** dialog. Type in **quote** for the **Name** of the Data Object.

5. To set the quote to the type Quote Business Object, select the **...** option. This brings up the **Type** window. Select **Component** from the list of types and then choose the **Quote** from the list of Business Objects.

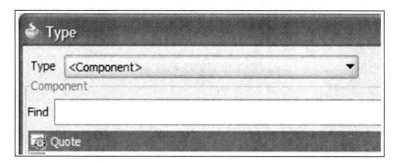

6. Click on the **OK** button and again click on the **OK** button in the next window.

7. The complete list of **Process Data Objects** for the Sales Quote process is captured in the following screenshot:

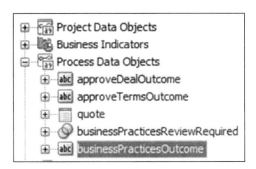

Implementing Interactive Tasks

Every Interactive Task has to be bound to a Human Task implementation artifact.

Defining the Task service

In Chapter 7, the process outline was defined and only the Name and Description for the activities was specified. In order to execute the process, the process activities have to be implemented. Browse for existing Human Task implementation artifacts in the Business Catalog or define a new one. Multiple Interactive Tasks can share the same Human Task implementation artifact. The following steps illustrate the association of a Human Task implementation artifact with the Enter Quote process step of the Sales Quote process:

1. Right-click on the **Enter Quote Details** user activity and select **Properties**.

2. In the **Properties** dialog, click on the **Implementation** tab.

3. Click on the + next to **Human Task**.

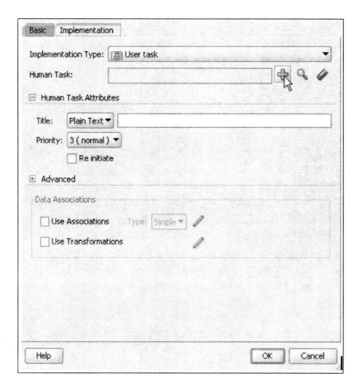

4. In the **Create Human Task** dialog type in **EnterQuoteDetails**.
5. Select **Initiator** for **Pattern**. This automatically sets the **Outcome** to **SUBMIT**.
6. Type in **Enter Quote** for the **Title**.
7. Click on the + next to **Parameters** to launch the **Data Object** dialog.
8. Drag quote from the **Data Object** window to the **Parameters** section.
9. Set the parameter to **Editable**.

10. Click on the **OK** button and the task definition gets created.

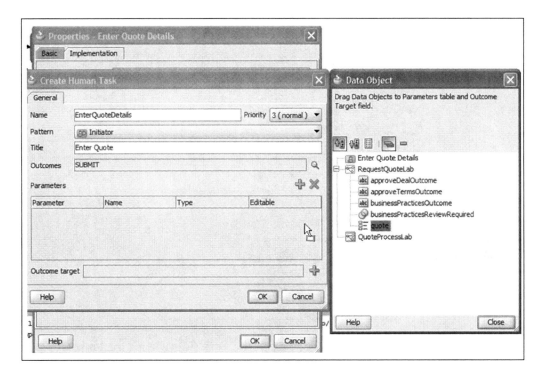

11. Click on the **OK** button again. This completes the creation of the
    EnterQuoteDetails Human Task implementation artifact.

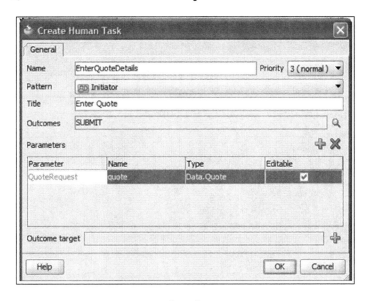

12. Expand the **Business Catalog | HumanTasks** folder to examine the newly created Human Task implementation artifact.

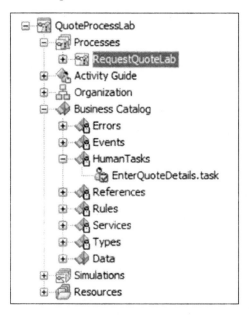

13. Double-click on the `.task` file to open the Task Editor with the Human Task implementation artifact definition. Set the **Title** of the task in a dynamic fashion based on incoming payload using the **Text and XPath** option.

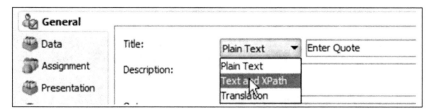

14. Click on the Expression Builder icon on the far right.

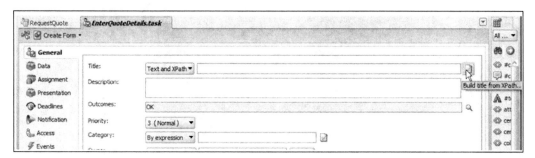

15. This opens up the **Expression Builder** window. Create the following XPath expression:

concat('Enter Quote Details for customer' , /task:task/task:payload/ns0: QuoteRequest/ns0:Summary/ns0:AccountName, 'Quote id = ', /task:task/ task:payload/ns0:QuoteRequest/ns0:Summary/ns0:OpportunityID)

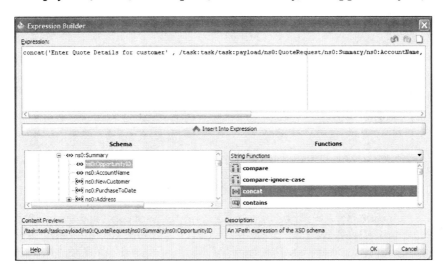

16. Click on the **OK** button.

Generating a form for the Human Task implementation

1. Click on the **Create Form** menu of the Task Editor and select **Auto-Generate Task Form**.

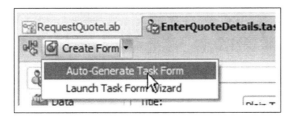

2. Enter the **Project Name** as **EnterQuoteUILab** and the **Directory** as **SalesQuoteLab\EnterQuoteUILab**. Click on the **OK** button.

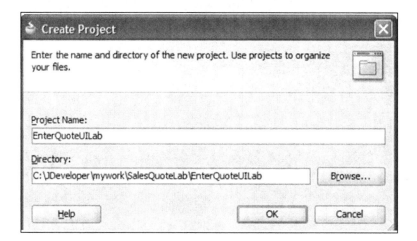

3. The user interface for the Human Task implementation is generated automatically. A number of dialogs open to provide an opportunity to do some customization. For this exercise, simply click on the **OK** button to all the dialogs. When the form generation is finished the taskdetails.jspx file is opened displaying the form. Save all open files and close all open task windows.

4. The configuration of the remaining four Interactive Tasks, namely Approve Deal, Approve Terms, Finalize Contract, and Business Practices Review can be completed in the same manner.

Key steps for the completion of Business Practices Review are as follows:

1. Right-click on **Business Practices Review** and select the **Properties** window and the **Implementation** tab.

2. Click on the **+** symbol to create the Human Task implementation artifact.

3. Enter the **Name** as **BusinessPracticesReview**.

4. Select the **Pattern** as **Simple**.

5. Enter the **Title** as **Business Practices Review**, and add the **quote** Data Object in the **Parameters** section with the **Editable** checkbox enabled.

6. The Business Practices Review properties dialog looks like the following screenshot:

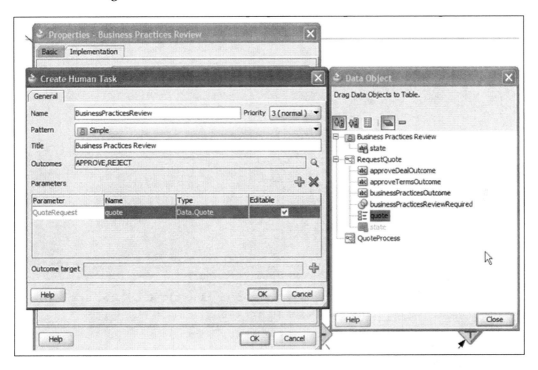

7. Click on the **OK** button and then click on the **OK** button again in the next window.

8. The configuration of Approve Deal and Approve Terms activities are the same as the configuration of the Business Practices Review activity (they have same outcomes—**APPROVE** and **REJECT**).

9. The configuration of the Finalize Contracts activity is the same except that it has a single outcome—**OK** instead of **APPROVE** and **REJECT**.

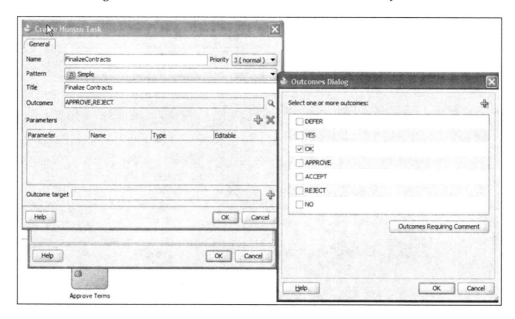

10. Now create the Task Forms as described for **EnterQuoteUILab** Task Form project. Use the suffix **UILab** for all the auto-generated task forms.

Task data mapping

Review and select the data associations for the activities.

1. For the Interactive Task activities, creating the Task also sets the input and output data associations automatically for the data defined in the task when possible. To view the associations, right-click on the **Enter Quote Details** and click on **Interactive Task | Properties** and in the **Implementation** tab click on the pencil icon next to it.

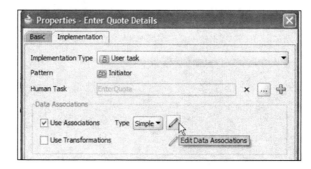

2. Note that for **Enter Quote Details** step, the output association is set while the input association is empty. The input for **Enter Quote Details** will be set manually towards the end of this chapter. For the other tasks, the appropriate output association for the **Outcome** output argument needs to be set as well. It's best to do data associations in the last part of implementation after all of the different elements have been built.

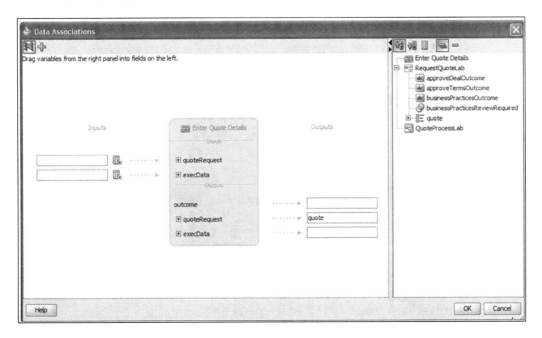

Mapping swim lane roles to LDAP roles

Process roles have to be mapped to LDAP roles for the process to run. The steps for pre-seeding users and groups in the LDAP of the Oracle WebLogic Application Server for the Sales Quote process are described in the installation chapter.

 The BPM engine (Oracle WebLogic Application Server) has to be running to map the Process Roles to the LDAP roles. Be sure your server is running before continuing.

1. In BPM Studio, navigate to **BPM Process Navigator**.

2. Right-click on **Organization** and select **Open**. In the **Organization** editor, select the **SalesRep** role from the list of **Roles**.

3. Click on the **+** within the **Members** subpanel.

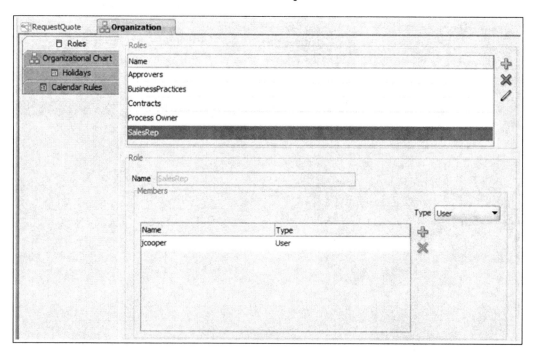

4. Choose the Application Server connection for your server. If there is not one already created, select the **+** icon to create it.

To create a Oracle WebLogic Application server connection: the default configurations use user **weblogic** and password **welcome1** with the port number **7001** and the domain1 for the domain.

5. Click on the Expression Builder icon on the far right. Check the **Realm** selection and change it, if necessary. Click on the lookup icon to search for users. Select user **jcooper** and click the **Select** button.

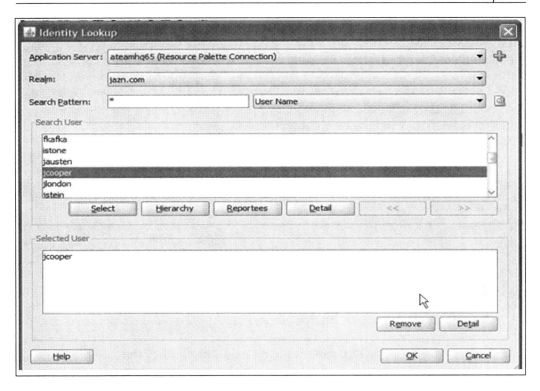

6. In a similar manner, perform role mapping as shown in the following table for the remaining process role:

Role	User
Approvers	cdickens
Business Practices	jstein
Contracts	wfaulk
Process Owner	jstein

Configuration of the Service Task

The Save Quote step saves the quote payload to a local file system. The Save Quote Service Task is bound to a File Adapter Service. The Oracle BPM Suite comes with a rich set of adapters and these enable connectivity to virtually any data source inside the enterprise. Oracle adapters are available for more than 300 packaged applications, for legacy and mainframes including Tuxedo, VSAM, CICS, and for technology and protocols including FTP, Files, Database, AQ, and JMS. Oracle adapters are standards-based and support both web services and JCA. The Adapters Services can be created in the Composite view.

The IT view of the BPM Project is the Composite view. Navigate to the Composite view from the BPM Project Navigator. The Palette on the Composite view contains all the implementation artifacts including the adapters bundled with the Oracle BPM Suite. The implementation artifacts created in the Composite view automatically gets added to the Business Catalog of the BPM Project. The process or IT Developer can thus populate the Business Catalog with implementation artifacts which serve as building blocks that can later be bound to process steps.

1. Navigate to the composite editor by clicking on the **Goto Composite Editor** button at the top of your BPM process.

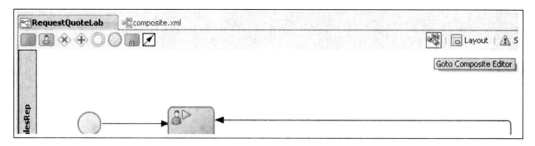

2. Drag-and-drop the **File Adapter** from the **Component Palette** to the right-hand **External References** pane in the composite editor.

3. Note that with the composite editor, you can drag the **File Adapter** and drop it on the **External References** pane.

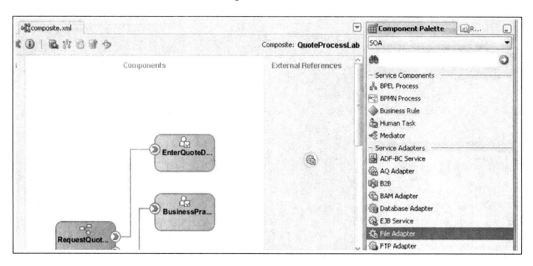

4. Walk through the steps in the File Adapter wizard and create a service called **SaveQuote** to write to a file. Enter **SaveQuote** for **Service Name**.

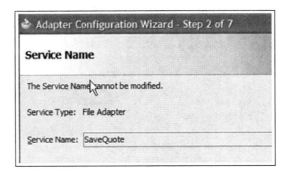

5. Choose the **Define from operation and schema (specified later)** option for **Interface**.

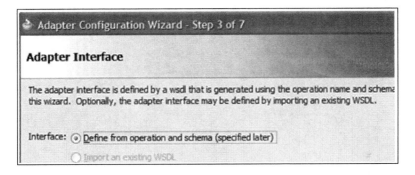

6. Choose the **Write File** for **Operation Type**.

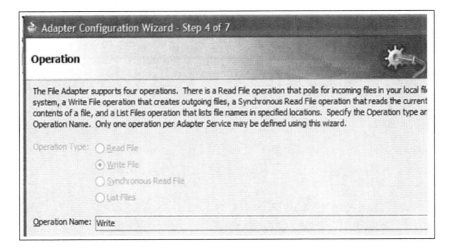

7. Choose **Physical Path** for **Directory specified as** and specify the destination file name and directory (it must be a directory accessible to the BPM runtime engine, such as `c:\temp`) for **Directory for Outgoing Files (physical path)**.

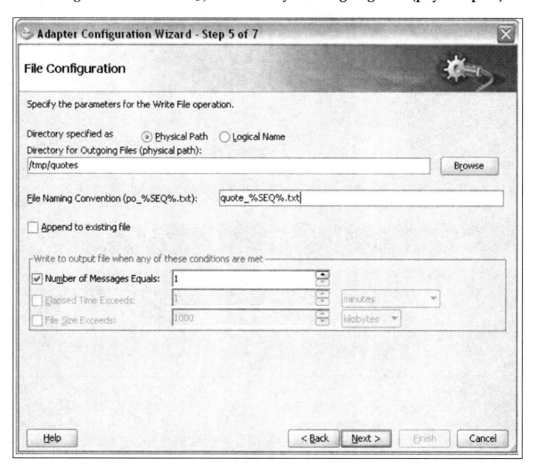

8. Do not select the **Native Format Translation Required** option, and for the
    Schema, choose the **QuoteRequest** schema.

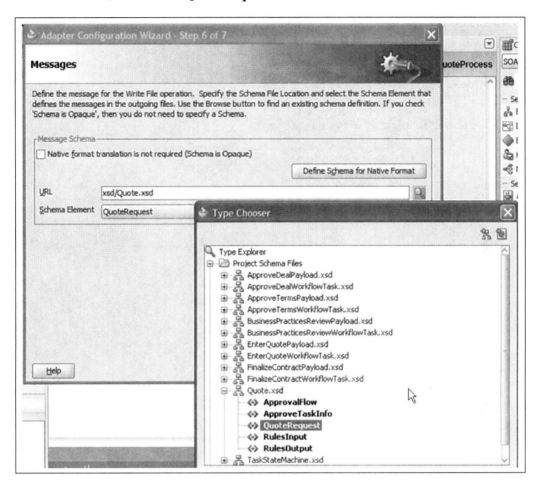

This completes the creation of the File Adapter service.

Bind File Adapter service to Save Quote step

The File Adapter service just created in the composite application gets promoted to the Business Catalog in the BPM Project Navigator automatically. The following steps illustrate the binding of the **SaveQuote** File Adapter service to the Save Quote step of the Sales Quote process:

1. Navigate to **BPM Project Navigator**.

2. Go to **Business Catalog | Services | Externals** folder and expand it. Verify that the **SaveQuote** service is present.

3. Open the **RequestQuoteLab** BPMN process.

4. Right-click on **Save Quote** step, select **Properties**, and click the **Implementation** tab.

5. Select **Service Call** in the drop-down menu for the **Implementation** field.

6. Click on the magnifying glass next to **Name** to search for available services and select the service **SaveQuote**. Click on the **OK** button to select the service.

Passing data to service

Set the data associations for the service activity.

1. Select the **Data Associations | Use Associations** section and select type **Simple**.

2. Drag-and-drop the **quote** data object from the right-hand panel to the **Inputs** area.

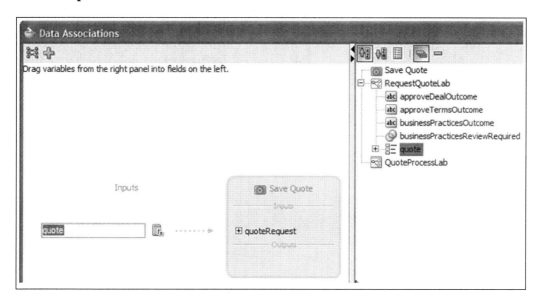

3. Click on the **OK** button and again click on the **OK** button in the next window. The Save Quote step is complete.

Data association configuration for conditional flows

All Interactive Tasks are associated with a list of possible outcomes. The outcomes are defined while configuring the associated Human Task implementation artifact. These outcomes are presented as actions on the Task Forms (Task user interfaces) to the process participant when they log on to the BPM Workspace work management application. The process participant has to choose from one of the Actions (outcomes defined plus default set of actions) in order for the Task to be completed. In the Sales Quote process, the Enter Quote step has only one outcome—**SUBMIT**, while the Business Practices Review, Approve Deal, and Approve Terms steps have two possible outcomes—**APPROVE** and **REJECT**. In the earlier section, three String Data Objects, namely `businessPracticesOutcome`, `approveDealOutcome`, and `approveTermsOutcome`, were defined to hold the value of the outcome property of the above steps and also mapped appropriately using Data Associations. These Human Task outcomes can be evaluated to perform conditional branching and split the sequential flow of the process in to conditional flows. The following steps illustrate the conditional evaluation of outcome for the Business Practices Review step:

1. Open the **Implementation** tab for the **Business Practices Review** step by right-click on **Properties** and map the task outcome as shown in the following screenshot. Drag-and-drop the **businessPracticesOutcome** data object into the field next to the **outcome** output argument. Click on the **OK** button and then click on the **OK** button again in the next window.

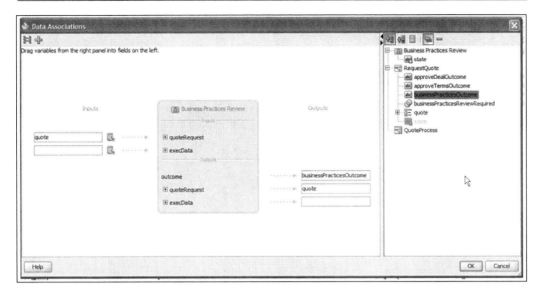

2. Map the outcome of the **Approve Deal** step in the same manner.

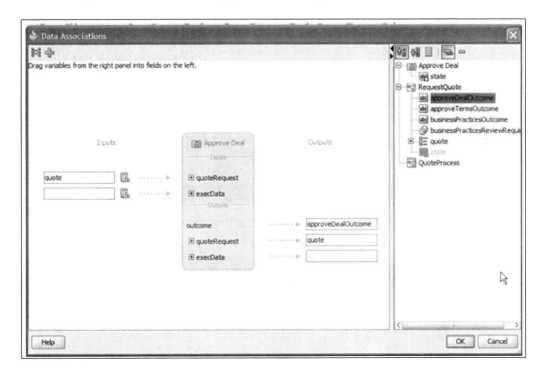

3. Map the **outcome** of the **Approve Terms** step as shown in the following screenshot:

4. Specify the data object based conditional expression for the **Business Practices Reject** and **Deal or Terms Rejected** paths as shown in the following screenshots. Right-click on **conditional path**, choose **Properties** tab, set **type** to **Condition,** and **Expression** to **Simple**. Enter the expression **businessPracticesOutcome == "REJECT"**.

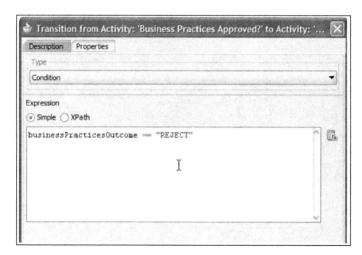

5. Follow the same steps for the **Deal or Terms Rejected** conditional path. Enter the expression **approveDealOutcome == "REJECT" or approveTermsOutcome == "REJECT"**.

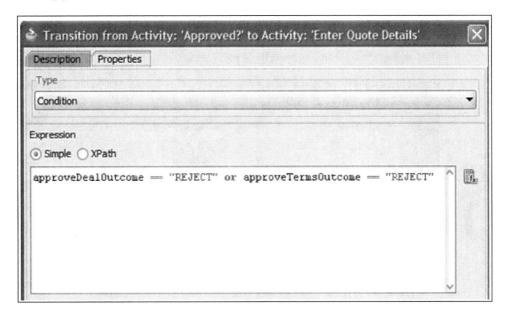

6. Add the condition for the **Yes** path for **Is Business Practices Review Required?** Enter the expression **businessPracticesReviewRequired == true**.

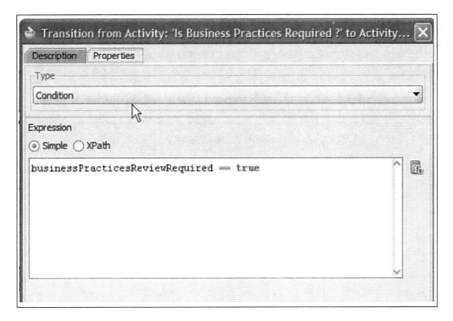

Configuration of Script Tasks

Add a Script Task to set the payload (the input data) for the Enter Quote Details task and to determine whether the Business Practices Review activity is required or not. The script goes right before Enter Quote Details. Using a script to set the input data makes testing this process easier but when running such a process in production, the user who initiates the task would enter the input data.

1. Click and drop a **Script Task** from the **BPMN Component Palette** and place it right before the **Enter Quote Details** step. Name it **Initialize Quote**.

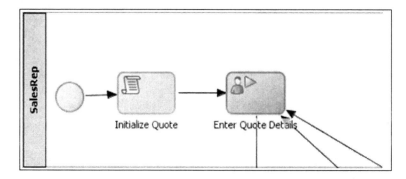

2. Click on the **Implementation** tab and select **Use Associations**.

3. Select the **XPath** option for **Type** and click on the pencil icon to edit.

4. Drag the **quote** Data Object into the **Custom Assignments** area under **Drag variables here**.

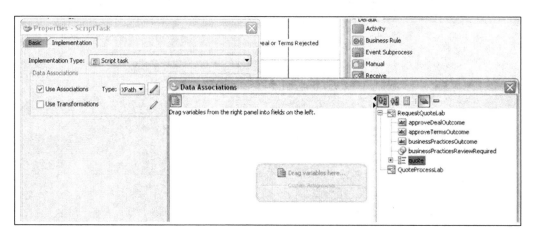

1

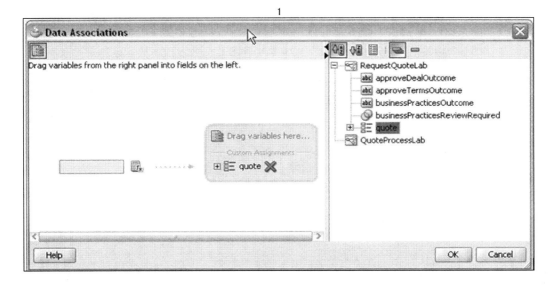

5. The XPath expression for the left-hand side is shown below. The input XML is also available as part of the lab artifacts.

```
oraext:parseXML('<ns1:QuoteRequest
xmlns:ns1="http://www.mycompany.com/ns/salesquote">
  <ns1:Summary>
    <ns1:OpportunityID>zzzz2</ns1:OpportunityID>
    <ns1:AccountName>Acme New</ns1:AccountName>
    <ns1:Address>
      <ns1:Street>Demo Way</ns1:Street>
      <ns1:City>Redwood Shores</ns1:City>
      <ns1:State>CA</ns1:State>
      <ns1:Zip>94065</ns1:Zip>
      <ns1:Country>USA</ns1:Country>
    </ns1:Address>
    <ns1:SalesRepId>jcooper</ns1:SalesRepId>
    <ns1:SalesRepName>James Cooper</ns1:SalesRepName>
    <ns1:ValidUntil>2010-05-30</ns1:ValidUntil>
    <ns1:EffectiveDiscount>0.0</ns1:EffectiveDiscount>
  </ns1:Summary>
  <ns1:QuoteRequestStatus/>
</ns1:QuoteRequest>')
```

6. Click the Expression Builder icon to open the Expression Builder and enter the XML string. Be sure to use the oraext:parseXML() function and enter single quotes around the XML string inside the brackets.

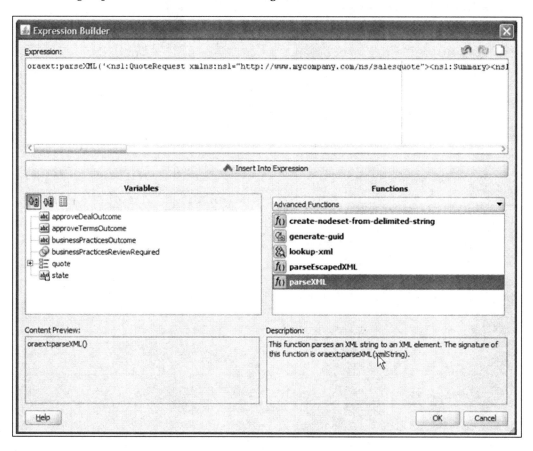

7. Add another custom data mapping by dragging **businessPracticesReviewRequired** in to the **Custom Assignments** area.

8. Set the **businessPracticesReviewRequired** to **false()** by either typing it into the Expression Builder or selecting it from the list of Logical Functions.

9. Go back to the **Enter Quote Details** step and set the input mapping to the quote Data Object as shown in the following screenshot. There is no need to set the outcome output data because this task has only a **SUBMIT** outcome.

This completes the implementation of the process.

Deploying the process

Now your application is ready to deploy.

1. Go to **Applications Navigator**.
2. Right-click the BPM Project **QuoteProcessLab** and select Deploy.

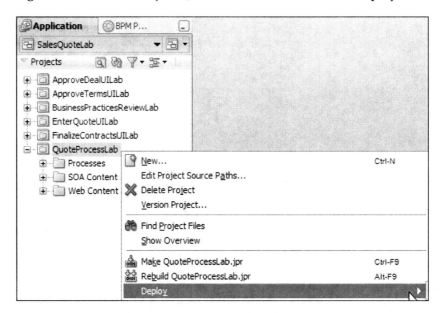

Follow the steps as shown in the following screenshots. Configure a connection to the BPM runtime engine along the way. In the **Deployment Action** step, select the **Deploy to Application server** action. In the **Deploy Configuration** step, enter **1.0** for **Choose Revision**. Select the **Mark Composite Revision as Default** and **Overwrite any existing composites with the same Revision ID**. Choose **Do not attach** for the **SOA Configuration Plan**.

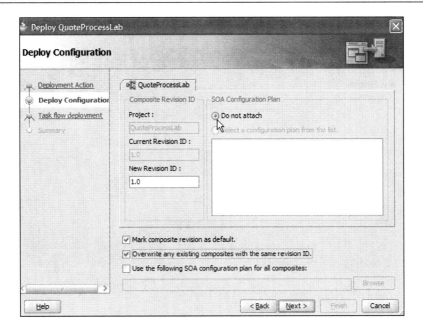

3. Configure the **Task flow deployment** step as shown in the following screenshot. Enter **FinalizeQuoteUILab** as the **EAR Profile Name**.

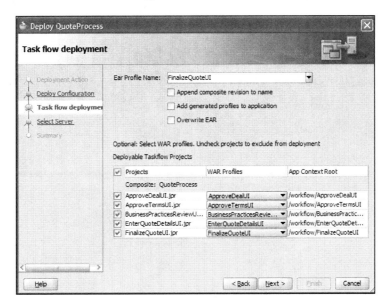

4. Choose the target server.

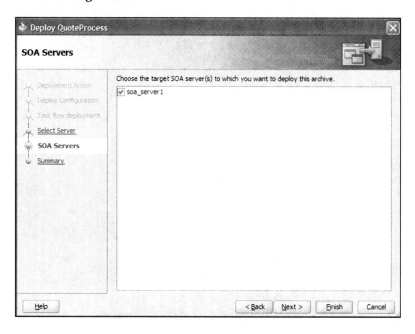

5. This completes deployment of the process and the process is ready to run. The next chapter provides instructions on running and testing the process.

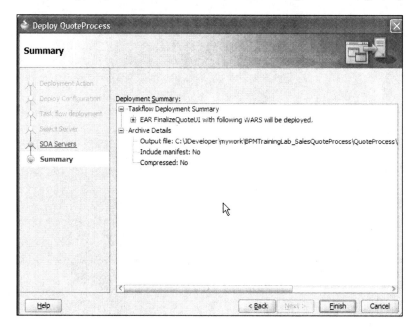

Summary

As you can see, BPMN 2.0 not only provides a business-friendly modeling notation, but also enables high fidelity mapping between a business process model and executable process. The model created by business is not just a requirements document but drives the implementation itself. BPM Studio enables business empowered model driven implementation via unified, zero-code, wizard-driven, business, and an IT-friendly modeling environment leading to agile process development.

11
Using Process Composer

In addition to BPM Studio, Oracle supports business empowerment through a second tool called Process Composer. Process Composer is a role-based, web-based BPMN 2.0 process modeling tool targeted at a business audience. Like BPM Studio, it also provides BPMN editing, but hides the complexity of defining implementation components, such as human tasks, services, or business objects.

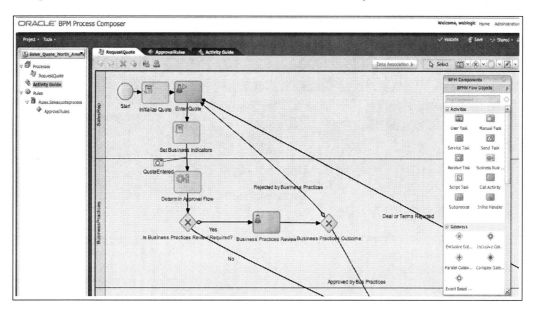

Process Composer can be used in either top-down or bottom-up process development. In the top-down mode of process development, the business user can use the Process Composer for creating BPMN-based, high-level process flows without implementation details. The BPM projects thus created can be published to **Metadata Services Repository (MDS)** and further refined and enriched for execution inside the BPM Studio. This facilitates the business community to participate in the requirements gathering and the definition of their business process and propagate that information to IT with high fidelity. In the bottom-up mode of process development, the process developer/IT developer populates the Business Catalog with implementation artifacts such as system services, human tasks implementations, rules, and data types. The BPM projects/BPM project templates created inside BPM Studio can then be published to MDS and further customized within certain constraints to meet specific business requirements inside Process Composer. This promotes reuse, enforcement of best practices, and governance across customizations. The customized BPM projects, if complete, can be deployed directly from Process Composer to the BPM runtime engine without requiring BPM Studio. This empowers the business by being able to make changes for their specific use case without requiring help from IT. A combination of top-down and bottom-up modeling approaches can be used to enable rapid process development. The MDS supports a shared work environment across multiple BPM Studio and Process Composer deployments.

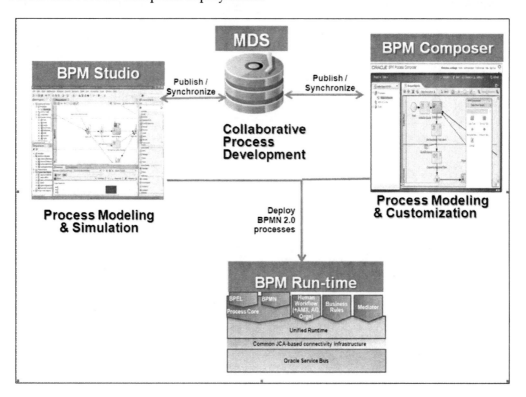

A third use case for the Process Composer is the ability for business users/business analysts/process analysts to design or modify activity guides and business rules. Process Composer can be used to edit the Oracle Business Rules in a running application. Oracle Business Rules are used to define business policies associated with the business processes using the business rules task. Rules enable business policies to be changed at runtime without having to remodel the business process or redeploy the business application. The business rules editor inside Process Composer enables viewing and editing of Oracle Business Rules. The business rules editor can be accessed by opening a business rule from the project navigator.

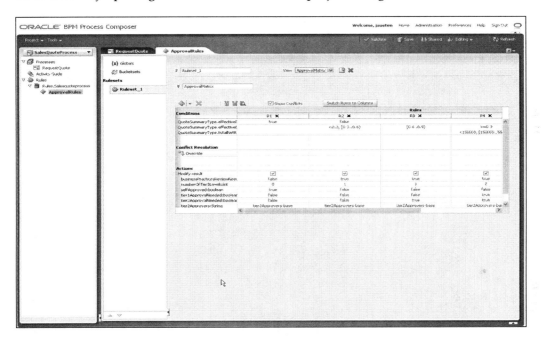

Signing on to Process Composer

Process Composer is a servlet that is deployed along with the BPM runtime engine on top of Oracle WebLogic Application Server 11*g*. The BPM runtime has to be up and running in order to access Process Composer.

The following parameters are required to sign on to Process Composer:

- **URL**: The location of Process Composer installation—
  `http://<host>:<port>/bpm/composer`
- **Username**: The username to access Process Composer
- **Password**: The security credential to access Process Composer

Oracle Application Server Single Sign-On is enabled by default in Oracle BPM Suite. It enables one single sign-on session to be used across multiple web-based applications.

The **Welcome Page** shows the **Open a Project** menu that displays various BPM projects and the associated folder hierarchy in MDS. Clicking on a BPM project displays information about it such as its description, when it was created, author, and so on. Double-clicking on the BPM project opens it. Process Composer is a role-based application and the privileges determine the access and editing capabilities across the BPM projects.

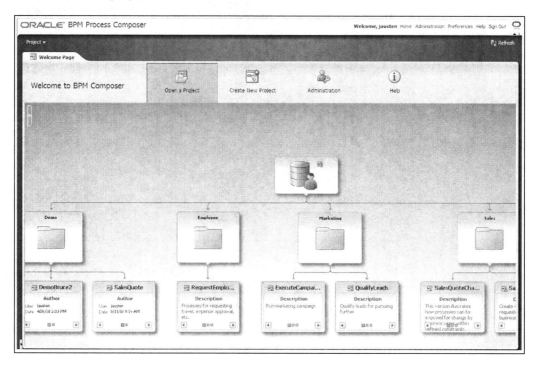

Process Composer can also be used to create a new BPM project from a published BPM project template. The **Create New Project** menu on the home page is used to create a new BPM project from a BPM project template in MDS.

The **Administration** menu is used to administer roles and privileges as well as to manage BPM projects.

Tutorial: Making changes to SalesQuote from Process Composer

MDS is used to store design-time configuration information, customizations, and persisted personalization for many Oracle Fusion Middleware products and Oracle Fusion applications. The metadata can be stored either in a file-based repository or relational database. MDS provides a shared, multi-user environment across distributed BPM Studio and Process Composer clients. In the customization use case, the BPM project template created inside BPM Studio is published to MDS and a customized BPM project based on the BPM project template is created inside Process Composer. The process developer/IT developer populates the Business Catalog with implementation artifacts and process models that in turn become building blocks for business to do process composition inside Process Composer to meet their specific business requirements. Permissions can be specified as part the BPM project template creation inside BPM Studio and these permissions determine what aspects of the BPM project can be changed and what cannot be changed.

The degree of customization to these BPM projects generated from BPM project templates are constrained by the permissions specified as part of the BPM project template. Thus, the BPM project template not only promotes reuse but also governance across processes. The following steps are required to generate and customize a BPM project from the BPM project template:

1. Create an MDS connection inside BPM Studio.
2. Generate a BPM project template inside Studio and publish it.
3. Create a BPM project from the BPM project template.
4. Customize the BPM project.

This part of the tutorial changes your project into a template. Therefore, you must save your project in its current state for use in the next lab where you continue to make project modifications. Exit JDeveloper, make a copy of your lab directory, and start JDeveloper again. At the end of this lab, restore your saved lab before moving on to the next lab.

Setting up an MDS connection

The first step is to create a connection to the MDS database. The second step is to use the MDS database connection to create a SOA MDS connection. These steps are outlined as follows:

1. Start BPM Studio.
2. Open the **Resource Palette** by selecting the menu **View | Resource Palette**.
3. Go to **IDE Connections**. Click on the folder with the **+** sign

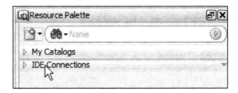

4. Right-click on **New Connection** and then **Database**.

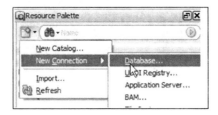

5. Create a database connection to the MDS as shown in the following screenshot. Enter the values for **Username** (default is **DEV_MDS** but it is whatever was used during installation), **Password** (default is **welcome1**), and **Host Name** where the database is installed. Check the connection by pressing the **Test Connection** button and a success message appears if the parameters are correct. Click on the **OK** button.

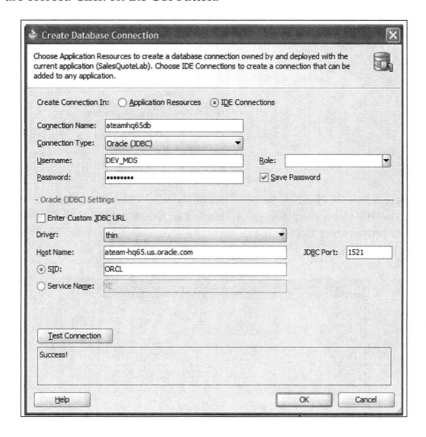

6. Now, click on the 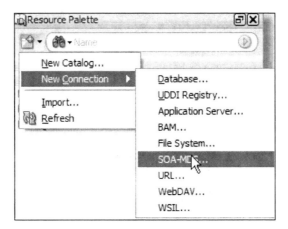 symbol again. Select **New Connection** and select **SOA-MDS**.

7. Create a new SOA MDS connection as shown in the following screenshot. Choose the database connection created in the previous step. In the **Select MDS partition** option, **obpm** should be automatically selected. Test the connection:

8. Go to **View/BPM MDS Navigator** to open the **BPM MDS Navigator**.

9. Open **Configure Connection** and choose the SOA MDS connection defined earlier for the **MDS Connections** field.

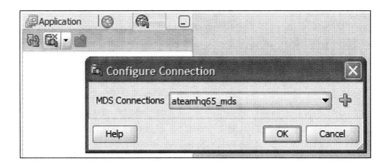

10. Check that root folders **Public** and **Templates** are shown in the **BPM MDS Navigator**.

Creating and publishing BPM project template in BPM Studio to MDS

Both BPM projects and BPM project templates can be published to MDS and the steps to publish are the same.

1. Go to **BPM Project Navigator**; right-click on the **Quote Process Lab** – BPM project. Select the **Convert to template** option. This converts the Quote Process Lab to a BPM project template.

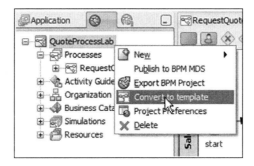

2. Go to **Request Quote Lab** process node. Right-click and select **Properties**. This brings up the **Properties Editor** for the BPM project template. Select **Advanced**. By default, the two fields **Flow Sealed** and **Activity Sealed** are selected. The **Flow Sealed** property when selected prevents the changes to the process flow of the BPM projects generated from the BPM project template. Process steps cannot be deleted and their ordering cannot be changed. In addition, new process steps cannot be introduced. The **Activity Sealed** property when selected prevents changes to the process steps. The binding of the process step to its implementation artifact, as well as associated data mapping, cannot be modified if the **Activity Sealed** property is set for the process step. The permissions at the process level can be modified and overridden at the process step level. In this example, the **Flow Sealed** and **Activity Sealed** properties are set to true at the process level.

3. Go to the **Approve Terms** step. Open the properties for that task (double-click or right-click, and then select **Properties**), and change permissions to **Must Implement**. Save the template.

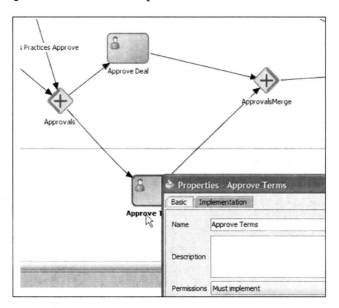

4. The **Approve Terms** step now has a special icon to indicate that it needs to be edited in the BPM Process Composer:

5. Right-click on the **QuoteProcessLab** node and select the **Publish to BPM MDS** menu item to publish the BPM project template.

6. The **Publish to BPM MDS** dialog pops up. Type a name for the **Project** field (the name of the BPM project template to be published in MDS) and choose a **Location** to publish the project. Create a destination folder by pressing the **+** button, as shown in the following screenshot:

7. Once you've chosen the destination folder press the **OK** button to publish the project; this operation can take some time to finish.

8. To see the project template just published go to the **BPM MDS Navigator** and expand the **Templates** root folder; the project template should be listed in the correct location folder. The published BPM projects go under the **Projects** root folder.

Creating a BPM project from a template inside Process Composer

1. Log in to Process Composer as a user who has write privileges (for example, weblogic user) at `http://localhost:7001/bpm/composer` (or `8001` for managed server configuration). Go to the BPM Process Composer home page. Select **Create New Project**. In step 1, choose the option **Create a Project based on a Template** and select the template **QuoteProcessLab** published from Studio. In step 2, give the project a name—**QuoteProcessLab_custom**, and select the **Begin editing now** option.

2. Choose a destination folder in step 4 and an approval workflow to be triggered before publish to MDS can be specified in step 5.

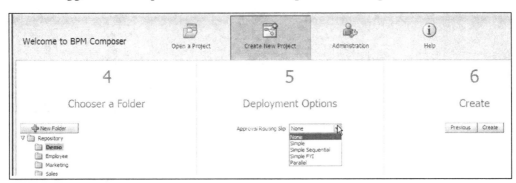

3. A navigator appears on the left with the project structure. Open the **RequestQuoteLab** process.

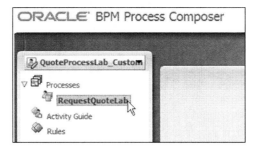

4. Locate the **Approve Terms** task, which should have a mark indicating what needs to be implemented.

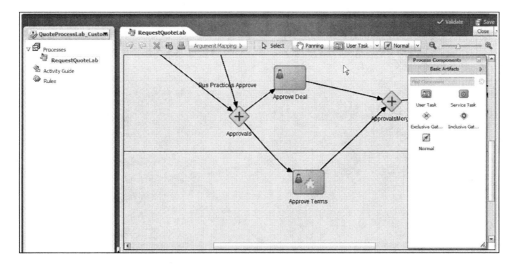

5. In order to implement this task, go to the palette on the right (dock it by dragging it to the right border of the application). The **Basic Artifacts** palette shows the most frequently used BPMN objects.

6. Click twice on the title to switch to **Business Catalog** palette.

7. Under the **Human Tasks** group, select the one with the name of **ApproveTerms**. Drag that human task to **Approve Terms** step on the process.

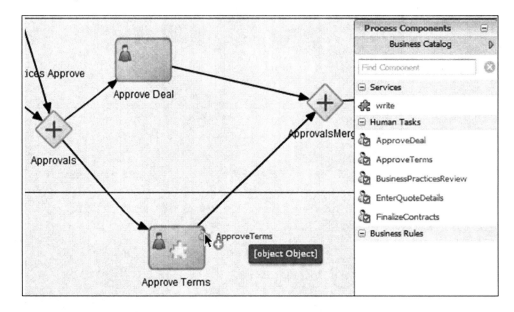

8. This automatically switches control to the data mapping—**Arguments Mapping** screen. From the variables list on the right, drag **quote** variable to the first **Inputs** field—**quoteRequest**. Drag **approveTermsOutcome** variable to the first **Outputs** field—**outcome** and **quote** variable to the second **Outputs** field **quoteRequest**.

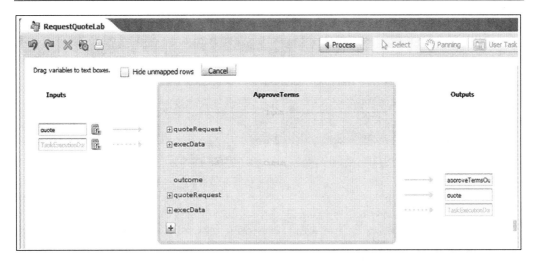

9. Click on the **Process** button on the toolbar on the top to go back to the process editor.

10. The **Save** option saves the changes made to the BPM Project locally to a file.

11. The BPM project needs to be validated for semantic correctness before deployment. Process Composer provides visual guidance on fixing errors. To validate the BPM project, select the **Validate Project** option under the **Tools** menu. The results of the validation are displayed on the panel on the bottom of the application. If the project validates correctly, it is ready to publish.

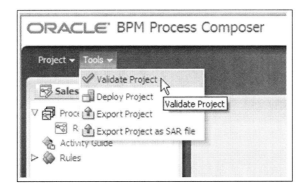

12. To publish the changes to MDS, select the **Publish** option under the **Editing** menu. Approval workflows if specified are triggered and have to have a successful outcome before the BPM project is published. The **Discard** option is used to roll back the changes and any changes saved locally are deleted.

13. Once it is published, the project can be deployed. Click on the **Deploy Project** option. To overwrite the existing deployed version of the BPM project with the new version, enter the same revision id as **Last Revision ID** for the **New Revision ID** field. Specify the username and password for the BPM runtime connection. To deploy a new revision of the BPM project in parallel to the existing revision, specify a different value for the **New Revision ID** field. Selecting **Mark composite revision as default** makes the newly deployed revision as the default.

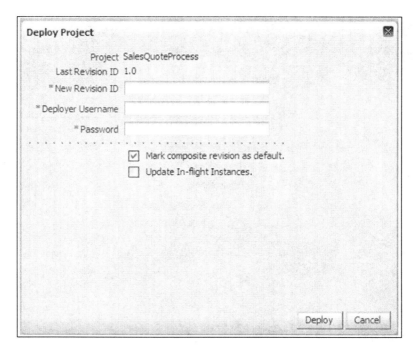

Process Composer Administration

The Oracle BPM Suite comes with pre-defined security roles for Process Composer.

Role mapping

The Oracle BPM Suite comes with pre-defined security roles for Process Composer. The Project Administrator is one of the pre-defined security roles for Process Composer and users/groups that are mapped to this role can delete projects, reset project locks, and manage security roles. This **Administration** menu is only visible to users who have been granted the **Project Administrator** security role. There are other pre-defined security roles and they are as follows:

- **Designer** — models process flows but cannot add implementation details to process steps
- **Developer** — models and implements process flows
- **Deployer** — deploys unlocked BPM projects
- **Project Creator from Template** — creates new BPM projects from BPM project templates
- **Project Creator** — creates new BPM projects from scratch as well as from BPM project templates
- **Project Viewer** — views BPM projects for feedback purposes but cannot create or edit process flows
- **Project Documenter** — views BPM projects and provides additional documentation (use case documentation) for process steps but cannot create or edit process steps
- **SOA Designer** — edits business rules

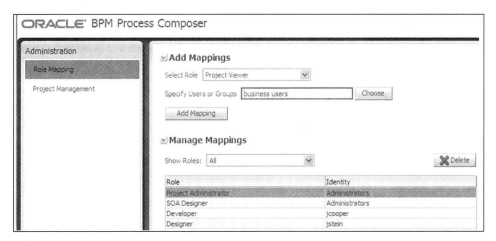

To assign users and groups to security roles use the following steps:

1. Click on **Administration**.

2. Select **Role Mapping**.

3. Expand the **Add Mappings** section.

4. Select the security role to add to the user or group. Click on **Choose** and then click on **Search**. This returns a list of all users of groups. Search for a specific user or group is also supported. Select the appropriate user or group from the **Available** column. Click on **Move**.

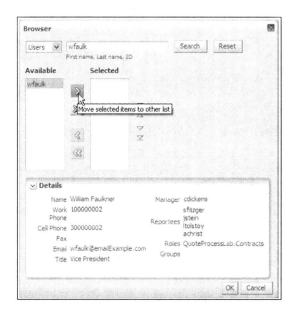

5. Click on **OK**.

6. Click on **Add Mapping** button.

Managing projects

Process Composer is used to perform BPM project management related tasks such as releasing project locks and deleting projects inside MDS. To perform project related administrative tasks:

1. Sign-on to Business Process Composer with the Project Administrator privilege.

2. Click on **Administration**.

3. Select **Project Management** from the left-hand side column.

4. Select the appropriate project from the right-hand side column, then select from the following:

- Delete: Deletes the selected project from the Oracle BPM Metadata Service repository.

- Release Lock: Releases the lock for the selected project. Other users with the appropriate permissions can lock and edit the project.

- Refresh Repository: Refreshes the project list from MDS.

Summary

The web-based Process Composer takes process modeling to a wider business audience and empowers business users across an organization to get involved with understanding and improving their own processes. Web-based Process Composer allows process owners to tailor processes and rules to their exact specifications. In addition, the product features many capabilities for process owners to manage and orchestrate successful completion of processes.

12
Using Process Spaces and Workspace Application

The end user interaction in Oracle Business Process Management Suite 11*g* is mainly offered through two out-of-the-box components named Oracle Business Process Management Workspace and Oracle Business Process Management Process Spaces. These two end user interfaces offer task management and process monitoring for in-flight work being orchestrated by the underlying Business Process Management Engine. The Oracle Business Process Management Workspace is a standalone web application while the Oracle Business Process Management Process Spaces leverages the Web Center Suite portal capabilities for exposing the same Workspace widgets through this collaboration environment.

Walk through the following chapters to understand these two different interfaces and what they offer in terms of functionality.

End user roles and concepts

Different types of persons within an organization can use the Oracle Business Process Management Workspace and Process Spaces. Among these types of persons we find:

- End users
- Supervisors
- Administrators

The end users represent the community in your organization performing the individual steps in a business process based on the roles and responsibilities delegated to them in the organization. These users will be processing the granular work that is pushed to them by the underlying Business Process Management Engine for processing.

The supervisors have the responsibility of overseeing the work performed by the end users. These users will be in charge of making sure the work is processed in a timeline manner and also manage the exceptions of having to delegate and reassign work as needed based on different conditions on their end user community.

The administrators are responsible for doing administrative tasks at the organization level, including operations such as role assignments, view management, and so on.

It is important to note that regardless of the responsibility of individuals in an organization where Oracle Business Process Management is deployed, the out-of-the-box Workspace and Process Spaces will provide the functionality needed by these persons to perform their work as needed in a collaborative environment.

Workspace application

The Oracle Business Process Management Workspace interface offers end users, supervisors, and administrators an interface for processing their work. The Workspace application will enable or offer functionality depending on the permissions these different users have based on their roles and responsibilities assigned within an organization.

When a person logs into the Workspace, the application will present the successfully connected user with three main tabs:

1. Tasks
2. Process Tracking
3. Standard Dashboards

The **Tasks** tab is the place where the end users will spend most of the time. This tab is where the end user's work is pushed to and where they will process the granular work assigned to them. The next screenshot shows the task interface for James Cooper following the Sales Quote example:

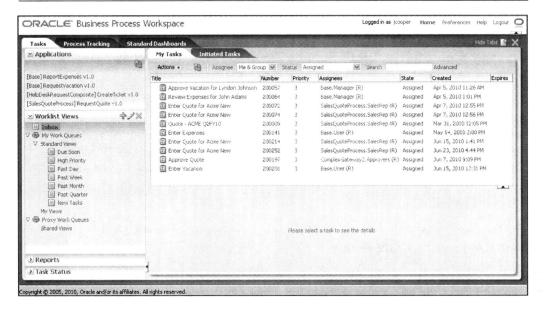

The **Tasks** tab will also offer a specific set of aggregations by using tabs on the main Workspace canvas. The most notable one is **My Tasks**. This will group all the tasks for the logged user that have been assigned to him or for which this person is a candidate (meaning that he can claim the task and execute it).

The other task tab offered out of the box to all type of users is **Initiated Tasks**. This will show a list of all tasks that have been started by the logged user.

If you are a supervisor, two new task tabs will become available as shown in the following screenshot:

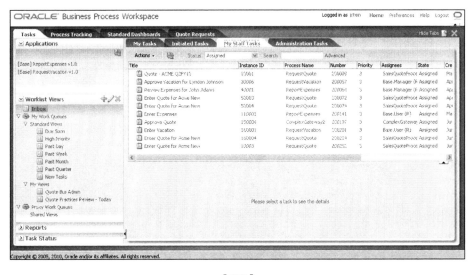

In the screenshot above, the **My Staff Tasks** tab will show the supervisor the tasks assigned to all the persons that report to him/her based on the organization hierarchy. Similarly, the **Administration Tasks** tab will bring visibility to all tasks for its management.

The **Process Tracking** tab is the place where the supervisors will spend most of their time as they need to oversee the in-flight work as process instances move from one business process activity to the next one. Generally speaking, what the end user will see in the instances list in this panel will relate to process instances in BPMN user activities. These activities will usually spawn work on the task list to end users. Still, the supervisors will need to see the instance in the context of the process and this is what this panel is all about.

The following screenshot shows the **Process Tracking** interfaces for Jeff Stein in the context of the Sales Quote example:

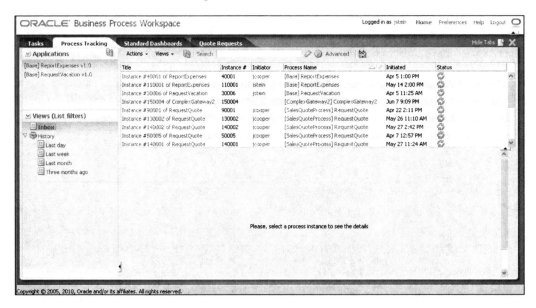

The **Standard Dashboard** tab is a way to expose supervisors with the ability to get process analytics in the context of the Workspace application. The **Standard Dashboard** panel will be composed of widgets containing dashboards showing standard process metrics common to all business process. These process analytics are workload and performance. These two relate to the accumulation of work and its distribution within a business process. The later one reflects the actual times for processing a business process from start to end as well as the break down at the activity level on a per process basis.

The following screenshot shows the Workload process analytics reflecting the distribution of instances on a per process basis and the break down associated for the example business process Sales Quote:

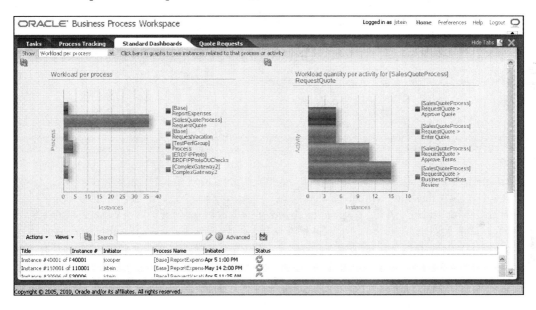

In addition to the three out-of-the-box tabs exposed in the Workspace, it is possible to create new tabs. These new tabs can be used to create new dashboards for tracking business process-specific metrics and provide better visibility and insight into the health of the deployed business processes. These new tabs are generally created by supervisors or administrators and the dashboards contained in them are created dynamically and on the fly within the Workspace application using KPIs or Business Indicators defined in the business processes at modeling time.

The following screenshot shows a custom made Dashboard showing distribution of Sales Quotes on a per industry basis and the associated list of instances for the selected aggregation on the right-hand side:

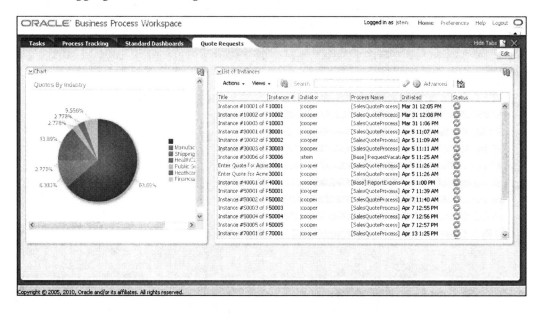

Administrators can also use the Workspace for performing administrative tasks. If a user has the Administrator role, when he/she logs in, they will see an **Administration** link in the upper right-hand side corner of the Workspace once they are successfully logged in. The following screenshot shows the interface an administrator will be presented with, after clicking on this link, in order to perform administration tasks.

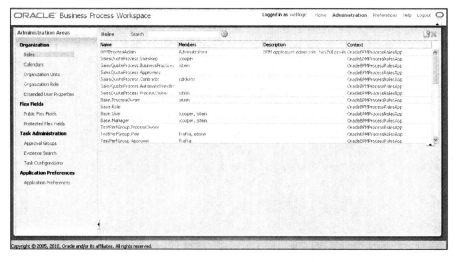

Process Spaces

Oracle Business Process Management Process Spaces offers the same capabilities previously exposed by the Workspace but in the portal context of Web Center. The Process Spaces presents three main templates out of the box:

1. Process Workspace Space
2. Process Instance Space
3. Process Modeling Space

The **Process Workspace Space** is most similar to the one in the **Tasks** and **Process Tracking** Workspace tabs in the sense that they include a list of tasks and instances to process and monitor. These widgets can be complemented with functionality offered by the Web Center Suite, including social and collaborative services such as chat, discussion forums, document management, dashboards, and so on.

The following screenshot shows James Cooper in the context of the Sales Quote example but connecting to the Process Workspace Space in Web Center:

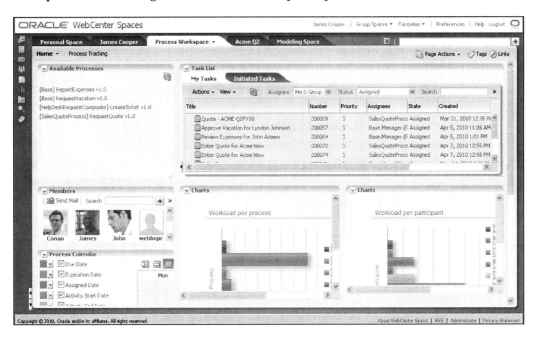

The Process Workspace **Space** offers an option for **Tasks** and **Process Tracking** tabs. These can be selected from the toolbar of this space on the upper left-hand corner. This panel offers discussion forums, document management, and others, as seen in the following screenshot:

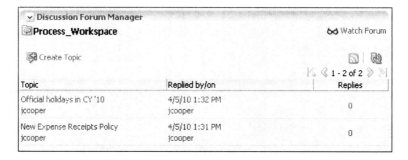

The next space to cover is the **Process Instance Space**. In the **Task list** of the **Process Workspace Space**, for each task or process instance, there will be a place to connect to the specific **Process Instance Space**. The following screenshot shows these links on the **Instance Space** column at the very far right:

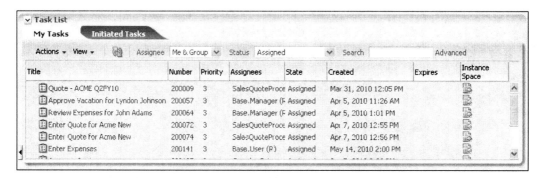

When the user clicks on this link, the flow will move to a new tab containing the details and information for the selected instance as shown in the following screenshot:

The first thing to note is the fact that the tab label is the name of the task or label associated to the process instance. This panel will also display all the process instance associated details such as the current state, the associated pending tasks, the audit trail, comments or notes, and the linked attachments. It can also incorporate Web Center services such as participant groups, document management, and discussion forums as can be seen in the preceding screenshot.

The following screenshot shows the audit trail for this process instance when the **Audit Trail** section is expanded (as seen in the preceding screenshot):

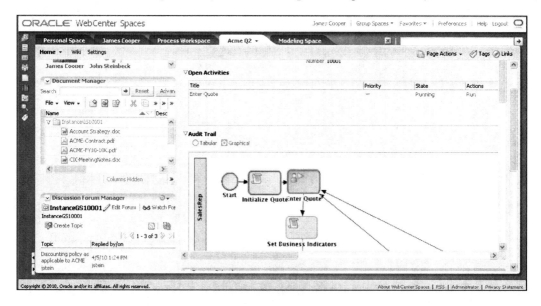

The third space offered by the Business Process Management Suite in Web Center is the **Modeling Space**. This will provide a collaborative environment at modeling time for different development groups to work together on the documentation and assembly of business processes. The **Modeling Space** is shown in the following screenshot:

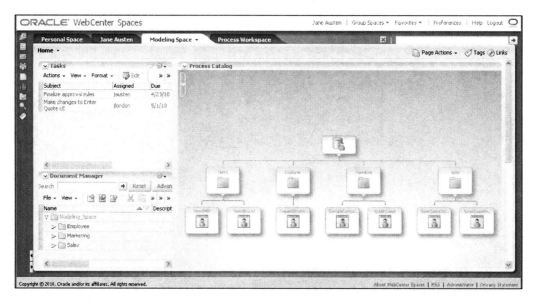

The **Modeling Space** offers a social and collaborative environment where different individuals can see the business processes available for consumption and usage and also the way to shared documents, discussions, and tasks as they work together in the lifecycle of bringing business processes to life, from their initial requirements gathering phase to their final deployment and execution.

The **Modeling Space** can be used to aid during this journey and provides the right interface and tools to facilitate these tasks, providing more agility and productivity with the ability to improve reusability and knowledge sharing.

Organizing, finding, and performing work

End users and administrators will spend most of their time processing tasks in the Workspace **Tasks** and **Process Tracking** panels per their specific responsibilities. The task processing will be more effective if these different audiences would have a way to organize their work and also combine it with search capabilities to process the important work first.

Oracle BPM Workspace offers out-of-the-box capabilities for organizing and finding the work (tasks) effectively by these different end user audiences.

Organizing the work

With more order comes better productivity and BPM is all about helping end users be better organized so that they can do their job in a clean, fast, and secure manner. For this, Oracle BPM Workspace offers a way to organize the work or tasks through the notion or concept of views. Views can group tasks based on particular search conditions, logically grouping together tasks with certain characteristics.

Oracle BPM Workspace offers some out-of-the-box views with general-purpose classification categories, but it is also possible for end users and supervisors to create their own views and also share these with other members in their groups.

Let's assume now that the supervisor wants to create a new view to organize today's work on the Business Practice Review's process activity so that end users, with this activity's role, can spot the approvals easily by selecting this view in the **Tasks** panel in the Workspace.

The supervisor (for example, J. Stein) can create this view by clicking on the **+** icon in the **Worklist Views** panel as shown in the following screenshot:

The view wizard starts with this action. The supervisor will need to fill in the different aspects that conform to the definition of the custom view by providing a name, the type of tasks to filter by this view, as well as its sharing setup. Let's navigate these aspects one by one.

1. Provide a name to the view: **Quote Practice Review - Today**. This will become the label shown in the **Worklist Views** panel.

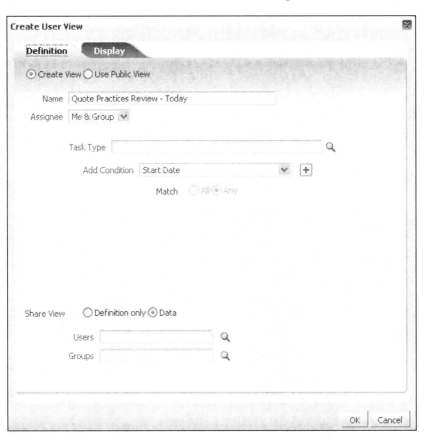

2. After specifying the label of the view, click on the magnifier icon on the right-hand side of the **Task Type** text field, as this view will only filter tasks that are pending on the task implementation associated to the **Business Practice Review** process activity whose implementation name is: **Business Practice Review**. When this icon is clicked, the following new dialog pops up. Click on the **Search** button to get the list of all available tasks.

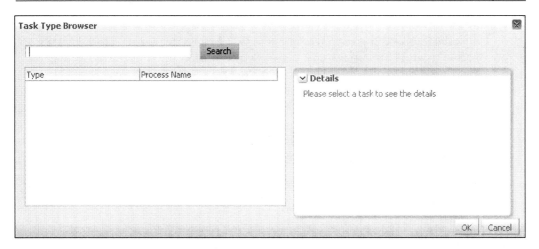

3. When all the available tasks have been listed on the left-hand side panel, select **BusinessPracticeReview** (which is the one we are interested in per the exercise at hand) and once selected, click on the **OK** button on the lower right-hand side of the dialog. This is shown in the following screenshot:

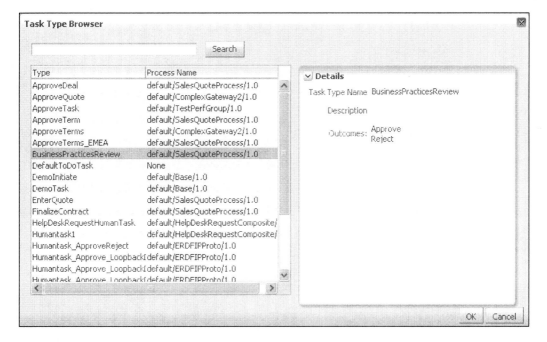

4. After the task has been selected (it is also possible to not select any specific task and the search scope will be all tasks the logged on user has access to), it is time to specify the search condition for those tasks in the **BusinessPracticeReview** task. Select the **Start Date** search condition and choose the **last n days** comparison operand. Enter the integer number **1** on the right-hand side of the expression. Add a new condition stating that the tasks to be filtered by this view should only contain tasks that are assigned. For this, use the **State** task attribute. These conditions should look like the dialog below when these operations have been completed:

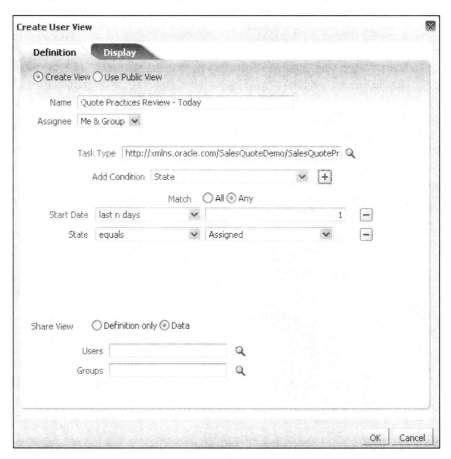

5. Although this exercise will not include sharing the view, it is possible to select any number of users or groups so that others can leverage this view for organizing the work in a team of people collaborating together in processing tasks of a specific nature.

6. Click on the **Display** tab on the header and select any additional columns associated with the task of displaying additional information that may be relevant for the end user processing and completing the task. The following screenshot shows this panel:

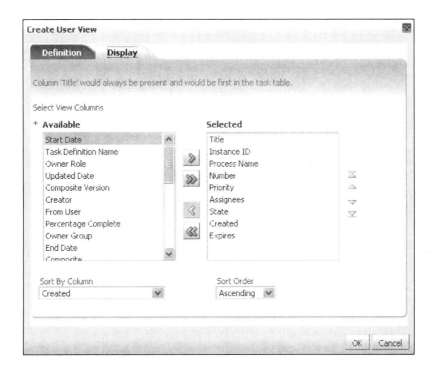

7. Click on **OK** to complete the creation of the custom user view. The final result will show the recently created view in the **My Views** section of the **Worklist Views** panel, as shown in the following screenshot:

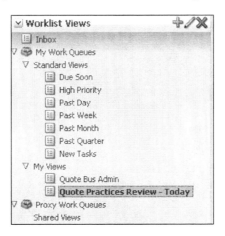

Finding the work

Often, the end users will have lots of tasks to process in their **Inbox** view and they need to be able to narrow down the list to find the tasks that need to be processes. This activity can only be done from the Inbox view and not on custom created views.

Let's use, for example, a case where the end user needs to find all tasks related to the **Acme** sales opportunity.

Follow these steps to find tasks under this condition:

1. Click on the **Inbox** view.

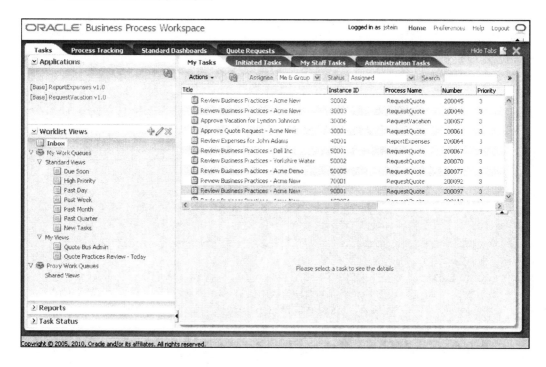

2. Enter the text string **Acme** on the **Search** text field on the upper right-hand corner of the **View** list as follows:

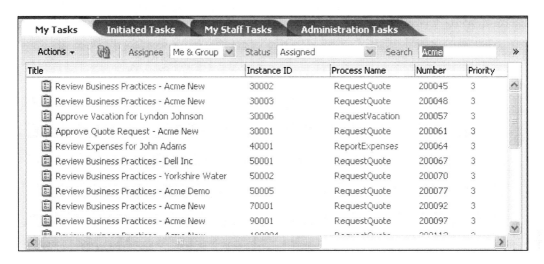

3. Press the *Enter* key and the list will be refreshed to only show those tasks with a title containing the **Acme** keyword as a substring of the task's title. This can be seen in the following screenshot:

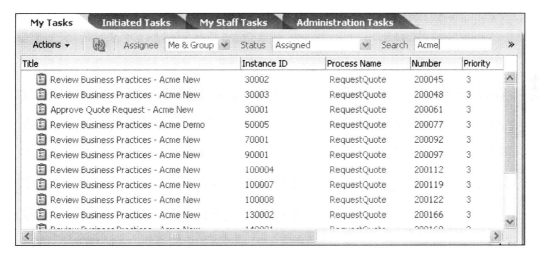

4. It is also possible to specify more advanced search conditions by clicking on the **Advanced** link to the right of the **Search** dialog.

Performing work

End users and supervisors will need to process the tasks once they have identified them by using views or the search Workspace capabilities. To process the task, simply click or select the task in the **Task List** and the lower section of the Workspace will automatically start rendering the execution of the associated task implementation. This is shown in the following screenshot using the Sales Quote example process:

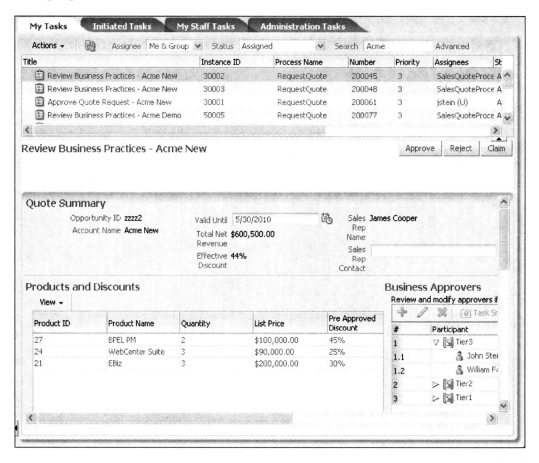

Alternatively, it is also possible to directly exercise the processing of the task from the **Actions** drop-down in the **View** toolbar of **Inbox**, as shown in the following screenshot:

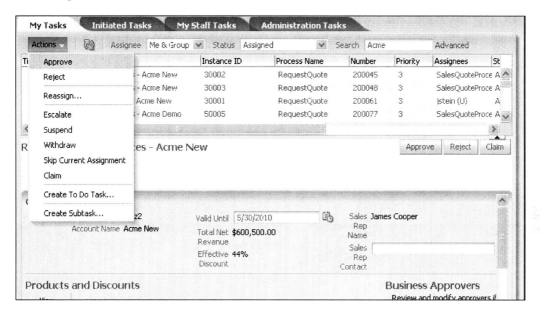

Managing vacations, and delegating and re-assigning work

In order to make an organization agile and self-service, it is necessary to delegate management tasks to the end users and supervisors so that they can perform their day-to-day activities easily and without too many barriers. In this category, we can distinguish how end users can manage their work while they are absent on vacations or how supervisors, for example, can reassign work as needed by different conditions.

Managing vacations

Let's suppose James Cooper, the Sales Representative from our Sales Quote needs to go on a vacation. It would be nice if while he is out enjoying his well-deserved vacation, he could delegate the processing of new incoming work to other peers in his team. Let's walk through the steps for James Cooper to set this up.

1. Log in with **jcooper** and click on the **Preferences** link on the toolbar as shown in the following screenshot:

2. In the new panel, select **Rules** and the vacation management entries will be ready to be set up as shown in the following screenshot:

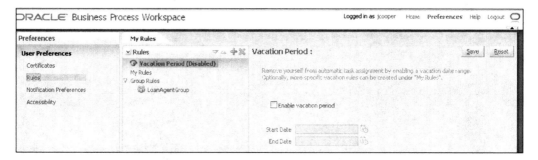

3. Select the **Enable vacation period** checkbox and then enter the beginning and end dates of his vacation.

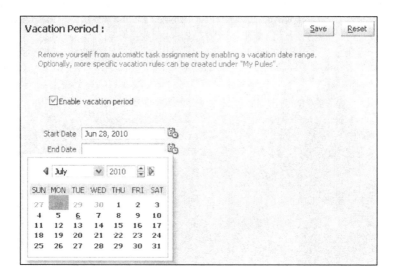

4. After saving the vacation settings (by clicking on the **Save** button), the end user will not receive new tasks within the specified vacation dates and James Cooper should see his vacation configuration as shown in the following screenshot:

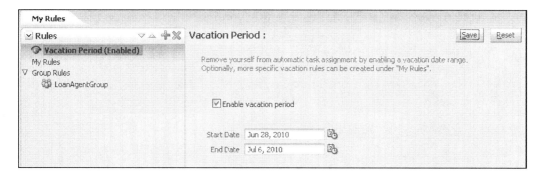

Delegating and re-assigning work

One of the responsibilities of a supervisor is to oversee that the end users participating the business process on his/her realm of responsibility are processing the work in a timely manner. For this main reason, it is very important to empower the supervisor with the capabilities to delegate and re-assign tasks based on people and team availability.

Let's assume there is an important sales opportunity escalated in the organization currently assigned to John Stein. John Stein happens to be the person responsible for approving this sales opportunity but he is busy with other internal tasks. In this case, John Stein decides to work this specific deal with his manager and delegates this work to him for the sales opportunity approval.

The following sequence of steps depicts how to manage the task re-assignment in this case and any other delegation or task re-assignment by a supervisor:

1. First, we need to identify the task to be delegated. Use the views or search capabilities to identify the task assigned to **jstein**, which is also associated with the deal at hand. For this example, John Stein will click on the **Administration Tasks** panel so that he can see all his work and the work of the people he supervises. This is shown in the following screenshot with the task that needs to be re-assigned and delegated for its expedited processing. In the **Assignees** column, **jstein** also shows as the person currently assigned this task:

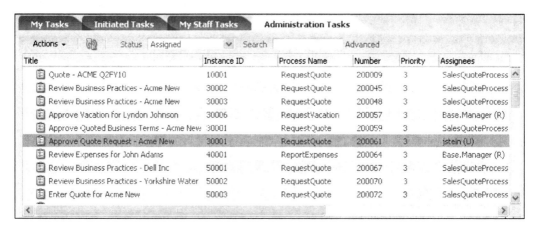

2. With the task selected, click on **Actions** in the upper left-hand corner and select the **Reassign...** option in the drop-down menu:

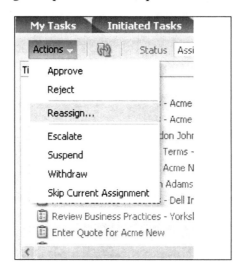

3. In the re-assign panel, click on the **Search** button to bring up all the users to whom the task can be re-assigned or delegated. Then select the target user. This will look something like the following screenshot:

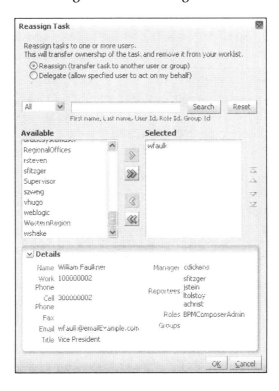

4. Click on the **OK** button to complete the reassignment. The task now will show as assigned to **William Faulkner**, who is John Stein's manager.

Managing and tracking processes

So far, we have been mostly concentrating on how end users and supervisors will process and administer the task granular work pushed through the Workspace.

The Workspace also offers the **Process Tracking** panel so that supervisors can track the work at the process level and not the tasks completely isolated from the process that created them.

The **Process Tracking** panel offers supervisors the ability to see where the process instance is in the context of a particular business process as well as the whole history of the process instance as it moved from activity to activity within the business process.

For one second, let's put ourselves in the shoes of John Stein, who is the person responsible for the overall behavior and health of the Sales Quote business process. John Stein needs to be armed with the capabilities mentioned before.

Let's walk the steps that John Stein would need to follow to find the instance and analyze its state:

1. John Stein would need to be logged into the Workspace and would then click on the **Process Tracking** panel. In there, John Stein would need to use the search capabilities or look for the instances that he wants to analyze. This can be seen in the following screenshot:

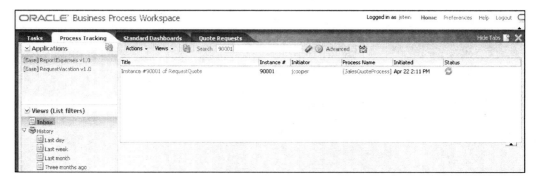

2. Select the instance and the lower panel will show the details of the selected process instance as seen in the following screenshot:

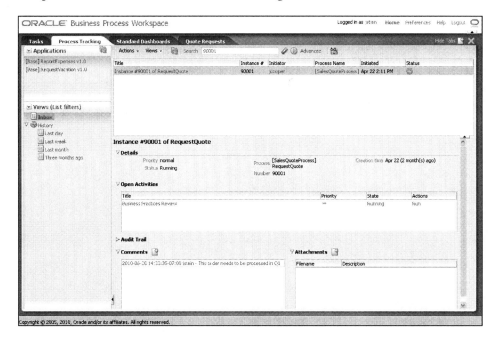

3. The **Details** and **Open Activities** sections will reveal where it is in the process as well as information about the process instance itself such as the process instance ID and status. Additionally, the **Open Activities** section will show the current activity in which the process instance is waiting its execution. If we link it back to its implementation, this activity (**Business Practice Review**) will have a task listed in the **Tasks** panel for the appropriate person to complete.

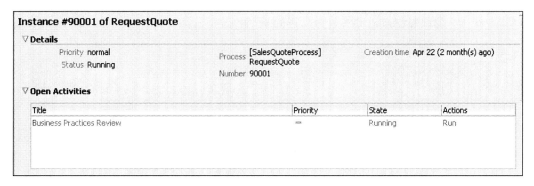

4. The next section will show the **audit trail** for the process instance in tabular text fashion. The individual entries can be expanded to get more details if needed.

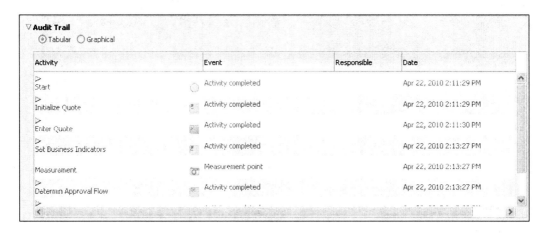

5. This **audit trail** can also be seen graphically and on top of the BPMN 2.0 business process picture with the painted path of the instance following the sequence flow. This particular view can be very useful in the context of a more complex diagram and the steps that lay ahead of the last executed business process activity.

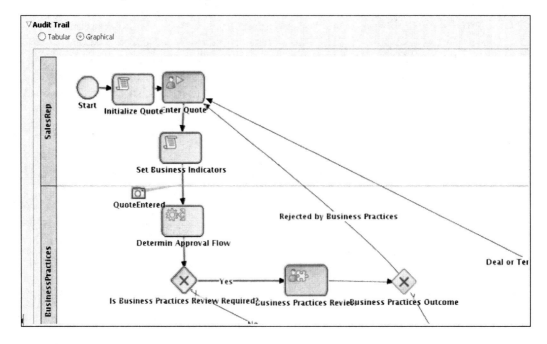

6. Last but not least, the supervisor can also see the **Comments** associated to the process instance at the business process level, as well as the ancillary files or **Attachments** associated to this in flight process instance.

Summary

In this chapter you learned about the two out-of-the-box interfaces that Oracle Business Process Management Suite offers to the different end user audiences, including the Workspace and Process Spaces in the context of Web Center Suite.

It also showed how the end users can be more productive organizing their work by using mechanisms such as views and search capabilities.

We also exposed some of the self-serve capabilities and looked at how the Workspace and Process Spaces can empower these end users for their own administration tasks.

13
Process Analytics and Business Activity Monitoring

Process analytics is an important part of BPM. Without metrics and analysis of metrics, the business processes cannot be measured and optimized. It is critical to your business success that you establish **Key Performance Indicators** (**KPI**s) and manage your **Service Level Agreements** (**SLAs**). Businesses will also leverage **Business Activity Monitoring** (**BAM**) to monitor and improve business processes. Oracle BPM offers two options to manage the metrics — BPM process analytics and **Oracle Business Activity Monitoring** (**BAM**).

The first part of this chapter is about process analytics and the second part is about BAM.

Concepts and architecture

BPM process analytics is comprised of standard and custom metrics, process cubes, BPM standard and custom dashboards, and integration with BAM. With these tools, the business analyst can monitor processes for optimization, KPIs, and SLAs.

The architecture for process analytics merges with the original BAM architecture, which was already in place. It has two primary pieces—measurements and actions. The BPMN engine feeds data to the measurements that makes that data available to BAM and cube actions, which in turn make data available to the business users in dashboards. The following diagram shows the architecture and related parts:

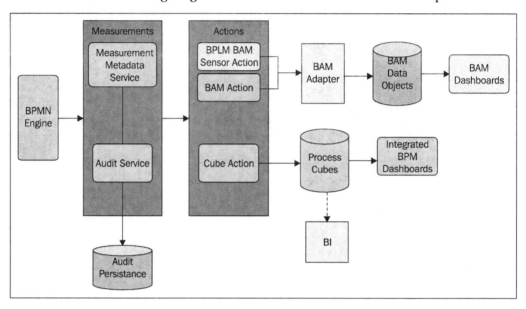

Default process analytics and dashboards

BPM Suite provides a set of default metrics that are always provided. The business user gains visibility into the process analytics with zero setup and configuration. The following are the default metrics:

- Cycle-time for completed activities
- Cycle-time for completed processes
- Number of active instances per activity, process, and participant
- Average and median time for activities and processes

Workload calculations consider all active instances and are used to provide aggregations for total quantity, average time, and median time. The information is sliced for all the dimensions.

These metrics are captured by default but this setting can be modified in process properties by turning off sampling as desired. Sampling information is captured when the execution of the corresponding artifact is completed.

There are two important properties that are configured using the Enterprise Manager Fusion Middleware control. If you are not aware of these property values, your metric data may seem incorrect.

- **CubeUpdateFrequency**: Determines how often to compute. Default value is 30 minutes.

- **CubeInstanceExpiration**: Determines the retention for the workload records. Default is 48 hours.

There are two types of dashboards provided as **Standard Dashboards** that are available from BPM Workspace. BPM dashboards use pre-computed data in process cubes aggregated by well-known dimensions such as participants and activities:

- Workload dashboards
- Performance (cycle-time) dashboards

Here is an example of a process workload dashboard with drilldown to workload by activity. The later section will show actual instances based on the selection in these charts:

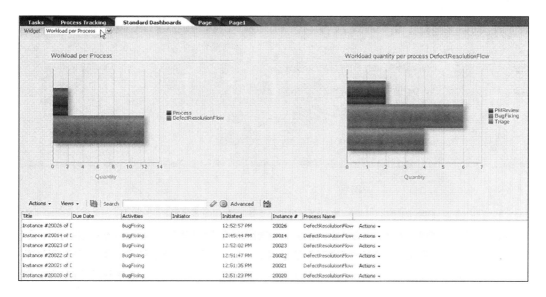

Business indicators and measurement marks

Process analytics capture standard data such as workload and cycle time and process-specific data. Business indicators are used to specify what process-specific data should be captured. There are three types of business indicators supported:

- **Measures**: These are numerical data that typically signify a value that is interesting in process analytics. For example, the sales total.

- **Dimensions**: These specify how process analytic data may be sliced. A dimension has to have a finite set of values. In cases where it does not, such as for numbers and date/time, a set of ranges must be specified for the data. For example, region, month, and sales total ranges (high, medium, low).

- **Counters**: As the name indicates, these are useful for counting iterations. The number of iterations is clearly an interesting data point for analytics. For example, the number of deals.

In addition to measures, **measurement marks** provide a way to add additional capture points. Moreover, measurement marks also provide a visual notation to indicate the capture point.

- Single measurement:
    - To sample business indicators at a specific point in the process
    - Specified on the transition
    - Samples list of measures specified

- Counter mark:
    - Used to define counter on an activity
    - Can samples the counters specified in the definition

- Interval (start and end):
    - Provides an ability to define a logical activity
    - Samples value at the end of the interval
    - Specified on the transitions
    - Only captures the measures specified in the definition

If it is someone's preference not to have measurement marks displayed on the canvas, it is possible to specify equivalent capture points by using the **Sampling Point** property of preceding activity.

Business indicators behave just like other data objects regarding data assignment (association). That is, data can be assigned to them either as part of an activity's output data association or within a script activity.

By default, process analytic data sampling is specified at the project level and there are three possible settings:

- Generate for interactive activities only
- Generate for all activities
- Do not generate

For all the artifacts, in addition to standard metrics, values for all the dimensions are captured. The following table summarizes how measures are captured:

Capture Type	What data is captured?
Activity	Values for all measures at the end of an activity (if enabled)
Interval	Value for specified measures at the end of an interval
Single measurement	Snapshot for specified measures
Counter mark	Snapshot for specified counters

Custom dashboards

BPM dashboards are ADF pages that are defined and accessed from BPM workspace. BPM dashboards provide charts and drilldowns. Drilldowns could be to another chart or to the final details.

End users can create custom (user-defined) dashboards by defining graphs in the BPM workspace and assembling those graphs to define a dashboard.

Custom graphs can utilize standard metrics and user defined dimensions and measures so the user can define new graphs that utilize business indicators. The user chooses the type of graph that will be created based on the metric data types. The three data type choices are:

- **Workload**: The workload tables capture workload and aggregated analytic data
- **Activity and measurement sampling**: This is essentially a snapshot of analytic data at the activity level
- **Process level sampling**: This is a snapshot of analytic data at the process level (and will be available only for completed instances)

Custom dashboards support various ADF graph types and these are assembled to create new dashboards.

Tutorial: Using standard and custom dashboards for the Request Quote process

At this stage in the tutorial, you have deployed and run the process. Using the Process Tracking feature of the BPM workspace you tracked and monitored the process. In addition to the standard tracking views, you can also create your own personalized dashboards. This tutorial will guide you in creating these dashboards. Starting with the adding of business indicators to the process and then using the data from these business indicators in BPM Process Workspace dashboards.

Adding process analytics specifications to a BPMN process

In this lab, you add process analytics information to the Sales Quote process.

For the purposes of this lab, you analyze discounts offered to understand its distribution across deal sizes (total net revenue) and industries. At the end of this lab, you will have created the following dashboard:

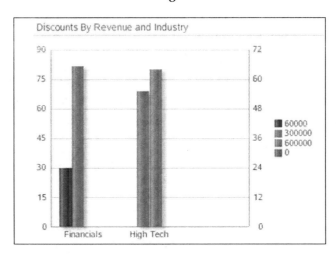

Adding business indicators

Now add the measures, dimensions, and counters for analyzing the process. In this scenario, you create a measure for *discount,* and dimensions for *industry* and *revenue,* where revenue is a numerical dimension and needs ranges to be specified. You also add a counter to count the number of times the quote needs to be revised.

The first step is to add a **dimension** business indicator for revenue:

1. In BPM Studio, open the version of the process you saved in *Chapter 11* before turning your process into a template, open the **RequestQuoteLab** BPMN process, and select it by clicking on an empty spot on the canvas. This opens the **Structure** panel with the BPM process context.

2. Navigate to the **Structure** panel; if it is not open, you can open it by pressing the *Ctrl+Shift+S* keys or by selecting **Structure** in the **View** menu.

3. Right-click on **Business Indicators** and select **New**.

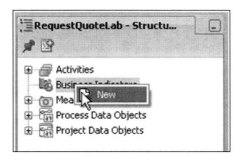

4. Specify the following values:

   ° **Name**: revenueDimension

   ° **Business Indicator**: Dimension

   ° **Type**: Int

 Revenue could be a **measure** as well; therefore name it with **Dimension** suffix to remind you how it is to be used.

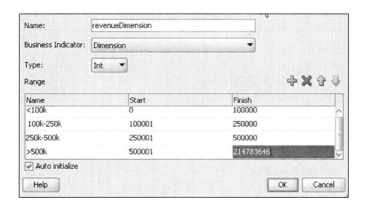

5. Specify ranges for dividing numerical revenue data into finite set of values:

Name	Start	Finish
<100K	0	100000
100K – 250K	100001	250000
250K – 500K	250001	500000
>500K	500001	214783646

 The above ranges are just suggestions; you can choose any values that make sense to you

 214783646 is the largest value possible (in the future, it will be easier to specify upper and lower ends of ranges).

6. Add another dimension business indicator for industry:
   ○ **Name: industry**
   ○ **Business Indicator: Dimension**
   ○ **Type: String**

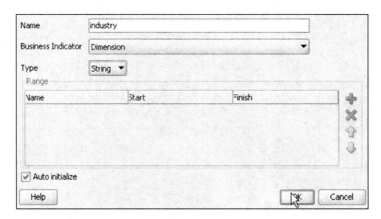

7. Add measure business indicator for discount:
   ○ **Name: discount**
   ○ **Business Indicator: Measure**
   ○ **Type: Int**

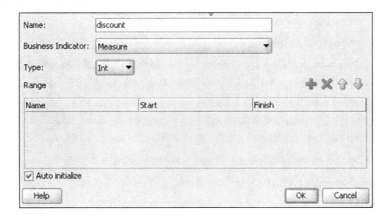

8. Add counter business indicator for counting the number of times the quote is revised, with name **numQuoteEdits** and type **Counter**:

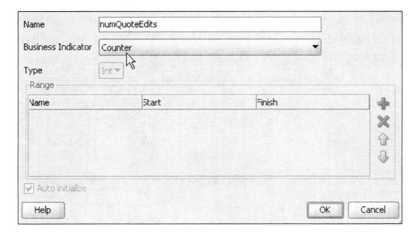

Assigning data to business indicators

Now that you have defined your business indicators, we need to assign data to them.

As, in this scenario, the **Enter Quote Details** output data association is already used for assigning to quote data object, use a script activity to assign data to the business indicators from the quote data object by using the following steps:

1. Click on the **Script** activity in the **Component Palette**.

2. Move the mouse over the connector between the **Enter Quote Details** activity and the **Is Business Practices Required?** gateway.

3. When the connector turns blue, click on it.

4. In the properties dialog box, specify **Name** as **Assign Indicators**.

5. Create data associations by selecting the **Implementation** tab of the **Properties** dialog box (if not open from the previous step, double-click on the **Assign Indicators** activity).

6. Select the **Use Associations** checkbox in the **Data Associations** sub-panel, leave **Type** as **Simple**, and click on the pencil icon.

7. Drag-and-drop **industry** into the variables panel.

8. Drag-and-drop **discount** into the variables panel.

9. Drag-and-drop **revenueDimension** into the variables panel.

10. In the right-hand side panel, expand the **RequestQuoteLab** node, then its **quote** child node, and then its **summary** child node.

11. Drag-and-drop **industry** to the source (left input textbox) for the **industry** indicator.

12. To set **discount**, click on the **Expression Builder** icon to the right of the left-hand input box for the discount indicator.

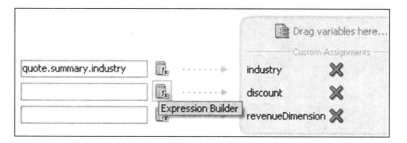

13. Enter the expression `round(quote.summary.effectiveDiscount * 100)` because the **effectiveDiscount** is set as a decimal value and the business user should see it as a normal percentage value between 0-100.

 This formula for the discount indicator expects that the **effectiveDiscount** value coming from the page is a percentage value in decimal form, that is, a value such as .25 for 25%. In a later lab, you customize this form so that the user can enter the integer value for the discount. *For now, you must enter the decimal value for analytics to work properly.*

14. Click on **OK**.

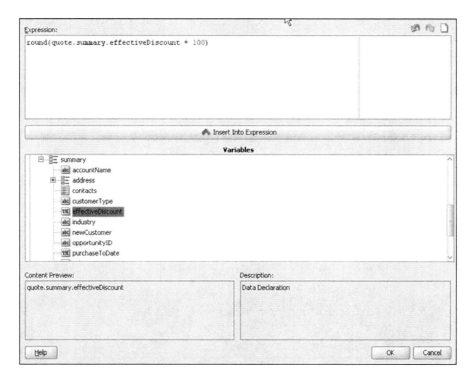

15. Again, use the **Expression Builder** to set the expression for **revenueDimension** indicator to `round(quote.summary.totalNetRevenue)` and click on OK.

16. The completed expressions look like the following screenshot. Note the changed syntax of the round function from what you saw in the **Expression Builder:**

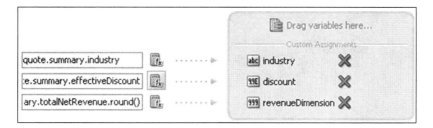

17. Click on **OK**, and click on **OK** again to close the **Properties** dialog.

Adding a measurement mark

In the previous section, you used a **Script** activity to assign data to business indicators. As process analytic data is by default not captured after automatic activities, unless you specify that it should be captured, it will not be captured until the next interactive activity is completed. As you want to track quotes as soon as they are entered, you need to specify a measurement mark. You can do so by using the following steps:

1. Expand the **Artifacts** accordion in the **Component Palette**.

2. Click on **Measurement**.

3. Move mouse over the connector between the **Assign Indicators** activity and **Is Business Practices Required?** gateway.

4. When the connector turns blue, click on it.

5. Specify measurement properties as follows:

   ° Measurement type: **Single Measurement**

   ° Name: **QuoteEntered**

   ° Move **discount** business indicator to selected

6. Click on **OK**.

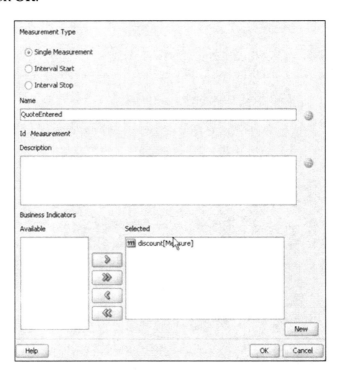

Adding a counter

In this scenario, you want to track how many times a quote has to be revised (due to rejections).

1. Right-click on **Enter Quote Details** and select **New Counter Mark**.

2. In **Counter Properties** dialog, select **numQuoteEdits,** and click on **OK**.

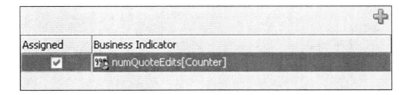

Once the counter is created you can view it from **Properties** on the **Counter** tab:

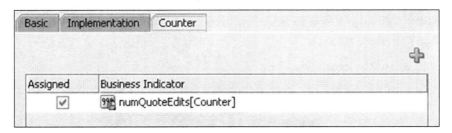

Running instances to create sample data

As described below, deploy the new version of the process and run a few instances so that during dashboard creation in the next section, some data is already available to view.

1. Deploy the updated project.

 As there are no changes to the UI, remember to deselect all task forms before deploying. You do not have to deploy them every time you deploy the composite; you only deploy them when they change.

2. Log in as **jcooper** and initiate a few instances; specify any interesting mix for the following fields:
   ° industry
   ° totalNetRevenue
   ° discount

 Because these fields are referenced in the process do not leave them blank or your process will have a fault.

3. Log in as **cdickens** and submit the **Approve Deal** task.

Creating dashboards

In this section, you will create the custom dashboard shown in the beginning of this lab—one that allows you to analyze *discounts* by *revenue* and *industry*. Use the following steps to do so:

1. Log in to **Workspace** as **jcooper**.

2. Click on the **New Page** icon (document with **+**) on the top-right corner.

3. Give the page a meaningful name and then click on the **Add Panel** button on the far right.

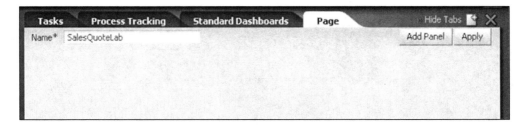

4. Click on the Search icon to add dashboard as the content for this page.

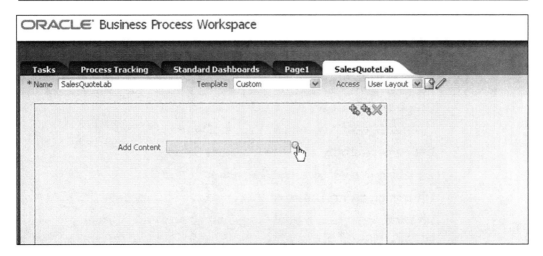

5. Select **Dashboard (Charts)** and select **OK**.

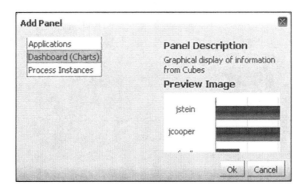

6. Enter a meaningful name and then click on the **Magnifying Glass** next to **Data Source**.

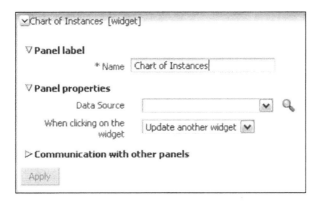

7. Click on the new icon and specify the following for the newly created data source:

   ◦ Name: **Discounts-Revenue-Industry**
   ◦ Title: **Discounts By Revenue and Industry**
   ◦ Graph type: **BAR_VERT_CLUST**
   ◦ Process: **[QuoteProcessLab] RequestQuoteLab**
   ◦ Data type: **Activity and Measurement Sampling**
   ◦ Dimension series: **revenueDimension**
   ◦ Dimension group: **industry**
   ◦ Measure variable: **discount**
   ◦ Measure operation type: **avg**

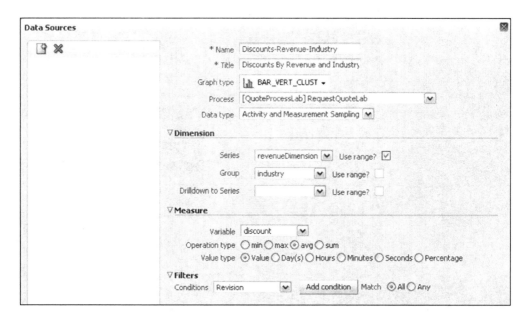

8. Click on **OK**.
9. Click on **Apply** within the **Panel** (not to be confused with **Apply** at the page level).
10. Click on the **View Mode** icon on the top right-hand side corner of the panel.

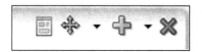

11. Click on **Apply** at the page level and you will see your new custom graph. If you do not see any data here, make sure you have completed more than one user activity per process and that your analytics properties are set to what you expect (see defaults in the overview section at the beginning of this document).

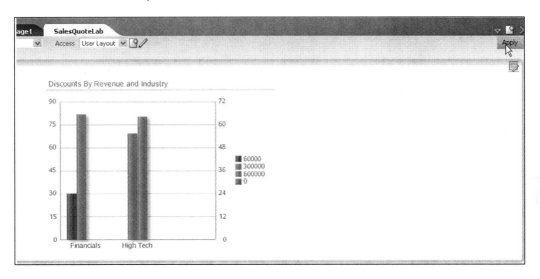

Integration with Oracle Business Activity Monitoring

BAM enables process visualization by providing real-time visibility into KPIs of the process through real-time dashboards and alerts. This is a vital area for BPM and BPM Suite integrates with BAM in a number of ways compatible with BPM process analytics. Primarily, BAM utilizes the same measurement capabilities for business indicators definition and sampling as what is used in process analytics.

BPM Suite utilizes the BAM adapter to communicate with BAM but this is done automatically and the developer does not need to configure the adapter except to point to the BAM adapter data resource.

BAM defines standard reports just like BPM does. BAM standard reports are called **Monitor Express Reports**. These reports become available by running a provided script. When using **BAM Active Studio** to create custom BAM dashboards from BPMN standard metrics, you will see the pre-created BAM data objects with the express terminology.

To create a BAM dashboard with the BPM business indicators that you created, you need a BAM data object for the business indicators you defined in your process. This is done by extending the express data object which is already defined for your process.

There are three steps for integrating BPM and BAM:

1. Get the BAM server ready:

    i. Import standard data objects and reports.

    ii. Create custom data objects and reports.

2. Configure the BPM server for BAM integration:

    i. Configure the BAM adapter to point to BAM server.

    ii. Enable BAM action in EM (disabled by default).

3. Enable the project to populate BAM:

    i. Enable BAM action for the project (disabled by default).

    ii. Optionally specify BAM adapter properties.

Tutorial: Using BAM reports for Request Quote process

In this lab, you continue the process analytics lab and use Oracle BAM to monitor the process analytic data in real time. Oracle BAM provides a real-time, event-based monitoring option. It can aggregate and correlate events from multiple sources and raise alerts on abnormal business condition, thereby, enabling end-to-end business process visibility.

Setting up for monitoring with Oracle BAM

In this section, you do the one-time setup needed for enabling Oracle BAM monitoring. This includes setting up the BAM adapter application to connect to the BAM server, telling the BPMN server to send data to BAM, and setting up the BAM data object for standard metrics. Later, the BPMN engine sends metrics to the adapter.

These steps are typically done by the person managing the installation.

Configuring the BAM adapter

The BPM server uses the BAM adapter to push events to BAM. This adapter needs to be configured so that it knows how to connect to the BAM server. Note that the BPM server and BAM server can be running in different environments but the adapter runs with the BPM server.

This configuration is done using the **WebLogic Server Console (WLS)** for the BPM server.

If you are using a pre-configured system for this book, you do not need to do this step. See *Oracle Technology Network BPM Suite* page for information about a pre-configured system.

1. Log in to the WLS for your BPM server, typically `http://bpmhost:7001/console` (where you would replace `bpmhost` with details specific to your environment).

2. Find the **Domain Structure** panel on the left-hand side bar, and click on **Deployments**.

3. In the **Deployments** table in the main panel, find **OracleBamAdapter** of type **Resource Adapter**

☐	oracle.wsm.seedpolicies(11.1.1,11.1.1)	Active		Library	100
☐	OracleAppsAdapter	Active	✓ OK	Resource Adapter	328
☐	OracleBamAdapter	Active	✓ OK	Resource Adapter	329
☐	⊞ OracleBPMComposerRolesApp	Active	✓ OK	Enterprise Application	382
☐	⊞ OracleBPMProcessRolesApp	Active	✓ OK	Enterprise Application	381

You may want to use the **Customize This Table** link at the top of the table and choose to filter out Libraries as well as increase the number of rows displayed to 100 to make it easier to find **OracleBamAdapter** and other applications. There are about 30 applications on a typical, newly installed server.

4. Drill into **OracleBamAdapter** by clicking on the name (not the checkbox).

5. Select the **Configuration** tab and within it the **Outbound Connection Pools** tab.

6. Expand **oracle.bam.adapter.adc.soap.SOAPConnectionFactory** and drill down into the **eis/bam/soap** link.

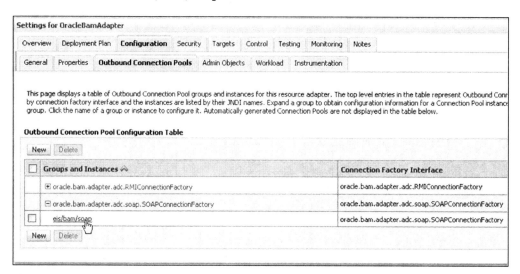

7. In the **Properties** tab, specify the connection information for the BAM server:

Property Name	Property Value
HostName	localhost (or as appropriate)
IsHTTPEnabledWebService	false
Password	welcome1
PortNumber	9001 (or 7001 if you have BAM on the AdminServer)
UserName	weblogic

You need to press the *Enter* key after entering a property value—moving out of the field without pressing enter, will cause changes to the field to be lost.

The clear text password is necessary here unless you use encryption for your adapter.

The connection properties look like this:

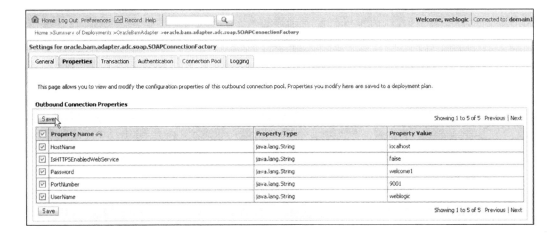

8. Click on **Save**.

   If this is the first time you are changing properties for the BAM adapter you will be asked to specify the deployment plan.

9. Create a directory, **BAMPlan**, in your **SOA_HOME/soa** directory.

10. In the dialog box, select **BAMPlan** in the locations list.

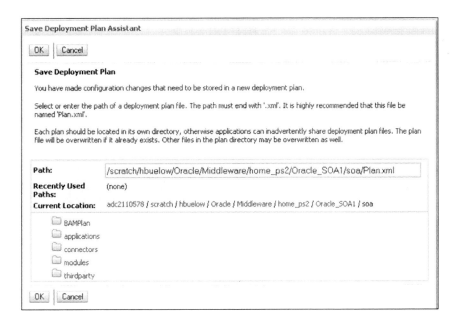

The **Path** field should be set as shown in the following screenshot:

Path:	/scratch/hbuelow/Oracle/Middleware/home_ps2/Oracle_SOA1/soa/BAMPlan/Plan.
Recently Used Paths:	(none)
Current Location:	adc2110578 / scratch / hbuelow / Oracle / Middleware / home_ps2 / Oracle_SOA1 / soa / BAMPlan

11. Click on **Save**.

    Now you need to update the BAM adapter with the new plan. Find **OracleBAMAdapter** in the **Deployments** table as seen in the preceding screenshot.

12. Select the checkbox for the adapter and click on **Update**.

13. In the **Update Application Assistant**, choose **Update this application in place with the new deployment plan changes. (A deployment plan must be specified for this option)**

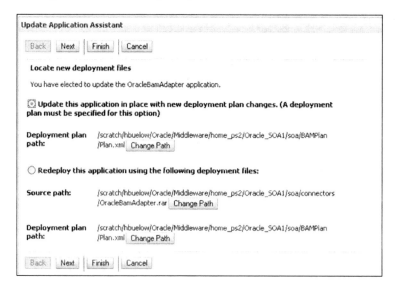

14. Click on **Finish**.

Configuring the BPMN engine for BAM integration

The BPMN engine has a configuration option to send events to BAM and this option is off by default. It needs to be turned on from **Enterprise Manager Fusion Middleware Control**.

 If you are using a pre-configured system for this training, you do not need to do this step. See the *Oracle Technology Network BPM Suite* page for information about a pre-configured system.

1. Log in to **Oracle EM Fusion Middleware Control**, typically `http://bpmhost:7001/em` (where you would replace `bpmhost` with details specific to your environment).

2. Expand **Weblogic Domain** within **Farm_domain**, select your domain, for example, **domain1**, and then select the BPM Server (typically, **soa_server1** if running managed servers; otherwise, **AdminServer**).

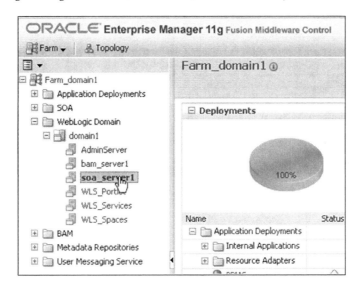

3. Click on **the WebLogic Server** drop-down menu, and select **System MBean Browser**.

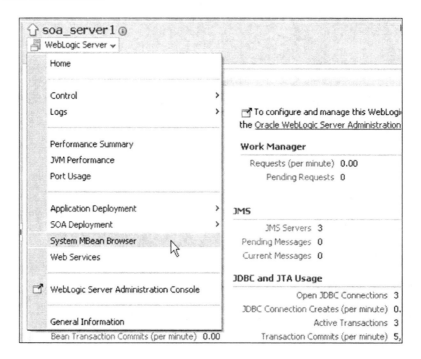

4. In the **System MBean Browser**, expand **Application Defined MBeans**.

 Collapsing other top-level nodes will make finding this easier.

5. Expand **oracle.as.soainfra.config**.

6. Expand **Server: soa_server1** (server: **AdminServer**, if not running managed server).

7. Expand **BPMNConfig**.

8. Click on the **bpmn** entry.

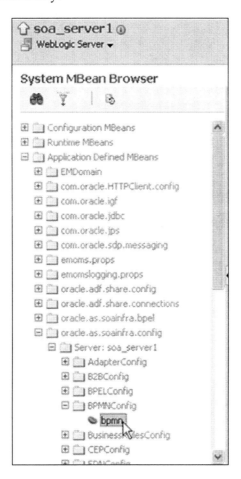

9. Set **Value** of **DisableActions** to empty.

10. Find the attribute **DisableActions**.

11. Clear its current value.

12. Click on **Apply**.

	Name	Description	Access	Value
8	CubeUpdateFrequency	Frequency in seconds at which cube action calculates the workload	RW	300
9	DisableActions	Comma delimited list of disabled measurement actions (e.g. "CubeCommand, BAMCommand")	RW	
10	DisableSensors	If set to "true" the engine will disable all calls to sensors. The default value "false".	RW	false
11	DispatcherEngineThreads	The total number of threads that will be allocated to process engine dispatcher messages	RW	30
12	DispatcherInvokeThreads	The total number of threads that will be allocated to process invocation dispatcher messages	RW	20

Application Defined MBeans: BPMNConfig:bpmn   Apply   Revert

Show MBean Information

Attributes   Notifications

Importing BAM monitor express

Oracle BAM ships with standard data objects and dashboards defined for BPMN and BPEL processes. However, these need to be imported into BAM after installation.

> If you are using a pre-configured system for this training, you do not need to do this step. See the *Oracle Technology Network BPM Suite* page for information about a pre-configured system.
>
> In these instructions $SOA_HOME refers to where you chose to install SOA, usually $MW_HOME/Oracle_SOA1

In order to eliminate having to manually enter the username and password multiple times during script execution, update the BAMICommandConfig.xml as follows. This is optional but recommended .

1. Edit $SOA_HOME/bam/config/BAMICommandConfig.xml file as follows.

2. Add the following two lines above the </BAMICommand> tag at the bottom. Replace the user_name and password value with your admin username and password:

```
<ICommand_Default_User_Name>user_name</ICommand_Default_User_Name>
<ICommand_Default_Password>password</ICommand_Default_Password>
```

3. Set `JAVA_HOME` environment variable:

   ○ Linux:
   ```
   setenv JAVA_HOME /scratch /Oracle/Middleware/home_
   ps2/jdk160_18
   ```

   ○ Windows:
   ```
   set JAVA_HOME=c:\Oracle\Middleware\home_ps2\jdk160_18
   ```

4. Find the monitoring express sample shipped with BAM and run the included setup script:

   ```
   cd $SOA_HOME/bam/samples/bam/monitoringexpress/bin
   ./setup.sh
   ```

 If you did not edit the `config` file in step 1, you will be prompted multiple times for the username/password; use user `weblogic`.

Later in this lab, you will review the dashboard you just imported.

Configuring the BPM project for BAM monitoring

In this section, you set up your BPM project for BAM, monitoring. This setup is simple and would usually be done earlier in process definition. For flow of tutorial purposes, you are doing it here as it is specific to this lab.

1. Open the BPM Project in JDeveloper (if not already open).

2. Navigate to the **BPM Project Navigator** panel (use **View** menu if needed).

3. Right-click on the project, **QuoteProcessLab**, and select **Project Preferences**.

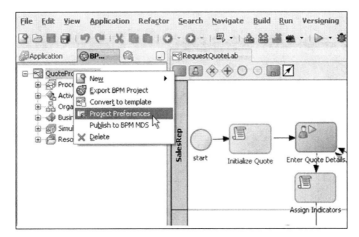

4. In the **Data Targets** tab, select **Enable BAM** as a data target for process analytics.

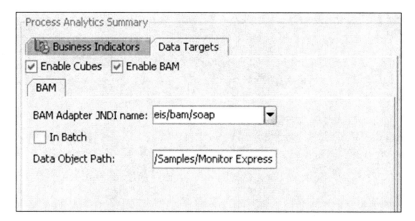

5. Select **eis/bam/soap** as the BAM adapter JNDI name.

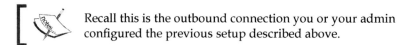

Recall this is the outbound connection you or your admin configured the previous setup described above.

6. Specify **Data Object Path** as **/Samples/Monitor Express**.

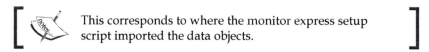

This corresponds to where the monitor express setup script imported the data objects.

7. Deploy the project.

Creating a process-specific BAM data object

For capturing process-specific process analytic events, you need to create BAM data objects for each process. The bulk of the data object is the same for every process so you import the common express data object and create the process-specific data object by adding process business indicators to it.

The following are the rules for creating a BAM data object for the BPM process:

- Name of the data object must be must be exactly `BI_DEFAULT_<Composite Name>_<Process Name>` (`Composite Name` is same as `Project Name`)

- For every business indicator, a column needs to be created in the data object:
    - Column name must be exactly `METRIC_<business indicator name>`
    - Types should match

- For a business indicator with ranges, that is dimension business indicators of numerical types, an additional column needs to be created to capture the range:
    - Column name must be exactly `METRIC_RANGE_<business indicator name>`
    - Type is String

The following instructions show how to update the BAM data object for the business indicators you created in the process:

1. Launch BAM Architect.

2. Using MS Internet Explorer, log in to Oracle BAM, `http://bamhost:9001/OracleBAM`, as `weblogic`. Use port 7001 if you have a single `AdminServer` configuration.

 BAM web tools require Internet Explorer.

3. Click on **Architect**.

4. Follow the steps to find the imported base data object and rename it to `BI_DEFAULT_QuoteProcessLab_RequestQuoteLab`

5. Drill down into the folder **Data Objects**, **Samples**, **Monitor Express**.

6. Select the data object as **BI_DEFAULT_Composite_Process**.

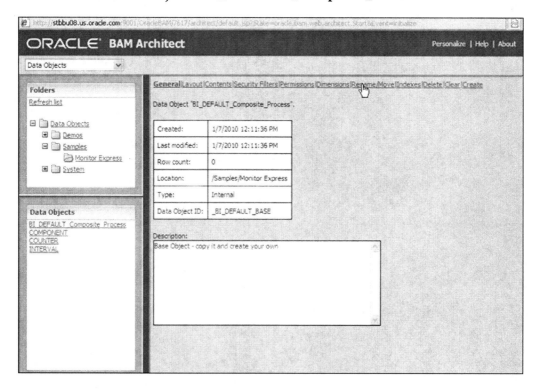

7. Click on **Rename/Move**.
8. Specify **Name** as **BI_DEFAULT_QuoteProcessLab_RequestQuoteLab**.
9. Click on **Save Changes** and then on **Continue**.

10. Click on **Layout**.

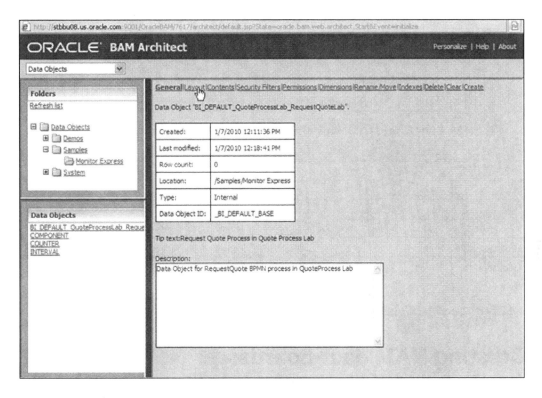

11. Click on **Edit Layout**.

12. Add the following fields by clicking on **Add a field** (at the bottom of the panel):

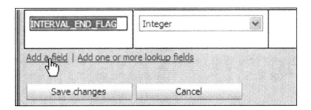

 See rules for creating Data Object columns for process business indicators at the beginning of this section.

Field Name	Field Type
METRIC_revenueDimension	Integer
METRIC_RANGE_revenueDimension	String
METRIC_discount	Integer
METRIC_industry	String
METRIC_numQuoteEdits	Integer

13. Save changes and click on **Continue**.

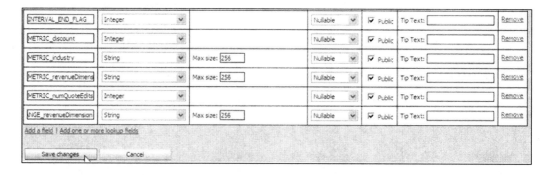

Creating BAM dashboards

Once you have your BAM data object and you have set the properties in your BPM project for BAM process analytics, it's time to create the BAM dashboard. While creating the dashboard, you can preview how it will look if you have data in your data object.

 In the BPM workspace as `jcooper`, submit a few instances of the process to put data in the data object. Be sure to enter industry, total revenue, and discount values. You need to submit the first form, Enter Quote Details, and the subsequent form, either Business Practices Review or Approve Terms. Make sure your discount percentage value is in decimal form, so 0.25 and not 25%.

1. Log in to **Oracle BAM**, `http://bamhost:9001/OracleBAM`, as `weblogic`. Use port `7001` if you have a single `AdminServer` configuration.

 BAM web tools require Internet Explorer.

2. Click on **Active Studio**.

3. Create a new report as follows:

    i.   Click on **Shared Reports** tab.

    ii.   Click on **Create a New Report** button.

    iii. Select the template with two horizontal sections.

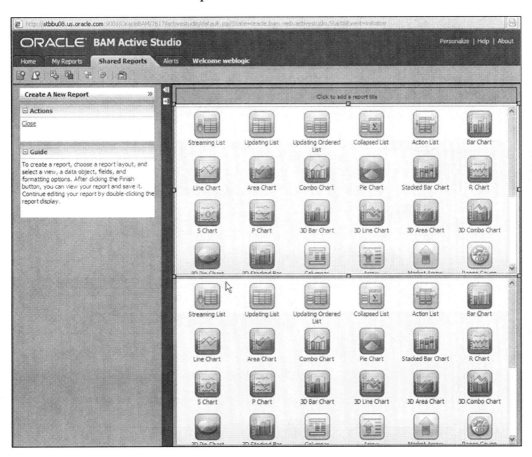

4. Click on **Click to add a report title** and enter **Request Quote Dashboard**.

5. Click on **3D Bar Chart**.

6. In **Choose Data Object** tab, drill down in to **Data Objects, Samples, Monitor Express**, and select **BI_DEFAULT_QuoteProcessLab_RequestQuoteLab**.

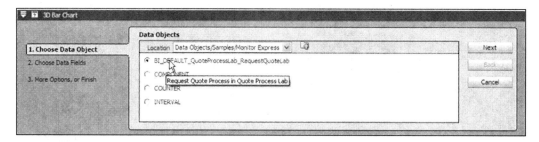

7. Click on **Next**.

8. In **Choose Data Fields**:

   ° Group by: **METRIC_RANGE_revenueDimension** and **METRIC_industry**

   ° Chart values: **METRIC_discount**

   ° Summary function(s): **Average**

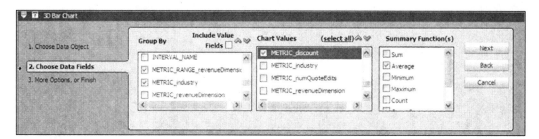

9. Click on **Next**.

10. Select **Change View Properties** and enter:

   ◦ View title: **Discounts by Revenue and Industry**

   ◦ Vertical axis label: **Discount%**

   ◦ Click on **Apply** to review

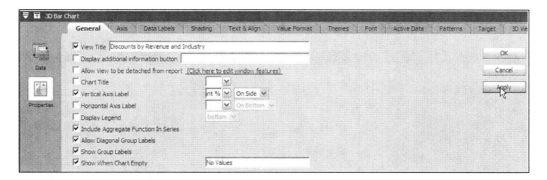

11. If you don't like the order of grouping on the X-axis, follow these steps:

   i. Click on **Data** and go to the **Fields** tab.

   ii. Use the blue arrows in the **Group By** column to re-arrange.

   iii. Click on **Apply** and review.

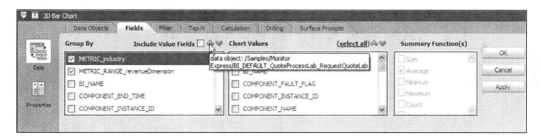

12. Specify a filter so that any orders with revenue as 0 are not shown in the dashboard (these are the orders at activation, before any data is entered).

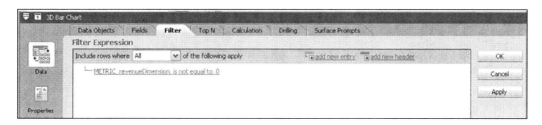

13. Click on **OK**:

Add a gauge to display discounts. For the bottom of your report, click on **Range Gauge** and choose **Data Objects** exactly as in previous step.

14. In **Choose Data Fields**:

    i.   Select **METRIC_discount** in the center picklist.

    ii. Select **Average** in the picklist below it.

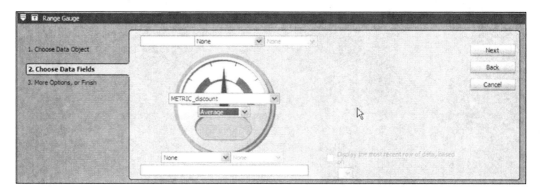

15. Click on **Next**.

16. Click on **Change View Properties**.

    i.   Specify **View Title** as **Discount Gauge**.

    ii. Specify **Value** display ranges as **0, 30, 65, 90**.

17. Click on **Apply** to review.

Specify a filter as you did with the 3D chart so that any orders with revenue as 0 are not considered in the discount average

18. Click on **OK**.

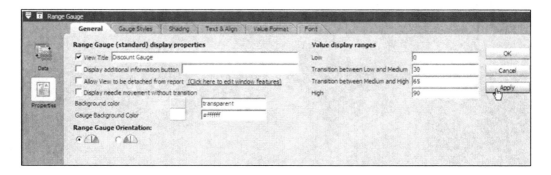

19. Save the report under **Shared Reports/Samples/Monitor Express**.

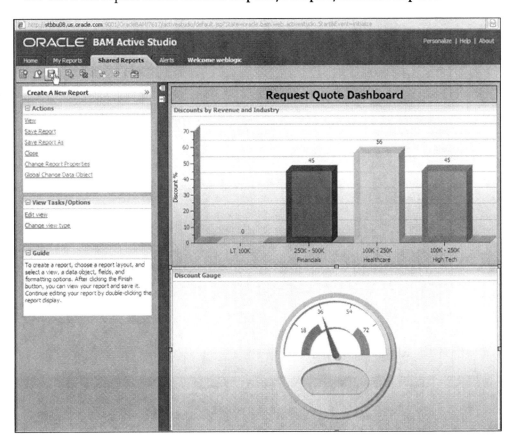

Viewing BAM dashboards

In this section, you use **BAM Active Viewer** to view both the standard dashboard, as well as the one you created in the previous section.

1. Log in to Oracle BAM, `http://bamhost:9001/OracleBAM`, as `weblogic`. (Use port `7001` if you have a single `AdminServer` configuration) and click on **Active Viewer**.

2. Click on **Select Report** and open the **Request Quote Dashboard**.

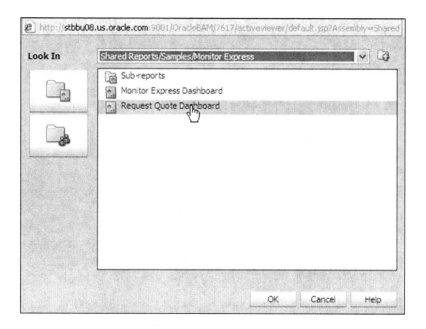

3. View the **Request Quote Dashboard**.

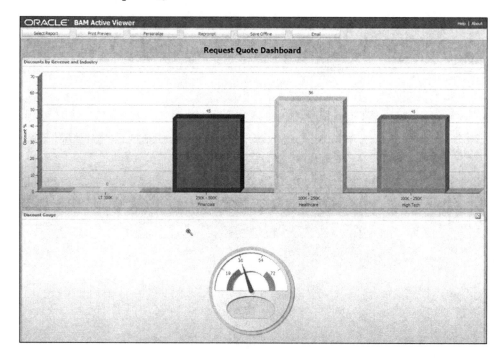

4. View the **Standard Dashboards** (monitor express sample) as follows:

    i.   Click on **Select Report**.

    ii.   Drill down into **Shared Reports/Samples/Monitor Express**.

    iii.   Select **Monitor Express Dashboard** and click on **OK**.

    iv.   Select the **Process View** tab.

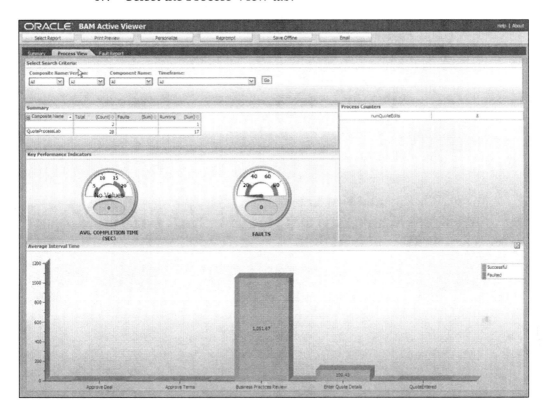

Creating an alert for a High Discount Sales Quote

In this section, you use **BAM Active Studio** to create an alert when the KPI for the average discount is in the red zone:

1. Launch **BAM Active Studio**.

2. Click on the **Alerts** tab.

3. Click on **Create a New Alert**.

4. Select **Create a Rule**.

5. Name the alert **High Discount Alert**.

6. Select **Event** as **When a data field in a Report** meets a specified condition.

7. In the rule expression:

   i.   Click on **Select Report**.

   ii. Select **Request Quote Dashboard**.

   iii. Click on **When this data field has a condition x**.

   iv. Select **DataObject BI_Default_QuoteProcesslab_RequestQuoteLab**

   v.   Click on the **Group Filter** tab.

   vi. Click on **Add New Entry**.

   vii. Set the filter for **AVG(METRIC_Discount) is greater than or equal to 65**.

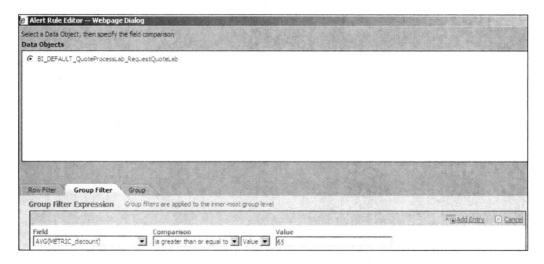

8. Click on **Add Entry** to save the group filter condition.

9. Click on **OK**.

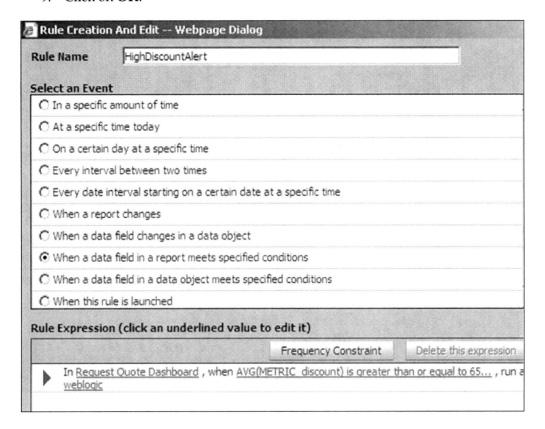

10. Click on **Next** to set up an action on the alert.

11. Under **Select an Action**, select **Send a message via e-mail** checkbox.

You can also invoke a web service or start an ODI scenario among other options as part of the action. One alert can kick off multiple actions.

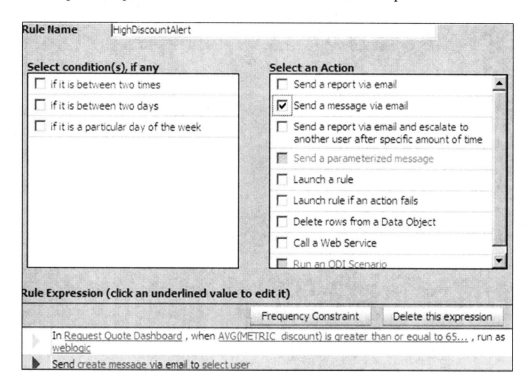

12. Under **Rule Expression**, click on **create message**.

13. Select the parameters to populate for the message as shown in the following screenshot:

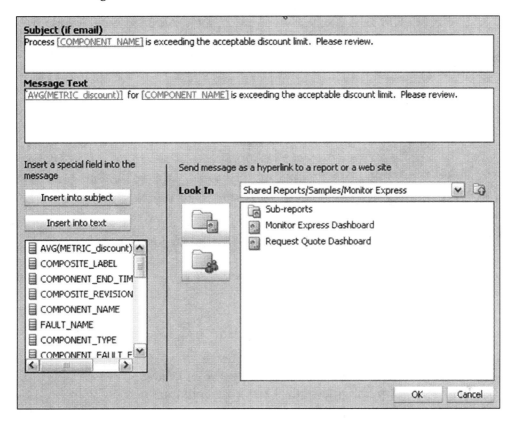

14. Click on **OK**.

15. Click on **Select User**, and select **weblogic**.

16. Click on **OK**.

17. Click on **OK** on the main **Alert** dialog.

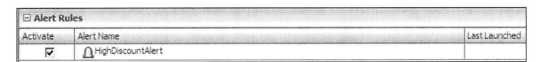

As you do not have an e-mail address configured, the following steps will show how alerts can be viewed on the dashboard. In production scenarios, the users will normally send the alert e-mail and keep the dashboard design to allow analysis of the situation for the alert recipient.

1. Go to **Active Studio** and open **Request Quote Dashboard**.
2. Click on **Edit**.
3. Resize the **KPI Dial Gauge** view by selecting it and dragging the window from the right-hand side corner to have it take up the left half of the lower part of the dashboard.
4. Click on **Insert View** on the top menu bar:

5. Select the **Action List** view.
6. Select the following **System/Alerts/History Data** object.
7. Click on **Next**.
8. Select **Subject Text** and **Sent Date** (re-order the fields with the arrows).
9. Click on **Next**.
10. Click on **Change View** properties.
11. Change **View Title** to **Alerts**.
12. Click on **Apply**.
13. Click on **OK**.
14. Select the **Alert Action List** view, the cursor will show up as a cross when placed on the edge of the view, click and drag the view to the lower right-hand side corner.

The alert view will appear next to the KPI as shown in the following screenshot:

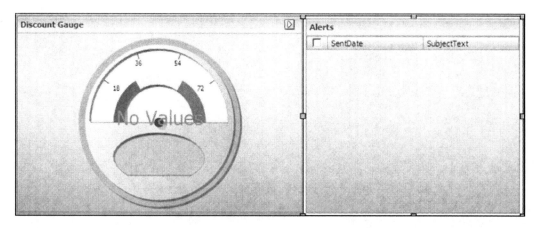

If you want to test the alert, enter a Discount metric such that the average is 65 or above.

You should see the following on the dashboard:

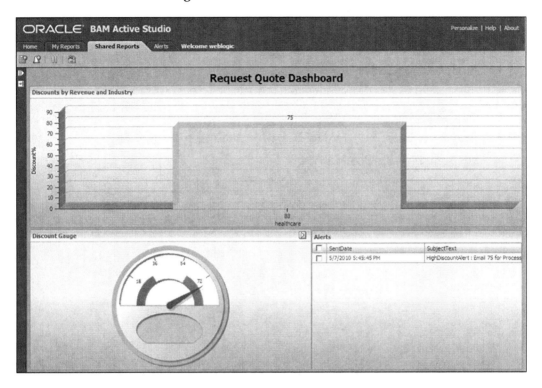

Use architect to edit the content of the data object so that you can test your dashboard with different data.

Challenge exercise: Create an alert that can invoke a web service in your BPM process to allow dynamic process handling based on real-time monitoring.

Summary

With this chapter, you have seen the process measurement capabilities defining metrics and doing analysis in the following areas:

- Defining metrics (in addition to standard ones)
- Specifying sampling points
- Analysis capabilities
- Process cubes with pre-computed data
- Out-of-the-box dashboards on standard metrics
- Support to build custom dashboards to analyze process cubes
- Integrations with Oracle BAM
- Out-of-the-box "Monitor Express" reports
- Support to build reports based on process-specific metrics

14
Using Business Rules

Business rules define the key decisions and policies of your business. They can be used to specify constraints and computations as well as policy and reasoning rules for making business decisions. Some examples are approval matrices, regulatory requirements, discounts, scoring, and coupons based on customer spending. With Oracle Business Rules, these decisions can be automated, enabling flexibility, agility, and equally important, transparency for your business rules.

Introducing Oracle Business Rules

Oracle Business Rules (OBR) provides automation for BPM business rules. This includes tight integration with BPMN process design and the right rules design tools for the business user.

With Business Rules automation, you extract business rules from processes and procedural logic, and express those business rules declaratively. OBR is business focused, letting business users edit business rules with the option to define the rules using BPM Studio or the browser-based BPM Composer. Additionally, you can create custom user interfaces for the browser or other applications.

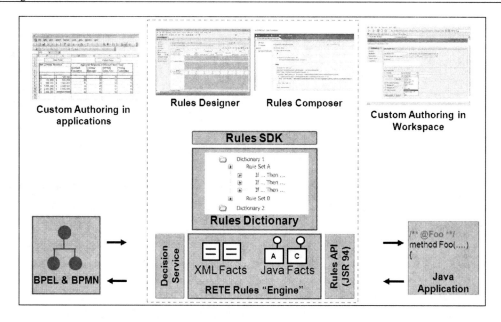

The rules that you create are defined in a **rule dictionary**. A rule dictionary contains multiple **rulesets** that are made up of **rules**. A ruleset can be defined as a service and accessed via API or Web services. Alternatively, the rule dictionary can be a component in the BPMN composite application and the rulesets accessed directly by the BPMN process.

OBR execution is in an inference capable business rules engine. The OBR engine runs in the Unified Runtime SOA Infrastructure along with the BPMN engine. This allows for optimal performance and simplified execution configuration.

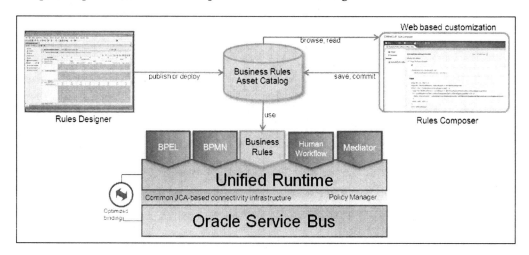

After publishing or deploying a BPM project, the rule resides in the **Business Rules Asset Catalog**, where it is accessed by BPM Composer for editing and by the composite runtime for execution.

Using business rules from BPM

Business rules are used throughout the BPM Suite. Not only are they a component in the BPMN process, but they are also used by BPM Workspace for user-defined task management and vacation rules. They can also be used by Human Workflow to identify the proper recipient for a task assignment and for dynamic service binding in the composite. The rules you define can be used throughout the product, not just in the process design.

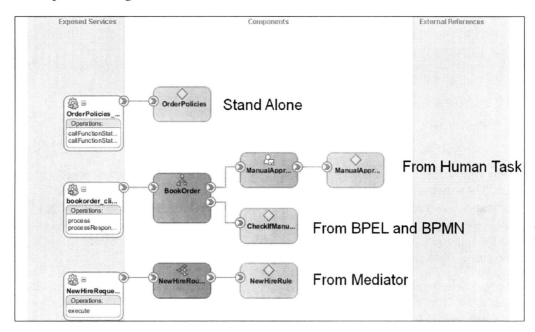

While complex rule definition is often done using BPM Studio, BPM Composer can handle these complex editing tasks as well. In addition, the browser-based BPM Composer is suited to the business user who needs to modify a rule due to changing business conditions. Business rules can not only be changed after being published for shared development, but also after deployment in a composite that is running.

The BPM Suite is built with the business user in mind and the Business Rules component is built with agility in mind. Together, the business user has flexibility and speed for managing business rules.

Business rules concepts

What is a business rule? A **business rule** contains the key decisions and policy computational logic that is separate from the process logic. When the business changes, the policies may change but the process logic typically does not. You still need, for example, a manager approval for certain types of expense reports but how you decide when you need that approval is a business decision. The expense report process stays the same.

Some examples of decision logic that is best moved to a business rule include the following:

- Risk determination — loan, insurance, credit
- Automation of decision steps — approval rules
- Product configuration
- Benefits determination — pensions, unemployment
- Assignment — leads, opportunities
- Order decomposition
- Customer privacy
- Sarbanes-Oxley

When you execute a business rule in OBR, you are executing a ruleset, a set of rules. These rules define your overall Business Rule decision logic. Because the rule engine is an inference engine, it controls the flow of the execution of the rules within the ruleset. You can control this in some ways but it is most effective to leave it to the inference engine as much as possible. This is much easier to maintain than procedural code and relates well to business users.

To begin, when you create a business rule in BPM Suite, you must determine what result you want and what information you need to get that result. The information you provide is called the **input facts** and the result is called the **output facts**. The input and output facts define the rule dictionary. All of the rulesets in a rule dictionary use these input and output facts.

Once the dictionary is defined, the rules can be created. A rule is defined using an **IF-THEN** construct or using a **Decision Table**.

Using IF-THEN rules

An `IF-THEN` rule has two parts—the condition and the action. An `IF-THEN` rule may be simple or complex.

The condition is an expression that can evaluate to true or false. The action sets the result data. Here is an example of a simple `IF-THEN` rule:

A complex `IF-THEN` rule utilizes additional functionality. This functionality is exposed when the user selects the **Advanced** checkbox. In this way, the normal case shows only a simplified list of actions and the rules designer has a simplified view to make rules editing easier.

When in Advanced mode, there are additional actions offered in the selection list, including the `while` loop, error handling, and others. This is appropriate for advanced users. The following example shows some advanced `IF-THEN` rules constructs:

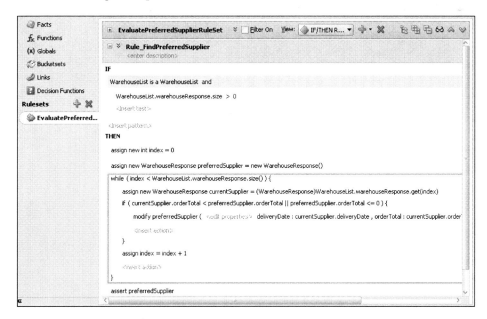

Using decision tables

Decision tables are an efficient way to describe a rule when there are many conditions and many result actions. You set up the table with each set of conditions in a column and for each, you specify the action. However, the decision table can also be utilized when there are few conditions. Sometimes, it's just more convenient.

Here is a simple, easy-to-read decision table:

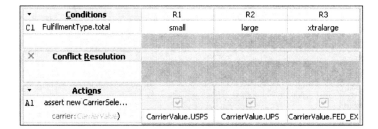

▾	Conditions	R1	R2	R3
C1	FulfillmentType.total	small	large	xtralarge
✕	**Conflict Resolution**			
▾	**Actions**			
A1	assert new CarrierSele...	☑	☑	☑
	carrier: *CarrierValue*)	CarrierValue.USPS	CarrierValue.UPS	CarrierValue.FED_EX

One of the additional benefits of using the decision table is that it calculates where there are conflicting cases, where your ranges overlap, and also calculates where your rules miss a value or range in the input data. The following decision table shows a conflict where the business user has selected to have **R5** override **R3**:

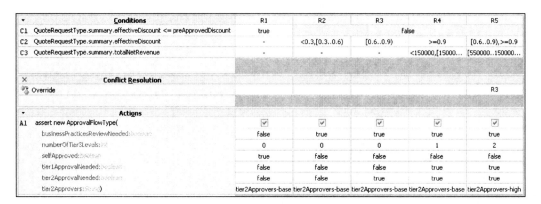

▾	Conditions	R1	R2	R3	R4	R5
C1	QuoteRequestType.summary.effectiveDiscount <= preApprovedDiscount	true		false		
C2	QuoteRequestType.summary.effectiveDiscount	-	<0.3,[0.3..0.6)	[0.6..0.9)	>=0.9	[0.6..0.9),>=0.9
C3	QuoteRequestType.summary.totalNetRevenue	-	-	-	<150000,[15000...	[550000..150000...
✕	**Conflict Resolution**					
⚙	Override					R3
▾	**Actions**					
A1	assert new ApprovalFlowType(	☑	☑	☑	☑	☑
	businessPracticesReviewNeeded: *boolean*	false	true	true	true	true
	numberOfTier3Levels: *int*	0	0	0	1	2
	selfApproved: *boolean*	true	false	false	false	false
	tier1ApprovalNeeded: *boolean*	false	false	false	true	true
	tier2ApprovalNeeded: *boolean*	false	false	true	true	true
	tier2Approvers: *String*)	tier2Approvers-base	tier2Approvers-base	tier2Approvers-base	tier2Approvers-base	tier2Approvers-high

Decision tables help you design your multi-condition business rules with conflict and gap analysis. This helps make the rule design easy to read and robust.

Using aggregates

Aggregates are essential when defining business rules that combine information. OBR includes out-of-box aggregation functions: `count`, `average`, `minimum`, `maximum`, `sum`, `collection`.

Aggregates are commonly part of a decision rule. An example: If an order has more than five items with a price less than 1000, then it requires manual approval. Here, the rule uses the `count aggregate` function:

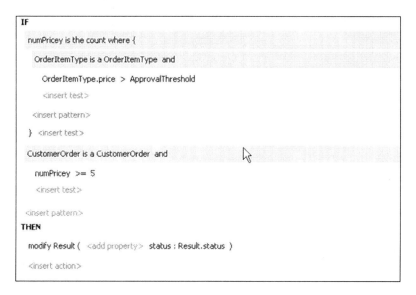

In addition to the provided functions, you can define a custom aggregation function.

Tutorial: Adding determine approvals to the Request Quote process

In this section of the tutorial, you add a business rule to determine how to manage the Approve Deal participant list.

Creating and using new business rules

The first step in this section is to add a new business rule activity to the process. Then, before defining the rule itself, you create the Business Object that defines the input fact, all of the information required to determine the rule result.

1. Add the activity and the business object and then the data object. The following figure shows transition between the **Enter Quote Details** activity and **Is Business Practices Review required?** gateway:

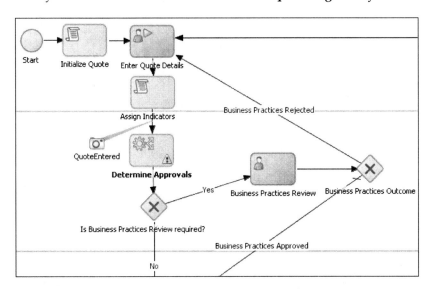

2. Specify the name of the activity as **Determine Approvals** and click on **OK**.

3. In the **BPM Project Navigator**, expand **Business Catalog** and right-click on the **Data** module. Select **New | Business Object**.

4. Add a new **Business Object**, **ApprovalFlow**, based on the schema element **ApprovalFlow** in **Quote.xsd**.

5. Close the **Business Object** window and select somewhere in the open BPM process in order to set the context for the structure menu in the lower left pane.

6. Right-click on **Process Data Objects** and add a new **Process Data Object** called **ApprovalFlow**, of **Business Object** type **ApprovalFlow** that you just created.

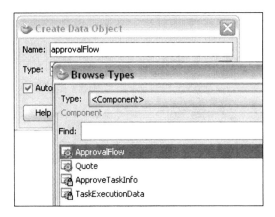

Once you have the Business and Data Object, you can create the rule.

1. Go to the **Implementation** tab of the **Determine Approvals** activity and click on the green **+** icon.

2. In the **Create Business Rule** dialog:

   i. Specify **Name** as **ApprovalRules**.

   ii. Click on the green + next to **Input and Outputs Data Objects**, select **Add Input Data Object**, and then drag **quote** element from the **Data Object** pane into the **Input and Outputs Data Objects** pane.

iii. In the **Direction** drop-down, select **Output**, and then drag **Approval-Flow** from the **Data Object** pane.

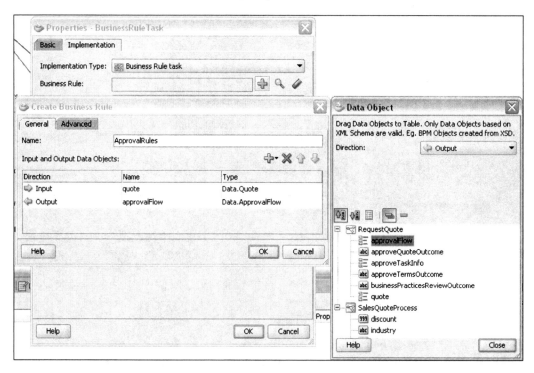

3. Double check that you have the input and output directions correct. Click on **OK**. This creates the rule dictionary. Click on **OK** again to close the dialog.

4. Click on **Save All**. Now, bind the Business Rules Activity to the implementation.

5. Double-click on the **Determine Approvals** Business Rules activity again and select the **Implementation** tab.

6. Click on the **Edit** (denoted by a pencil icon) next to **Use Associations** and in the **Data Associations** dialog, notice the data associations are set properly. Click on **OK**.

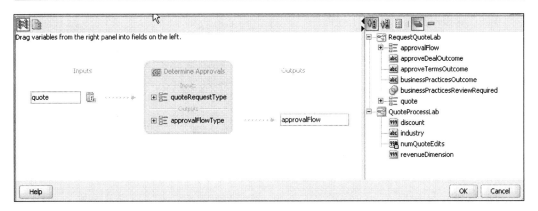

Defining rules

Now it's time to define the rule within the dictionary you just created.

Typically, you want to write rules such that a business user can alter the rule behavior without actually touching the rule logic. This can be achieved in OBR using **Globals**. In this section, you define three Globals to facilitate rule authoring and maintenance. These are as follows:

Global	Type	Value	Final
preApprovedDiscount	Double	0.3	Yes
tier2Approvers-base	String	"wfaulk"	Yes
tier2Approvers-high	String	"wfaulk, jlondon"	Yes

1. Go to the **BPM Project Navigator**, expand the **Business Catalog**, the **Rules** category, and the dictionary folder. Double-click on **ApprovalRules.rules**. This opens the rules editor.

2. Create a new **Global** called `preApprovedDiscount` to model what level of discount does not need any approvals. Discounts greater than this will need approvals. Complete the following:

    ° Select the **Globals** tab and click on the green + to add a new global.

    ° Specify **Name** as **preApprovedDiscount**.

    ° Select **double** for **Type**.

    ° Click on the **Launch Expression builder...** icon next to **Value**, and specify **0.3** in the **expression** section.

    ° Make sure that **Final** checkbox is selected.

3. Create Global `tier2Approvers-base` to configure tier2 approvers as follows:

    ○ Select **Globals** tab and click on the green **+** to add a new global.

    ○ Specify **Name** as **tier2Approvers-base**.

    ○ Select **String** for **Type**.

    ○ Click on the **Launch Expression builder...** icon next to **Value**, and specify `wfaulk` in the **expression** section.

    ○ Make sure that **Final** checkbox is selected.

4. Create **Global** `tier2Approvers-high` to configure tier2 approvers as follows:

    ○ Select **Globals** tab and click on the green **+** to add a new global.

    ○ Specify **Name** as **tier2Approvers-high**.

    ○ Select **String** for **Type**.

    ○ Click on the **Launch Expression builder...** icon next to **Value**, and specify **wfaulk,jlondon** in the **expression** section.

    ○ Make sure that **Final** checkbox is selected.

Defining bucketsets to use in the decision table

A decision table works by dividing each of its condition variables into a finite set of possible values or ranges, called **Bucketsets** in Oracle Business Rules. Bucketsets are another mechanism, similar to globals, by which a business user can change rules without actually editing them. In this section, you define Bucketsets for discounts and revenues. You use these two Bucketsets in a decision table later in this lab.

1. Create **Bucketset** `DiscountBuckets` as follows:

    ○ Click on **Bucketsets** tab.

    ○ Click on the green **+** and select **list of ranges**.

    ○ Select the entry just created and click on the edit (pencil) icon.

    ○ Specify **Name** as `DiscountBuckets`.

    ○ For **Data Type**, select **double**.

    ○ Click on the green **+** next to **Range Bucket Values** 3 times for a total of 4.

      ○   For the three entries just created, change the **Endpoint** column to **0.3**, **0.6**, and **0.9**.

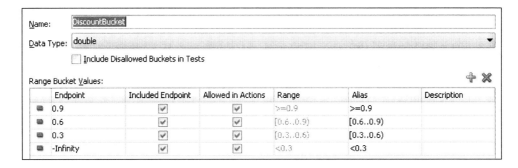

2. Create Bucketset as follows:

      ○   Click on the **Bucketsets** tab.

      ○   Click on the green **+** and select **list of ranges**.

      ○   Select the just created entry and click on the edit (pencil) icon.

      ○   Specify **Name** as **RevenueBuckets**.

      ○   For **Data Type**, select **double**.

      ○   Click on the green **+** next to **Range Bucket Values** three times for a total of 4.

      ○   For the three entries just created, change the **Endpoint** column to **150000**, **550000**, and **1500000**.

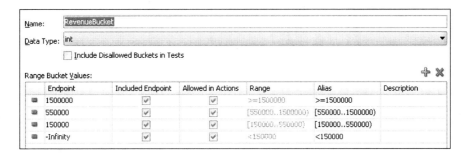

 If you wanted, you could have given some meaningful aliases; however, in these scenarios, the default aliases are descriptive and so you do not need to specify any aliases.

Creating a new decision table

This rule is defined by a decision table.

1. Click on **Rulesets** `Ruleset_1`.

2. Click on the pull-down arrow next to the green **+** and select **Create Decision Table**.

3. Click on **DecisionTable_1** and change the name to **ApprovalMatrix** (remember to hit the *Enter* key).

4. Add the condition `QuoteSummaryType.effectiveDiscount <= preApprovedDiscount` as follows:

   ° Click on the green **+** and select **Condition**.

   ° Double-click on **edit condition** and then click on the **Expression Builder** icon.

   ° From the **Variables** tab of the **Expression Builder**, select **QuoteSummaryType**, expand it, select **effectiveDiscount**, and click on **Insert Into Expression**.

   ° Type **<=**.

   ° From the **Constants** tab, select **preApprovedDiscount** and click on **Insert Into Expression**.

   ° Click on **OK**.

5. Add the condition **QuoteSummaryType.effectiveDiscount** as follows:

   ° Click on the green **+** and select **Condition**.

   ° Double-click on **edit condition**, expand **QuoteSummaryType**, and select **effectiveDiscount**.

   ° Add condition **QuoteSummaryType.totalNetRevenue**.

   ° Click on the green **+** and select **Condition**.

   ° Double-click on **edit condition**, expand **QuoteSummaryType**, and select **totalNetRevenue**.

   ° Click on **Save-All**.

6. Select the second condition, **QuoteSummaryType.effectiveDiscount**, click on the **Local List of Ranges** pull-down, and select the earlier created **Bucketset DiscountBuckets**.

7. Select the third condition, **QuoteSummaryType.totalNetRevenue**, click on the **Local List of Ranges** pull-down, and select the earlier created **Bucketset RevenueBuckets**.

Specifying actions for the decision table

After specifying the conditions, specify the actions for each rule.

1. Click on the green **+** and select **Action | Assert New**.

2. Double-click on **assert new** in the **Actions** section.

3. Select **ApprovalFlowType** for **Value**.

4. Check **Parameterized** column for all parameters.

5. Click on **OK** and click on **Save All**.

6. Add rules **R1** to **R4**, as shown in the following screenshot.

   Add each rule completely, one at a time, and set each of the three conditions. The new rule appears first in the left-most column and then moves right as you enter each of the three condition values, so that you can see how it fits in the big picture as you add the condition values. This is an optimization while you enter the rules.

7. Click on the **?** in the first row and check **true**.

8. Click on the green **+** and select **Rule**.

9. Click on the **?** in the first row and check **false**.

10. Continue adding rules and the values shown in the following screenshot. For the cells with no values, right-click the **?** and select **Don't Care**.

11. After adding the rules, add the actions, as shown for each rule:

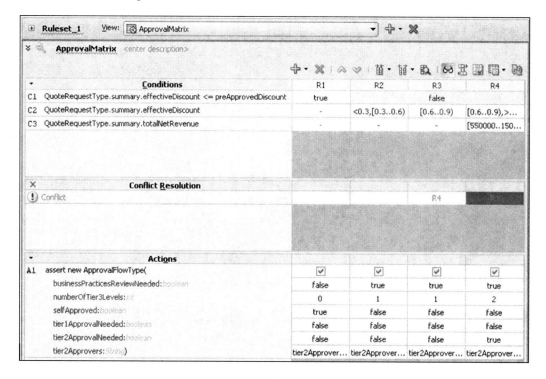

	Conditions	R1	R2	R3	R4
C1	QuoteRequestType.summary.effectiveDiscount <= preApprovedDiscount	true		false	
C2	QuoteRequestType.summary.effectiveDiscount	-	<0.3,[0.3..0.6)	[0.6..0.9)	[0.6..0.9),>...
C3	QuoteRequestType.summary.totalNetRevenue	-	-	-	[550000..150...

	Conflict Resolution				
⚠	Conflict			R4	

	Actions				
A1	assert new ApprovalFlowType(	☑	☑	☑	☑
	businessPracticesReviewNeeded: *boolean*	false	true	true	true
	numberOfTier3Levels: *int*	0	1	1	2
	selfApproved: *boolean*	true	false	false	false
	tier1ApprovalNeeded: *boolean*	false	false	false	false
	tier2ApprovalNeeded: *boolean*	false	false	false	true
	tier2Approvers: *String*)	tier2Approver...	tier2Approver...	tier2Approver...	tier2Approver...

Using conflict detection

Notice that there is a conflict between **R3** and **R4**. In this case, **R4** is a more specific rule and you want it to override **R3**.

1. Double-click on the **Conflict** cell in **R4** column and select **Override** as the conflict resolution method.

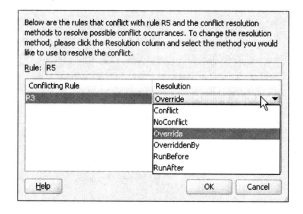

2. Click on the **Gap Analysis** icon, and select the identified gap to be added to the decision table by selecting the checkbox above the set of conditions.

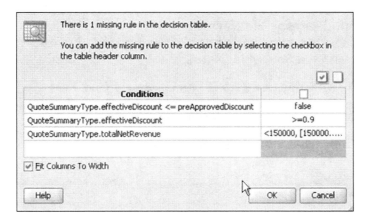

3. Specify the action values for the rule added by gap analysis. At the end, the decision table should look like the following:

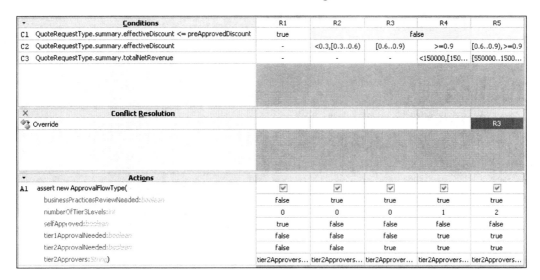

4. Save and close **ApprovalRules**.

Changing branch test for Business Practices Review required

Now that the rule determines if Business Practices Review is required, you need to change the expression for the **Yes** branch. Remember this is hardcoded to always be false, based on the value you set in the **Initialize Quote** script activity.

1. Open the properties for the **Yes** branch coming from the **Is Business Practices Review required?** gateway to the **Business Practices Review** activity.

2. On the **Properties** tab, set the expression to test the value returned from the rule.

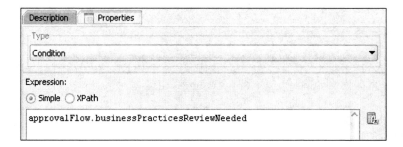

Testing

Now, test your new business rule.

1. Re-deploy the composite project.

2. Initiate a new instance.

3. Log in to Enterprise Manager and click on the instance ID of the newly created QuoteProcessLab instance. This pops up the **Flow Trace** window.

4. In the **Flow Trace** window, click on the **Approval Rules**.

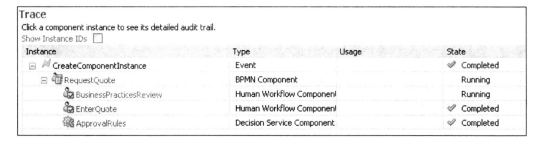

5. You see the input data to the decision service and the result returned by it.

6. You can also select the BPMN component, `RequestQuoteLab` and view the process flow. Expand the rule activity here and select the link for **instance left the activity** to view the payload of the rule result.

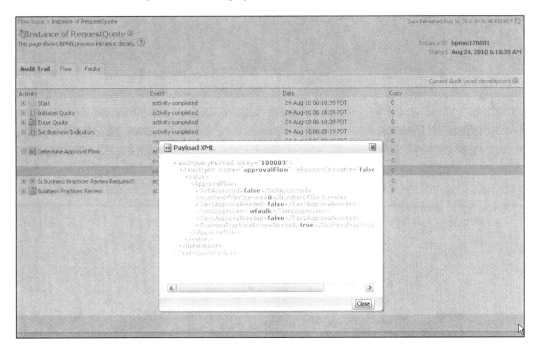

Summary

Business Rules are used to extract business logic from procedural logic. In this section of the tutorial, you created a Business Rule for the process that defines the approval flow and approval participants. In the next chapter, you will use the results of this Business Rule to define the process flow and Human Workflow participants. Once the Business Rule is in place, it can be changed without changing the process logic.

15
Using Human Task Patterns and Other Concepts

Human workflow — the ability to manage work assignment, routing, and completion in accordance with business policies and rules — is an integral component of Oracle Business Process Management. The **Human Task** component implements interactive human workflow in the business process.

Introducing Human Task

In Oracle Business Process Management, the Human Task is represented by the **BPMN Interactive Task** activity in the BPMN process. This refers to a step in the business process that is managed by the Human Task workflow engine.

A Human Task can be a single task activity for a single user or it can represent a complex participant pattern involving users and groups in sequence and in parallel. These patterns could be implemented by the process flow itself but using the functionality provided in Human Task, these patterns are defined declaratively and can be dynamic.

The **Human Task Participant** defines the business users who need to carry out the Interactive Task. The task is presented to the users through a browser-based worklist application. The associated task is shown in the inbox of the assigned users when the Interactive Task is triggered. In addition to assigned users, two additional participants optionally can be defined for a task, **Error Assignee**, and **Reviewers**. The error assignee receives the task if there is an error in the participant definition. The reviewers receive the task but do not affect the task outcome or process flow.

The **Human Workflow Service** implements the Human Task component. It runs as an engine on the unified runtime, SOA infrastructure. When the BPMN component triggers a Human Task, the Human Workflow Service is responsible for routing the task to the user, or set of users, notifying them and so on. Once the final user approves or completes the task, the Human Workflow Service returns to the calling process and the calling process is free to continue.

The Human Workflow Service is made up of a set of workflow components including the Task Management Service, Worklist Service, User Metadata Services, Task Rules Service, and Task Routing Service, and utilizes several components itself such as the User Messaging Service, Identity Management Service, and Rules Service to perform the various actions required. Internally the workflow services use these components through their public APIs, just as any other service would. In addition, the User Messaging Service, Identity Service, and Rules Service are all pluggable so you are free to replace the standard functionality of those with your own specialized functionality if desired.

Using Human Tasks from BPM

In BPM Studio, a Human Task is added to a business process by dragging and dropping the Interactive Task activity from the component palette onto the process flow. The Participant is set automatically to the role associated with the swim lane into which the Interactive Task is dropped. There are five different Interactive Task activities in the palette that set different Participant patterns for common assignment and routing patterns and a sixth Interactive Task used for complex patterns.

A Human Task has three parts to it:

- Interactive Task activity
- Task definition
- The task form for the browser user interface

In the Interactive Task properties, the process variables are mapped to and from the task payload to specify the data provided to and received from the human participants.

In addition to the participant, the task definition includes the data payload associated with the task, notifications, routing, and other properties. The task definition is stored outside of the business process in a separate task file and is reusable by other processes. In addition to triggering and waiting for the task completion, the process may choose to receive finer grained events during task execution and react to them.

Every Human Task has to be bound to a task definition. You can either browse for existing task definitions or create one on the fly. Multiple Interactive Tasks can share the same Human Task definition.

The user interface is an ADF form which binds the task payload to the form data controls. The form can be generated automatically, which is especially helpful during development and testing. Later, for production, the form is usually customized for the purposes of the business process.

Human Task participant patterns

The following are the set of selected Human Task patterns provided by Oracle BPM Studio. These are based on the Interactive Task BPMN construct and makes it easy for the designer to use the different participant patterns. These are shortcuts for the designer. Any of these could be defined manually by setting the correct property values during task creation.

- **Initiate Task** (User Initiate Task) — when this type of task appears in a swim lane, the users who have that swim lane role see a link in Workspace to initiate the process.

- **User Task** (Single Approver) — this is a simple pattern where the participant is defined by the swim lane. This is the default pattern.

- **Management Task** (Sequential Management Chain) — this pattern is a set of users defined by a specified number of levels of management.

- **Voting Task** (Parallel Voting Group) — with a voting pattern, the users receive the task at the same time and the process waits until the specified number of tasks are completed.

- **FYI Task** (FYI pattern) — with this pattern, the process does not wait for task completion but continues on ahead.

- **Complex Task** (for combination patterns) — here is where the designer can specify pattern combinations; for example, Management Chain and FYI might be used to inform but not wait for one user but the process does wait for the managers to complete the task.

A Human Task Participant List specifies who gets the task assignment. Except for the Complex Task, for all of these patterns, the participant is defined by the swim lane role. For the Complex Task, specify the Participant List using combinations of participant patterns and users or groups specified by value or expression.

Human Task completion outcome

When a user completes a Human Task in the browser worklist application, the Human Task has a result value called **Outcome**. The user selects the desired outcome to complete the task. The outcome determines what happens next in the process. The designer uses the outcome for conditional branching.

There are predefined outcomes as well as custom outcomes. A custom outcome is a string value added during the task definition.

Predefined outcome choices are: YES, NO, OK, APPROVE, ACCEPT, REJECT, and DEFER.

A custom outcome might be: Submit or Continue.

The semantics of the different outcomes are up to the process designer. A conditional branch can be based on the value of the outcome but where that branch goes and what happens next is part of the process design.

Using Management Chain

Management Chain is a commonly used participant pattern that is sequential and defined by specifying a starting user and either the number of levels of management or the title of the highest manager desired in the chain. The starting user, levels, and title can all be declared dynamically using an expression or Oracle Business Rule.

The task is passed to each user in the management chain. Each user takes action on the task until the end of the chain is reached and the Human Workflow Service returns control to the calling process.

In BPM Studio, when selecting the Management Interactive Task, the starting user is predefined by the swim lane. After the Task definition gets created, the designer specifies the levels of management in the Task definition properties.

Using parallel approvals

The group participant pattern allows users to receive the task in parallel. Tasks in parallel appear in the inbox at the same time for all users defined by the Participant List and can be completed in any order. The participant is by default the swim lane role. The outcome of a parallel task is defined by the **Voted Outcome**.

The Voted Outcome can be defined in two different ways. Either the final result outcome is specified, such as ACCEPT, or the outcome is defined as ANY. When the outcome is specified, the percentage of that outcome must be reached for it to be the result outcome. Otherwise, with ANY, any outcome that reaches that percentage will set the result outcome.

In addition, there is a **Default Outcome** which is used when the specified outcome percentage is not reached, another outcome is used, or the task has expired. For example, set the Voted Outcome to ACCEPT and 67% and set the Default Outcome to REJECT if there must be at least 67% ACCEPT outcomes from the group for the voted outcome result to be ACCEPT. Then, if at least 67% of the users all submit their tasks with ACCEPT, the result outcome is ACCEPT. If say, only 60% submit with ACCEPT, the result is REJECT. For a dynamic result, use ANY and do not set the Default Outcome.

The Voted Outcome specifies how to define the outcome as well as how to continue—either waiting until all of the users have completed their tasks or waiting until only some of them have completed them. Use the radio button selection to immediately trigger the Voted Outcome when the minimum percentage is met or to wait until all votes are in before triggering the voted outcome.

Using Approval Groups

One of the options for building a Participant List is the use of **Approval Groups**. The Approval Groups participant allows for a group to be defined using BPM Workspace Administration instead of requiring it to be defined in LDAP. This means that your BPM processes can have groups specific to the process and defined by the BPM administrator without the need to make group LDAP changes through IT. In this way, the Approval Groups can reflect the business process and the business modeller has the flexibility to define groups on a per process basis. Members of the Approval Group can be defined statically or dynamically. The Approval Group's name can be specified as a value or expression.

Using Notifications

The Human Workflow Service can send notifications when the task changes status such as when the task is assigned or when it is completed. In the task definition **Notifications** tab, select the desired task status and then specify the **Recipient**. The recipient can be defined by type, such as assignees or owner, it can be set to a specific user or group using an LDAP lookup, or it can be specified by an expression.

Finally, define the header that is to be sent with the notification. The header is defined using an expression and can include elements from the task definition such as payload data.

Enter as many rows as you like for whatever status-recipient-header notifications you want to include in your task. By default, three notifications are defined for Interactive Tasks in BPMN, as shown in the following table:

Status	Recipient	Header
Assign	**Assignees**	`Task <%/task:task/task:title%> requires your attention.`
Complete	**Initiator**	`Task <%/task:task/task:title%> requires your attention.`
Error	**Owner**	`Task <%/task:task/task:title%> requires your attention.`

End users who receive notifications must specify how they want to receive them using the preferences link in **BPM Workspace**. This could include e-mail, SMS, pager, or whatever has been configured on the server.

Using escalations and expirations

A task definition can optionally include **Deadlines** by using duration settings specified as expiration or escalation. In both cases, the time is specified as an absolute amount of time or as an expression to compute the duration of time and optionally the business calendar can be used.

The expiration can also be set on a per-participant basis. In this case, it overrides the setting at the task level. When using the participant expiration, the duration settings at the task level can specify a **Renew** option to allow an expired task to be renewed a specified number of times.

When using escalation, specify the management chain as a number of levels or top participant title, such as Manager, or CEO. In addition, you can specify a custom java class to take care of other escalation actions as desired.

In the **Deadlines** tab you can also set a deadline. This would let the user know that the task would be expiring soon.

Tutorial: Using pattern-based, rule-driven approval routing in the Request Quote process

In this part of the tutorial you will add some complexity to the Human Task activity that was created earlier.

1. Open the **SalesQuoteProcess** composite in JDeveloper.

2. Double-click the **ApproveDeal Human Task** from the **Business Catalog** to open it.

3. Ignore the **General** tab for the moment and select the **Data** tab.

4. In the **Data** section, click on the green plus (+) icon and select **Add other payload**.

5. In the **Add Task Parameter** dialog, make sure **Variable** is selected.

6. Select **Element**.

7. Click the browse icon on the right of the **Element** field.

8. Select **Quote.xsd | ApprovalFlow**, and click on the **OK** button.

9. In the same way as just shown in steps 3 to 8, add the following element:

   ° Quote.xsd | ApproveTaskInfo

10. Your **Data** tab should look like this:

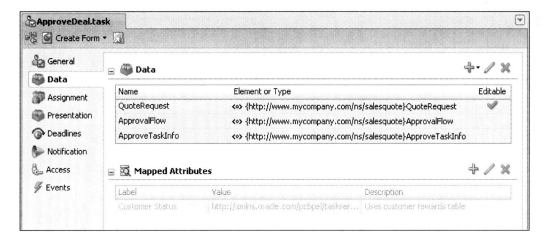

> The **Data** tab lets you specify the data that will be available to the Human Task. Typically the data listed here is what you want to expose to the end user in a task form. But it doesn't have to be. This data can be a superset and you can choose which fields the end user should see.

11. Select the **General** tab.

12. Set type of title to **Text** and **XPath**.

13. Click on the **XPath** editor button on the right of the **Task Title** field.

14. In the **Schema** section, expand **task | payload | QuoteRequest | Summary** and select **AccountName** and click on the **Insert Into Expression** button to add it to the expression.

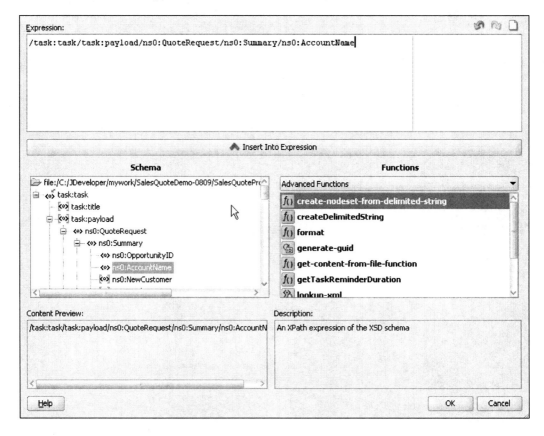

15. Click on the **OK** button.

16. The **Task Title** field is now populated with a reference to that element. Click in the field and put the cursor at the front, and add **Approve Deal for** in the front. At runtime the variable will be replaced with the account name and say something like, "Approve Deal for Big Bank".

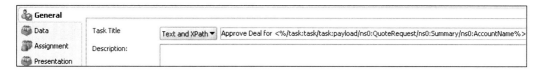

17. In the **Owner** field, select **User** from the drop-down list.

18. Click the browse icon to the right of the **Owner** field to browse users and groups.

19. Make sure that the correct **Application Server** connection is selected. If you have your application server selected, the **Realm** field will have **jazn.com** selected.

20. Click the browse icon on the far right of the **Search Pattern** field and to search.

21. In the **Search User** field, choose **jstein** and click on the **Select** button.

22. Click on the **OK** button.

   Your **General** tab should look like this:

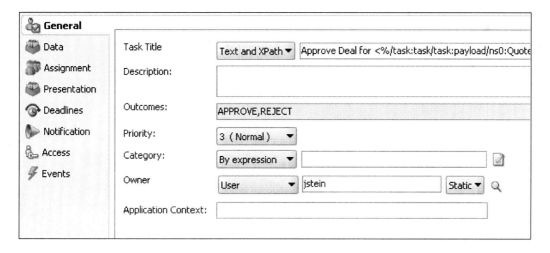

23. Select the **Assignment** tab.

24. Double-click on the stage name (for example, **Stage1**) to edit the name.

25. Change it to **Tier3** and click on the **OK** button.

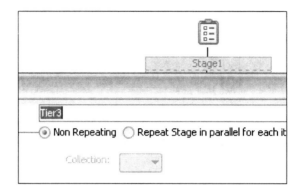

26. Click on the **Participant** box (with the person icon) to select it.

27. Click on the **Edit** button next to the green plus icon. Alternatively you can double-click the **Participant** box to edit it.

28. Specify the following values:

    ° Type: **Serial**

    ° Label: **Sales Management**

    ° Build a list of participants using: **Management Chain**

    ° Specify attributes using: **Value-based**

29. In the **Starting Participant** box, click the green plus icon and select **Add User**.

30. In the **Data Type** field, select **By Expression**.

31. Click on the **...** button in the **Value** field.

32. In the **Expression Builder**, change the **Functions** poplist to **Identity Service Functions**.

33. Select **getManager** and click the **Insert Into Expression** button to add it.

34. In the **Expression** field, put the cursor between the parentheses.

35. In the **Schema** section, select **task | payload | QuoteRequest | Summary | SalesRepId** and add it to the expression.

36. Enter a comma followed by `'jazn.com'` for the realm.

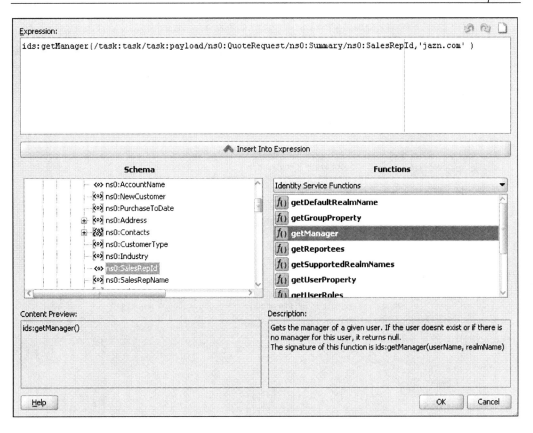

37. Click on the **OK** button.

38. Back in the **Edit Participant Type** dialog, change the **Number of Levels** to **XPath**.

39. Click on the **Expression Builder** icon to the right of the **Number of Levels** field.

40. From the **Schema** field, select **task | payload | ApprovalFlow | NumberOfTier3Levels** and add it to the expression. This value is set at runtime.

41. Click on the **OK** button.

42. The **Edit Participant Type** dialog should look like this:

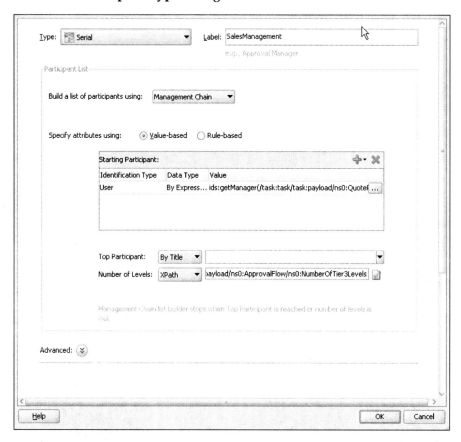

43. Click on the **OK** button to return to the Human Task.

44. Click on the **Tier3** box to select it. Then click on the green plus icon and select **Sequential Stage** to add a new one.

45. Double-click the new stage name (for example, **Stage1**) and rename it to `Tier2`.

46. Double-click on the **Edit Participant** box to open it.

47. Specify the following values:
    ° Type: **Parallel**
    ° Label: **Tier2Approvers**
    ° **Voted Outcomes | Value**: **100**
    ° **Default Outcome**: APPROVE
    ° Wait until all votes are in before triggering outcome: **Selected**
    ° Build a list of participants using: **Names and expressions**
    ° Specify attributes using: **Value-based**

48. Click on the green plus icon in **Participant List** and specify the following values:
    ° Identification Type: User
    ° Data Type: **By Expression**
    ° Value: **/task:task/task:payload/ns0:ApprovalFlow/ns0: Tier2Approvers**
    ° (Use the **Expression Builder** because your namespace might be different)

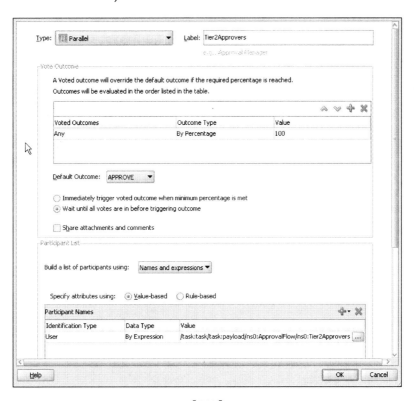

49. Click on the **OK** button.

50. Click on the **Tier2** box to select it. Then click the green plus icon and select **Sequential Stage** to add a new one.

51. Double-click on the new stage name (for example, **Stage1**) and rename it to **Tier1**.

52. Double-click on the **Participant** box to open it.

53. Specify the following values:

    ° Type: **Single**
    ° Label: Tier1.Participant1
    ° Build a list of participants using: **Approval Groups**
    ° Specify attributes using: **Value-based**
    ° Name: **Tier1ApprovalGroup** (you create this group later in the lab)

54. Click on the **OK** button and close the task definition window.

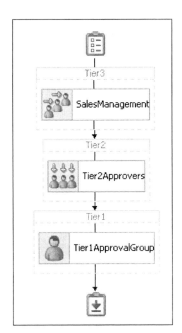

Adding a data assignment

As one of the first steps of this lab exercise, you added two more data items, namely ApprovalFlow and ApproveTaskInfo, to the task definition. The task flow in this human task uses values from the ApprovalFlow data item that were set by the business rules activity earlier in the process. You need to update the Approve Deal task activity in the process to assign these values:

1. Open the BPM process from the **BPM** Navigator.

2. Double-click on the **Approve Deal** activity to open the properties window.

3. Navigate to the **Implementation** tab.

4. Edit the data association to add the **approvalFlow** as one of the inputs:

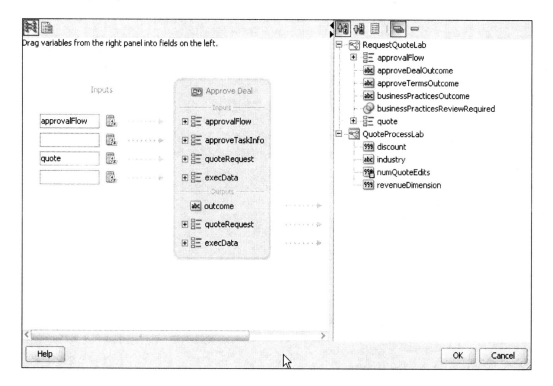

Deploying the application

Deploy the application. You can do this in the **Application Navigator** and deploy the QuoteProcessLab project. See the steps in Chapter 10 for a refresher on how to deploy.

Running

Before you can instantiate a new process, you need to create a new approval group called Tier1ApprovalGroup. Recollect that you defined the Tier 1 approval based on approval groups and defined the group name as Tier1ApprovalGroup. This group needs to be created and members added to it using the BPM Workspace.

Creating the approval group

Using the BPM Workspace you create a new group and add one member cdoyle to it. The following steps will guide you through setting up this new group:

1. Log in to the **BPM Workspace** as weblogic.

2. Click on the **Administration** link at the top of the page.

3. In the **Administration Areas** panel on the left, click on **Approval Groups**.

4. In the **Approval Groups** panel click on the button next to the **+** icon and select **Create Static**.

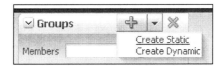

5. Enter **Name** in the **Details** panel as **Tier1ApprovalGroup**.

6. Click on the + to add member cdoyle to this static group.

7. Click on the **Apply** button.

Hierarchy of users

You may find it useful to refer to the following figure during the lab. It shows the demo users and who their managers are. For example, the manager of jcooper is jstein.

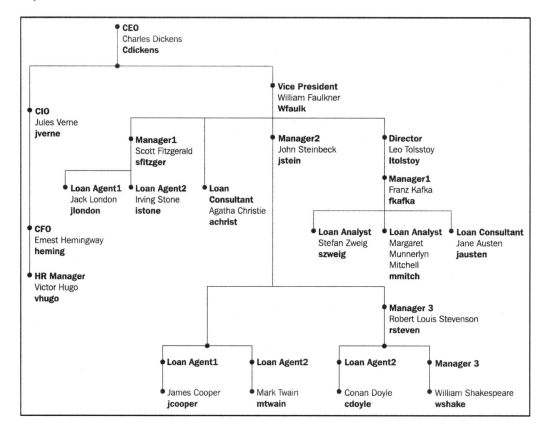

Instantiating a new process

Now you will run a new instance to see the effects of the business rules on the human workflow approvals.

1. Open **BPM Workspace** in a browser: `http://hostname:7001/bpm/workspace` (or port `8001` if you have a managed server).

2. Log in as jcooper/welcome1 (or whoever you set as the SalesRep user).

3. From the **Applications** panel on the left, click on **RequestQuoteLab v2.0**. (Or whatever version you just deployed.)

4. When the **Enter Quote** screen appears, specify the following fields:

   ○ Account Name: Change this from Acme to something memorable and unique to you. For example, `My Cool Company`. If you use a different name each time you run it will be easier to tell the tasks apart later during the approval steps.

   ○ Sale Rep Id: `jcooper`

   ○ Sales Rep Name: `James Cooper`

   ○ Industry: `Media`

   ○ Total Net Revenue: `275000` this value causes the right rule result for this test

   ○ Effective Discount: `0.94` this value causes the right rule result for this test

5. Click on the **Submit** button (on the upper-right).

 According to the business rules, a business practices review is needed. According to the BPM diagram, business practices reviews need to be approved by the Business Practices role, which is jstein.

6. Log out from BPM Workspace and re-login as jstein/welcome1.

7. There should be a task called **Business Practices Review** in the inbox. Click on it and in the details you should see the **Account Name** and other details that you had entered previously.

8. Click on the **Approve** button.

 From the BPM diagram, there are now two approval steps: Approve Deal and Approve Terms. Take a look at Approve Deal first.

In the lab you just completed, you implemented Approve Deal and gave it three assignees. The first assignee is a management chain that goes up a certain number of levels as specified by the business rules. For a deal size of $275,000 and effective discount of 94%, NumberOfTier3Levels is set to 2. So the next approval is jcooper's manager, and then two managers above them.

From the user hierarchy, you can see that jcooper's manager is jstein, whose manager is wfaulk, whose manager is cdickens.

9. Log out from BPM Workspace and re-login as `jstein/welcome1`.

10. There should be a task called **Approve Deal** for BigCorp (or whatever you named your account) in the inbox. Click on it and in the details you should see the **Account Name** and other details that you entered earlier.

11. Click on the **Approve** button.

12. Log out from BPM Workspace and re-login as `wfaulk/welcome1`.

13. There should be a task called **Approve Deal** for BigCorp (or whatever you named your account) in the inbox. Click on it and in the details you should see the **Account Name** that you entered earlier.

14. Click on the **Approve** button.

15. Log out from BPM Workspace and re-login as `cdickens/welcome1`.

16. There should be a task called **Approve Deal** for BigCorp (or whatever you named your account) in the inbox. Click on it and in the details you should see the **Account Name and** other details that you entered earlier.

17. Click on the **Approve** button.

 That completes the first assignee of Approve Deal. The second assignee is Tier2 approvers. According to the business rules, the Tier2 approver is wfaulk.

18. Log out from BPM Workspace and re-login as wfaulk/welcome1.

19. wfaulk will actually have two tasks. That's because he's the approver for the second assignee of the **Approve Deal**, but is also the approver for **Approve Term**, which is assigned to the **Contracts** role, which wfaulk is a member of.

20. There should be a task called **Approve Deal** for BigCorp (or whatever you named your account) in the inbox. Click on it and in the details you should see the **Account Name** that you entered earlier.

21. Click on the **Approve** button.

22. As you're here, approve the other task which is for the same instance.

23. Select **Approve Terms** task and approve it.

24. Now you are up to the third assigned of the **Approve Deal** task, which is assigned to the **Tier1ApprovalGroup** role. Earlier in the lab you created this role and made cdoyle a member.

25. Log out from BPM Workspace and re-login as cdoyle/welcome1.

26. There should be a task called **Approve Deal** for BigCorp (or whatever you named your account) in the inbox. Click on it and in the details you should see the **Account Name** that you entered earlier.

27. Click on the **Approve** button.

28. From the BPM diagram, both **Approve Deal** and **Approve Terms** are now complete. So the process flow has moved to **Finalize Contracts**. The contract approver is `wfaulk`.

29. Log out from BPM Workspace and re-login as `wfaulk/welcome1`.

30. There should be a task called **Finalize Contracts** (or whatever you named your account) in the inbox. Click on it and in the details you should see the **Account Name** that you entered earlier.

31. Click on the **OK** button (remember the outcome was set to **OK** instead of **Accept/Reject**).

32. The process is now complete. You can log on to **Enterprise Manager** (for example, `http://localhost:7001/em`) and see if the instance is complete.

33. Click on the **ApproveDeal Human Workflow Component** link to see the task progression through the different approvers.

Why did wfaulk have to approve the Approve Deal task twice? It's because he is in the management chain for jcooper and is also a Tier2 Approver. You can use a different user for SalesRep and get a different result. Just change the SalesRep role using BPM Workspace. Try vhugo.

Other scenarios

You can run other scenarios by seeing the options in the business rules. For example, create an instance with an effective discount of higher between 0.3 and 0.6, or greater than 0.9, or with revenue higher than 150,000, or over 550,000 and so on.

This is left as an exercise for the reader.

Summary

In this chapter, you learned about some of the more advanced concepts of Human Task functionality and how you can create a complex participant pattern in the task definition.

16
User Interface Development for Human Tasks

In the previous chapter, you created complex user task routing and assignment using the human workflow services that are available in Oracle BPM 11*g*. Most user tasks require a user interface to the task details that will help the user complete his assigned tasks. As you know, BPM Workspace provides a comprehensive task-list application for doing just that. In the previous exercises, you autogenerated task forms for each of the user tasks in your process.

If you noticed, these autogenerated forms were single-page forms and all used the same layout. This may be good enough for tasks with simple user interface requirements but for a significant number of use cases, a single page with the default layout may not be good enough. You may also need to have your task forms comply with standard look and feel and branding. The default autogenerated forms may not meet these requirements.

A good case in point is our Sales Quote process. The process starts with the sales representative entering a new quote. A typical quote would require the user to provide some header-level details such as the opportunity information, customer information, and so on. He then needs to enter the products for which the quote is being prepared, followed by the addition of terms and conditions, if any. As you can see, this form needs to be a multipage form. A multipage form means that it will most likely also need to have some page-flow logic implemented so that the user can easily navigate between the different parts of the sales quote being created.

Such a use case would require a significant amount of UI programming. Fortunately, Oracle BPM 11*g* with the use of Application Development Framework or ADF makes this task much simpler.

It is difficult to cover ADF in a few pages so we will try to give you a quick primer on ADF that will provide you with a basic understanding and help you to complete the hands-on exercises in this book.

Introducing ADF

Oracle Application Development Framework provides a complete application development and runtime environment for creating rich web-based applications. ADF provides a declarative and model-based approach to creating web applications using the **Model-View-Controller (MVC)** pattern.

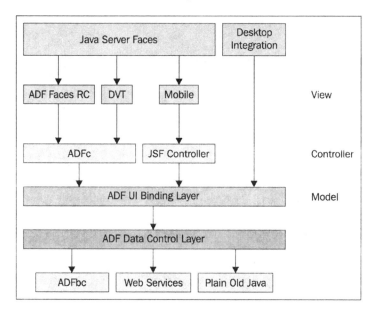

Key components in ADF

Following are the key components that make up ADF:

- **ADFv** is the view layer of the MVC pattern and includes Java Server Pages (**JSP**), Struts, Java Server Faces (**JSF**), and **ADF Faces Rich Client (ADF Faces RC)**, and Data Visualization Tool (**DVT**) components

- **ADFc** provides the page controller functionality and is an extension of the JSF navigation model that adds, among other features, declarative transaction handling

- **ADFm** is the model in this MVC-based framework and provides data to the view layer by way of **data controls**

- **ADFbc** is an object-relational mapping framework that allows you to create rich web applications that work with relational databases via entity and view objects

- **ADFdi** or ADF Desktop Integration lets you integrate ADF applications with Microsoft Office 2007

The ADF Controller

In a Model-View-Controller pattern, the controller is responsible for receiving input and interacting with the model layer to provide responses that the view layer can then render in a suitable form. At its core, it is a page flow controller. MVC framework works such that Struts and JSF provide just such a controller.

Since ADF is based on JSF, why did Oracle create the ADF Controller? JSF handles basic page flow tasks and is probably sufficient for basic web applications. When it comes to creating Rich Internet Applications (**RIA**) it doesn't address a number of core requirements such as:

- Navigation within a single page. RIAs aim to provide the same user experience as a desktop application. This means that the standard, whole page navigation will not work. You would need to manage flows between fragments of a single page.

- Out of the box, the JSF controller only deals with pages, but in any non-trivial application you may need to execute code in between two view pages. You may also need to handle conditional branching between pages. Although this is possible in JSF, you need to either code for it or extend the controller and implement your own extensions to handle these cases.

- JSF doesn't allow for reuse of flows. Although you can define multiple flow definitions, at runtime it is compiled into one single flow.

The ADF Controller extends JSF and fills these gaps and also adds more features. One of the most important concepts ADF introduces is that of bounded and unbounded task flows. Before we look at the types of task flows, let us quickly look at the components that make up a flow.

Task flow components

A task flow is the definition of how control passes through the pages of a web application, though in an ADF task flow, you can define more than just pages. A task flow can contain one or more of the following components:

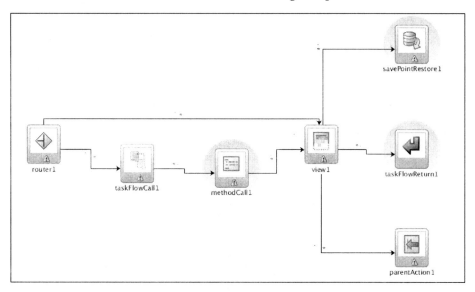

- Router—conditional routing based on expression evaluation
- Task Flow Call—calls another bounded task flow from this task flow
- Method Call—allows you to call a Java method
- View—corresponds to a JSP page or a page fragment
- Task Flow Return—returns from the calling task flow (available only for bounded task flows)
- Parent Action—navigates to the parent task flow
- Save Point Restore—restores a save point in the current transaction

Unbounded task flow

These types of task flows (or page flows) have no explicit start or end and therefore have multiple entry points. A user can navigate directly to any page in an unbounded task flow. This corresponds to the page flow that JSF supports. ADF applications can only have one unbounded task flow at runtime. It is possible to define multiple unbounded task flows in different flow definitions but at runtime they are merged into a single logical flow. Typically, you would use an unbounded task flow as your main entry point. This in turn can call appropriate bounded task flows as required.

Bounded task flow

As the name suggests, bounded task flows have a boundary and have only one entry point and one or more exit points. They can be called from other unbounded or bounded flows. They can also be nested in pages or page fragments using special ADF components called **region components**. Bounded task flows can also take parameters and are stateful. This allows a bounded task flow to be reused. Since a bounded task flow can also have exit points, it can also return data when it returns.

ADF Business Components (ADFBC)

ADFBC provides a simplified, yet powerful, framework for using relational database objects such as tables and views in Java. ADFBC uses a metadata-based, declarative approach that makes it easy to create complex database-based Java EE applications by using SQL queries to defined database access. The tooling also autogenerates SQL queries based on user selection and manages master-detail relationships between tables by introspecting foreign key relationships. ADFBC provides full transaction control with support for locking and state management.

Not only can ADFBC be used in standard Java programs, but one can also expose **Application Modules** in ADFBC as services as **Service Data Objects** (SDO).

ADFBC plays an important role in BPM projects, especially when creating complex task forms. Another very useful feature is the ability to use ADFBC view objects as facts in Oracle Business Rules.

Tutorial: Building the ADF task forms

You will now build an ADF application using the Human Workflow task data controls that provide a user-friendly and rich user interface for your workflow tasks.

Oracle BPM Suite fully leverages the ADF framework for its workflow application. Naturally, task forms associated with a task are also ADF pages. These task forms are user-defined ADF pages created as part of a task flow and registered with the workflow application so that when the user navigates to the task, the appropriate task form is displayed alongside the task.

In this lab you will implement user interfaces for the following three task flows:

- Forms for entering a quote
- Forms for reviewing the quote
- Forms for approving the deal

Although you can use the Create Form wizard from the human task definition to create task forms, you are limited to a default task flow with a single page. Of course, you can then add more pages to the flow, but these additional pages will have to be created using the standard ADF page designer only. For this lab, you are creating moderately complex UI, hence you won't be using the automatic form generation feature.

To ease the page design, you are provided with page templates that already have the basic page layout completed. You will be using these templates to create your task form pages. Make sure that you follow the instructions for each task flow for copying in the appropriate templates.

Task forms for entering a quote

One of the first activities in the Sales Quote process is creating a new sales quote and is initiated as a user task. You created this task as a simple approval task with a default task form.

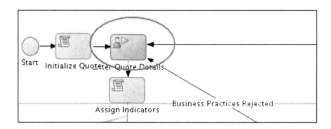

You will now create a custom user interface for this user task for capturing the details of a quote.

Setup

You have created default UI forms for all the human tasks in the process in the previous exercises. In this lab you recreate those same forms from ground up. In order to start from a clean slate, you need to delete all the UI projects from the JDeveloper application work space. Follow these steps for removing the default UI projects:

1. Exit JDeveloper and save your existing application by copying it to another folder or archiving it as a ZIP file. Make sure that you copy the full directory tree starting with the directory that contains the application workspace file, `SalesQuoteLab.jws`.

2. Start JDeveloper, open the **Application Navigator**, right-click on the **ApproveDealUILab** UI project, and select **Delete Project**.

3. In the **Confirm Delete Project** dialog window, select **Remove project and delete all of its contents**.

Repeat this for the following UI projects:

- BusinessPracticesReviewUILab
- EnterQuoteUILab

Do not delete the following UI projects:

- ApproveTermsUILab
- FinalizeContractsUILab

Creating a new UI project

Start by creating a new project that will contain the form for entering the quote:

1. Create a new project from the **Application** menu.

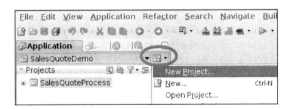

2. In the **New Gallery** window select **Generic Project** and click on the **OK** button.

3. The project dialog opens. Name your project **EnterQuoteUILab** and click on the **Finish** button.

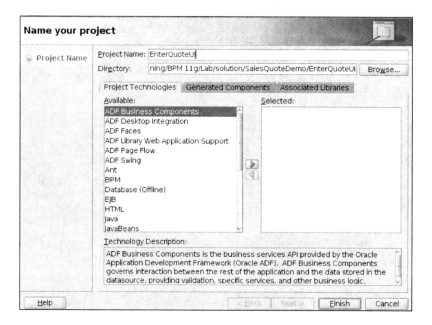

4. Click on **Save All** to save.

Creating ADF business components

To create a sales quote you will need, in addition to other data, products that you are creating the quote for. In the task form, the user should be able to select products to add to the quote. Typically, this list would come from an item master or price list in a database.

For this lab, you use ADFBC view objects that provide this product data. You also create a second view object for providing the different terms and conditions that one can choose to add to the quote.

 If you have not already created the QUOTE database schema, run the SQL scripts `c:\bpm\sql\create_user.sql` and `quote.sql`.

If you are using the pre-configured Amazon EC2 instance, these scripts have already been run. You can verify that the scripts have run by creating a database connection in JDeveloper for a user named **quote** with **quote** as the password.

The following steps illustrate how to create the business components for the products and license terms:

1. Right-click on the **EnterQuoteUILab** project in the **Application Navigator**, and select **New Gallery**.

2. In the **New Gallery** window, select **ADF Business Components** in the **Categories** panel and **Business Components from Tables** in the **Items** panel and click on the **OK** button.

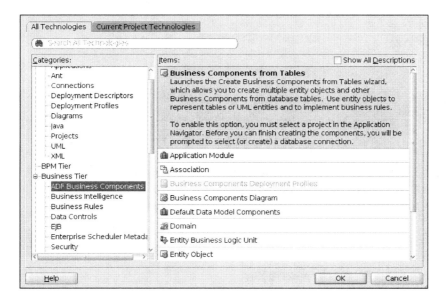

3. Create a new database connection to the quote schema that you created. This connection is part of the project. You can also browse for and copy the connection if you already created one in the IDE.

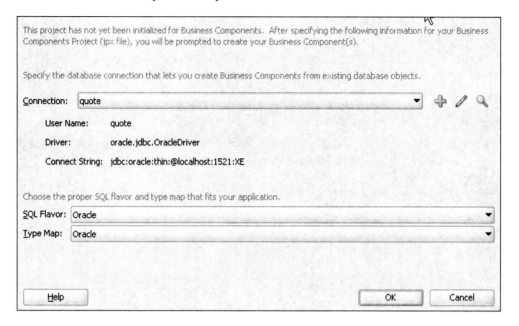

4. Click on the **OK** button.

5. In the **Entity Objects** window, enter **Package** name as **enterquoteui.adfbc** and select **PRODUCT** and **TERM** tables. If you don't see the tables in the **Available** list, click on the **Query** button to query the database.

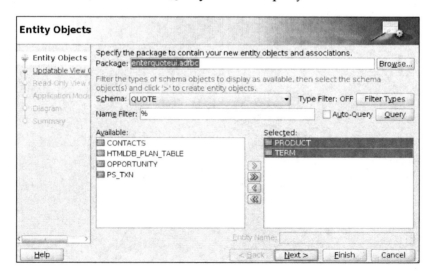

An **Entity Object** (EO) maps to a database table and an instance of it represents a row in that table. It also implements any constraints defined for the table. The Entity Object can be customized for runtime behavior and for implementing validation rules.

6. Click on the **Next** button.

7. Click on **Next** in the **Updatable View Objects** window, without selecting any object.

8. In the **Read-Only View Objects** window, click on **Query** to retrieve a list of available objects and select **PRODUCT** and **TERM** and click on **Next**.

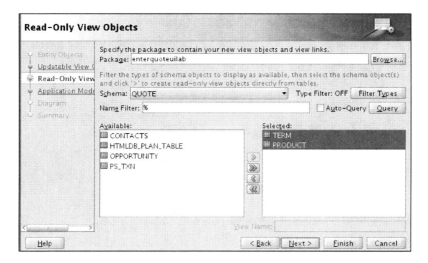

A **View Object** (VO) provides a view of your data represented by the entity objects. A view object can define which attributes are visible and can also set filter criteria and sorting for the query represented by the entity object. A View Object can provide a view over one or more tables (one or more entity objects) and can do master-detail coordination.

9. Click on **Next** on all subsequent windows and then click on **Finish**.

10. Click on **Save All**.

11. You now have entity objects and corresponding view objects created for the underlying **PRODUCT** and **TERM** tables. You use these via **ADF Data Controls** in the task form later in this lab. Before you move on to creating the task forms, you need to update the application module configuration to use the JDBC data source for the **QUOTE** schema.

Creating JDBC data source

The following steps guide you thorough creating a new JDBC data source using the WebLogic console:

1. First, create the JDBC data source using the Weblogic Console.

 You can skip the Creating JDBC data source steps if you are using an Amazon EC2 instance as the quoteDS data source has already been created in the image.

2. Open `http://localhost:7001/console` to start the Web Logic Server (WLS) console and log in using `weblogic/welcome` (replace the host and port and username/password to match your own configuration).

3. On the left navigation bar, click on **Services | JDBC | Data Sources**.

4. At the top of the data source table, click on **New**.

5. Enter the data source information as given in the following table:

Property	Value
Name	quoteDS
JNDI Name	jdbc/quoteDS
Database Type	Oracle

6. Click on **Next** on the subsequent windows three times.

7. Enter the database information.

Property	Value
Database Name	XE
Host Name	localhost
Port	1521
Database User Name	quote
Password	Quote

 If you are using the BPM **Amazon Machine Image (AMI)**, use the database name as **soa11gdb** and the EC2 public host name of your instance for the host name

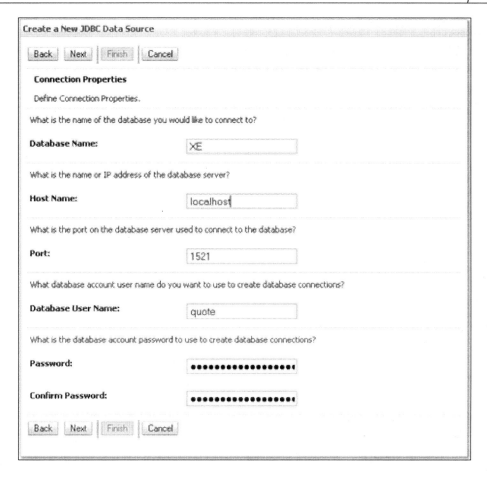

8. Click on **Next**.

9. Click on **Test Configuration**. Confirm the success message at the top of page.

10. Click on **Next**.

11. Select the **Target server** where your BPM component is running: **soa_server1** or **AdminServer**.

If you are using an Amazon EC2 instance, your target server should be **soa_server1**. If you installed your own with all servers running in one admin server, then the target should be **AdminServer**.

12 Click on **Finish**.

Updating the application module configuration

An **Application Module (AM)** is the highest level component in ADFBC and consists of one or more view objects. It manages database connections and is responsible for controlling the database transactions. You need to update the AM to use the JDBC datasource defined in the **WebLogic** console, rather than hard-coding it in the AM.

1. Double-click on **AppModule** under **EnterQuoteUILab | Application Sources | enterquoteui.adfbc** to open the application module.

2. Click on **Configurations**.

3. Select **AppModuleLocal** and click on the Edit icon.

4. Change the **Connection Type** to **JDBC DataSource** and enter **Datasource Name** as **jdbc/quoteDS**.

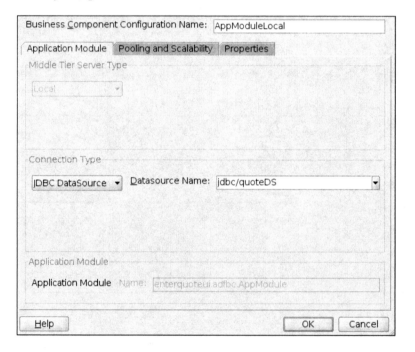

5. Click on **OK**.

6. Repeat the previous step for **AppModuleShared**.

7. Click on **Save All**.

Creating task flow form

The sales quote requires the following information to be captured from the user:

- Header-level information such as customer address, contact information, type of customer, sales representative associated with this deal, industry type and so on.

- A list of products for which the quote is being prepared.

- Information about any discount being given. The discount could be different for each selected product.

- Any terms and conditions that need to be added to the quote.

Rather than capturing all this information in a single page, you can design four separate pages, each capturing one type of information. Completion of one page will take the user to the next until the quote is completed and ready for submission for approval. The user should also have an option of going back and forth between the various parts of the quote.

Using a bounded task flow

This can be done by creating a bounded task flow with four views arranged in a proper sequence.

To create a bounded task flow that will be rendered as part of the Oracle BPM Worklist application, JDeveloper provides a convenient wizard for creating a new ADF task flow based on a human task definition. The following steps will guide you in creating such a task flow:

1. Right-click on **EnterQuoteUILab** in the Application Navigator and select **New…**.

2. In the **New Gallery** window, switch to the **All Technologies** tab and select **JSF** under the **Web Tier** node.

3. In the **Items** panel, select **ADF Task Flow Based on Human Task** and click on **OK**.

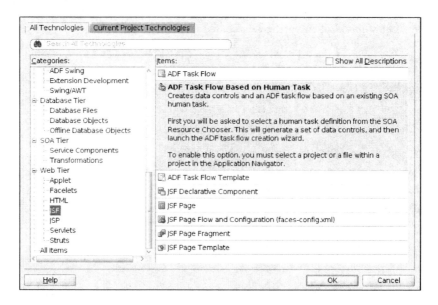

4. In the **SOA Resource Browser** window, go one directory up and double-click on the **QuoteProcessLab** folder.

5. Select **EnterQuoteDetails.task** and click on **OK**.

6. You should now see the **Create Task Flow** window. Select **Create Train** and click on **OK**. Selecting **Create Train** creates a special type of task flow that allows sequential flow of pages, which the ADF Controller manages. It also provides visual clues on the progress of the train represented by train stops which the user can click to progress through the flow.

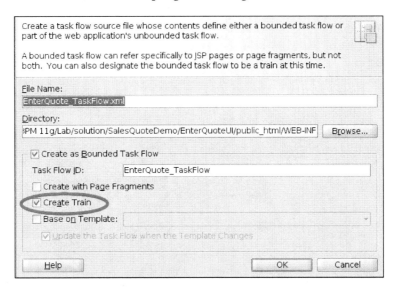

You should now see a basic flow as shown in the following diagram:

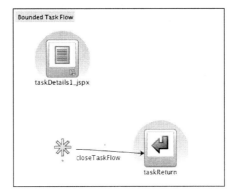

7. Delete the **taskDetails1_jspx** view from the flow by right-clicking on the view icon and selecting **Delete** from the pop-up menu.

8. Drag-and-drop a **View** from the components palette. Name it **enterHeader**.

9. Similarly, drop in a view for the remaining pages. Make sure you drop them in the right sequence and they will automatically get connected to each other in a flow. Name them **selectProduct**, **requestDiscount**, **requestTerms**, and **submit**.

10. Click on **Save All**.

You just created the pages for each train stop. The last page, **submit**, should return from this bounded task flow. To do that drag a **Control Flow Case** from the palette and drop it on the **submit** page. This will allow you to connect that page to `taskReturn`. The control flow can have an event associated with it. In this case, name the event `endTaskFlow`.

Your flow diagram should look like this:

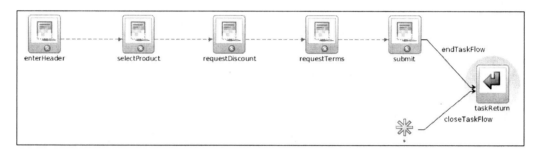

 A **Wildcard control flow** is used to specify a control flow case that can originate from any activity whose IDs match a wildcard expression.

In this case. Wildcard control flow ID is set to *****, which allows the task flow to return to the calling flow from any of the pages.

At this point you have the required task flow defined. The next step is to create pages for each of the views in the task flow.

Creating a form for entering the quote header data

Views in the task flow are JSF pages that you design using the ADF page designer. JDeveloper provides an extensive list of UI components, layout containers, and operations to create very complex pages.

Depending on the richness and complexity of the page design, the layout of the page can take some planning. There are a number of layout containers to choose from and each provides different ways to render UI components.

To reduce the time required to complete the lab, you are given JSF page templates with basic page layout already completed. You can use these templates to build out all the required pages.

> A **Page Template** provides layout and behavior. The layout is created using standard ADF Faces layout managers. You can also add custom facets to the templates that allow for adding your own UI components at specific locations in the layout when you create a page from a template. A big advantage of using a template-based approach is that, templates are referenced, not compiled. What this means is that you can make changes to the template layout both at design time and runtime without rebuilding or redeploying.

Before you begin creating the pages, you need to register the ADF Library that contains these templates in your project. Follow these steps to register the ADF Library:

1. Open the **Resource Palette** from the **View** menu.

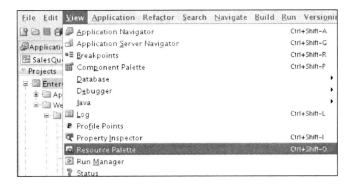

2. Create a new **File System** connection by clicking on the New Folder icon in the **Resource Palette** as shown:

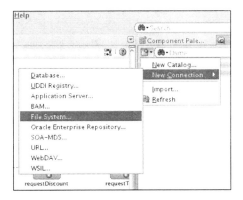

3. Enter the connection name as **SalesQuoteUIadflib** and choose the directory **adflib**. You will find this directory at the same level as your lab docs folder.

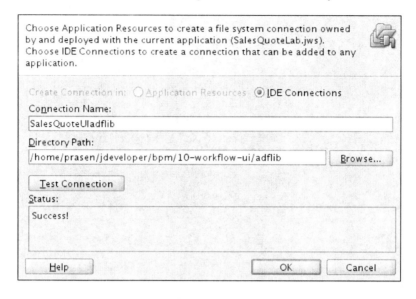

4. Click on the **OK** button.

5. Now, make sure that the **EnterQuoteUILab** project is selected.

6. Expand the **SalesQuoteUIadflib** folder.

7. Right-click on the DF library and select **Add to Project**.

8. Click on **Save All**.

9. Now design the first page for entering the quote header information.

10. Open the task flow, if not already open, by double-clicking on **EnterQuoteDetails_Taskflow** under **Page Flows** in the Application Navigator.

11. Double-click on the **enterHeader** view in the flow.

12. In the **Create JSF Page** window, select the page template **Oracle BPM 11*g* Training – Enter Header Template**, leave other fields as they are, and click on the **OK** button.

13. A new JSF file `enterHeader.jspx` is opened in the ADF designer. This template has four facets defined. Drag-and-drop **EnterQuoteUILab_ EnterQuoteDetails** data control from the **Data Controls** panel as explained in the following steps.

> A **Data Control** provides the abstraction layer between the data source-specific API and the standard set of APIs that are exposed through ADFm (ADF Model). This allows you to work with the model APIs without knowing the details of the actual implementation.
>
> The Task data controls you are using in this lab, encapsulate read/write access to the task information and its payload. These data controls were automatically created for you when you created an ADF Task Flow project with Human Task.
>
> Without this feature, you would need to call the appropriate task APIs or task services to display/modify task details.

14. Drag-and-drop the **Task** data control on the **task-action** facet. When you drop the control, a pop-up menu appears. Select **Human Task | Task Action**. Click on **OK** in the two pop ups that follow.

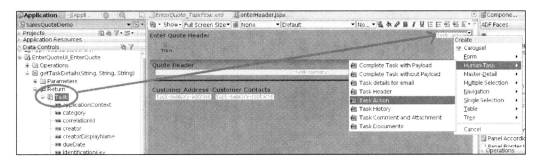

This adds the task action UI components with appropriate action and action listener setup.

15. Next, drop the **Summary** data control into the **task-summary** facet and select **Form | ADF Form**.

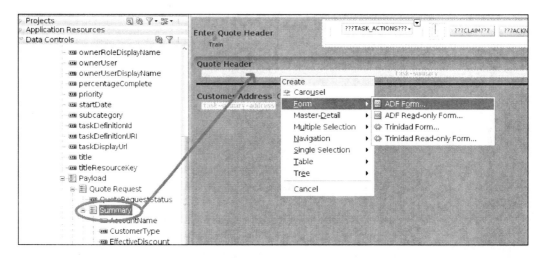

16. In the **Edit Form Fields** window, delete the following fields and click on the **OK** button:

    ◦ **NewCustomer**

    ◦ **TotalNetRevenue**

    ◦ **EffectiveDiscount**

17. The default form is laid out in a single column. You can have the fields laid out in three columns. To do that, click on the form in the editor window to set the structure panel context and then select **af:panelFormLayout** under **task-summary** in the structure panel. In **the Property Inspector** (on the right side), set the **MaxColumns** to three and **Rows** to one.

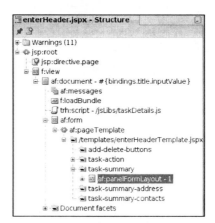

18. Drag-and-drop the **Address** data control from under the **Summary** data control to the **task-summary-address** facet.

19. Choose **Form | ADF Form** and then click on **OK** in the **Edit Form Fields** window.

20. Now add the **Contacts** data control to the page. This time you want to create a table so that the user can add multiple contacts.

21. Before you drop the control onto the page, drop a **Panel Collection** from the **Layout** section of the **Component Palette** to **the task-summary-contacts** facet. A **Panel Collection** layout container is useful for rendering collection types such as tables. Drag-and-drop **Contacts** data control to the new panel just added and choose **Table | ADF Table**. Click on **OK** on the **Edit Form Fields** window.

22. Your first form is nearly complete, and just needs a few more additions. Your contacts table needs a couple of buttons to add and delete contacts. The next few steps show you how to do that.

23. Add a **Toolbar** from the components palette to the **toolbar** facet.

24. Expand the **Contacts** data control, and do the same for the `Operations` folder within it. Drag-and-drop the **Create** and **Delete** operations to the toolbar. Choose the **ADF Button** as the UI component to use for these operations.

25. Select the **CreateInsert** button you just created and change the **Text** property in the **Property Inspector** to **Add**.

26. Your form is now ready and should look like this:

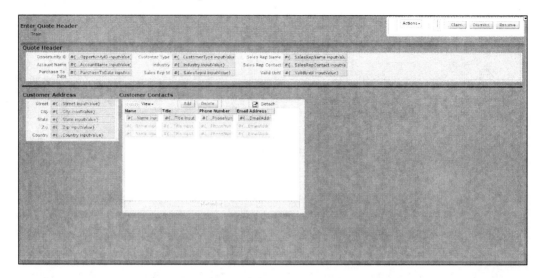

Creating a form for adding products to the quote

Now create a form for selecting products for the quote. This form uses the drag-and-drop feature of ADF to drag the required product and drop it into the selected products table. For the source product list, use the ADF BC view ProductView that you created earlier.

There are a number of ways one can use drag-and-drop in ADF. The simplest is dragging content or the value of an attribute and dropping it on a target. This typically requires no coding. In this case, though, you need to drag a row containing product item details and drop it to a target of a different structure. For such a drag-n-drop operation a bit of Java coding is required. Since advanced ADF Java coding is not the focus of this lab, you are given a JAR file with the required code already written. You can call methods in your Java class by registering these classes as managed beans.

Registering Managed Beans

When building complex UI, you come across instances where you may need custom sources of data for your components or may need custom handling of events generated by components in your UI. In ADF this is provided by way of JavaBeans registered with the task flow called **Managed Beans**. Once registered, components can invoke methods on these beans as well as `get` or `set` properties exposed by the beans. In your lab, you use beans for providing both values from custom data sources as well as custom functions for handling drag-and-drop functionality.

To ease the development of these, you are provided with a pre-built JAR file that contains all the required JavaBeans. The following steps will guide you through registering these classes as Managed Beans:

1. Open the **EnterQuoteUILab Project Properties** (right-click on the **EnterQuoteUILab** project).

2. In the **Project Properties** window, click on **Libraries** and then **Classpaths**.

3. Click on **Add JAR/Directory** and browse to `c:\bpm\lib` and select `bpm-training-salesquote.jar`.

4. Click on **Select**, then click on **OK**, and click on **Save All**.

5. Open the **EnterQuoteDetails_TaskFlow task flow** and switch from the **Diagram** view to the **Overview** view by clicking the tab at the bottom of the flow window.

6. Select the **Managed Beans** tab and add a new managed bean called **dropProduct**.

7. Set the class to `enterquoteui.backing.DropProduct` (just start typing and then select the class when it appears in the drop down). You can also browse the class hierarchy and select the class by clicking on the **v** that appears to the right of the **Class** field when you click on it. Set the **Scope** to **session**.

8. Similarly add the following and click on **Save All**:

Name	Class	Scope
discountHelper	enterquoteui.backing.DiscountHelper	session
termChoices	enterquoteui.backing.TermChoices	session

Building the form

The following steps describe the process for building the form for entering the products:

1. Open the **EnterQuoteDetails_TaskFlow** task flow diagram view (**diagram** tab).

2. Double-click on **selectProduct** view to create a new JSF page.

3. Select **Oracle BPM 11gR1 Training – Select Product Template** as the **Page Template**.

4. Click on the **OK** button.

5. As before, create the task action buttons by dragging and dropping the task data control from the **EnterQuoteUILab_EnterQuoteDetails** data control, to the task-action facet. Select **Human Task | Task Action** from the pop-up menu that appears. Click on **OK** in the two pop ups that follow.

6. Add a **Panel Collection** layout container to the **available-products** facet.

7. Drag-and-drop **ProductView1** data control from the **AppModuleDataControl** to the panel collection. This data control is for the ADF BC view you created at the beginning of this lab.

8. Choose **Table | ADF Read-only Table** as the UI component for this data control.

9. In the **Edit Table Columns** dialog, delete the following fields:
    ◦ **Category**
    ◦ **ImageURL**

10. Check the **Row Selection** checkbox and click on **OK**. You now have a table of products to select from.

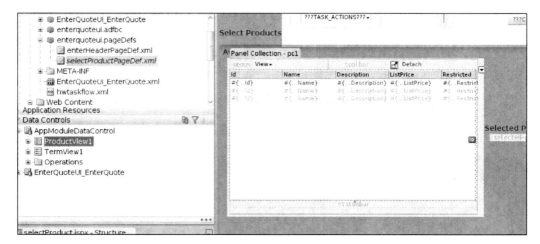

11. Now create the target table which will refer to the product list in the human task payload.

12. Add a **Panel Collection** to the **selected-products** facet.

> A **Panel Collection** is a type of layout manager that aggregates collection components like table, tree-table, and tree to display standard menus, toolbars, and status bar item.

13. Drag-and-drop the **Product Item** data control from within the **Task** payload to the new panel.

14. Choose **Table | ADF Read-only Table** as the UI component.

15. In the **Edit Table Columns** delete the following columns:

    ○ **RequestedDiscount**

    ○ **ControlledAvailability**

16. You now have the form completed and it should look something like the following screenshot:

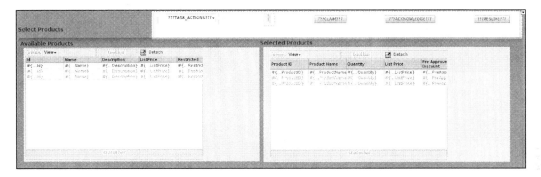

There are a few more steps you still need to complete to enable the drag-and-drop operation so that the user can select a product in the **Available Products** table and drop it into the **Selected Products** table.

17. In the **Component Palette**, open the **Operations** section and drop **Drag Source** onto the **Available Products** table portion of the **Available Product** facet.

18. With the **Drag Source** selected in the **Structure Panel**, in the **Property Inspector**, set the **Actions** to COPY, the **DefaultAction** to COPY, and the **Discriminant** to **productItem**.

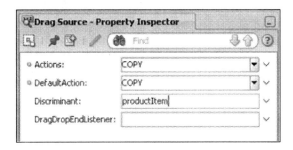

19. Drop the **Collection Drop Target** to the **Selected Products** table. This will pop up a dialog for specifying a **DropListener**. Click on the **v** to the right of the field to open the expression editor and click on **Method Expression Builder**.

20. Clear any expression in the **Expression** box. Under the **ADF Managed Beans** folder, expand the **dropProduct** node and select **HandleDrop**. Click on **OK** and click on **OK** again to return to the designer.

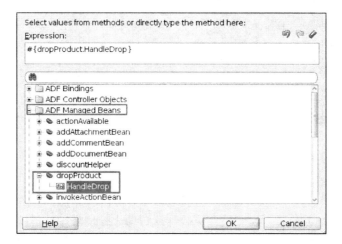

21. With the **Collection Drop Target** selected in the **Structure Panel**, in the **Property Inspector**, set the **Actions** to COPY, and the **ModelName** to **productItem**.

22. Click on **Save All**.

You now have a drag-and-drop enabled task form for selecting products for a sales quote.

Creating a form for requesting a discount

In this form, you allow the user to request a discount for each product selected in the product selection form.

1. Open the task flow and double-click on **requestDiscount** view.

2. Select **Oracle BPM 11gR1 Training – Request Discount Template** for the **Page Template**.

3. Click on the **OK** button to create a new JSF page called **requestDiscount.jspx**.

4. Create the task action button at the top of the page as you did for the previous pages.

5. Add the **Summary** data-control as an **ADF Form** to the **summary** facet. In the **Edit Form Fields** window, delete all fields except the following:

   ◦ **TotalNetRevenue**

   ◦ **EffectiveDiscount**

6. Change the form to have the fields laid out in two columns by changing the **MaxColumns** and the **Rows** property of the form.

   The effective discount and net revenue are calculated fields and should get updated as the discount is applied to each product. This requires a managed bean to do the computations. The JAR file you registered earlier already, has JavaBean, which will do these computations. In the following steps you will use that bean as the source for these fields' values.

    With this change, the user can enter an integer percentage value instead of a decimal value. Once this form is in use, enter 25 instead of .25 for 25%.

7. Since these are calculated fields, make them read only by selecting each field and changing the input field's **ReadOnly** property to **true**. This property can be found in the **Behavior** section in the property inspector.

8. Click on the **Net Revenue** field.

9. In the property inspector, click on the property menu icon for the **Value** property to open the **Value** window.

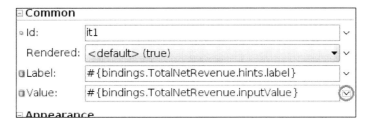

10. Click on **Expression Builder** to open the **Expression Builder** window.

11. Clear the existing expression.

12. Select **discountHelper | netRevenue** under the **ADF Managed Beans** node.

13. Similarly, set the value for **Effective Discount** by selecting **discountHelper | effectiveDiscount**.

14. Add a **Panel Collection** layout that will hold the product items table to the **discounts-table** facet.

15. Now add the selected products as an ADF table by dropping the **Product Item** data control to the new panel.

16. In the **Edit Table** window, delete the following columns:

    ° **RestrictedItem**

    ° **ControlledAvailability**

17. Click on **Save All**.

18. Set all columns except **Quantity** and **Requested Discount** to read only. It may be easier to use the **Structure Panel** to select the column's input text field.

19. Move the column **Requested Discount** to be after **Quantity**.

20. Change the component type of **Quantity** from a text input field to a number spin box so that the user can increase or decrease the value instead of typing it.

21. Right-click on **Quantity**, select **Convert To…**, and then select **Input Number Spinbox**.

    Whenever the quantity changes or the discount changes, the fields in your **Summary** should also automatically change. You have already associated the appropriate properties in the **discountHelper** managed bean. But that value needs to be rendered every time it changes. This is achieved using ADF's partial page rendering feature. To use partial page rendering to update these values follow the next steps:

     Partial Page Rendering (PPR) uses Ajax under the hood, which allows for refreshing a component or an area on a page without reloading the full page.

22. Set the **Behavior** property **AutoSubmit** to true for both **Quantity** and **RequestedDiscount** input fields.

23. Select the **Quantity** column and change its **Id** property to **cQuantity**. Similarly, change the **Id** of the **Requested Discount** column to **cRequestedDiscount**. Make sure you select the whole column and not the individual field. Use the **Structure Panel**, if necessary.

24. Select the **netRevenue** input field and edit the **PartialTriggers** property to pop up the **Edit Property: Partial Triggers** window and select the fields under the columns **cQuantity** and **cRequestedDiscount**.

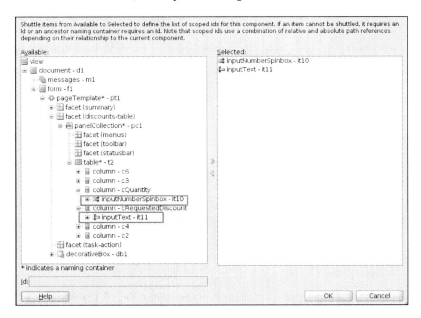

25. Note that the IDs of the fields may not be the same as in the last screenshot.

26. Click on the **OK** button.

27. Repeat the same steps for the **Effective Discount** field.

    Now do a bit of tidying up and you will have completed your third form. Notice that the table width doesn't fully occupy the page. To adjust that you need to carry out the next steps.

28. Change **StyleClass** property of the panel collection that holds the table to use the style **AFStretchWidth**. You can type this style name in or select it from the **StyleClass** browser by clicking on the **v**.

29. Select the **ADF Table** and in the **Appearance** section of the property inspector, set **ColumnStretching** property to the **Product Name** column. This change will stretch the product name column so that the table width occupies all available space.

30. To make this change, first select the **Product Name** column (not the **input** field in the column) and note down the ID. Select this ID in the **ColumnStretching** property by first selecting the table.

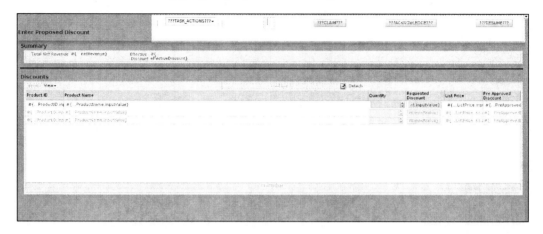

31. Click on **Save All**.

Creating a form for adding terms and conditions to the quote

In this form, you provide the user pop-up based choices for adding pre-defined terms and conditions to the quote. As with the Product Items ADF BC data control you used earlier, you will now use the TermView ADF BC data control, which will get the terms from the underlying database table.

The form needs to be designed in a way that shows only the terms that are valid for the category selected. For example, if the user selects the category as **PriceHoldOptions** then the terms choice list should only contain terms that are valid for it.

To achieve this, a bit of Java code is needed. This has already been done for you and the JavaBeans that implement the filtering logic were registered by you earlier as managed beans.

1. Open the task flow and double-click on the **requestTems** view and choose the page template as **Oracle BPM 11g Training – Request Terms Template**.

2. Add the task action buttons as you did for the earlier pages.

3. Add a **Panel Collection** layout container to the business-terms facet and set the **StyleClass** property to **AFStretchWidth** as you did for the panel in the previous form.

4. Drop the **License Term** data control from the **Quote Request** to the panel collection container as an **ADF Table**.

5. Select the **Description** column and note down its ID from the **Common** properties.

6. Select the table and change the **ColumnStretching** property to the ID of the **Description** column.

   Instead of the text fields that were generated for the **Category** and **Type** fields, you want to use drop-down lists of term categories and corresponding types from a database table that the user can choose from. The following steps show how to do that.

7. Select the **Category** text field (not the whole column) and copy the contents of the **Label** and **Value** properties from the **Property Inspector**.

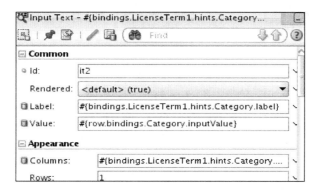

8. Delete the existing text field under the **Category** column.

9. Drag-and-drop a **Select One Choice** component onto the **Category** column (make sure the full column is highlighted as you drop the component).

10. This pops up a window for selecting the source to be used for the value displayed in the drop-down list. Click on **Bind...** and under the **ADF Managed Beans** node select **termChoices | categoryChoices** and click on **OK** and click on the **Next** button.

11. In the **Common Properties** window set the **Label** property to the value copied earlier from the property inspector and click on **Finish**.

12. Select the new field and in the **Property Inspector**, set the **Value** property to the value copied earlier from the deleted text field.

13. Repeat the above steps for the **Type** column; this time select **termChoices | termTypeChoices** for the **Bind** value.

14. You need to provide a way to add new terms or delete existing ones. So add a **Toolbar** to the toolbar facet from the components palette.

15. To this toolbar add **CreateInsert** and **Delete** operations as **ADF Button** from the **Operations** node in the **LicenseTerm** data control.

16. Change the **Text** property for **CreateInsert** button to **Add**.

As mentioned at the beginning of this section, the form only needs to show the terms associated with the selected category. What is required is a forced reload of the terms every time the user selects a category but without reloading the whole page. This is done by using a PPR. To force the refresh of the Terms component whenever the selection in the Category component changes, you will set the Category component to do an immediate submit as soon as a category is selected, and set the Terms component to watch the Category component for this auto submit. The following describes the steps required to set this up:

1. Select the Category component and set the **Auto Submit** property in the **Property Inspector** to **true**.

2. Note down the ID of the component displayed in the property inspector for the **Category** component.

3. Select the **Terms** component and enter the ID of the **Category** component in the **Partial Triggers** property in the **Property Inspector**.

4. Click on **Save all**.

You should now see the completed form as shown in the following screenshot:

Creating a submit form

The last form in this page flow is for reviewing the quote before submitting it for approval.

1. Open the task flow and double-click on the **submit** view to create a new JSF page. Select the **Oracle BPM 11g Training – Submit Template** as the page template.

2. Add the task action to the **task-action** facet.

3. Add **Summary** data control from the Quote Request to the **quote-summary** facet as an **ADF Form**. Keep the following fields from the **Edit Form Fields** window and delete the rest:
   - **AccountName**
   - **SalesRepName**
   - **TotalNetRevenue**
   - **EffectiveDiscount**
   - **ValidUntil**

4. Set **Effective Discount** and **the TotalNetRevnue** fields to be read only.

5. Update the form layout so that the fields are laid out in three columns.

6. Add a **Panel Collection** to the **products-discount** facet.

7. To this panel add the **Product Item** data control as a read-only **ADF Table**. Keep the following columns and delete the rest:
   - **ProductId**
   - **Productname**
   - **Quantity**
   - **RequestedDiscount**

8. Add another **Panel Collection** to the **license-terms** facet.

9. Add **License Term** data control to this panel as a read-only **ADF Table**.

10. Drag-and-drop the top level **Task** data control onto the **comments** facet. In the pop-up menu select **Human Task | Task Comment And Attachment**.

11. Click on **Save All**.

12. Your page is now complete and should look something like the following screenshot:

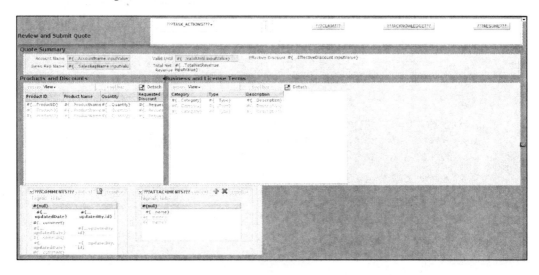

13. The last step is to set the default activity for this page flow. Open the **EnterQuoteDetails_TaskFlow Overview** tab (tabs are at the bottom) and select the **General** tab on the left.

14. Select **enterHeader** for the **Default Activity**.

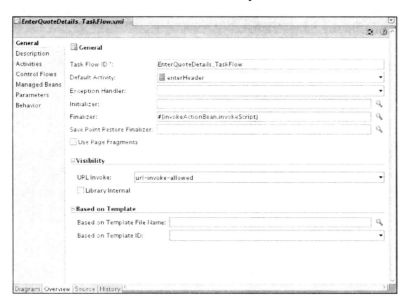

15. Click on **Save All**.

Task form for reviewing the quote

The next activity in the Sales Quote process that requires human workflow is the Business Practices Review activity where the quote is reviewed and the next task in the workflow is set. In this lab, you create a form that shows the sales quote details as entered by the sales representative.

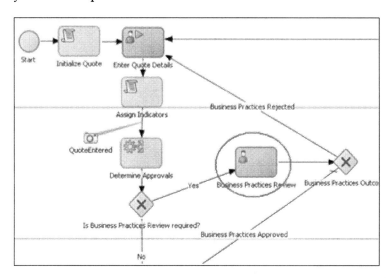

Creating a task flow for the Business Practices Review task

The following steps guide you through creating a new ADF task-flow and associated view pages for presenting the business practices review task:

1. Create a new **Generic Project** in the **SalesQuoteLab** application. Refer to the beginning of this document for detailed steps.

2. Enter the name of the project as **BPReviewUILab**.

3. Add a new **ADF Task Flow Based on HumanTask**. Refer to steps starting from 2 under 10.2.4. Follow those steps, except for the following points here.

4. Select the **BusinessPracticeReview.task** for the task definition.

5. Do not select **Create Train**.

6. You should see a basic flow as before.

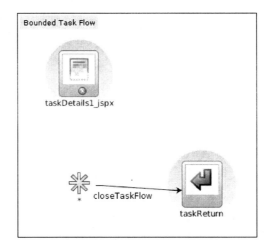

7. Delete the **taskDetails1_jspx** view from the flow by right-clicking on the view icon and selecting **Delete** from the pop-up menu.

8. Drag-and-drop a **View** from the components palette. Name it **review**.

9. Select the wildcard control flow indicated by the blue asterisk and delete it. With this change, you are ensuring that the task flow will exit only through the **review** page.

10. Click on the **Control Flow Case** in the **Control Flow** section of the component palette and connect **review** to **taskReturn**. Name the flow **closeTaskFlow**.

11. Your flow should look like the following image:

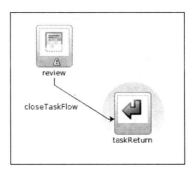

12. Click on **Save All**.

13. Add the templates library to this project the same way as you did for the earlier one.

    ○ Make sure you select the project **BPReviewUILab** in the **Application Navigator**

    ○ In the **Resource Palette**, select the **adflibSalesQuoteUITemplates.jar**, right-click, and select **Add to Project**

14. Click on **Save All**.

15. Double-click on the **review** view to open the **Create JSP Page** window.

16. Select the **Oracle BPM 11gR1 Training - Business Practices Review Template**.

17. Drag-and-drop the **Task** data control from **BPReviewUILab_BusinessPracticesReview** to the **task-action** facet.

18. Drag-and-drop the **Summary** data control from **BPReviewUILab_BusinessPracticesReview** to the **quote-summary** facet as a **Read-only ADF Form**. Keep the following fields and delete the rest:

    ○ **Opportunity ID**
    ○ **AccountName**
    ○ **ValidUntil**
    ○ **TotalNetRevenue**
    ○ **EffectiveDiscount**
    ○ **SalesRepName**
    ○ **SalesRepContact**

19. Change the **Rows & Columns** property of the form to layout the fields in three columns.

20. Select the **TotalNetRevenue** text field and right-click and select **Convert to…**, then select **Output Formatted**.

21. Make sure that the **TotalNetRevenue** field is selected and open the **Structure Panel**, if not already open. In the **Structure Panel**, select **af:convertNumber** and set its **Type** property in the **Property Inspector** to **currency**.

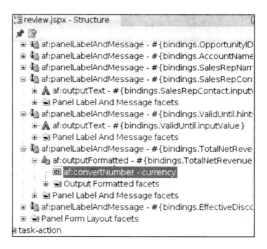

22. Add a **Panel Collection** to the **product-discount** facet. To this panel add the **Product Item** data control as an **ADF read-only table**.

23. Add a **Panel Collection** to the **license-terms** facet and add the **License Term** data control as an **ADF read-only table** to this.

24. Click on **Save All**.

25. Drag-and-drop the **Task** data control to the **task-history** facet. Select **Human Task | Task History** from the pop-up menu.

26. Set the **Default Activity** as you did for the previous form.

27. Click on **Save All**.

This completes your review form.

Creating the UI for quote approval

This is a challenge exercise. You need to create a form that looks like the following screenshot:

Hints to help you with the challenge exercise

The ADF TaskFlow is the same as the BPReviewUILab.

1. Start with a **Decorative Box** layout.

2. In the **top** facet of the **Decorative Box**, add a **Panel Header**, which will have a **toolbar facet** for the task action components.

3. In the **center** facet of the **Decorative Box**, add a **Panel Group Layout** and set the layout to **scroll**.

4. Within this panel add a **Panel Header** for the quote summary, and two **Panel Group Layout** containers with layout set to **horizontal**.

5. In one of the containers, add two **Panel Group Layout** containers for **Product Item** and **License Terms**. Both these containers should have layout set to **vertical**.

6. In the other container, add **Task Comments and Attachments** and **Task History**.

7. Set the **Default Activity**.

Deploying the UI

You can deploy the UI projects along with the composite as in earlier labs or you can create a single EAR and deploy it separately. This allows you to deploy the UI separately from the composite.

Since there is already an EAR deployed with the same root context set for these tasks, you must undeploy that one first. Undeploy it by right-clicking on the EAR and selecting undeploy. You can do this from an application server connection in JDeveloper, from the WebLogic server console, or from Enterprise Manager.

1. Create a new deployment profile for the application from the **Application** properties menu.

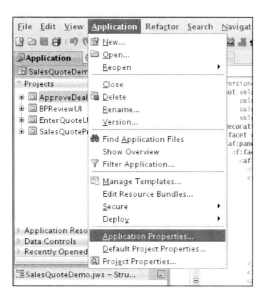

2. Select **Deployment** and **New**. Name the EAR as **SalesQuoteUILab**.

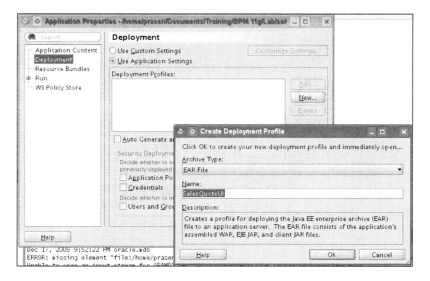

3. Select the **UI projects** in the **Application Assembly**.

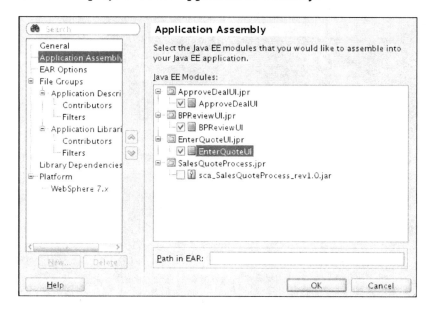

4. Deploy using the **Deploy** command on the **Application** menu.

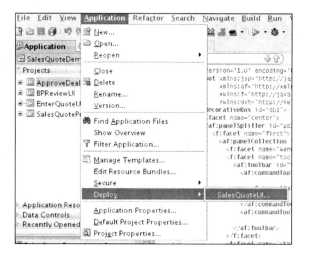

Summary

In a BPM implementation, it is not enough that one designs and implements complex process flows to make a business process more efficient. One has to also ensure that all the human-related tasks can also be easily and efficiently performed. This requires designing and implementing highly user-friendly user interfaces that are tightly integrated with the user tasks in the business process. ADF provides all the necessary functionality and requires tooling to achieve just that.

References

"Oracle Fusion Developer Guide, Oracle Press", *Frank Nimphus, Lynnn Munsinger, The McGraw-Hill Companies,Inc.(Publisher).*

"Oracle JDeveloper 11g Handbook, Oracle Press", *Duncan Mills, Peter Koletzke, Dr. Avrom Roy-Faderman, The McGraw-Hill Companies,Inc.(Publisher).*

17

Events and Exception Handling

A BPMN event is something of note that happens to a business. It can be caused by external triggers such as the arrival of a message, certain time conditions being satisfied, errors being caught, and so on. The event can also cause a result and generate a message, publish a signal, and lead to errors being thrown. One of the salient features of BPMN is the rich support for events. The events can occur at the beginning — Start Events, at the end — End Events, or in the middle — Intermediate Events, of the process. All events are represented by a circle symbol. This chapter provides an overview of BPMN events and exception handling.

Start and End Events

The start and end events in the process can be of various different types that affect how the process can be started and also how it ends

Start Events

The **Start Event** represents the start of a process or subprocess and is used to listen to external triggers to instantiate a process. The Start Event always receives or catches triggers and never throws one. There are various types of Start Event to indicate the triggering mechanisms by which the process instance can be instantiated. They are distinguished by symbols called **markers**. The Start Event is denoted by a thin circle.

None Start Event

The **None Start Event** is not associated with any trigger and is usually used to start a main process by a process participant and is followed by an **Initiator Task**. The None Start Event does not have a marker. The Initiator Task is a type of Interactive Task—human step managed by the BPM runtime engine—and is used to trigger the process from the Human Task user interfaces. The Initiator Task is always preceded by a None Start Event and the assignee or process participant for the Initiator Task is the role associated with the swim lane. A subprocess (embedded subprocess) must always start with a None Start Event.

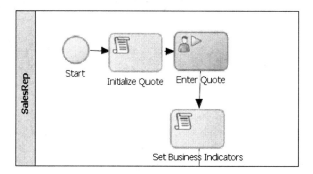

The None Start Event does not have any special properties. It can be easily converted into other Start Event types. To convert a None Start Event into another type of Start Event in BPM Studio, right-click and choose the **Change Trigger Type** option and select the appropriate trigger.

Message Start Event

The **Message Start Event** is used to trigger the process instance upon arrival of a message. Message is a special type of data and is used to show data exchanges in the context of process interactions. The source of the message is well known and the message can originate from various sources such as another BPMN process or BPEL process or Adapter Event or external web service client. For example, the Sales Quote process can be triggered by the arrival of a quote request message as shown in the following image:

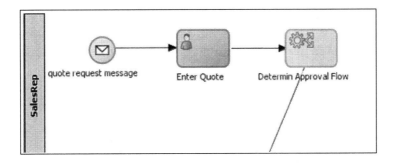

Implementation of Message Start Event

The Message Event is always associated with the operation of a service interface. The following steps illustrate the configuration of a Message Start Event in BPM Studio.

1. Right-click on **Message Start Event** and choose **Properties**. This brings up the **Properties** wizard. Go to the **Implementation** tab. There are two ways to define the service interface. You can either define the interface from scratch using the **Define Interface** option or browse the Business Catalog for an existing interface by choosing the **Interface from Catalog** option. In this example, the **Define Interface** option is used for specifying the interface for the Message Start Event.

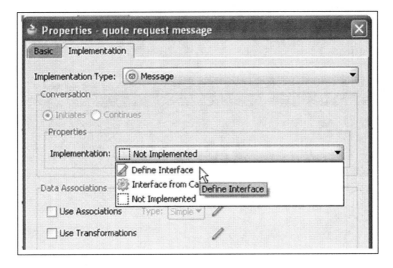

2. Click on the **+** symbol to define input argument(s) for the interface. In this example, the argument name is **quote**. Select **....** to browse the complex data types defined in the Business Catalog.

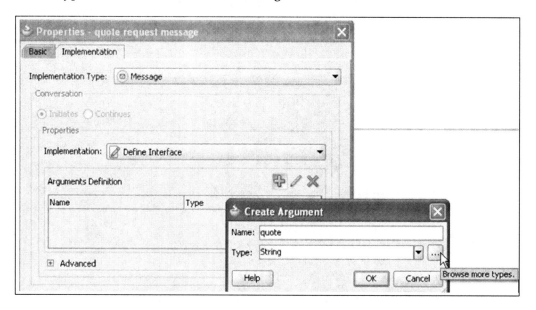

3. This brings up the **Browse Types** window. Select the **Component** option for **Type** and choose **Quote** from the list of complex data types displayed at the bottom.

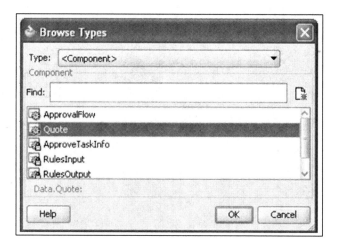

4. Expand the **Advanced** section. Choose the type of operation, **Asynchronous** versus **Synchronous**, and enter a meaningful name for the **Operation Name** field.

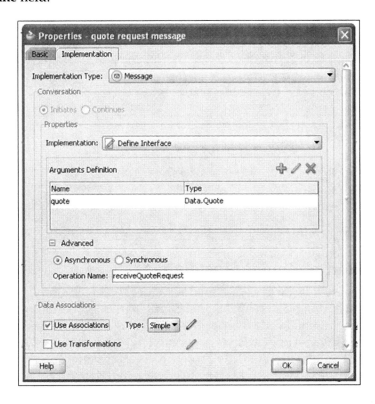

5. Use the **Data Associations** section to map the incoming message to process data objects. This completes the configuration of the Message Start Event.

Signal Start Event

The **Signal Start Event** is used to trigger the process instance upon the arrival of a subscribed signal via broadcast mechanisms. The sender is unknown in this case and the Signal Start Event listens on a well-known topic. For example, the Order Processing Application might publish a signal indicating successful completion of the order, and the various processes down the line need to subscribe to this signal to perform the next set of activities. For example, the Sales Quote process can be triggered upon arrival of the quote request event.

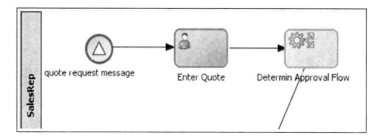

Configuration of Signal Start Event

The Signal Start Event is always associated with an event definition. The following steps illustrate the configuration of a Signal Start Event in BPM Studio once you create an event definition inside the **Application Navigator** view. Any Event Definition added in the **Application Navigator** view automatically shows up in the `Business Catalog` folder of the **BPM Project Navigator** view. Please refer to the Oracle SOA Suite documentation on how to create event definitions.

Right-click on **Signal Start Event** and choose **Properties**. This brings up the **Properties** wizard. Go to the **Implementation** tab. Browse from a list of events available from the Business Catalog.

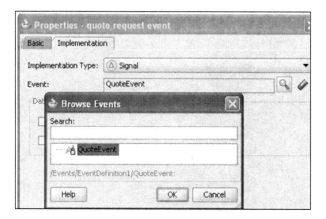

Timer Start Event

The **Timer Start Event** is used to trigger the process instances based on some schedule. It can be a fixed timestamp or a regularly occurring event or a combination of both. For example, a process can be scheduled to occur at the end of the month, at New Year, or bi-weekly after 1st June.

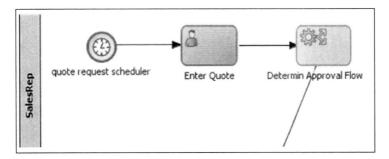

Configuration of Timer Start Event

To set a timer event, complete the properties as follows:

1. Right-click on **Timer Start Event** and choose **Properties**. This brings up the **Properties** wizard. Go to the **Implementation** tab.

2. To schedule the process instance to kick off every day choose the **Time Cycle** option and enter **0 Months 1 Days 0:0:0** to represent a one day time interval.

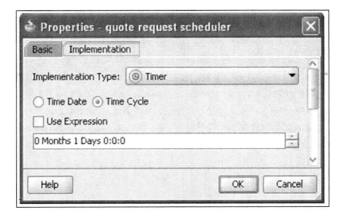

Multiple Start Events

There can be multiple exclusive ways to instantiate a process and hence there can be multiple Start Events. The process instance is instantiated when one of the Start Events becomes active and the alternative triggers are ignored. For example, the Sales Quote process can be triggered by the arrival of either a quote request event (Signal Start Event) or by the arrival of quote request message (Message Start Event) or by the Sales Rep creating a task for the Enter Quote step (Initiator Task).

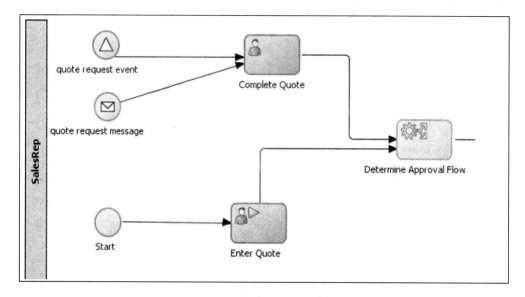

End Events

The **End Event** signals the end of all or portions of the process/subprocess and defines the result generated by the process upon completion. The End Events always send or throw triggers and never catch one. The End Events are represented by thicker circles. Similar to Start Event, there can be multiple flavors of End Event and they are distinguished from each other by symbols called markers.

None End Event

The **None End Event** does not produce any trigger when the process completes. Unlike the condition that the Start Events of a subprocess have to be of "None" type only, the End Events of a subprocess can be of any type. The triggers thrown by the subprocess have to be caught at the parent process up the hierarchy. The control passes to the subsequent step in the main process if a subprocess has a None End Event and completes normally. The Sales Quote Process in the case study has a None End Event.

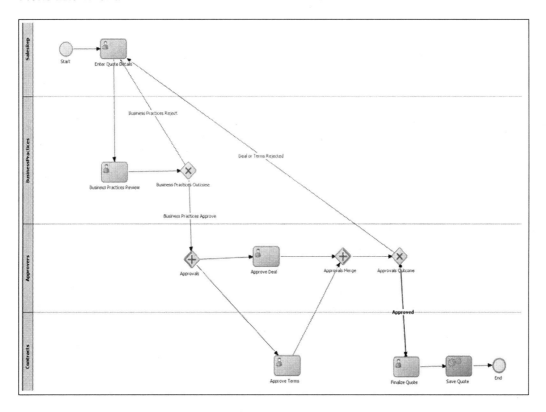

Message End Event

Upon process completion, the **Message End Event** is used to send a message to another process or application. The destination of the message is well known.

The following figure shows an example configuration of a Message End Event in Oracle BPM Studio.

- The **Conversation** field is always set to **Continues**. Since the Message End Event is of throw type, it should have a corresponding catch event. This catch event can be either a Message Start Event or a catch Message Intermediate Event.

- The **Initiator Node** is used to point to the corresponding catch event. The drop-down list shows the Message Start Events as well as Message Intermediate Events of type catch.

- The **Arguments Definition** section is used to specify the payload for the operation. Use the **+** symbol to launch the Data Object browser and add the appropriate data types.

- If the **Initiator Node** is asynchronous, then the **Asynchronous** radio button is automatically selected under the **Advanced** section. In addition, a meaningful operation name must be specified for the **Operation Name** field.

- If the **Initiator Node** is synchronous, then the **Synchronous** radio button is automatically selected under the **Advanced** section and the **Operation Name** field is disabled.

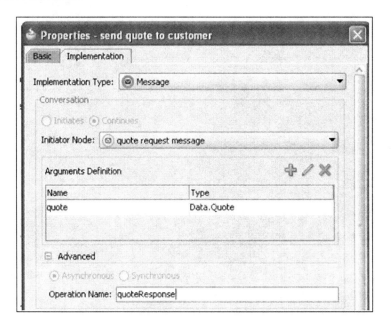

BPMN process as a service

The BPMN process with a Message Start Event and a Message End Event is itself a service provider that can be invoked from a Service Task of another BPMN process, a web service client, or invoked from a BPEL process. The BPMN process is an asynchronous service if the operation type of its Message Start Event is asynchronous and the BPMN process is a synchronous service if the operation type of its Message Start Event is synchronous. In the following screenshot, the Customer BPMN process is an asynchronous service that receives input message of type quote and replies back with the output message of the same type quote.

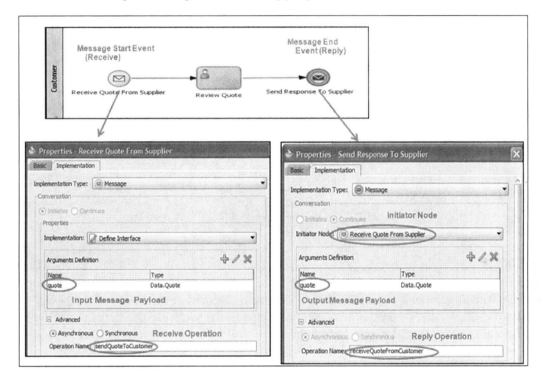

Signal End Event

The **Signal End Event** publishes a broadcast signal. The receivers are not known and the Signal End Event publishes the event to a well-known topic or subject.

Error End Event

The **Error End Events** are used for propagation of errors from the subprocess to the parent processes up the hierarchy. Error End Events are meaningful only in the context of a subprocess. To be caught by the parent process, there should be an associated Error Intermediate Event attached to the boundary of the subprocess. Boundary events and exception flow are discussed in later portions of this chapter.

Terminate End Event

The **Terminate End Event** is used to end the process or subprocess abruptly. It does not generate any result.

Multiple End Events

There can be multiple End Events for different end states. For example, the Customer process, shown in the following image, can review the quote sent by the Sales Quote process and can either accept or reject it.

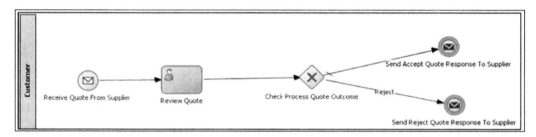

All parallel paths of a process or subprocess must be completed before the process or subprocess can be completed. The exceptions to the same are the Error End Event and the Terminate End Event. When the Error End Event or Terminate End Event is encountered, the process or the subprocess is abruptly terminated irrespective of whether there are other parallel paths which are still being executed. However, unlike the Error End Event, the Terminate End Event does not throw a trigger and is not caught by the parent process. If the Terminate End Event of a subprocess is reached, the execution at the subprocess level ends and the next activity in the parent process is executed.

Intermediate Events

Intermediate events occur in the middle of the process.

Throw and Catch Intermediate Events

The **Intermediate Events** occur in the middle of the sequence flow of the process in between the Start and End Events. Unlike Start Events, which can only catch triggers and End Events, which can only throw triggers, the Intermediate Events can catch as well as throw triggers. The Intermediate Events can be produced by the process (throw type) or they can be consumed by the process (catch type). There can be multiple Intermediate Events of catch and throw type in a process. To distinguish the throw type of Intermediate Events from the catch type of Intermediate Events, the throw type of Intermediate Event is represented by shaded markers while the markers for the catch type of Intermediate Events are not shaded. There are multiple types of Intermediate Events similar to Start and End Events.

Message Intermediate Event

The **Message Intermediate Event** is used to send and receive messages to external processes and often used for process interactions. The **throw Message Intermediate Event** followed by the **catch Message Intermediate Event** is used to model the asynchronous request response scenario. The catch Message Intermediate Event followed by the throw Message Intermediate Event is used to model the receive-reply scenario. In the following example, the Supplier process sends a message to the customer process and waits for a response.

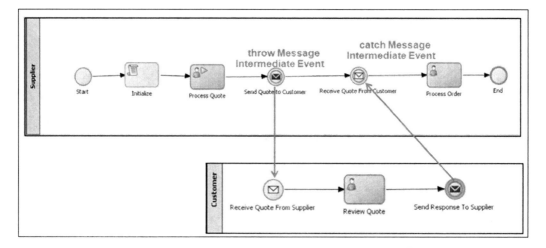

There can be more than one possible response. An **XOR Event Gateway** together with Message Intermediate Events is used to receive mutually exclusive events.

Only one of the events can be received. In the following example, the Sales Quote process sends a quote to the Customer process and waits for a response. The Customer can either accept or reject the quote and hence, there are two mutually exclusive responses that can be received. The XOR Event Gateway is used to perform mutually exclusive conditional splits based on incoming event.

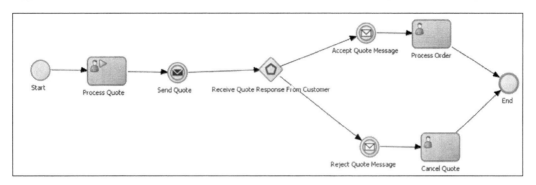

Signal Intermediate Event

The **Signal Intermediate Event** is used to publish and subscribe to signals using broadcast mechanisms. Unlike Message Events, which can be used for communication across processes, a Signal Event can be used to send a trigger both inside—activities inside the same process can subscribe to the signal event published by the process— and outside the process.

Timer Intermediate Event

The **Timer Intermediate Event** is used to wait for a certain time period or wait until a certain date time. It is of catch type only.

 Error Events and Terminate Events cannot occur in the middle of the sequence flow of the process.

Boundary Events

Certain Intermediate Events of catch type can be attached to the boundary of an activity (Task or subprocess) and can listen to internal as well as external triggers. These events are referred to as **Boundary Events**. When the Boundary Event is triggered, the process execution flows through the outgoing path, also referred to as exception flow. The Boundary Event is active and listening to the trigger only as long as the activity to which it is attached is active.

The Boundary Event can be of two types—interrupting and non-interrupting. The non-interrupting Boundary Events have a dashed border to distinguish them from interrupting Boundary Events. In the interrupting case, the process execution proceeding on the normal sequence flow is interrupted and instead proceeds on the exception path. In other words, the normal execution flow and the exception flow are mutually exclusive.

In the non-interrupting case, the process execution continues on the normal sequence flow and in parallel also executes the exception flow. Care must be taken when the exception flow is merged into the main flow of the process. In most cases, the exception flow should end with its own End Event. Oracle BPM 11*g* supports various Boundary Events such as Message Boundary Event, Signal Boundary Event, Error Boundary Event, and Timer Boundary Event. It supports both interrupting and non-interrupting Boundary Event types.

Timer Boundary Events

The **Timer Boundary Event** is used to handle timeout exceptions. They can be used to catch service invocation timeouts in the case of system steps or catch Human Task related events such as deadline violation in the case of human steps. When attached to the boundary of the subprocess, they can be used to interrupt process execution if the time taken to execute the subprocess exceeds beyond a certain time limit. In the interrupting Timer Boundary Event, the process execution along the normal sequence flow is interrupted and the execution continues on the exception flow path. For example, in the following Sales Quote Process screenshot, an interrupting Timer Boundary Event can be attached to the Save Quote step to interrupt the process flow if the File Adapter service invocation exceeds 10 minutes. The exception flow consists of a User Task to manually enter the quote by the Admin role.

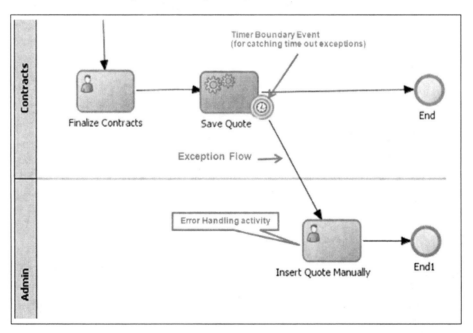

Follow these steps to configure an interrupting Timer Boundary Event and the associated exception flow:

1. Switch to **Component Palette** and select **BPM**. Go to **Catch Events** under **Events**.

2. Drag-and-drop the **Timer** event from the **Catch Events** section on to the **Save Quote** step in the Sales Quote model. Enter **timeout** for **Name**. Right-click and select **Properties** to bring up the **Properties** editor. Select **Interrupting Event** and **Time Cycle** option. Type in 10 minutes for the time cycle.

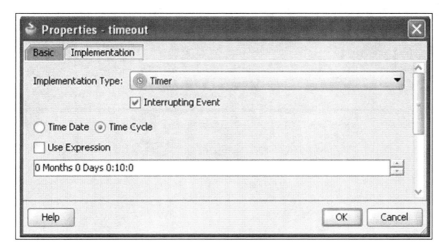

3. Add a swim lane under **Contracts** and type in **Admin** for the new **Role**.

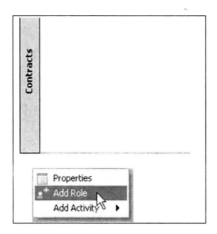

4. Drag-and-drop a **User Task** from the **Component Palette** under the **Interactive Tasks** section into the **Admin** swim lane. Enter **Insert Quote Manually** for the **Name**. Drag-and-drop an End Event and connect the outgoing sequence flow of the User Task to this newly created End Event.

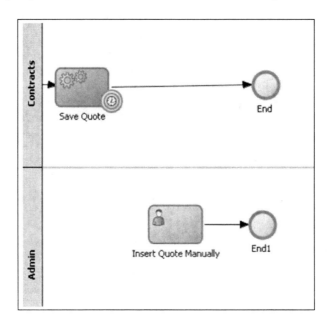

5. Right-click on the **Boundary Timer Event** and select **Add Default Sequence flow** option and connect it with the **Insert Quote Manually** process step.

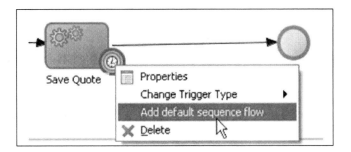

In the non-interrupting Boundary Timer Event, the process execution continues on the normal sequence flow and in parallel executes the exception flow path. A non-interrupting Boundary Timer Event is usually used for notifying or escalating when the deadline associated with an Interactive Task is violated. In the following Sales Quote example, the non-interrupting Boundary Timer Event attached to the Approve Terms step can be used to notify the process administrator when the deadline for the Approve Terms Human Task implementation is reached.

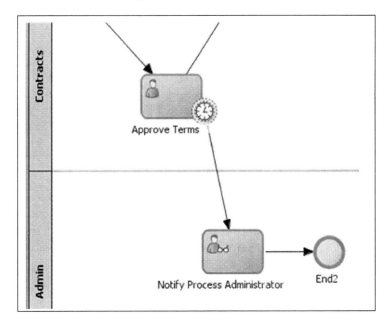

Error Boundary Events

The **Error Boundary Event** can only be of interrupting type and the process execution along the normal sequence flow is aborted and instead the exception flow is taken.

Using Error Boundary Events to catch system exceptions

The Error Boundary Event attached to a system step such as Service Task, Send Task, and Receive Task is used to catch service invocation exceptions or system faults. The service might not be available or the data passed to the service or data received from the service might be invalid. In these situations, the Boundary Error Event is attached to the system step to trap system exceptions.

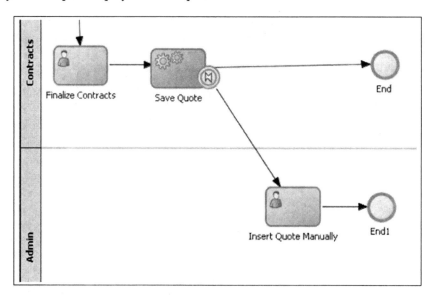

The following steps illustrate the configuration of Error Boundary Event to catch system exceptions:

1. Right-click on the **Error Boundary Event**. Select **Properties** to open up the **Properties** wizard. Go to **Implementation** tab. Select the **Browse..** icon.

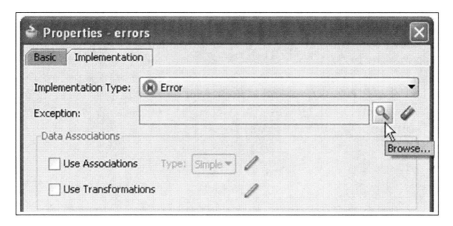

2. Select **Show System Faults**. A predefined list of system faults is displayed. The two most commonly used system faults are **Binding Fault** and **Remote Fault**. Binding Fault is used to capture service unavailable errors and Remote Fault for all other system errors such as bad data.

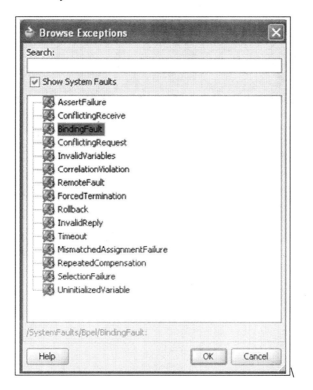

3. Once you select the system fault, you can map it in the Data Association section to process data objects.

Using Error Boundary Events to catch business exceptions

The Error Boundary Event can also be used to trap business exceptions. The service invoked by the Service Task has to throw a Message Fault in order to be caught as a business exception. In the following example, the Customer process reviews the quote and accepts or rejects the quote. The Accept Quote Message is configured as a regular Message End Event. However, the Reject Quote Message is configured as a Message Fault and is tied to a Business Exception.

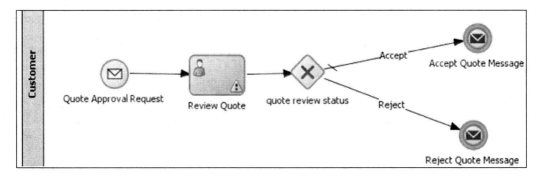

The following steps illustrate the configuration of a Message End Event as a service fault:

1. The Business Exception artefact needs to be created first. Go to **Business Catalog** in the **BPM Project Navigator** in BPM Studio. Right-click on the **Business Catalog** and select **New** and then **Business Exception**.

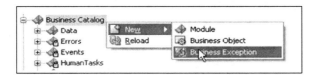

2. Specify a name for the Business Exception (**Name** field) and the folder (**Destination Module** field) inside the Business Catalog that it should be created in.

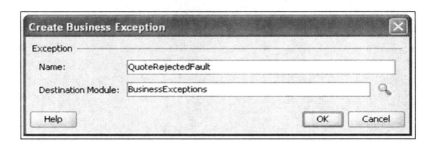

3. The Business Exception is created as String type. The type can be changed by going to the Business Exception in the Business Catalog and opening the Business Exception editor.

4. Use the **...** browse button to change the type as shown in the following image:

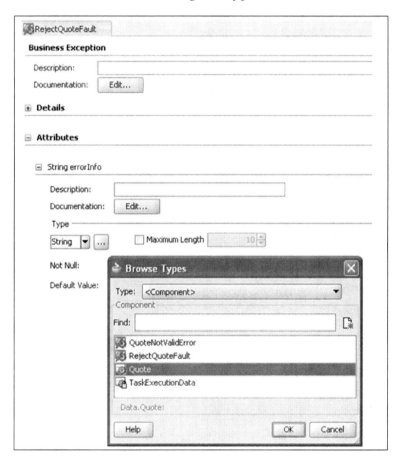

The Sales Quote process has a Send Task for sending the quote approval request message to customer and a corresponding Receive Task for receiving the quote approval response message from customer. The Customer process returns a normal message response in the case of quote acceptance and throws a fault in the case of quote rejection. The Receive Task has an Error Boundary Event to catch the fault thrown in the case of a quote reject by the Customer process.

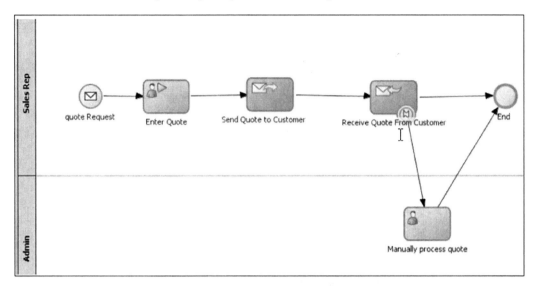

The configuration of the Error Boundary Event for catching the fault is shown in the following screenshot.

1. Use the browse button at the end of the Exception field to browse the list of Business Exceptions in the Business Catalog.

2. Choose the appropriate Business Exception.

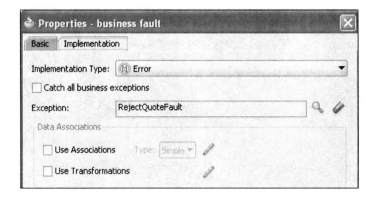

Using Error Boundary Events for propagation of subprocess errors

The Error Boundary Events of a subprocess is used for propagation of error messages thrown inside the subprocess scope to be caught and handled by the parent-level process. The following example is a slightly modified version of the Sales Quote process to illustrate how to catch an exception thrown by the subprocess. The Approvals subprocess throws the **quote reject error** (Error End Event) if the outcome of either **Approve Deal**, or **Approve Terms**, or both is **REJECT**. The error thrown inside the subprocess is caught at the parent process by the Error Boundary Event attached to the border of the subprocess. The exception path is executed in this case and the Cancel Quote step is executed.

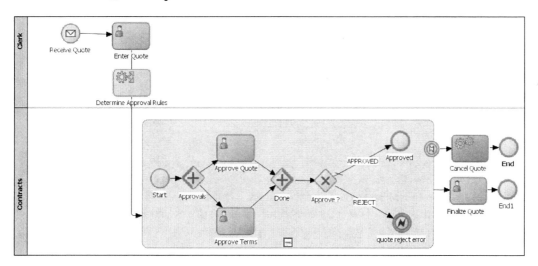

Event Subprocess

The **Event Subprocess** is contained within a process or a subprocess. It is not applicable to a Task. It is marked with a dotted line boundary and triggered by a Start Event. The Start Event is followed by activities. It does not have incoming or outgoing sequence flows. It can be collapsed or expanded. When collapsed, it has the marker of the Start Event. Types of Start Events for Event Subprocess are Message, Error, Timer, and Signal. The Event Subprocess has access to the data of its parent scope. Just like boundary events, it listens for external signals but instead of transferring outside of the activity it runs within the activity (process / subprocess).

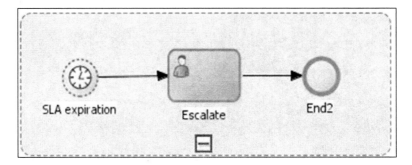

The Event Subprocess is active only if the subprocess or process in which it is contained is active. When the Start Event of the Event Subprocess is triggered, the activities following the Start Event is executed. The Start Events can be interrupting or non-interrupting type. The only exception to this rule is Error Start Event. It is always of interrupting type. In the interrupting case, the process execution proceeding the normal sequence flow in the process or subprocess gets halted and the process activities following the Start Event in the Event Subprocess is executed instead. In the non-interrupting case, the normal process execution continues and in addition, the Event Subprocess is executed.

In the following Sales Quote process example, the Quote Process Exceptions Event Subprocess is shown expanded and is used to catch Quote Exceptions, notify the process administrator, and then end abruptly. The Error Start Event is interrupting and when triggered, the normal execution is broken and the process executes the activities contained within the Event Subprocess.

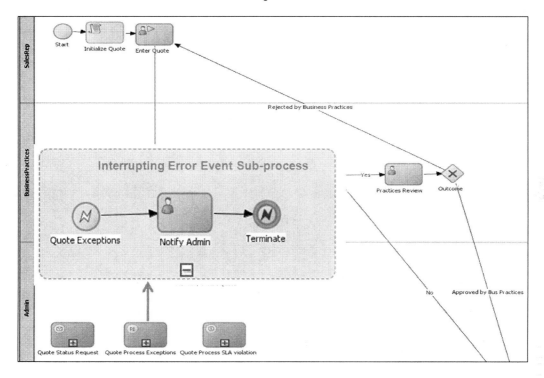

In the following screenshot, the Quote Process SLA violation Event Subprocess is shown expanded and is used to send an escalation to the administrator upon violation of process SLA. The Start Event is of non-interrupting type and hence the normal process execution continues and in parallel the Event Subprocess is also executed.

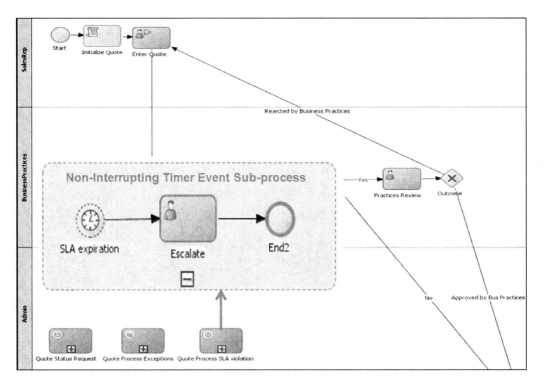

Summary

The support for describing event-triggered behavior for handling inter-process communications and exception handling directly in the diagram distinguishes BPMN from other modeling notations and makes it a business-friendly modeling-cum-execution language. An event in BPMN can do many things — trigger a process, block a process, resume a waiting process, abort a process activity, propagate exceptions, and change the flow. The BPMN specification has many event types but learning a few common patterns is all you really need to do to handle most of the exception scenarios.

18
Customizing and Extending Process Spaces

Process Spaces provides a rich collaborative interface for process participants. Basic usage of Process Spaces is covered in Chapter 12, *Using Process Spaces and Workspace Application*. One of the salient benefits of using Process Spaces is the ease with which it can be customized as well as, the depth of customization allowed. Such customization enables optimization of process interfaces for every process participant. This chapter illustrates some of the customization capabilities.

Concepts

Process Spaces leverages the deep customization capabilities offered by WebCenter Spaces. Some of the customization and extension capabilities available are:

- End User process participants can personalize their Group Spaces and pages. Such personalization may include moving around page components using drag-and-drop interfaces.

- Moderator and Administrator process participants can customize out of the box Group Spaces and Group Space Templates as well as create new spaces leveraging out the box or custom templates. Such customization may include adding of new pages or modifying existing pages by rearranging components or adding new components.

- Administrator process participants can customize the behavior of services including discussion and document services.

- Administrator process participants can customize who has access to what pages and services.

- Administrator process participants can customize the look of the application including the branding logo, application display name, skin, and so on. Some customization, such as skin, may also be done at a Group Space level.

- Developers can customize the WebCenter Spaces application itself. Such customization may include custom landing page, additional skins, additional languages, and so on.

This chapter focuses on customization from an Administrator perspective.

Tutorial: Customizing and extending Workspace

While this tutorial will customize Workspace, the same steps apply to customizing other spaces. For the purposes of this tutorial, it is assumed that you are logged in to `http://orabpm-server:8888/webcenter/` as **weblogic** user and have the **Home** page of the **Workspace**, **Group Space**, open. The starting state is assumed to look like the following screenshot:

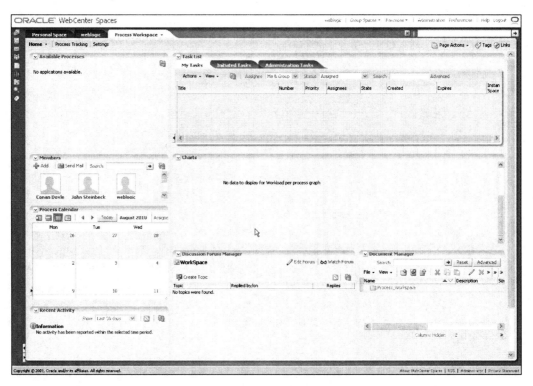

Customizing layout and components

This section illustrates customization of a Group Space by laying out components differently, changing the behavior of included components, and adding new components. In this section, the **Process Calendar** component is moved to a different position, the **Task List** component is customized using parameters, and a new **Chart** component is added.From **Page Actions** menu, select **Edit Page**.

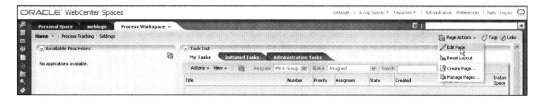

Rearranging layout

First, move the calendar panel:

1. Hold **Process Calendar** component from its title bar.

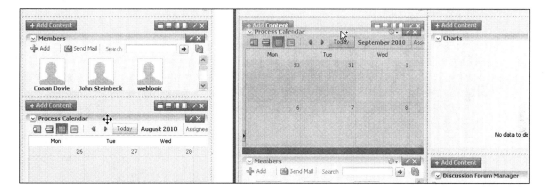

2. Drag it above the **Members** component and release.

> **Source view**
>
> Some users may find it easier to use the source view to edit. Select **Source** option from **View** menu. In this mode, **Cut** and **Paste** (**Paste Before**, **Paste After**, or **Paste Into**) can be used to rearrange the layout.

3. Click on the **Save** icon to save.

Saving Work

Save periodically to avoid timeout issues. If any issue is encountered during edit, please log out of Process Spaces to close the editing session and log in back. You may also want to periodically backup the Group Space from the **Administration** menu; this will allow you to revert back to a known good state.

Changing component attributes

Now, edit some of the component attributes:

1. Click on the **Pencil** icon of the **Task** List component.

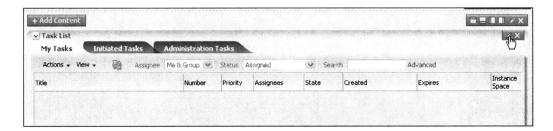

2. Review the **Parameters** tab of the **Component Properties** dialog box. These are the various customization options exposed by the Task List component. For example, **View Filter** can be used to limit the list to a particular view definition.

Parameter Descriptions

For documentation of the parameters, please see the *Passing Worklist Portlet Parameters* section of the *Configuring Task List Portlets* chapter of *Oracle® Fusion Middleware Developer's Guide for Oracle SOA Suite*.

3. For **Show Views Panel**, specify **true**. This will add an additional panel to the left-hand side of the task-listing panel to allow the selection of views. Note that by default, views are available from the **menu** bar of the Task List component.

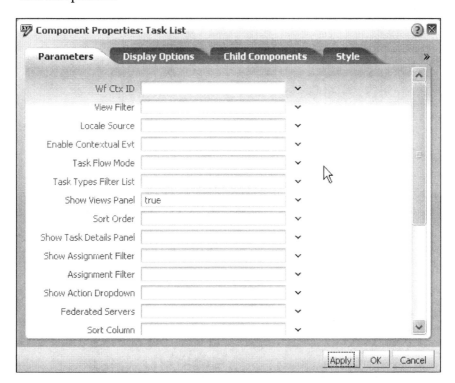

4. Select the **Display Options** tab of the **Component Properties** dialog box.

5. Change the **Text** property to **BPM Inbox**.

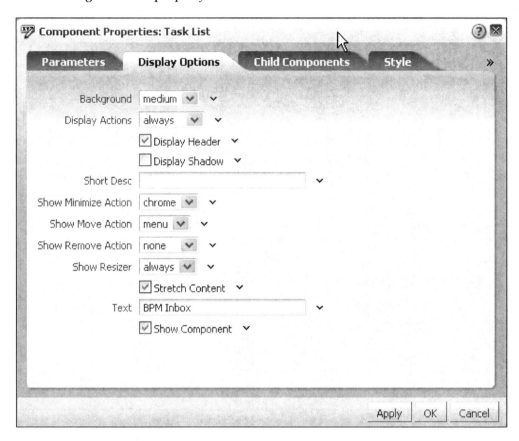

6. Click on the **Save** icon to save.

Adding Components

In this section, you add some components:

1. Click on the **Add to Right** icon (the one with the grey box on the right-hand side) in the box containing the **Charts** component.

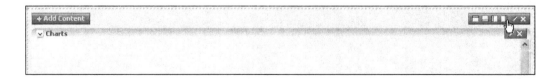

2. Click on the **Add Content** button in the box just added.

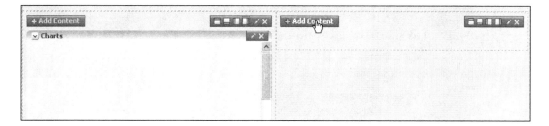

3. In the **Catalog** dialog box, click on **Open** in the **Process Workspace** row. Next, click on **Add** in the **Charts** row. (Ignore any error you may get.)

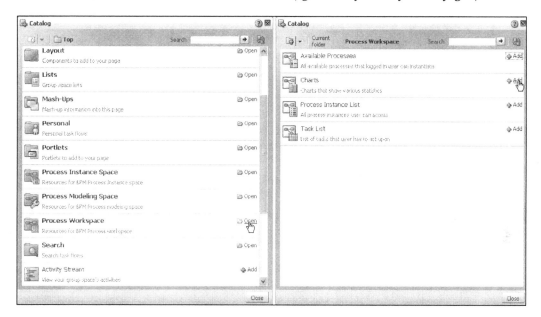

4. Click on the **Pencil** icon for the newly added **Charts** component.

5. The **Widget Id** property can be used to choose a particular standard or custom dashboard. Specify **Widget Id** as **SPpPar-20091229115500**. Alternatively, **Show Selector** may be set to **true** to enable a selector pick list of available dashboards.

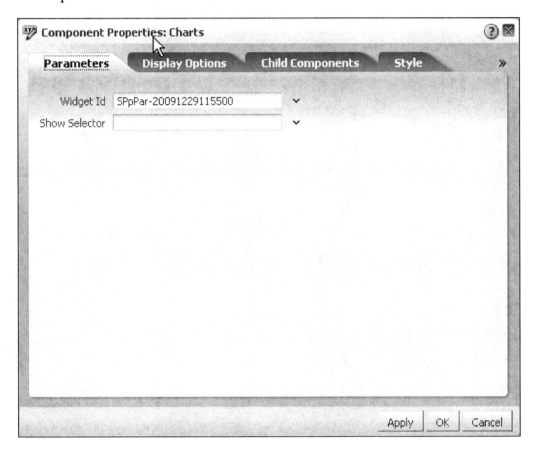

Widget IDs for Standard Dashboards

Performance per Participant: `SPpPar-20091229115500`

Performance per Process: `SPpPro-20090902103700`

Workload per Participant: `SWpPar-20091229115500`

Workload per Process: `SWpPro-20090902103700`

6. Select the **Display Properties** tab and specify **Text** as `Performance per Participant`.

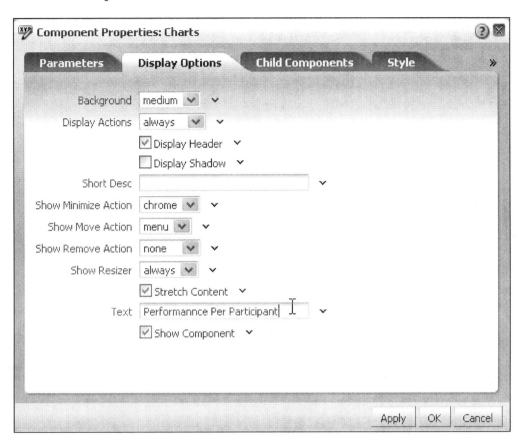

7. Click on **OK, Save,** and **Close** in that order.

At this point, customization of the **Home** page in the **Process Workspace** Group Space is complete and it should look like this:

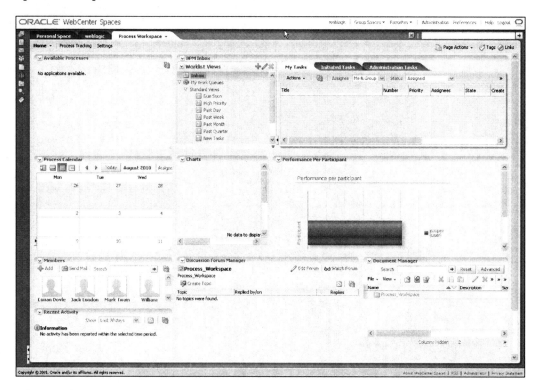

Customizing services

This section illustrates customization and configuration of WebCenter Services. In this section, **Discussion Services** is configured and a **List** is created to manage improvement proposals from process participants.

1. Click on the **Settings** sub tab of the **Process Workspace**.

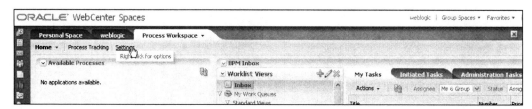

2. Navigate to the **Services** tab within the **Settings** page.

3. Select **Announcements** and then click on the **Search** (looking glass) icon next to **Forum Id**.

4. Review the forum setting. Create and select a new forum, if needed.

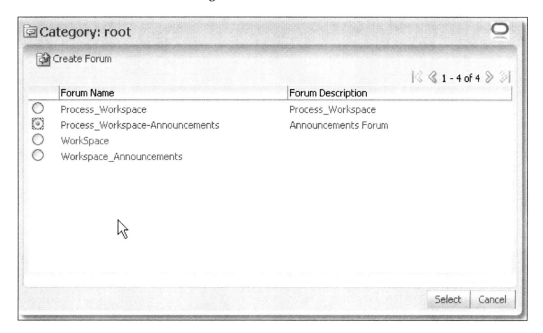

5. Navigate to the **Pages** tab.

6. Click on the **Lists** item in the pages list.

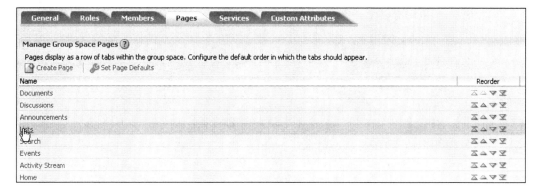

7. Click on the **Create a New List** icon in the Lists page.

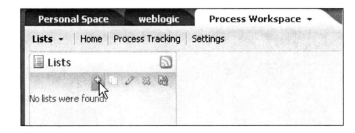

8. Specify the following:

   ° Name: **Improvement Proposals**

   ° Description: **List of process issues that are candidates for process improvements**

   ° Template: **Issues**

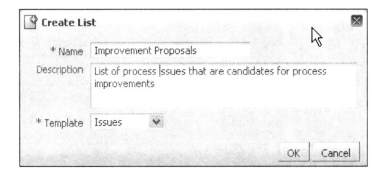

9. With **Improvement Proposals** selected, click on the **Edit List** (pencil) icon.

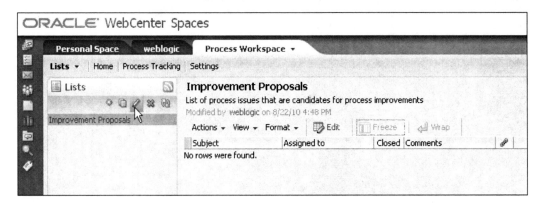

10. Click on the **Create** icon under **Columns**.

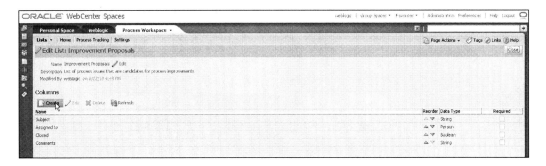

11. In the **Create Column** dialog box, specify the following:

   ° Name: **Process**

   ° Required: selected

   ° Allow Links: selected

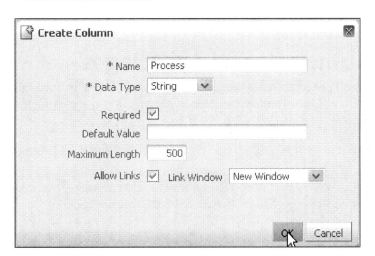

Links

Links are a powerful mechanism for attaching information to list items. Documents, discussions, notes, and so on. can be attached to a list item as links.

12. Click on **Close** on the right-hand side of **Edit List: Improvement Proposals**.

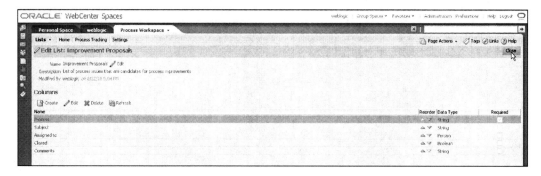

A list has been created to track improvement proposals. It is left as an exercise to the reader to add this list to the Process Workspace using earlier described steps for adding new components to a page.

Customizing roles and privileges

This section illustrates customization of roles and privileges. In this section, view and create access to **Document Services** is customized and a user is granted the **Administrator** role as well.

1. Click on the **Setting** sub-tab of the **Process Workspace** Group Space and then on the **Roles** tab.

2. In the **Documents** section, select **View** for **Participant**, **Public User**, and **Viewer** checkboxes. Select **Create** for **Participant** checkbox. Make other changes as desired.

3. Click on **Apply**.

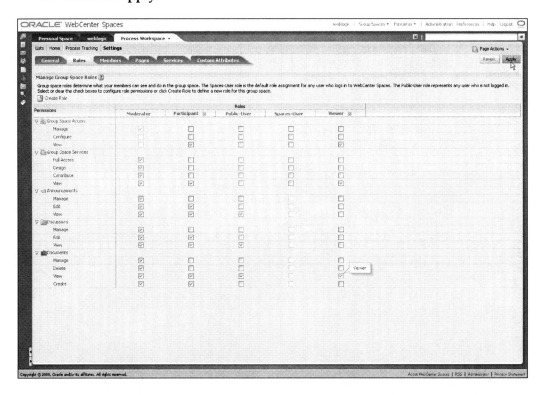

4. Navigate to **Members** tab.

5. Click on the **Member Actions** (gear) icon in the box for **John Steinbeck**. Select **Change Role**.

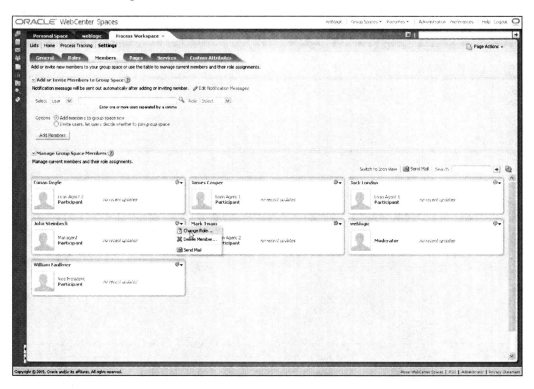

6. In the **Change Role** dialog box, select **Moderator**.

7. Navigate to the **General** tab, find the **Self-Subscription / Change Membership** section, and make any desired changes. For example, select **Approval Required** checkbox within **Change Membership** for the **Participant** role.

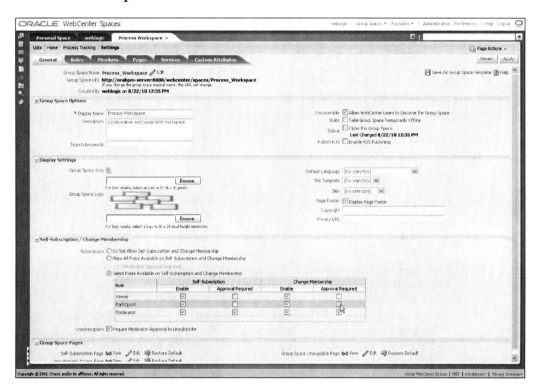

8. Click on **Apply**.

Saving as Template

In this section, the customized **Group Space** is saved as a **Group Space Template** so that it can be used to create new spaces with the customization.

1. The earlier sequence of steps would have the **General** tab of **Settings** within **Process Workspace** open. If needed, navigate there.

2. Click on **Save as Group Space Template**.

3. In the **Save as Group Space Template** dialog, specify the following:

   ° Template Name: **Process Workspace Custom**
   ° Description: **Customized version of Process Workspace**
   ° Publish: Enabled

Saving a new Instance Space Template

Since instance spaces are created based on a template with the name **Process Instance Space Template**, customizations should be saved with this name. Before saving a new template with this name, delete or rename the existing one from **Web Center Administration | Group Spaces | Templates**. Also, remove the group space attribute **instanceId** from **Settings | Custom Attributes** page of the Group Space being saved as template.

Tutorial: Customizing WebCenter's look

In this tutorial, some basic changes are made to the application's appearance, including the logo, name, and skin.

1. Navigate to the **WebCenter Administration** pages. If they aren't open, click on the **Administration** menu item on the top-right corner of WebCenter Spaces.

2. Select the General sub tab; specify the following:

- ° Application Name: **Process Spaces Customized**
- ° Application Skin: **Deep Sea FX**
- ° Application Logo: path to `Acme-Logo.png`
- ° Page Footer: deselect the checkbox

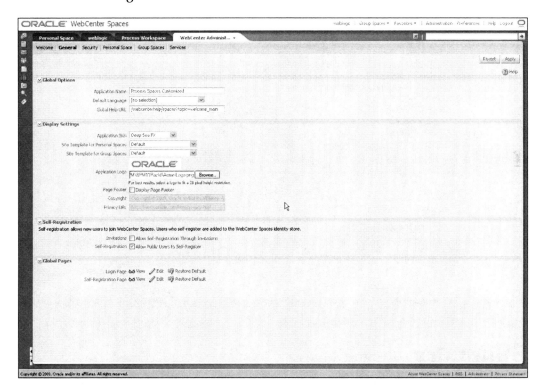

Additional Skins

Developers can add additional skins as described in the *Extending WebCenter Spaces* white paper available from `http://www.oracle.com/technetwork/middleware/webcenter`.

3. Navigate to the **Home** page of Process Workspace. It now looks like the following screenshot:

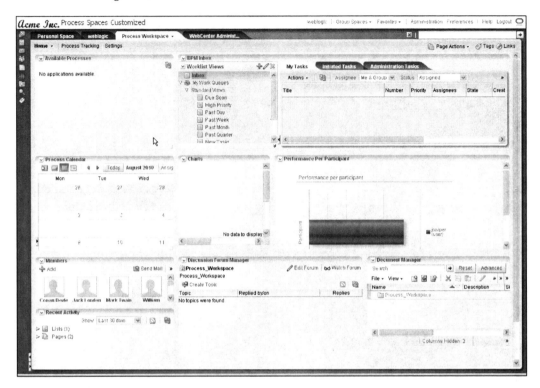

Summary

This chapter provided a summary overview of the customization capabilities available to a Process Spaces administrator and moderator. WebCenter exposes deep customization capabilities to developers, including the ability to change the landing page, add or customize skins, modify resource catalog, add custom task flows to the resource catalog, add additional languages, and so on. These capabilities are described in the *Extending WebCenter Spaces* white paper available from http://www.oracle.com/technetwork/middleware/webcenter.

19
Administering the BPM Environment

You have seen that the BPM life cycle involves multiple types of roles, such as the Business Analyst who models the business process, the BPM/SOA developer who adds implementation details to it, the business users who participate in the process as task performers, and so on. When it comes to administering the BPM runtime environment, there are two distinct roles that come into play. One is that of a BPM administrator and the other is that of the system or infrastructure administrator, who is responsible for keeping the BPM runtime environment up and running and providing the expected quality of service.

BPM administration

A BPM administrator's task is to manage the non-technical, business process-focused activities such as:

- Organization definitions
- Task administration

Managing organization definitions

One of the most common administrative tasks is managing the organization-related information such as **Roles** and **Organizational Units**.

Managing roles

You have already seen how process roles are defined while modeling the Sales Quote process. You created a swim lane for each role that was responsible for performing the appropriate user tasks that are modelled in that lane. You then associated a set of users with these roles. This was all done during the modeling process. But role assignments are not static—they can and do change when users' responsibilities change or when they leave the organization. You also have new users that may need to be associated to a particular role after the process is deployed. It would be an unnecessary overhead if you had to redeploy the process just to update such role assignments.

Oracle BPM 11*g* provides a convenient way to manage roles through the BPM Workspace at runtime. For example, assume that a person named Jack London, with a user ID of `jlondon` is now part of Sales and will also be creating sales quotes. This means that, in addition to `jcooper`, you also need to add `jlondon` to the `SalesRep` role. To add the new user to the role, follow these short steps:

1. Log in to the Business Process Workspace as the user **weblogic**.

> You need to have administrative privileges to gain access to the Administration page in the workspace. By default, the user `weblogic` has the privileges. You can grant this privilege to other users by adding the user or a group to the `SOAAdmin` application role using the Oracle Enterprise Manager Fusion Middleware Control.

2. Click on the **Administration** link.

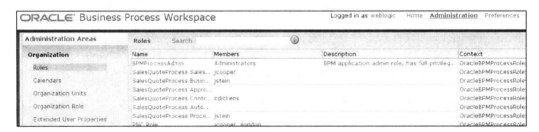

3. Click on **Roles** in the **Administration Areas** panel on the left. This will list all the different roles across all the deployed processes.

4. Select **QuoteProcessLab.SalesRep** from the list. The bottom half of the page should show `jcooper` as the only user assigned to this role.

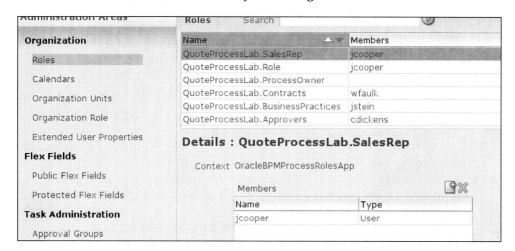

5. Click on the **New** icon to add the new user.

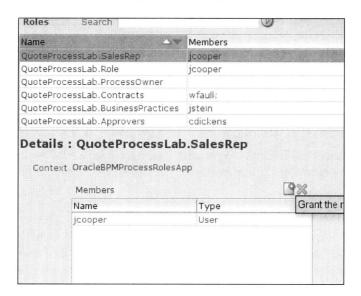

6. Search for `jlondon` and move it to the **Selected** panel in the pop-up window and click on the **OK** button.

7. Click on the **Apply** button to save the new changes.
8. Log out as `weblogic` and log in as `jlondon`. Do you now see the link for creating a new sales quote in the **Applications** panel on the left?

Organizational units

Oracle BPM 11*g* allows you to define hierarchical organization structures that are relevant to the processes being modelled. You can either do this during the modeling of the process or after the process has been deployed. During modeling, each project can define different organizational units organized in a hierarchy appropriate in the context of the BPM project. These hierarchies may represent a subset or a full representation of the enterprise organizational hierarchy, but do not have to.

You can map a project to an organizational unit. Associating an organizational unit with a project restricts the visibility of the processes and tasks in the project to only those users that are members of the associated organizational unit and its child units. By default, a project is not mapped to any unit.

The following figure shows a definition of an organizational unit structure in the BPM Studio:

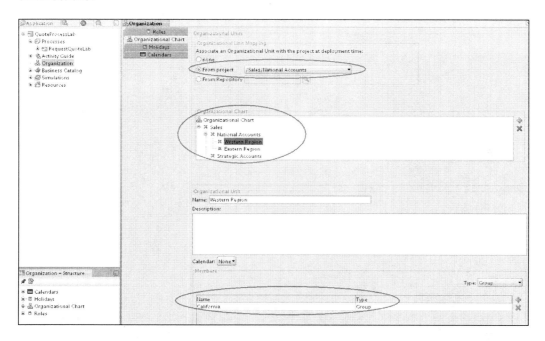

This example shows that the organization hierarchy is defined as starting with **Sales**. The **Sales** unit has two child units—**National Accounts** and **Strategic Accounts**. **National Accounts** in turn has two more units—**Eastern Region** and **Western Region**.

It also shows that this project is mapped to the **National Accounts** organization unit. This means that when this process executes, only users assigned to **National Accounts**, **Western Region**, and **Eastern Region** units will have visibility into the process and can be performers of any tasks assigned.

A BPM Administrator can also define organizational units using the BPM Workspace. Organizational units defined using the workspace can be associated with any project since these definitions are not restricted to a BPM project.

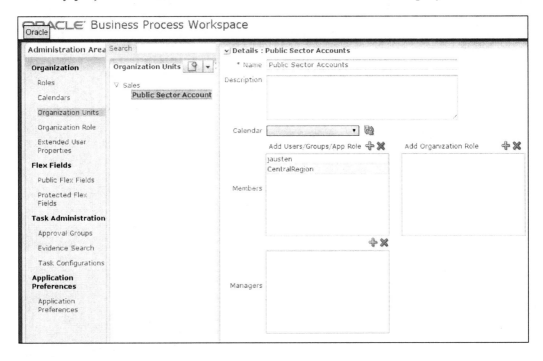

The preceding screenshot shows the definition of an organizational unit called **Public Sector Accounts** under **Sales**. This unit has one user (**jausten**) and one group (**CentralRegion**) as members. This organizational unit can now be mapped to any project and will automatically inherit the memberships defined. This way the BPM administrator, rather than the BPM developer, has control over who has access to and can participate in the process. The following figure shows the organizational unit **Public Sector Accounts** being mapped to another project:

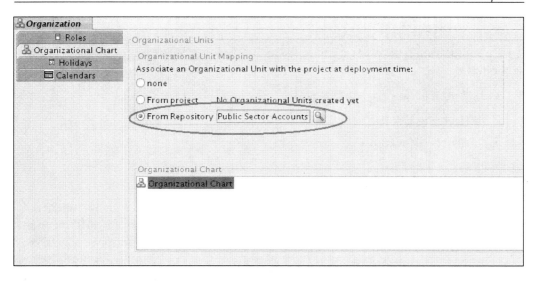

Challenge exercise

You can try using these features and see for yourself how you can manage the BPM environment. If you have completed the mini lab in this chapter for adding `jlondon` to the `SalesRep` role, you now have two people who can create the sales quote. `jcooper` is in the `California` group whereas `jlondon` is in the `CentralRegion` group. Your challenge exercise is to allow only the sales representatives from `Calfornia` to create the sales quote.

Here are some hints that will help you with this exercise:

1. Create a new organizational unit using the Administration page in the BPM Workspace.

2. Add the group `California` as a member to this organizational unit.

3. Using JDeveloper map the new organization unit from the repository to the project and redploy the project.

4. Log in as `jlondon` to the BPM Workspace. Do you see the link for creating the sales quote?

5. Now log in as `weblogic` and replace the group `California` with `CentralRegion`.

6. First log in as `jlondon` and then as `jcooper`. Who has the permissions for creating the quote?

Task administration

Task administration involves managing human task related configurations and covers:

- Administering approval groups
- Managing flex fields
- Task configuration

Administering approval groups

You have already defined an approval group called `Tier1ApprovalGroup` with the lab exercises in *Chapter 15, Using Human Task patterns and other concepts*. Although in those exercises you defined only one user as the member of this group, Oracle BPM 11*g* allows you to define much more complex grouping. For example, you can have multiple users as members of an approval group and can sequence them such that the task will flow though each user in the sequence flow. This is very similar to the Management Task flow described in *Chapter 15* but adds one more level approval flow.

For example, assume that business policies have changed and deal approval now requires two Tier 1 approvers. Once `cdoyle` approves, it should go to `wshake` before it can proceed to the next step. You don't need to make any changes to the project to address this new requirement. You update the `Tier1ApprovalGroup` and add `wshake` to the list using the BPM Workspace Administration, as shown in the following screenshot:

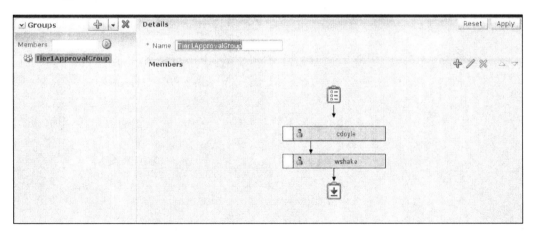

The above definition is using a static list of users. Approval groups can also be dynamic. This allows you to create approval list at runtime and requires writing a custom Java class that implements the `IDynamicApprovalGroup` interface. You register this class when defining the dynamic approval group.

> You can find the Java API reference documentation for human task workflow on Oracle OTN website at `http://download.oracle.com/docs/cd/E14571_01/apirefs.1111/e10660/toc.htm`

Configuring tasks

Oracle BPM 11*g* allows you to configure the task at runtime without having to modify the BPM project and to redploy. The changes can be done for each individual human task that is part of deployed process from the Administration page of the BPM Workspace. Most the of the attributes of a human task that you would set up while designing the workflow task in the BPM Studio are available to be changed at runtime. Using this administration function you can:

- Modify the assignment and routing policy. For example, you can allow participants to edit future participants, provided the task form display the task history component.
- Change expiration and escalation policy.
- Change the notification setting.
- Manage task access permissions.

Managing the BPM infrastructure

Oracle BPM 11*g* is an integrated and unified platform based on SCA, where the BPMN engine is one of the core SCA component engines that runs inside the SOA Infrastructure. Since this is a unified infrastructure, you manage all aspects of BPM and related software components from a single monitoring and management console—the Oracle Enterprise Manager Fusion Middleware Control. This section provides a quick tour of some of the important functions in EM relevant to BPM administration.

You can access EM by navigating to `http://your-host-name:7001/em`. The default installation of Oracle BPM 11*g* has the EM running on port 7001 and the default user is `weblogic`. If you have installed your `AdminServer` on a different port, please use that port instead of 7001. The password for `weblogic` is set during the time of installation.

If you are using the BPM Amazon Machine Image on Amazon EC2 or the VirtualBox SOA/BPM appliance from Oracle Technology Network, all passwords are set to `welcome1` and the port for EM is 7001.

Managing your business processes

In Oracle BPM 11*g*, the unit of deployment and management is an SCA composite. BPM processes in a project are components in a composite and therefore, for monitoring and managing BPM processes, you manage the composite that contains these processes. The following screenshot shows the list of deployed composites on Oracle BPM 11*g* server:

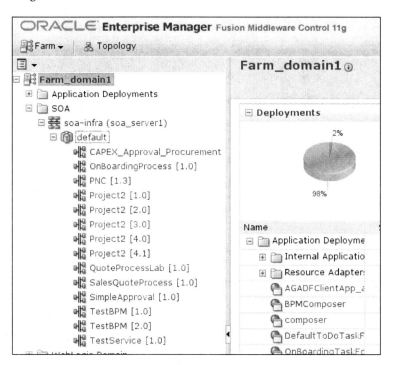

In the screenshot, **soa-infra** is the SOA Infrastructure running on the WebLogic managed server named **soa_server1**. The **default** below **soa-infra** is the default partition. You can have multiple partitions in a server and composites are deployed to a particular partition. Composites deployed to a partition are listed under each partition.

You can get more information on SOA Partitions here:
`http://download.oracle.com/docs/cd/E14571_01/`
`integration.1111/e10226/soasuite_intro.htm#SOAAG97248`

You can undeploy and deploy composites from EM by right-clicking on the composite and selecting **SOA Deployment** from the pop-up menu, as shown in the following screenshot:

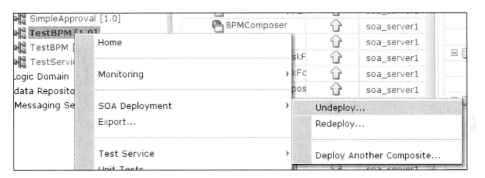

Once a composite is deployed it is in an active state. If you want to temporarily stop a BPM process from creating new instances, you can shutdown the composite. Shutting down the composite stops any instances that are currently running and prevents new instances from being created. If you would like to stop creating new instances but don't want to stop current running instances, you retire the composite instead of shutting it down.

Monitoring your business processes

Oracle Enterprise Manage provides full end-to-end tracking of execution of your business processes. A typical composite that contains BPMN processes also has other components wired to it, such as rules engines, human workflow tasks, service references to adapters or other web services, BPEL, and so on. As these components get executed, the system keeps track of the invocation chain across all components in a composite. If a component, such as BPMN invokes another BPMN process in a different composite, that invocation and any components that are part of the other composite are also tracked in the same chain. This way you can get true end-to-end view of all BPMN and non-BPMN execution.

You can view the execution flow trace by clicking on the appropriate instance ID in the dashboard for the selected composite.

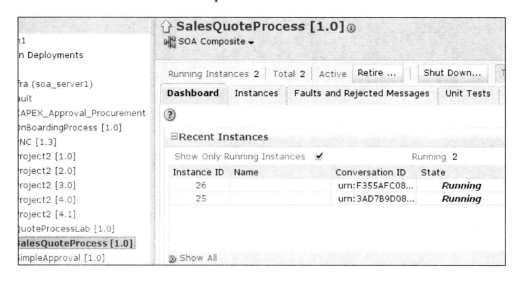

Clicking on the instance ID link pops-up a flow-trace window showing the components that are executing or have completed execution.

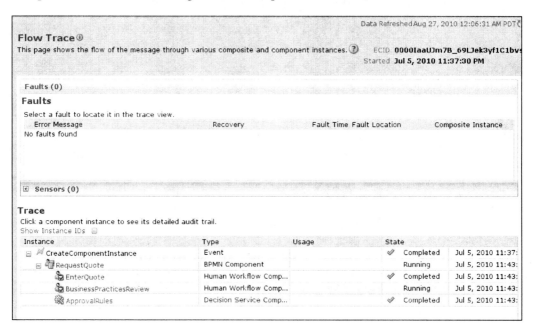

You can further drill down into each of the components to get component-specific details. For example, to see the flow trace of the BPMN process, click on the BPMN component instance. You should see the following screenshot in the flow trace window:

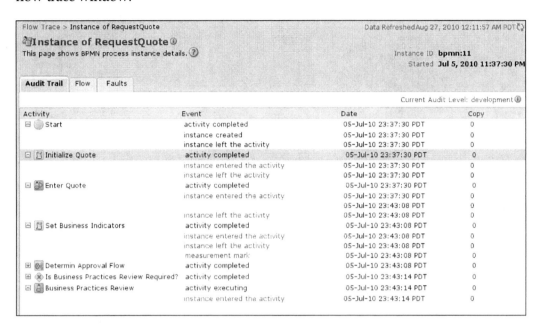

When you expand each activity you can further drill down and inspect the input to and output of the activity.

Note that these details are only available when the **Audit Level** is set to development. You can set the audit level at the SOA Infrastructure level or at the composite level. To set the composite's audit level to development, select the composite, and using **Settings...**, set the required audit level.

You can also get a graphical view of the audit trail by switching to the **Flow** tab.

The main page for the composite also provides basic statistics on each component in the composite, such as the number of running instances per component, total instances, and faulted instances.

Name	Component Type	Total Instances	Running Instances	Faulted Instances Recoverable	Non Recoverable
EnterQuote	Human Workflow	2	1	0	0
RequestQuote	BPMN	2	2	0	0
ApprovalRules	Decision Service	1	0	0	0
ApproveTerms	Human Workflow	0	0	0	0

If the BPMN process or any associated components in the composite encounter an exception, the composite instance shows up as a faulted instance. If the fault is a recoverable fault the Enterprise Manager console allows the administrator to take manual action on the faulted instance by retrying it or aborting it.

Summary

Oracle BPM 11*g* provides a complete solution with strong management and monitoring features that are designed for both business users responsible for the BPM and for system administrators. Since Oracle BPM 11*g* is part of the unified SOA infrastructure, system administrators do not have to use multiple consoles for managing different pieces of the BPM solution.

20
Concluding Remarks

Congratulations! If you completed the exercises in this book, or even most of them, you are well versed with the breadth of functionality offered by Oracle BPM Suite 11*g*, one of the most comprehensive BPM Suites in the market. Through these exercises you not only learned BPMN process modeling and implementation but also business rules and user interface development for human tasks (or activities). While the main focus of these exercises was on developing BPM applications, you also learned about the end user facing functionality and how to customize and extend them as well as the administration concepts and tasks. If you are a Business Analyst and you followed this book, maybe skipping many of the implementation details and focusing on process modeling, simulation, and process patterns, you have acquired a level of BPM understanding that will enable you to steer BPM initiatives in your organization.

With the knowledge acquired, you are now ready to start your first BPM project with Oracle BPM Suite 11*g*. As you encounter new scenarios or need solutions to specific problems, please visit the Business Process Management page at Oracle Technology Network: `http://www.oracle.com/technetwork/middleware/soasuite/index-098806.html`. Here you will find many samples and tech-notes that may help with your questions. You may also want to leverage the community of BPM experts through the extremely responsive BPM forum: `http://forums.oracle.com/forums/forum.jspa?forumID=560`.

Oracle BPM components are layered on top of other Oracle Fusion Middleware (FMW) components such as Oracle SOA Suite, Application Development Framework (ADF), and so on. While this book does not assume any prior knowledge of these underlying products you may want to increase your expertise by learning more about these components. Process developers are often responsible for application integration and related tasks such as data transformations; knowledge of Oracle SOA Suite is essential for such tasks. Developers needing to go beyond auto-generated or wizard-generated user interfaces (or forms) will find an understanding of ADF (and Java Server Faces) extremely useful.

BPM promises many opportunities with rapid implementation of business applications and quick return on investment (ROI). However, please bear in mind that the true potential of BPM is realized only through more effective participation of business stakeholders in BPM initiatives. In this book, you learned about tools and technologies that enable business to engage, including BPMN modeling and simulation and the use of Process Composer. Armed with this knowledge, plan out how business and IT can collaborate more effectively in your next BPM project.

Finally, BPM success depends on organizational factors beyond technology and implementation. Encourage Business Analysts or sponsors of your BPM initiative to take the BPM lifecycle assessment available at `http://www.oracle.com/us/technologies/bpm/index.htm`.

Index

Workspace customization

components, customizing 469
layout, customizing 469
New Instance Space Template, saving 484
privileges, customizing 480-483
roles, customizing 480-483
services, customizing 476-480
starting state 468
template, saving as 483, 484

X

XOR Event Gateway 452

Z

ZIP archive, structure

adflib 69
input 69
lib 69
schema 69
solutions / chh# 69
sql 69

Thank you for buying
Getting Started with Oracle BPM Suite 11gR1 – A Hands-On Tutorial

About Packt Publishing

Packt, pronounced 'packed', published its first book "Mastering phpMyAdmin for Effective MySQL Management" in April 2004 and subsequently continued to specialize in publishing highly focused books on specific technologies and solutions.

Our books and publications share the experiences of your fellow IT professionals in adapting and customizing today's systems, applications, and frameworks. Our solution based books give you the knowledge and power to customize the software and technologies you're using to get the job done. Packt books are more specific and less general than the IT books you have seen in the past. Our unique business model allows us to bring you more focused information, giving you more of what you need to know, and less of what you don't.

Packt is a modern, yet unique publishing company, which focuses on producing quality, cutting-edge books for communities of developers, administrators, and newbies alike. For more information, please visit our website: www.packtpub.com.

About Packt Enterprise

In 2010, Packt launched two new brands, Packt Enterprise and Packt Open Source, in order to continue its focus on specialization. This book is part of the Packt Enterprise brand, home to books published on enterprise software – software created by major vendors, including (but not limited to) IBM, Microsoft and Oracle, often for use in other corporations. Its titles will offer information relevant to a range of users of this software, including administrators, developers, architects, and end users.

Writing for Packt

We welcome all inquiries from people who are interested in authoring. Book proposals should be sent to author@packtpub.com. If your book idea is still at an early stage and you would like to discuss it first before writing a formal book proposal, contact us; one of our commissioning editors will get in touch with you.

We're not just looking for published authors; if you have strong technical skills but no writing experience, our experienced editors can help you develop a writing career, or simply get some additional reward for your expertise.

Getting Started With Oracle SOA Suite 11g R1 – A Hands-On Tutorial

ISBN: 978-1-847199-78-2   Paperback: 482 pages

Fast track your SOA adoption – Build a service-oriented composite application in just hours!

1. Offers an accelerated learning path for the much anticipated Oracle SOA Suite 11g release

2. Beginning with a discussion of the evolution of SOA, this book sets the stage for your SOA learning experience

3. Includes a comprehensive overview of the Oracle SOA Suite 11g Product Architecture

Oracle SOA Suite 11g R1 Developer's Guide

ISBN: 978-1-8496801-8-9   Paperback: 540 pages

Develop Service-Oriented Architecture Solutions with the Oracle SOA Suite

1. A hands-on, best-practice guide to using and applying the Oracle SOA Suite in the delivery of real-world SOA applications

2. Detailed coverage of the Oracle Service Bus, BPEL PM, Rules, Human Workflow, Event Delivery Network, and Business Activity Monitoring

3. Master the best way to use and combine each of these different components in the implementation of a SOA solution

Please check **www.PacktPub.com** for information on our titles

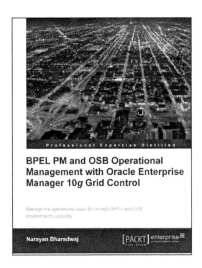

BPEL PM and OSB Operational Management with Oracle Enterprise Manager 10g Grid Control

Manage the operational tasks for multiple BPEL and OSB environments centrally

Narayan Bharadwaj

[PACKT] enterprise

BPEL PM and OSB operational management with Oracle Enterprise Manager 10g Grid Control

ISBN: 978-1-847197-74-0   Paperback: 248 pages

Manage the operational tasks for multiple BPEL and OSB environments centrally

1. Monitor and manage all components of your SOA environment from a central location

2. Save time and increase efficiency by automating all the day-to-day operational tasks associated with the SOA environment

3. Step-by-step exercises to set up the framework to effectively manage Oracle SOA products

Middleware Management with Oracle Enterprise Manager Grid Control 10g R5

Monitor, diagnose, and maximize the system performance of Oracle Fusion Middleware solutions

Foreword by Ali Siddiqui, Vice President, Product Development Fusion Middleware Management, Oracle Corporation

Debu Panda   Arvind Maheshwari   PACKT

Middleware Management with Oracle Enterprise Manager Grid Control 10g R5

ISBN: 978-1-847198-34-1   Paperback: 350 pages

Monitor, diagnose, and maximize the system performance of Oracle Fusion Middleware solutions

1. Manage your Oracle Fusion Middleware and non-Oracle middleware applications effectively and efficiently using Oracle Enterprise Manager Grid Conrol

2. Implement proactive monitoring to maximize application performance

3. Best practices and troubleshooting tips to manage your middleware and SOA applications for optimal service levels and reduced down time from Oracle Product Managers

Please check **www.PacktPub.com** for information on our titles

9 781849 681681